HISTORY, TRUTH, LIBERTY

HISTORY, TRUTH, LIBERTY

Selected Writings of Raymond Aron

Edited by
Franciszek Draus

With a Memoir by
Edward Shils

The University of Chicago Press
Chicago and London

The University of Chicago Press, Chicago 60637
The University of Chicago Press, Ltd., London

© 1985 by The University of Chicago
All rights reserved. Published 1985
Printed in the United States of America

94 93 92 91 90 89 88 87 86 85   5 4 3 2 1

Library of Congress Cataloging in Publication Data

Aron, Raymond, 1905–83
  History, truth, liberty.

  Includes index.
  1. History—Philosophy—Addresses, essays,
lectures. I. Draus, Franciszek. II. Shils,
Edward Albert, 1911–   III. Title.
D16.8.A73   1985   901   85–8590
ISBN 0–226–02800–3

Contents

Raymond Aron, 1905–1983
A Memoir

Edward Shils

Raymond Aron had many great virtues as an intellectual and citizen. Among these numerous virtues were a penetrating, pervasive intelligence operating over a very wide range, an exceptional speed in focusing his mind on fundamentals in the midst of a chaos of particular facts, an immense stock of knowledge in philsophy, history, economics, sociology, and politics, a vast capacity for unceasing and strenuous work, a quiet and tenacious courage, and sobriety and lucidity of outlook and style. All of these were in the service of a steady, matter-of-fact patriotism and a firm and discriminating devotion to the ideals of the Enlightenment. Yet what made him unique among the intellectuals of his time was his practice as a scholar, observer, and analyst, year in, year out, day in, day out, of what Max Weber called the ethics of responsibility—*Verantwortungsethik*—in contrast with the ethics of conscience—*Gesinnungsethik*. The ethics of responsibility requires the unflinching effort to discover the truth and the readiness to accept disagreeable truths; it requires the courage to act in the light of knowledge, and to be aware at the same time of the inadequacy of that knowledge, while bearing in mind the limited range of possibilities of action and the costs as well as benefits of any action. It presupposes freedom of action within these limits. The primacy of the obligation of intellectual, ethical, and political responsibility that lay upon politicians and citizens, teachers and students, literary men and philosophers was the dominant note in Raymond Aron's active career as a university teacher, scholar, and publicist—a career that ran for more than half a century.

Raymond Aron's inquiry began in his dissertation, *Introduction à la philosophie de l'histoire,* which was a study of the possibility and the limits of knowledge of history and society as these were treated by four German authors of the late nineteenth and early twentieth centuries; it was also a study of the historical consciousness and of the place of historical—and sociological—knowledge in action. It was a work of clarification regarding the powers of the mind to apprehend the reality of human actions and institutions in the past and in the present.

The central theme of Raymond Aron's dissertation—the conditions and limits of valid knowledge of history and society—remained with him throughout his unusually variegated career. It was joined with an active, practical concern for the dignity of his country and the well-being of his fellow countrymen, which was not merely a contemplative interest. That interest was inseparably intertwined with the knowledge of the inevitable imperfection of knowledge itself and the ineluctability of choice and decision. It began to take form in the 1930s after he returned from several years in Cologne and Berlin. That combination was brought more sharply to the forefront of his consciousness in 1932, when he first began to give form to his political views in writing. He had been given an audience by an undersecretary of the Ministry of Foreign Affairs at the Quai d'Orsay. He had expounded his strongly held views about National Socialist Germany and French foreign policy and especially about the danger of war if Hitler came to power. The undersecretary replied, "The Minister of Foreign Affairs is a very exceptional person and he enjoys much authority. The moment is propitious of any initiative. But what would you, who have spoken to me so well about Germany and the dangers which are looming, do if you were in his place?"

That question never left Raymond Aron's mind. That question was always present in his analysis of contemporary politics in France and in the world. Decisions must be made, and the actions that they require are always taken under the constraints of limiting conditions and of limited resources and with very imperfect knowledge; decisions, moreover, must be made with an awareness of risks and costs—but they must be made. Such decisions require courage in politicians, and they require courage in those who analyze the actions of politicians and who attempt to understand the world as an intelligent politician would see it. Raymond Aron very early came to know the sterile vanity of moral denunciations and lofty proclamations, of demands for perfection and of the assessment of existing situations according to the standard of an unrealizable perfection.

Although he was a socialist (in fact, he was a member of the Section française de l'Internationale ouvrière, the French socialist party) while he was a student at the École normale supérieure, and although throughout his life he retained the humanitarian, secular, democratic, and progressive views of social-democracy, Raymond Aron also saw from the beginning that the government of the Popular Front of the middle 1930s was pursuing unattainable ends by ineffective and self-defeating means. He retained his sympathy and admiration for Léon Blum and for the kind of socialism Blum represented, and he preserved his intellectual interest in Marxism until the end of his life; but he became, in fact, the most persistent, the most severe, and the most learned critic of Marxism and of the socialist—or more precisely Communist—order of society of the present century. It was not prejudice that led Raymond Aron to perform this task. He accepted the task because of his respect for truth, his devotion to freedom and to the kind of society that sustains freedom and well-being, and his recognition that the world is a hard place, where ideals can be approached but can never be fully realized.

In an important sense, Aron was a man of his time but not a product of the opinions that prevailed in the intellectual circles of his time. He was an anguished witness to the weakness—decadence, he called it later—of French society in the 1930s and of its humiliation under conditions of defeat and occupation in the Second World War. When he returned to France in 1944, the agenda for the rest of his public life was made firm. It included the rehabilitation of French society, the effectiveness of its political conduct, the renewal of its self-respect, the protection of its unity in a regime of liberal democracy that makes provision for free disagreement, its integration into the wider civilization of humane and progressive liberal democracies, and the protection of that civilization from the encroachment of totalitarianism and the destructiveness of war. These were his daily preoccupations from 1947 to 1977 as publicist in *Figaro*, as well as in many other journals, and in *l'Express* from 1977 until his death. They were also his preoccupations in the academic career that he resumed in 1955, when he became professor of sociology at the Sorbonne, and later, when he became a director of studies at the École pratique des hautes études in 1960, and when he was professor of the sociology of European civilization at the Collège de France from 1969 until his retirement in 1978.

Raymond Aron did not direct his mind to the ultimate problems of human existence—he was too much an heir of the Enlightenment to think about transcendental realities; he directed it to the problems of his time, and he did so from a stable point of view. This point of view was defined by the prizing of reason and liberty and of the institutions, the society, and the civilization in which reason and liberty could be practiced and maintained and in which human beings could lead a decent life and have some influence on their fate.

II

At the time of his death on October 17, 1983, Raymond Aron was the most prominent and the most esteemed writer in the world on modern society and contemporary international politics. He was accepted as a towering figure in intellectual circles in France, Great Britain, Germany, and the United States, in Italy, Israel, and Latin America—indeed, wherever reason, learning, and moral responsibility are respected. He was never confined to the academic world by his professional obligations, which he observed with animated devotion and with a genuine concern for the university as an intellectual institution. He was known and deeply appreciated far beyond the boundaries of academic sociology. He had, in fact, become a celebrity known by the broad public that knew of Arnold Toynbee, Albert Schweitzer, and Teilhard de Chardin. He was the author of forty books, most of which were translated into English and many of which were translated into other languages both in Europe and in Japan. For a third of a century he regularly wrote many hundreds of articles on the current political and economic problems of France as well as of the whole world. He was an honorary graduate of Oxford, Cambridge, Jerusalem, Chicago, Columbia, and other universities. Honorific lectureships, above all the Gifford lectureship, and honorific prizes—the Goethe Prize, the Erasmus Prize, the Tocqueville Prize, the Ordre pour le Mérite, and countless others—were conferred on him. He was a member of the Académie des sciences morales et politiques and a foreign member of the British Academy, the American Philosophical Society, the American Academy of Arts and Sciences, and numerous other honorific learned bodies.

I think that no academic of this century—certainly no academic social scientist, with the possible exception of John Maynard Keynes —was so widely known and appreciated as Raymond Aron. In France, above all, leading politicians read his articles and sometimes invited him to discuss their problems and their policies. When he came to the United States, he was sought out by the highest officials in the fields of foreign policy and national security. He was listened to attentively by the political elites of France, and by Robert McNamara, Henry Kissinger, and many others in the United States.

With all his eminence, with all the attention he received in high political circles, he was nonetheless isolated in the French intellectual world. Of his close friends at the Ecole normale, one, Paul Nizan, became a Communist, two others, Jean-Paul Sartre and Maurice Merleau-Ponty, became arrant, if singular, fellow travelers of the Communist party and powerful and popular proponents of the Soviet Union. *Le Monde,* when it was not hostile, kept him at a distance. It was common, when a fellow-traveling, highbrow leftism ruled the roost in the French intellectual barnyard, to speak of Raymond Aron as a "reactionary." In the 1950s, I heard a refined young Trotskyite call him a "fascist." This same young man, when he became older and more sensible, became a devoted "Aronian." It was hinted, because Aron was critical of the Soviet Union, that he was an American agent. His entry into the Sorbonne was not an easy one. Some professors did not want him because he was, so they said, a journalist; others did not want him because he was critical of Marxism and the Soviet Union.

His life was not an easy one. It was sustained by the warmth of his domestic circle and a small number of affectionate friends, some of his own generation, like André Malraux and Manès Sperber, others of a younger generation, like Jean-Claude Casanova, François Bourricaud, and the group that gathered around him first at *Contrepoint* and then at *Commentaire.* It was only in the last ten years of his life that French intellectual opinion about him became more positive; there had always been a certain fearful awe before his intellectual power and his vast, easily summoned knowledge. The new attitude was more respectful, more admiring, even reverent. It was certainly not respect for age—he never gave the impression of being an old man—which caused this change. It was a genuine appreciation of the power of his mind and character.

Raymond Aron himself attributed the change in French opinion— not about himself but about Marxism—to the obvious gap between Marxist promises and the squalid record of the Soviet Union. He attributed the change in French opinion to the undermining of Marxist beliefs following Khrushchev's speech of February 24–25, 1956, and the shock of Solzhenitsyn's *Gulag Archipelago.* Aron himself never drew any conclusions about his own rise in standing before French opinion from his observations of the changes in the standing of Marxism. Some of the change in attitude toward him should undoubtedly be attributed to these two large causes. In my view, however, the change in the French intellectuals' attitude toward Aron was simply that, even in an intellectual stratum as frivolous and as irrational as it has been in France for some decades, a vein of seriousness and rationality is inexpungible. That seriousness could not resist the evidence of three decades of rigorous reasoning and dispassionate mastery of facts, fairness to opponents in argument, and, above all, integrity and liberality. Raymond Aron finally gained a more just assessment from French intellectuals because even they could not long deny the force of his imposing virtues or the claims of their own long-repressed, better selves.

III

Raymond Aron's life, like all lives and especially those in the twentieth century, was much affected by accidents and by events over which he had no control. After the superlative achievement at the Ecole normale supérieure, where he stood out among the most brilliant young men of his generation, including Sartre, Merleau-Ponty, Lagache, and Nizan, and taking first place in the *agrégation* of that year, he went to Germany. He took advantage of the opportunity to go there in a junior post at the University of Cologne because he was uncertain about what to do with the rest of his life. In Germany, he interested himself in the philosophy of history, discovered Max Weber, perfected his fluency in German, and witnessed the descent of the Weimar Republic and the rise of National Socialism. After a stay of about three years, he returned to France and taught at a lycée as a replacement for his classmate and friend, Sartre. For several years he accepted miscellaneous academic employments, and in 1939 he was appointed to a professorship at Toulouse. He could not take up this appointment, however, because he was called to military service. After the disintegration of the French army, he managed to make his way to London. Shortly after his arrival, General de Gaulle, under the influence of André Labarthe, decided that an intellectual review to uphold the idea of France in cultural matters should be published in England. Aron, who had meanwhile rejoined the French forces, became the review's political commentator, each month writing an article and a survey of the internal situation in France; he was also in effect the managing editor until his return to France in 1944.

There he became a publicist, at first with *Combat* and then with *Figaro*. He was pressed to join the staff of *Le Monde*, but he chose *Figaro* because, being a morning paper, its schedule of work would allow him to concentrate on his scholarly studies in the mornings and to give the later part of each day to journalism. During much of this time he also lectured at the Ecole nationale d'administration and the

Institut d'études politiques. When he returned to the university, he continued his career as a publicist with undiminished activity.

It was a unique career. There were academics who had been journalists—Franklin Giddings at Columbia and L. T. Hobhouse at the London School of Economics, among the sociologists of the two generations before Aron, had been editorial writers—and there were academics who became journalists. There were many academics who wrote frequently in newspapers: Harold Laski and Denis Brogan and Arthur Schlesinger, Jr., in English-speaking countries, Alfred Grosser and Maurice Duverger in France. Max Weber was an illustrious predecessor in this kind of occasional journalism by scholars. There has, in fact, been no shortage of these academic occasional journalists. This crossing of the boundaries between journalism and the university has indeed become a commonplace phenomenon, and television has further blurred the boundary between journalism and university teaching in history and the social sciences. In the case of Raymond Aron, the remarkable thing is not that he did both but that he did both so extraordinarily well.

This combination of two different kinds of activities and the unremittingly high level at which both activities were carried on undoubtedly contributed to his fame. The fact that he was known to be a productive and scrupulous academic philosopher and sociologist must have formed around his publicistic writings the aura that is even now seen as encircling a great savant. Whatever the dominant leftist literati in France said about him throughout the 1950s and 1960s and well into the 1970s, he was always regarded with great respect in the main academic circles of the United States, Great Britain, and Germany. His sociological achievements were justly known; the deference accorded to him was heightened by awareness of his subtle and realistic analysis of the affairs of the great world.

IV

Raymond Aron's combination of academic and publicistic careers was unique. He was a university teacher from the time of his resettlement in Paris after the Second World War until his retirement at the age of seventy-two from the Collège de France. Even before that he was an academic, in charge of a research center—the Centre de la documentation sociale—at the Ecole normale supérieure from 1934 to 1939, when he entered the French army. It was indeed only during the war that he was not active in academic life.

He began his publicistic activities very hesitantly in the 1930s; they began in earnest when he became editor de facto of *La France libre*. Thereafter they went on steadily until his death, being interrupted only by his illness in 1977.

Aron himself felt a tension between these two careers; he sometimes thought that he had not done the right thing in becoming a publicist. He yearned to devote himself exclusively to his academic work. He would have liked to produce more books like the two that he wrote in the 1930s on the epistemology of historical knowledge and the two major works on war and peace that he wrote in the last two decades of his life. That was what he would have preferred. But for nearly four decades he regularly and frequently wrote short articles on topics of the political arena, domestic and international. He also wrote numerous long sociological and philosophical essays, and he published many books, some of which were formed from his already-published longer essays. None of these books is simply a gathering of unconnected papers within a single binding. Each is unified by a common theme, and all are integrated by the "signature" that is always present in whatever an important artist or writer does.

In his later years, Aron felt occasional regret about his failure to write those longer, deeper, more scholarly works that could not be written because of that obligation to comment regularly on public questions which he had imposed upon himself. Yet such was the force of his intellectual personality that there was, in fact, no separation of these two different occupations. The same fundamental values, the same way of thinking, the same preoccupations were present in all he wrote.

Something should also be said about the wide diversity of Raymond Aron's intellectual interests. In his journalistic work, he wrote with the detail of an expert and the penetration of a sage about the economic problems and internal political affairs of the United States, Great Britain, the Federal Republic of Germany, Italy, the Soviet Union, Israel, Japan, Communist China, and India. He wrote with equal mastery of detail and wide perspective about the international economic and military order. He discussed military strategy and military weapons. His writings commanded the careful attention of specialized scholars and persons in responsible positions in many countries, yet they could be instructively understood by the intelligent layman. As an academic, he wrote with unquestionable scholarly authority on the main German thinkers in historical and sociological theory, on the structures of modern societies, on military strategy and international relations, on

Thucydides, Montesquieu, and Machiavelli, on Marxism in its variant forms, on intellectuals, on economic and social development, and on current economic policies. The list of topics he wrote on could be much extended. He did not experience any tension in keeping in balance this exceptionally broad range of subjects, each of which has its own large body of literature. There were good reasons why he felt no strain in mastering so many different fields of intellectual interest.

Yet he did experience a tension about the duality of his professional life. My own view is that he had, despite his own feelings about it, no grounds for a sense of strain in contemplating his dual career. There was a genuine unity that embraced all his activities; it was imposed by the unity of outlook that pervaded all his very diverse intellectual interests. That same unity of outlook made his dual professional career into a complex but single intellectual activity.

There were other heterogeneities in Aron's existence about which he at times felt a strain. One of these was his consciousness of being Jewish while at the same time being a Frenchman. This was not at all salient in his mind until his first sight of National Socialism in the last years of the Weimar Republic. Although he was a nonpracticing, nonbelieving Jew, he was conscious of being of Jewish origin, but he did not regard that in itself as setting him apart from other Frenchmen. Nevertheless, in the 1930s he was inhibited from trying to tell Frenchmen the truth about Hitler because he was apprehensive lest, because he was a Jew, his objectivity would be questioned. So it continued until President de Gaulle in 1967 made his disparaging statement about the Jews. This evoked in Aron's mind the anti-Semitism of Drumont and of Vichy France, and he wrote a powerful denunciation of De Gaulle's statement. But by this time he had ceased to fear that his objectivity or good faith could be placed in question.

There was another heterogeneity in Raymond Aron's intellectual constitution about which he had no reservations or doubts whatsoever. The inner heterogeneity of being French, European, and "Transatlantic" was one that he accepted entirely without self-consciousness. He was a Frenchman and a French patriot to the depth of his spirit. He was attached to France as a whole and positively; he was not one of those spurious patriots who espouses his own country only as a reflex of rancor against other countries. He was also a citizen of Europe—not in the narrow sense of being in favor of the Common Market, but in the way in which it was once said of Georg Brandes that he was a "good European." Aron was practically as at home in Great Britain and in Germany as he was in France. He was as at home in the United States as he was in Germany and Great Britain. He was more than a "good European"; he was a citizen of Western civilization.

He had never been in Great Britain until 1940, when he went there from Bordeaux to rejoin the French army, scattered elements of which had reassembled in England after they escaped from Dunkirk. He scarcely knew English when he arrived, but in a fairly short time he became very fluent in the language. He did not live in the confinement of exile; he soon became well known to leading British academic figures. The tradition of sympathy with British institutions that ran from Voltaire and Montesquieu through Tocqueville and Halévy became part of Aron's second nature. After the war he went frequently to England in various capacities to deliver lectures and to receive honorary degrees. Thereafter Britain joined Germany as part of his wider spiritual homeland.

Aron's relationship with the United States began later. I think he went there for the first time to participate in the summer school that Henry Kissinger conducted at Harvard. From the latter 1950s for the rest of his life, he was frequently in the United States and was very much at ease there. He understood American politics in the same quick and sympathetically realistic way that he grasped all situations.

No other intellectual of the present century has had the familiarity and sympathy with the major Western countries that Raymond Aron had. Denis Brogan knew France and the United States, and Isaiah Berlin acquired a very acute knowledge of America in the war years. But neither of them knew Germany as deeply as Aron did, and neither of them took the welfare of these foreign countries into their care in the way in which Aron did. They were part of his larger family—they were not kinsmen who intermittently entered into his consciousness, they were steadily there. They were a third circle—beyond his own immediate family and his intimate friends, and France—a circle of wide radius, the perimeter of which was always close to the center of his own existence.

The fact is that, despite the multifariousness of his activities, the diverse objects of his intellectual exertions, the duality of his professional careers, and the plurality of his attachments, there was a fundamental harmony in Raymond Aron's life and in his outlook. Without that harmony, he probably would not have been able to sustain himself so fruitfully in the face of his own sense of the tragic character of human history, his isolation from the long-dominant circles of French intellectuals, the attacks made against him by those intellectuals, and the obstacles placed in his way by the academics among them.

V

Raymond Aron, once he found himself in Germany, had wanted to be a scholar, a philosophic contemplator of the world as it really is, with his contemplative powers strengthened by his knowledge of modern sociology and economics. First the war intervened. Then, after the war, his attachment to and solicitude for France impelled him to attempt to contribute in his own intellectual way to the rehabilitation of French society by the clarifying guidance of public opinion and the constructive criticism of politicians and of governmental actions. Nevertheless, during his first decade as a journalist, he did succeed in writing several books that were not collections of articles but were in fact elegantly constructed, eloquently argued books: one on the wars of the nineteenth and twentieth centuries, another on nuclear warfare, and another—the most famous and perhaps the most enduring—*L'Opium des intellectuels,* on the alienation of intellectuals from their own society and their negativistic self-indulgence in the politics of perfection.

All this was not enough for him. He wished to be a professor, to teach intelligent young men and women, and to write books of depth of analysis and scholarly thoroughness. When, finally, in 1955 he was elected to a professorship of sociology at the Sorbonne against some resistance, he entered a period of even greater productivity. He published a major book on the great figures of sociological thought from Montesquieu to Max Weber, which is now one of the most authoritative works on the subject, and three small books on modern liberal-democratic and totalitarian societies. These four books were based on lectures delivered to his students, and they are evidence of his sense of pedagogical responsibility as well as of the power of his thought. He also published at this time a work that has since become a classic on peace and war among states. During this decade and a half of extraordinary intellectual exertion, he continued his publicistic activity in *Figaro* at the same high level and with unchanged frequency, ceasing only because of changes in the ownership and control of that newspaper. Three of his most impressive achievements as a publicist occurred in this period. These were his writings on the necessity of French decolonization of Algeria, on President de Gaulle's disparagement of Israel and the Jews, and on the "student revolution."

Aron was not, however, satisfied with these accomplishments, and he resigned from *Figaro* in order to concentrate on his scholarly works. In 1970 he was elected to the Collège de France, a distinction that had not been accorded to even the renowned Durkheim. During his tenure there he wrote his great book on Clausewitz and military strategy that showed what the learned world had lost, through the publicistic diversion of his enormous energy and his powerful mind, to the hurly-burly of politics.

In 1977, after the vexatious experience of his last months at *Figaro*, he suffered a stroke that deprived him of the power of speech and, indeed, threatened his life. He recovered completely all of his powers of speech and mind, resumed his journalistic activity in *l'Express* and *Commentaire*, and continued to write with his habitual clarity and fluency. His *Memoires*, which appeared in the last year of his life, is in itself a monumental account of the substance of sixty years of European and American intellectual life. It is also a vivid, often touching portrait of a very exceptional moral and intellectual personality.

Toward the end of his life, Raymond Aron permitted to be published a series of interviews, fragments of which were broadcast on French television. Two young persons, both of leftist political convictions, undertook to cross-examine him. They had studied his writings, of which they disapproved, and they were determined to put him in the dock. The result, *Le Spectateur engagé*, is a fascinating, quietly dramatic unfolding of the history of Raymond Aron's intellectual and political development and a fresh revelation of his constancy of demeanor and conviction. It is also a portrait of a noble moral personality, modest and self-questioning, of a delicate courtesy, of frankness and courage. It is such a testimonial to Raymond Aron's transparent and unshakable honesty, his patent determination to know and tell the truth, and above all his willingness to discuss—not just to expound—his convictions that, by the end of the interviews, the two young leftists who had come to demonstrate his faults, became his friends and admirers.

VI

Raymond Aron's accuser-interrogators repeatedly intimated in these interviews on television, as their elders had said before, that Raymond Aron had no heart, that he was without compassion, that he was a conservative without any feeling of sympathy for the poor in France and elsewhere in the world. His response to their charges and all his writings on modern societies showed just the opposite.

Indeed, one reason why he was such an outstanding observer of French life was that he had an embracing consciousness of his fellow countrymen. Without that fellow feeling he could never have understood his countrymen, including those with whom he disagreed, such as the conservatives and the socialists before the war, the Vichyites, and, to some extent, the Gaullists during the war, and the Communist leftist intellectuals after the war.

Raymond Aron in his lifetime was accused by his detractors, who became fewer and fewer as the years went on, of being indifferent to the unhappiness of human beings. Nothing could have been further from the truth. He had, on the contrary, a remarkable tenderness and refinement of sentiment; it was expressed with such dignity and courtesy that persons who were not in his most intimate circle of friends might mistake it for no more than a polished instance of the *politesse française* that has now become so rare. Others, who knew him only from his writings and who had become used to the emotionally effusive rhetoric of those who think that passionate sentiment is all, and who think that a good purpose is served by wearing their bleeding hearts on their sleeves, also thought that Raymond Aron was a detached observer of an icy coldness. They were wrong. They mistook a dispassionate consideration of the merits and defects of alternative possibilities of action for moral indifference.

Raymond Aron never engaged in moralistic denunciations of those with whom he disagreed. He wrote against their arguments, not against them personally. He distinguished between persons and arguments. He did not discuss the motives of his adversaries; he examined their arguments. He was never abusive even when he was abused; he wrote polemics, but they were factual and logical, and he never insulted his adversaries as they insulted him. The same courtesy that was characteristic of his conduct in dealing with whomever he met was present in his dealings with those with whom he contended in writing. There was a tone of deep sentiment in his voice, but what that voice said was invariably about intellectually stated arguments, his own and those of others. He was profound and affectionate in his personal attachments, and he remained faithful to the friends of his youth even when, as in the case of Sartre, the friend made himself into an abusive adversary.

It has always been a charge of the romantics against the Enlightenment that its cold rationality had driven enchantment out of the world. Raymond Aron was a direct continuator of the Enlightenment. He believed in and practiced the exercise of reason and the realistic assessment of possible courses of action in public life.

The virtues that he praised were impossible to realize in societies in which rulers thought they had the ultimate and correct answer to every problem and would not permit the free exercise of reason and the free pursuit of truth that might lead to conclusions differing from their own. He also prized the freedom of the individual to pursue, within the limits of his resources and his obligations to others, ends that he thought right. That is why he espoused the cause of a pluralistic society, competitive political parties, free elections, representative institutions, and a free press. That is why he opposed those who regarded the Soviet Union or some variant of it as the ideal. That is also why he opposed the expansion of the Soviet system to other societies.

Although he regarded the free exercise of reason, the free pursuit of truth, and the freedom of action of individuals and groups as among the chief criteria by which the merit of a society should be assessed, he was acutely aware of the imperfection of even the best societies—and Western liberal-democratic societies, not least. He had no confidence in claims of perfection. No society, he thought, could be perfect, and every society was justly subject to criticism. He did not exempt Western liberal-democratic societies. He was well aware of their imperfections with respect to equality and justice, but he thought that their merits and demerits must be realistically assessed in the light of plausible alternatives.

He was not a rationalist. He was conscious of the possibility of error in reasoning; he was, above all, conscious of the insufficiency of knowledge of the present and of the unforeseeability of the future. Theories or doctrines that claimed certainty were intellectually and temperamentally repugnant to him. That is why Marxism-Leninism and their variants, which confidently claimed to foresee the future as the culmination of an inevitable historical process, were even more unacceptable. He was a man of reason and truth who understood the frailty of reason and the obstacles to gaining knowledge of reality. Doctrines that asserted "the meaning of history" and expounded the correct way to realize that meaning were inimical, he was convinced, to the free exercise of reason and to the free pursuit of truth as well as to responsible and realistic action.

Utopias did not attract him because he thought that their proponents avoided, for the sake of an ultimate and unrealizable condition of perfection, a seriously taken responsibility in judgment and action. He himself eschewed the unqualified censure of politicians from the standpoint of an ideal that he regarded as unrealizable. He emphasized constantly the constraints of political action and decisions. He was always simultaneously critical and constructive. He knew that no politician or government could act without constraints; in every situation there were, according to his view, a small number and a narrow range of alternatives, and every one of these carried with it costs that should be borne in mind in the making of decisions. A government or any politician in office had to consider the state of opinion, the attitudes of rivals and adversaries, and the strength of the support that could be mustered for the realization of a decision. The limited power of politicians and governments, arising from ignorance—from inevitable ignorance, not avoidable ignorance—the impossibility of foreseeing the future, and the limits imposed on its powers by the limits of the support it enjoyed from its supporters and allies and the resistance of its adversaries, whether they were domestic or foreign, confirmed Raymond Aron in his conviction that no government, and least of all a government in a liberal-democratic society, could act in a way that would satisfy intellectual opponents whose criticisms postulated the realizability of a vaguely conceived but nonetheless absolute and ultimate ideal.

These are among the reasons why he so patiently and painstakingly remonstrated with the intellectuals of the left. It was not that he was unsympathetic with humanitarian ideals—quite the opposite—nor that he was unsympathetic with the more recent demand for "human rights." It was not at all that he ignored the misery of human beings or that he viewed with indifference their death from starvation and disease or their extermination by the brutality of war. On the contrary, justice in distribution of rewards and opportunities was in fact for him a vital criterion in the assessment of the goodness of a society.

In one sense Raymond Aron was the heir of the best elements in the outlook of the Third Republic. He retained a deep sympathy for those who came to the support of Captain Dreyfus and who continued that tradition. He retained, in a somber, less optimistic way, their appreciation of progress—progress in the sense of the increasing material well-being of humanity—their belief in the rightness and goodness of freedom, their conviction that reason and knowledge are proper guides of choice and action, and their French patriotism. Of course Raymond Aron was more aware of the seamy side of the technological progress that was necessary to the material well-being of mankind; he was far more aware of the limits of knowledge. He was even a "man of the left" in his humanitarianism and in his hatred of war. But he had no confidence that the "international working class" could be counted upon to prevent wars, and he had no confidence at all that public ownership of the instruments of production would improve the lot of men and increase their freedom. He had studied the writings of Marx and Engels too closely to believe that they were valid. He knew too much economics, he knew too much history, and he had studied international politics and military strategy and technology too closely to continue to accept the traditional doctrines of international and French socialism and communism. And of course he was never in the slightest degree a man of the left as that term came to be understood after the formation of the Communist International. He was never blind to the mendacity and deceitfulness of the Communist party, and he was too intelligent not to see through the manipulation of the gullibility of the fellow travelers.

Nevertheless, although it was the left that reviled him and ostracized him, he had a soft place in his heart for it. It was his strong intelligence, his acute scholarship, and his moral courage that caused him to reject its false beliefs and its lighthearted self-deceptions.

VII

It is very difficult for me to take a just and final leave of a man whom I knew for over forty years, with whom I agreed on nearly everything he wrote and said, whom I admired greatly, whom, especially in later years, I saw infrequently, toward whom I was drawn by warm affection, and from whom I was nonetheless remote. I had so many common intellectual interests with him. I shared intellectual traditions that were very important to both of us in our separate ways. It has therefore not been easy to attain the detachment necessary to do justice to such a complex and many-sided character, to such a richly learned and such a polymorphous and yet utterly straightforward intelligence.

I first encountered Raymond Aron in his little book, *La Sociologie allemande contemporaine,* which was published by Alcan in 1935. As soon as I learned of its existence, I ordered it from G. E. Stechert, who at that time was the major importer of European books into the United States. I myself was spending a lot of my time on the writers on whom Aron wrote, and my judgments had been much the same as those he arrived at. The prominence he gave to Max Weber, at a time when very few sociologists knew how important Weber's work was, caused me to feel a kinship with him over the four thousand miles that separated us. The book was very much a *Jugendschrift.* Yet even at that early date, I could sense the courage that was one of his major characteristics over the remainder of his life. There was almost no interest in German sociology in France in the middle of the 1930s and no more knowledge; among the German sociologists whom Aron came across in Germany in the early part of that decade, Weber had nothing like the prominence he now possesses. It needed courage for a young man, in his first book, to fly in the face of his elders by praising so fully, in France, an almost unknown German writer and by praising, in Germany, a dead writer whom living Germans did not want to appreciate.

I met Aron for the first time in the early months in 1943. We were introduced to each other in front of the offices of *La France libre,* which were in a fine residential building in Queensbury Place. I had come there with a Polish friend, Eugene Friedwald—a "petroleum journalist" who wrote on economic subjects for *La France libre.* Friedwald, or perhaps Karl Mannheim, must have told him about me; he appeared to know that I had studied Max Weber's writings carefully and had translated some of them. He knew that I had translated Mannheim's *Ideologie und Utopie.* He made a brief reference to our common admiration for Max Weber. He seemed pleased by my passing reference to the chapter on Weber in his little book. Then he went off with Mme Moura Budberg, the fabulous, then still beautiful friend of Maxim Gorky, H. G. Wells, and Bruce Lockhart, who performed some sort of administrative function at *La France libre.* I went off with Friedwald. Our meeting was very brief, but I still retain my original impression of his quick, yet sad and gentle smile, the fraternal benevolence of his brief conversation.

After his return to France in the late summer of 1944, I did not see him again until the spring of 1947. Thereafter I saw him frequently in Paris throughout the remainder of the 1940s and until 1967, when there was a temporary suspension. He never varied from his, at least for me, somewhat shy friendliness and his humor, which was never injurious. There was a melancholy sonorousness in his voice. He never slipped into "personalities." He never flaunted his connections with prominent politicians. If he knew secrets, he never disclosed or hinted at them. He did not tell me things "in confidence." He avoided giving any impression of being on the "inside." Just as in his writings, in his conversation he drew on information that was openly available to anyone who went to the trouble to obtain it. The only time I ever heard him refer with pride to any of his writings was just after he had completed *Paix et guerre entre les nations;* his reference was not to its content, of which he could very well have been proud, but rather to the fact that he had written that very thick book, based on much study, in what was for me an astonishingly short time. He never referred to the honors that had been conferred on him or made other acknowledgment of his achievements.

Although during much of the period when I was often in his company he was treated by most French intellectuals almost as a leper was treated in antiquity, I cannot recall his ever voicing a grievance against his detractors. I remember a lunch in the late autumn of 1951 in a *cabinet particulier* at Lapérouse. Present were Georges Davy, a dreary Durkheimian professor of sociology at the Sorbonne and dean of the faculté des lettres; Georges Friedmann, a very decent, once-Communist professor of sociology at the Conservatoire des arts et métiers; Aron; another person, whom I do not recall clearly; and myself. At the time, the "Gilson affair" was much talked about in the press and in conversation. Etienne Gilson earlier in the year had been visiting Notre Dame University. Gilson, who was a great authority on medieval philosophy, was much preoccupied with politics and was a vehement "neutralist." He had been writing for several years in a furious style against American foreign policy and most recently against the North Atlantic Treaty. Early in 1951 there appeared in *Figaro littéraire* an "open letter" addressed to Gilson by Waldemar Gurian, then professor of politics at Notre Dame, in which Gurian said that Gilson had declared that Aron was a "paid American agent." Gurian admitted that he himself had not heard Gilson say this but had it only at second hand. I knew Gurian well and he came often to see me in Chicago; on one of his visits he told me of the incident and he assured me of the reliability of the person who had reported Gilson's remark to him. This was well before the "open letter" was published in France. The discussion about Gilson's charge reverberated in France for a long time after the appearance of the "open letter," and it emerged in the course of our lunch. Aron uttered no recriminations against Gilson, although he did not deny that Gilson might have made the charge; nor did Aron attempt to refute the charge, which was obviously baseless. I recall above all that Aron insisted that Gurian should not have written as he did on the basis of secondhand evidence and that he wished to dissociate himself from Gurian's accusation, regardless of whether it was true or untrue. He was pained by the introduction of personal considerations into a political discussion. Although his own honor had been impugned, he would not accept a vindication by improper means.

I have, of course, not read all of Raymond Aron's hundreds and hundreds of articles in *Figaro* or even the smaller number in *l'Express.* I have, however, read a very large number over the years, and I have also read most of his writings published in book form. What impressed me most, along with their sense of responsibility, their cogency, their complete sobriety of judgment, and their amazing informedness, was the avoidance of any display of his "personality" and the absence of any claim to authority other than the authority of facts and rational arguments.

His reticence about himself was equaled by his consideration for others. His patience with Sartre, along with his generosity toward him, despite Sartre's brutal denunciations of him, is only one instance of his freedom from rancor. He always tried to speak of others in an understanding way. I once asked his opinion of Bertrand de Jouvenel's conduct in the first year or two of the German occupation. Jouvenel had been accused of being a *collaborateur* and in 1941 had written a problematic book that accepted the unification of Europe under German hegemony. Aron answered in something like the following words: "The defeat of the French army and the subjugation of France by Germany had deeply shaken and disordered the spirits of those who had to live under it. It was easy for me because I had to leave France, being a Jew, and so I could maintain my intellectual equilibrium. But for those who remained behind, the situation was very much harder. Furthermore, well before the Germans were driven out of France, Jouvenel had made amends by serving the *résistance*." His appearance in court on Jouvenel's behalf in a legal action instituted by Jouvenel against an author who had accused him of having been a fascist in the 1930s was another instance of his determination to be never less than truthful or just. (Aron died almost immediately on leaving the courtroom.)

I could go on and on in trying to be just to this extraordinary man, this model of civility, of selfless sobriety, and of deep and learned reflection. What stands out in my mind, in addition to his great qualities as a scholar and as a philosophical observer of human societies, was his indomitability. He was indomitable in the face of personal misfortunes, public obloquy, and the severe trials of the society and the civilizations that he sought to serve and strengthen. One of the greatest sons of the Enlightenment, he believed that reason could not be extinguished from the human mind and that his appeals to the reason of others would not be in vain.

Many years ago, Raymond Aron, Professor Arvid Brodersen, and I were standing on a street corner in Paris after lunch, continuing our conversation about the affairs of the human race. In response to a remark of my own, he said laughingly, "*C'est un pessimiste jovial.*" I now return the compliment but without doing anything like full justice to the richness of his mind and character, by saying, "*C'était un optimiste triste.*" With that I take my unhappy leave of Raymond Aron.

Introduction

Franciszek Draus

The work of Raymond Aron may be seen as a confluence of two different traditions: the classical, philosophical tradition, and the modern, analytic tradition. In an age of specialized scholarship and empirical research, Aron managed to maintain a breadth of vision and depth of thought characteristic of an era long since past. Whether focusing on the particular or on the historical, his perspective always remained broad as well as sharp. His philosophy of the historical condition of man is not an apology for transient things but a defense of wisdom and of prudence in history.

Aron's literary production was vast. The length and variety of his bibliography might lead one to wonder whether there is any unity in his work. The diversity of his writings, which include philosophy, economics, sociology, and journalism, is such that this huge intellectual achievement may be seen as heterogeneous, at best.

The impression of heterogeneity disappears, however, as soon as one undertakes a serious study of Aron's work. Its unity first of all is that of Raymond Aron himself, devoted to the ideals of liberty and dignity of man. By his life and by his work, Aron manifested a commitment to the free pursuit of truth in the intellectual sphere, and honesty and fidelity in the political sphere. Politically, Aron was committed to the struggle for tolerance and liberal democracy, with the conviction that humanity could be given expression only in a system that allows doubt and dialogue.

Even more important, perhaps, Aron's work has a philosophical unity. This unity is expressed by a certain mode of reflection, a certain

Translated by Charles Krance

attitude with regard to history, and a certain philosophical approach to the historical condition of man.

In my choice of Aron's writings for inclusion in this volume, I have intended to make clear the philosophical foundation of Aron's intellectual and political commitment. I used this criterion because the philosophical foundation of Aron's thought has, until now, been ignored. We have seen Aron the sociologist, the journalist, the university teacher, and the political thinker; consequently, this variety of interests and activities has been seen as the expression of temperament or of turns of fortune. Without denying the occasional character of many of Aron's writings, I emphasize the coherence and depth of his work. My goal in this collection is to present the enduring qualities of Aron's work.

On the Intelligibility of History

Aron's essential contribution to contemporary social and political thought consists of an elaboration of the principles and criteria of a mode of thought or reasoning which has nothing to do with either resignation or naïve optimism; it is a mode of thought which both embodies and expresses lucidity and moderation.

Aron's philosophy is not a logical system, but neither is it an incoherent aggregate of opinions. There is no explicit system of thought in Aron's work, in the sense of a construction of general propositions inferred from axiomatic principles; his thought is nevertheless marked by a comprehensive unity of philosophical, analytic approaches to diverse domains of social life, including international relations, diplomacy in the twentieth century, ideology, and class structure. All of it stems from a certain number of philosophical propositions and analytic criteria. Aron never formulated his point of view as an intellectual system, constructed by logical deductions. Rather, it is a philosophy in motion. It proceeds by applying a few fundamental propositions to diverse objects.

The main problem to which Aron's work addresses itself is that of *historical intelligibility.* The understanding of history was the task that determined the character and content of all of Aron's investigations, just as it determined the directions of Aron's career. Aron carried out his research on historical intelligibility on two levels: the strictly theoretical—reflection on historical knowledge—and the practical—research intended to deepen his understanding of European and world politics in the twentieth century. It is no surprise, then, that he was at once philosopher, sociological theorist, professor, historian of ideas, engaged political thinker, and journalist. The richness of Aron's life and work is the outgrowth of an original intellectual intention to grasp the intelligibility of history in its different aspects.

How can history be made intelligible? In pursuit of the answer, Aron conducted a minute analysis of historical understanding, inspired, moreover, by the ideas and analytic schemata of German hermeneutics at the beginning of the twentieth century, such as are to be found in the writings of Wilhelm Dilthey and Max Weber. Aron revived the analytic distinction between understanding and causal explanation, and through logical analyses of these two modes of cognition he formulated his own philosophical theses concerning history.

Historical understanding, for Aron, is both an act of awareness and a practical act (decision, action). This twofold aspect of history springs from the word *history* itself. *History* sometimes designates a reality, and sometimes the knowledge that we come to have of that reality. But Aron does not infer from this a duality of historical being. According to him, historical understanding is not separated from historical reality, and what is called "historical reality" does not exist totally apart from our understanding. Aron defines history as movement or becoming, which is both movement of consciousness and movement of actions. Moreover, in the processes of history, events and cognition are reciprocally connected with and condition each other, without constituting a total, logical system. Historical becoming unfolds in time, the beginning and end of which we do not know. It is a constituent of man. Man does not exist outside of history; there is no other history than that of man. Man is the subject of history and defines himself through history.

Consequently, historical understanding is movement, both spiritual and material, suspended between the unknown of the origin and the unknown of the end, a movement that acquires a meaningful direction insofar as it is a movement of self-determination and self-constitution of man by himself. To make history intelligible therefore implies grasping the sense of concrete history, not in terms of a finality, a law, or a structure, but in terms of man's historical freedom. It is from this type of general perspective that we must view Aron's investigation into the meaning of history, both his strictly political inquiries and those of a theoretical nature.

Epistemologically, to make history intelligible presupposes understanding and explanation. To understand, according to Aron, means to draw immanent meaning from the real, to grasp those intentions or thoughts that are part of any given historical event, to try to rethink or reconstitute the meaning as it was experienced and as it was expressed by a given historical act. How is such an understanding possible? Aron would answer: by an effort of detachment and a respect for facts. But is detachment possible? Under what conditions? Furthermore, how can one claim to respect facts if they are not completely independent of the historian's intentions?

Aron defines the ideal or the objective of knowledge—the search for truth—by detachment and respect for facts; but he immediately establishes the limited validity and relative character of such knowledge. Historic understanding does not exhaust the meanings expressed in historical actions. Facts, indeed historical reality itself, appear equivocal and inexhaustible. To the impossibility of exhaustiveness another obstacle is added: the impossibility of total detachment. The ideal of understanding is said to be that of participation, but "one only is oneself—one thinks or imagines others" (Aron, *Introduction to the Philosophy of History* [Boston: Beacon Press, 1961], p. 154).

Just as Aron's analysis of historic understanding shows us that meaning is never definitive, and thus spiritual (or noëtic) history is never determinate, so his analysis of causality attempts to demonstrate the inconclusiveness of action and the indeterminateness of factual history.

Historical action would be conclusive if it were inscribed in a determined order of facts, or events. But, as Aron demonstrates, such an order cannot be known. Discerning the causal links between events can lead, at the very most, to the recognition of contingent determinism, pointing to a partial and probable causality. For lack of absolute knowledge, the historical actor views himself as within the categories of probability. He must imagine the possibilities that reality offers him in one moment or another of his action. He must calculate the probability of success or failure in his undertaking.

Although the historian's situation is not the same as the actor's, historical understanding, which is subsequent to the event, does not differ essentially from that of the actor who participates in the event. According to Aron, both historian and actor must perceive historical reality in terms of degrees of probability. Here, Aron is in full agreement with Max Weber, and accepts the latter's conception of retrospective probability or objective possibility. This theory of objective possibility dispels the illusion of historical determinism at the same time that it emphasizes the relativity of action. It is an expression of an antinomy between historicity and the absoluteness of decision.

By his analysis of understanding, Aron intended to show the possibility of spiritual freedom, the freedom of choosing our spiritual destiny. By his analysis of historical causality, he made clear the existence of freedom of action and hence the freedom of political choice. While

the former rejects dogmatism, the latter resists fatalism. To make history intelligible, therefore, requires grasping at once the direction of our thought and the meaning of our liberty: "History is free because it is not written in advance, or determined as is a sector of nature or a fatality; it is unpredictable, as man is to himself" (ibid., p. 320).

The first two parts of this collection attempt to illustrate Aron's search for historical understanding. As I have already suggested, this search led him along two paths at the same time: a theoretical one and a practical one. First, Aron determined the categories and conditions of understanding; then he applied them in interpreting and commenting on the history of contemporary politics.

How is European history of the twentieth century to be understood? Was the First World War inevitable? Did the Treaty of Versailles increase the likelihood of a Second World War? Was the division of Europe after 1945 inevitable? For Aron, certainly, history—such as it has been—was not inevitable. His steadfast rejection of historical determinism has a double meaning. It is a refusal to accept the inevitability of yesterday's holocaust at the same time as a rejection of the inevitability of totalitarianism today or communism tomorrow. Aronian rejection of inevitability is an expression of hope. Just as there was no destiny predetermining the self-destruction of European states at the beginning of this century, there is no inevitable victory, either military or peaceful, for the Soviets tomorrow.

Indeed, Aron's historical probabilism insists on its educational function with regard to will and hope: "There is no such thing as global determinism. The transcendence of the future, for man in Time, is an incentive to will his own destiny and a guarantee that, whatever happens, hope will not perish" (Aron, *The Opium of the Intellectuals* [Garden City, N.Y.: Doubleday, 1957], p. 182).

Aron denied all assertions of historical inevitability; that was the ground for his argument against Marxism-Leninism and the ideologies allied with it. His struggle was relentless, for its stakes were hope and historical freedom.

Aron laid the philosophical foundations of his thought in his *Introduction to the Philosophy of History* (1938). The scope of the present volume permits no excerpt from that fundamental work. Nevertheless, I have included texts which, while in no way lacking the philosophical rigor of the *Introduction,* contain most of the major philosophical propositions. Compared to the 1938 book, the texts I have selected enjoy the advantage of having been written in a more accessible language. But the interested reader should not take them as a substitute for the *Introduction.*

Tocqueville and Marx

The third part of this anthology can be interpreted in several ways. It represents Aron's critique of the Marxism of Karl Marx as well as that of Marx's descendants; it is a critique of a mistaken understanding of history, of which Marxism is one example. Indeed, Aron's major criticism of Marx is focused on the latter's mistaken philosophy of history and, consequently, his erroneous idea of historical intelligibility.

Did Marxism, in fact, make it easier to understand historical reality in the nineteenth century? Do we still need Marxism today? Aron attempts to answer these questions through a dialogue between Tocqueville and Marx, a dialogue which Aron himself had to devise, since the two authors were in all likelihood unaware of each other; in any case, Tocqueville had not known Marx's writings.

Both Tocqueville and Marx wanted to make the reality of modern society intelligible. For each of them, this society was to be essentially democratic, but they did not take democracy to mean the same thing. Tocqueville was a liberal, Marx a dialectician of the Hegelian type. The former had a legal background, the latter was a born philosopher. But, paradoxically, it was Tocqueville who tried to grasp the true meaning of the dialectics of liberty and equality, while Marx, for his part, was set on suppressing it. Tocqueville was too much of an aristocrat to accept all the consequences of egalitarianism; he foresaw, nevertheless, the general extension of well-being through democracy. Marx, rebelling against his own social origins, condemned liberal society; his condemnation, however, perhaps unintentionally, entailed a condemnation of liberty itself. Tocqueville saw the possibility of salvation in political liberties and so-called categorical democracy, while Marx prophesied the coming of a real democracy, which would be the self-fulfillment of humanity. Today, after a century of historical experience, and in full awareness of the achievements of modern society, how, in political matters, could we maintain our honesty and not decide against Marx?

It would oversimplify the dialogue between the two simply to declare Tocqueville right and Marx wrong. The significance of the dialogue increases when we see it as a confrontation between two systems of historical understanding rather than between two historical predictions or visions. The Tocquevillian method was one of historical probabilism; Marx's method, on the other hand, was deterministic. Whether judgments are to be lucid or erroneous ought therefore to depend on the philosophical choice between probability and necessity, between indetermination and inevitability. Tocqueville, who analyzed the conditions and consequences of modern democracy, foresaw our era as egalitarian; but he left open the choice between liberty and servitude. He said that the future will depend on ourselves, the egalitarian impulse being the determining factor only for the conditions in which political choice will be exercised. By contrast, Marx arbitrarily proclaimed historical inevitability, and the only choice he allowed was between revolution and counterrevolution. Instead of giving hope to the underprivileged and thereby proposing reasonable means of action, Marx offered them a false certainty. Tocqueville did not promise liberty for all, only the equality of conditions. Marx proclaimed universal liberation, and thus neglected the fundamental concern of all human existence, namely, that of being able to choose one's own destiny.

If, at the end of this dialogue, Aron decided for Tocqueville's ideas, it was because he found in him a kinship of spirit and values. Both Tocqueville and Aron kept hope alive, as they placed their stakes on the free and clear-minded action of historical man. Both were convinced that political liberties are the condition of liberty in general.

Toward a Sociology of Modern Societies

The dialogue between Tocqueville and Marx could be read as a prelude to Aron's own effort to understand modern industrial societies. It shows us the general orientation of Aron's thought in this area: probabilistic philosophically, and liberal-democratic politically. But here his approach will be shown to be primarily analytic, with occasional references to theorists who were both the witnesses and the first analysts of industrial society at its inception. He used Saint-Simon's and Auguste Comte's ideas and predictions as points of reference; he accepted neither without reservation.

Both Saint-Simon and Comte emphasized the economic aspect of modern social transformations. They brought to light the fundamental difference between the old society and the new, the former being hierarchical and military, the latter scientific and commercial. They both considered phenomena such as science, technology, labor, and primary education to be new and decisive for the future of Western civilization. Aron, without attaching the same importance to the economic factor as these two authors did, nonetheless carried forward some of their analyses and propositions, and as one who lived in the period of the triumph of industrialization he examined their prophecy.

Aron's studies on industrial societies have a double significance. On the one hand, Aron summarizes, discusses, confirms, or refutes the questions and propositions of modern sociologists (Saint-Simon, Comte, Tocqueville, Marx, Pareto, Max Weber). On the other hand, he attempts to grasp the specific characteristics, the meaning of modern achievements, and the dangers of industrial civilization in the nuclear age. These studies, which partake of the history of ideas and statistical analyses, present a curious blend of philosophical debate and sometimes give the impression that Aron wanted to stay within the limits of his generation.

Three types of propositions may be distinguished in Aron's works on modern sociology: propositions about the general characteristics of modern societies; propositions which establish the categories of an adequate sociological analysis; and propositions bearing on the social and methodological status of sociological knowledge.

The distinctive traits of modern societies are science, technology, and industry. Aron uses the term *scientific societies* because the point of origin of modern social change and the condition of economic development are, in fact, based on science.

According to Aron, modern society, seen as a social model, has a doubly Promethean ambition: it aims to control nature in order to exploit it for the benefit of mankind, and to control "social matters" so as to mold them with an eye to the advancement of individual liberties. Modern society was formed, essentially, by two revolutions, the one scientific and technological, the other democratic. In Aron's view, the advent of these two revolutions was not a simple coincidence. Characteristic features such as the freedom to work, the striving for self-betterment, or social mobility all implied, in so many ways, a democratization of the entire society; at the very least, they implied the destruction of rigid social structures and traditional forms of political subordination which was to lead toward democracy. With these developments in mind, it is clear that modern transformations have been inseparable from the egalitarian and democratic impulse. The ideal of *equality*—social, political, economic—had become both the goal and the legitimation of modern society.

But the same ideal of equality, for which so many battles have been fought, became both a source of hope and a source of conflict. Egalitarian society thus became a society-in-conflict. And Aron strongly emphasized the conflictual character of modern industrial societies.

Aron's principal contribution to contemporary sociology is his thesis concerning the *fact of oligarchy* in the midst of modern democracies. The modernization of societies has markedly increased opportunities for education and economic prosperity for individuals, but it has also created new forms of power and hierarchy. Modern societies have proclaimed the democratic ideal, in the strictly political sense of according power "of the people, for the people, and by the people" as well as in the sense of material equality. Yet social differentiation and stratification, which were inevitable, have contradicted the ideal of material equality, while the formation of ruling categories such as politicians, economic leaders, leaders of the masses, and intellectual authorities with their considerable power has been inconsistent with the "power of the people."

Aron's belief in the fact of oligarchy in modern societies should not be interpreted as antidemocratic. He intended only to point out an irresolvable disparity between the ideal and its realization, between the intention and the effect. Modern societies have proclaimed the democratic ideal as their goal, but they have not achieved full democracy. The oligarchic element seems to be inseparable from the nature of society, but it does not necessarily nullify democracy as such. In democratic society, oligarchy is not an absolute negation of democracy—as long as it does not take the form of a ruling class, reproducing itself and maintaining its own internal cohesion from generation to generation; instead, it is a phenomenon of *ruling categories*, which are themselves divided and in a state of permanent conflict. Thus, as long as the element of oligarchy itself remains pluralistic, as is the case in Western societies, and as long as democracy insists that the rulers, i.e., those who govern, know and take into account the demands of the ruled, i.e., those who are governed, it will not, Aron reminds us, necessarily nullify democracy. "Free discussion between the controlling majority and its opposition, between labour unions and pressure groups, between intellectuals and those in power—despite the iron law of oligarchy—assures the ruled those guarantees which they may reasonably expect and gives the rulers little opportunity to misunderstand the profound desires of the masses" (Aron, *Progress and Disillusion* [New York: Praeger, 1968], pp. 35–36).

Aron's affirmation of the fact of oligarchy in democracy is therefore an appeal to realism, without which there can be no understanding or equitable judgment.

On International Politics

The fifth part of this volume also lends itself to a dual reading. The politician will find reflections on the nature of international relations, including their moral and strategic aspects. And the philosopher will find Aron's philosophical reflections on the antinomies of historical action.

For Aron, all thought and action contain antinomies since each, thought and action alike, is a human effort which, although never completed and always renewed, seeks to surpass either the limits of knowledge or the limits of action. The historical condition of man is expressed, among other ways, in the fact that he formulates goals and ideals which, although never reached, require his self-sacrifice. In Aron's thought, the tragic dialectic of historical man is the very condition of noble projects, glorious intentions, and their imperfect realization. This theme already makes its mark in Aron's theory of the fact of oligarchy; in the context of his theory on international relations, however, it is even more explicit.

The political ideal is always justice and peace. But no political regime has ever wholly attained its own ideals; consequently, those rare periods of peace have been little more than the absence of war. Aron's statement that man "creates cities, but he does not know the cities he creates," that "his children or his children's children recognise in them the familiar traits of the domination of man by man" (*History and the Dialectic of Violence* [Oxford: Blackwell, 1975], p. 216), is not free of a certain amount of pessimism.

It would be a mistake, however, to see this philosophy of the essential imperfection of the historical universe as an admission of a basic pessimism. To admit to the imperfection of human and historical endeavors is a sign of realism and modesty. This is how I interpret Aron's phenomenology of history. Man, in order to think clearly and act effectively, does not need absolute knowledge or the assurance of success. What he does need is an awareness of what man really is. Man is a historical being, that is, he is incomplete and free. What he has left, in such a situation, is hope and responsibility, which can have no other foundation than that of reason.

Like all human action, diplomatic action contains antinomies. This is the basis of Aron's theory of international relations. The primary antinomy of politics is that of ethics and effectiveness. Ethics prescribe the rejection of violence, while effectiveness, in prescribing peace, for example, often requires violence. But there is more to it than that: any state which intends unconditionally to follow the imperatives of ethics may very well run the risk, in a given situation, of being the victim of its own morality.

Diplomatic action contains antinomies because it seeks an ideal of peace in a universe where recourse to violence is legitimate. What ensues is a fragile, unstable peace and the impossibility of genuine peace. Furthermore, diplomatic action lays claim to a calculated rationality, but its calculations are based on the risk of war, and not on any quantifiable data.

For Aron, the first step toward understanding political action is to grasp its antinomies. Reality cannot be understood by denying antinomies; we must recognize and try to understand them. This intellectual attitude toward history and action allows Aron to formulate an ethics based on wisdom, and a strategy based on prudence. Wise judgment, according to Aron, "attempts not only to consider each case in its concrete particularities, but also not to ignore any of the arguments of principle and opportunity, to forget neither the relation of forces nor the wills of peoples" (below, p. 283). On the other hand, a prudent strategy is one that "takes into account the whole of reality, dictates diplomatic-strategic conduct adapted not to the finished portrait of what international politics would be if statesmen were wise in their selfishness, but to the nature of the passions, the follies, the ideas and the violences of the century" (below, p. 282). But neither an ethics based on wisdom, nor a strategy based on prudence, can guarantee absolute security. They express no certainty, only the hope that by complying with the principle of realism and reason men will at least bring about a decrease in the amount of historical violence.

Aron and Max Weber

Aron's thought cannot be fully understood without a recognition of its affinities with that of Max Weber. Indeed, Aron's work is an almost unceasing discussion of Weber's views about society and history.

The *Introduction to the Philosophy of History*, Aron's major work, was written under the influence of Weber's ideas. But it is much more than an extension of Weber's thought. Aron accepts, in principle, Weber's epistemological theses, but he does not extend them into a philosophy. He considers that "the relativist theory of historical knowledge does not necessarily lead to a relativist philosophy" (ibid. [Boston: Beacon Press, 1961], p. 291). This point seems to me to be of the utmost importance, both for Aron's criticism of Weber's views and for understanding what is central in Aron's thought itself. Was he justified in separating relativist epistemology from a relativist philosophy?

The intellectual relations between Aron and Max Weber underwent changes, and I shall try to trace these changes by focusing on three themes: the phenomenological description of history; the theory of knowledge; and world vision.

What links Aron and Weber is the phenomenology of history. Recognition of the limits of knowledge, and of the antinomies of thought and action, are fundamental to both Weber and Aron.

The same is not true, however, of epistemology. In his *Introduction,* Aron accepted Weber's theory of the incoherence of reality, the subjectivity of historical knowledge, and the relativity of scientific theories. In the late 1950s he revised his attitude toward Weber's view of scientific relativism.

> In fact, in Max Weber's thought relativism was linked with his idea of the real, and this idea originated in a neo-Kantian philosophy. He believed that all social reality lacked form, and was simply an accumulation of scattered facts. When faced with these incoherent facts the sociologist creates order with the aid of his concepts. The concepts enable him to understand reality, but his interpretation is obviously linked with his conceptual system, and this system is itself connected with his personal situation. But a society is not just a mass of incoherent elements. Social reality is neither a completely integrated whole nor an incoherent mass, and so it is impossible to be dogmatic either about the universal validity of social types, or about the relativism of every theory. (*Eighteen Lectures on Industrial Society* [London: Weidenfeld and Nicolson, 1967], p. 27)

By rejecting the extremes of theoretical dogmatism and relativist dogmatism, Aron proposed another interpretation of sociological knowledge. His proposition expressed a kind of compromise: "Social reality appears neither incoherent nor completely ordered; it contains innumerable semi-organized parts, but no obvious total order. The sociologist does not arbitrarily create the logic of the social behaviour which he analyses. . . . The sociologist brings out the categories and regularities of his subject, but he always makes a choice between these categories and regularities" (ibid., p. 28).

It is inevitable, therefore, that knowledge, whether historical or sociological, should be tinged with partiality; but if this partiality is perceived and acknowledged, it is quite compatible with the ideal of objectivity. The real danger for the objectivity of knowledge, according to Aron, lies in the failure to recognize its partiality.

Aron's revision of Weber's epistemology went even further. In striving to determine the conditions of scientific objectivity, Aron repudiated Weber's idea of evaluative neutrality, the idea of *wertfreie Wissenschaft,* and the objectivity of knowledge supposedly achieved by the construction of ideal types. According to Aron, objective knowledge is achieved neither by evaluative neutrality, which he regarded as impossible in itself, nor by intellectual rationalizations which are often ineffective, but rather by *fairness*—respect for facts and respect for others. From a strictly logical point of view, the best way to achieve fairness is by means of "an analytic theory that would at least indicate the principal determining factors and allow for a reconstruction of the whole" (below, p. 219).

But the major area of disagreement between Aron and Max Weber lies in their respective views of the world. Aron rejects the Weberian view of inexpiable and eternal conflicts and struggles between values. According to Aron, Weber was wrong to draw philosophical or quasi-religious conclusions from an epistemology of the relativity of knowledge and the plurality of scientific theories. He thought Weber was wrong to conclude that, because of the limits of knowledge and the ultimate indecisiveness of actions, various theories under consideration can have equal weight, and all actions are equally ineffective. In Aron's view, some theories better reflect the meaning of reality than others, just as some actions are more effective in furthering human dignity and respect than others. The wisdom of a sage and the prescience of a madman are no more alike than are the commitment of a moderate and the action of a fanatic.

Aron's criticism of Weber's philosophical vision culminated in a profession of faith and humanistic hope; he did not despair because of the indecisiveness or inconclusiveness of action and the limited powers of historical man, but placed his stakes on fragmentary yet sober knowledge and on moderate, reasonable action. Aron's ideal is a reasonable politics, one based on realistic and honest analysis of the social order rather than on some certitude or other.

In this Introduction I have mentioned only the principal themes and have only hinted at the philosophical depth of Aron's thought. The study of Aron's works has been a demanding experience for me, both intellectually and emotionally. I hope, therefore, that the reader of this book will find in it rewards similar to those that I have gained from editing it.

Part One

Man and History

The texts that follow were written approximately at the same time. The first was written in 1951 for the Congrès des sociétés françaises de philosophie but was not published until 1972. The second was published in French in 1951.

Despite the apparent difference between these two pieces—one strictly theoretical, the other an analysis of the history of European diplomacy in the first half of the twentieth century—they form a coherent whole. In the first, Aron reflects on the intelligibility of history in general; in the second, he attempts to apply the principles elaborated in the theoretical reflection to the understanding of European politics in our time.

1

Three Forms of Historical Intelligibility

The question of the *intelligibility of history* is itself ambiguous since each of these two terms involves multiple meanings and covers various realities.

If we agree to call history, in the sense of the object to be known, the whole past of human societies, and to call history, in the sense of the knowledge to be developed, the reconstruction of the past in its unique development, then the question of intelligibility can be raised apropos of any aspect of human existence taken individually as well as collectively. Perceiving the past of one's own consciousness, perceiving other lives, and perceiving the relations between minds as they occur at the moment or are reflected in institutions—each of these endeavors contains an element of the problem of historical intelligibility. One cannot claim to have examined this problem completely without having exhausted each of these endeavors and brought out the consequences of their interaction.

The definition of intelligibility is just as prone to controversy. We are referring not only to the distinction, as classical as it is controversial, between *explaining* and *understanding* (in one case revealing a unique succession within a regular framework; in the other, discovering the significant relation, intrinsic to what is given). The specific difficulty of historical intelligibility results from the plurality of levels on which the questioning must be repeated. Where is one seeking intelligibility: in the soldier's action on the battlefield, in the decision of the war leader, or in the sum total of thousands of actions and thousands of decisions taken by leaders large and small? The example is a crude

From *Politics and History: Selected Essays by Raymond Aron*, edited and translated by Miriam Bernheim Conant, pp. 47–61. © 1978 by The Free Press. Reprinted with permission of The Free Press, A Division of Macmillan, Inc.

one: depending on the historical realities considered, the dimension and character of potentially intelligible totalities vary. Nevertheless, it remains true that in historical matters the problem of intelligibility is related first of all to the totalities one is seeking to understand, from an individual life to a battle, a civilization, and finally the whole of history. In moving from elementary examples to ever vaster ones, intelligibility slips from a practical meaning to a properly metaphysical one, from an intrinsic understanding of man's behavior toward the ultimate meaning of the human adventure, accessible only to God or to those who take themselves to be His confidants.

We will therefore be content in the following pages to give the broad outlines of the problem without justifying the distinctions adopted at the outset. We propose to investigate, in turn, history as a *train of events,* history as a *succession of works,* and finally history as a *series of lives.*

A human act becomes an *event* when it is seen as the result of a choice among several possibilities, as a response to a given situation. It becomes a *work* when it reveals itself as a creation whose end is inherent in the creation itself yet whose meaning is never limited to the one consciously or unconsciously given it by its creator. Just as each life includes acts that are *choices* and others that are *works,* so history, taken as a whole, offers itself to the historian both as a train of events and as a succession of works. But it leaves the historian free to base these two interpretations on the essence of reality or to perceive them as two different forms of the historian's curiosity or inquiry. It also suggests to him the search for a possible reconciliation of these two perspectives at a higher level, for although they are not contradictory they are basically different.

*   *   *

Human acts, and therefore events related to human beings, involve intelligibility as such. When they lose it, the actors set themselves so to speak outside humanity; they become alienated, strangers to their own and to our humanity. But the intelligibility of human acts does not come under a single heading.

The simplest scheme, the one the historian is always tempted to use, is the relation between ends and means. Why did Caesar cross the Rubicon? Why did Napoleon leave his right flank exposed at the Battle of Austerlitz? Why did the speculator sell francs at the beginning of 1962? Why does the peasant replace his horse with a tractor? In all these cases, the simplest answer consists in connecting the decision taken with the goal pursued: the seizure of power in Rome, military victory, anticipation of a devaluation of currency, superior efficiency of tractors and reduction of farming costs, and so on.

The ends and means pattern usually turns out to be too simple. It bestows on human action only a partial intelligibility; it calls forth other considerations that in any case set the framework within which the act is reduced to a choice of means. Indeed, one must consider (1) the plurality of goals, from short-term to distant, from tactics to strategy; (2) the actor's knowledge of the situation, as well as the relative effectiveness of means (the behavior of a speculator is intelligible only to a person who knows the workings of currency and the stock market, the behavior of a peasant to one who knows the economics of farming, and so on); (3) the nature, lawful or unlawful, praiseworthy or not, of the end or means in relation to religious, mythological, or traditional beliefs; and (4) the duly psychological motivations of the act, which is sometimes appropriate but sometimes apparently irrational with respect to the actor's objective.

The total intelligibility of a historical act requires the progressive exploration of the knowledge, value system, or symbols of the actor. Decisions as to means are rarely the result of a strict plan; rationality, approached but never realized in the economic life of modern societies, seems to be the ultimate end of an always unfinished evolution; economic man, as such, would aim for maximum pecuniary profit without regard to other values. Max Weber, and more recently the American sociologists Talcott Parsons, Edward Shils, and others have attempted a detailed analysis of the basic concepts or the frames of reference (knowledge, values, symbols, drives) necessary for the intelligibility of human conduct. We are not concerned with furthering these analyses but with indicating some ideas that follow directly from our previous remarks.

Human acts can be understood in a variety of ways depending on the aims of the observer. One understands a course of action in depth only after one has laid bare the system of knowledge, values, and symbols that structures the mind of the actor. The meaning the act would have for us, whether or not we were ourselves the actor, does not necessarily coincide or rarely coincides with the meaning it had for the actor and his contemporary. In his first impulse, the historian must therefore go toward others, emerge from himself, and recognize the other in his otherness.

But, at the same time, this discovery of the other as other suggests that he and I have something in common. I can understand the mental universe in which the other lives only if I can discover, at whatever level of formalization or abstraction, the categories of that strange universe. In this way and at this level, the intelligibility of history implies the unity of human nature. No one has demonstrated this thesis more brilliantly than Lucien Lévy-Bruhl himself, inspired at one time in his life by the opposite thesis—which allowed him to extend self-detachment and sympathy for the other to the utmost, thereby, by inference, demonstrating community, the indispensable condition for understanding the other as other.

The real question of historical intelligibility, at this point in our analysis, is thus concerned with the search for the abstract elements—psychological drives, categories of judgment, typical situations, symbols, or values—constituting community among humans and consequently the conditions whereby their acts become intelligible. Another question arises at this point. If it is agreed that an individual act becomes intelligible only when placed in its proper context, can one at a higher level understand the diversity of religions, mythologies, or social organizations? Does *diversity* represent the sum total of responses to a single problem or is it the expression, indefinitely renewed, of creative genius or of tireless imagination?

*   *   *

Let us come back for the moment to human events. The action of a general can be understood only with reference to army organization, techniques of weaponry, his knowledge of his own troops and of the enemy, and of course the military rules that have excluded certain maneuvers and permitted others. With the disappearance of these rules, war loses its character as a game, or at least as a regulated social institution, to move closer to natural combat; it becomes more rational in appearance—reduced to a reckoning of ends and means without regard for symbols or values—and less human. Whatever the degree of intelligibility attained by seeing events in their context, any act by an individual considered in itself will retain an element of contingency in relation to the environment and the past. Certainly one has only to invoke the banal formulas of determinism to assert that given the whole of reality at moment A in the history of Rome, the whole reality of moment B would follow. But historical determinism, in the regular meaning of this concept, does not derive from the general principle of determinism. Rather, it would tend to deny it. For, according to the current interpretation of historical determinism, only certain economic or social factors have a decisive effect or necessarily give rise to other historical phenomena (or perhaps to interesting phenomena, but such a concession would lead the determinist further than he would wish).

Let us keep to what can be experienced.

Given a historical situation, no one can prove theoretically and without exception that the act of an individual or a decision taken was inevitable, leaving aside the psychology of the actor; that this psychology was completely determined by economic, social, or intellectual factors in the environment; or finally that the consequences of individual choice do not go beyond a certain point, so that in the end "it would have all come out the same." Phenomenologically, the understanding of history as a train of events obviously implies the retrospective grasp of what was *possible* at the moment of decision but *did not happen;* it implies also the oscillation between massive phenomena tending to push history in one direction and individual acts, minority initiatives, or accidental phenomena (not determined by the whole situation) that straighten or turn back the course of history. History as a train of events belongs by nature to what we have called *probabilistic determinism.* The event, as related to the actor, is defined as such as a decision: no one takes, after having hesitated, one of those decisions that historians will later speculate about, telling themselves it could not have been otherwise for reasons independent of the actor's will; on the other hand, as soon as the historian becomes interested in actors or fragmentary facts, he has to wonder what role individuals and accidents play in relation to what are called profound forces, the massive data of the economic and social structure.

Here it is no more a question of asserting or denying the influence of great men or accidents (fragmentary facts, not made inevitable by the situation). A priori denial of their importance is contradictory, unthinkable; a posteriori denial can be but relative, valid only for this or that particular period in history. Depending on the dictates of their curiosity, as well as their habits, historians are inclined to stress or play down the importance of contingent factors. But this tendency, in one direction or another, does not and must not constitute a philosophy: it is a simple prejudice or mental orientation. Analysis shows that history is inherently made up of events, and it justifies probabilistic determinism by the structure of reality as well as by the goal of retrospective inquiry. As for the conclusions allowed by historical knowledge of the relative importance of massive and fragmentary facts, they do not coincide with the generalization of results reached by causal analysis in a small number of cases. Indeed, there is no reason why the possible margin of effectiveness of individuals should be the same in all periods—always broad, always narrow, or even the same in different sectors.

Explanation in terms of contingency, as opposed to deterministic explanation, has been thought to block intelligibility under the notion that the latter would seem to imply and the former exclude understanding the whole at a higher level. The victory of Austerlitz does not become mysterious or impenetrable if the historian attributes part of it to Napoleon's genius. There is the objection that the victories of revolutionary armies become intelligible only by reference to massive evidence (numerical superiority, popular conscription, revolutionary enthusiasm, novel tactics, etc.); similarly, the triumphs, and later the final downfall, of Napoleon can be understood, it is argued, only by supposing or detecting a connection at some higher level. But why should this connection deny a role to individuals and accidents?

The intelligibility of the whole does not imply a determinism other than the one we have called probabilistic. The relationship between two events, fragmentary or total, remains equally *comprehensible* if it appears, on the causal level, contingent or necessary. The relation between popular conscription, numerical superiority, and tactical maneuvers and the success of revolutionary troops is neither more nor less intelligible than that between the genius of Napoleon and the victory at Austerlitz. The fact that at a higher level one finds a chain of events following satisfactorily one after another does not prove that accidents cancel each other out and that the course of the enterprise, in its broad outlines, was what it had to be, given the profound forces of European society and politics. This would be a logically false conclusion. Even supposing that the conquests of Napoleon, from a certain time onward, were bound to arouse the unappeasable hostility of England and as a result indefinitely to prolong a war inevitably to be lost against the coalition of a maritime power and one or more land powers, the basic facts of the situation would still not allow one to determine when or at what price the final collapse would come. Nor could one affirm a priori that differences in dates and modalities, once certain broad lines of events had been recognized as necessary, exercised only a limited influence and finally were wiped out. Depending upon the date at which it broke out, the war beginning in 1914 could have taken a very different course, provoked or not provoked European revolutions, and so on.

Let us go further and say that the main lines of history are and can only be, on the causal level, a series not strictly necessary but nevertheless probable to a certain degree and impossible to calculate exactly. After the Battle of Leipzig, the final defeat of Napoleon appears in hindsight to have been inevitable: the disproportion between the forces of the coalition, on the one hand, and those of imperial France, on the other, leaves no doubt about the outcome. Napoleon had no other chance but the breakup of the alliance facing him or the loss of resolution on the part of the allies, a chance that became all the weaker as the likelihood of allied victory came closer and seemed more certain. On the other hand, before the Russian campaign and the destruction of the Grande Armée, one could not have asserted that the collapse of the Napoleonic empire was inevitable or close. One can understand that Napoleon was swayed by the mechanism of the continental blockade and by a conqueror's ambitions toward the immense plains of Russia. One could also understand if he had resisted the temptation. Likewise, several of Hitler's advisers recommended another strategy for 1941, an attack on Alexandria, Malta, and Gibraltar and the intensification of submarine warfare, instead of Operation Barbarossa: even if the same final result had thereby occurred, what should one call the final result—the fall of Hitler or the occupation by the Russian army of half of Europe?

In other words, one can trace, at a certain level, a totality in the chain of events, but the recital does not imply that this history, the only one possible, was determined, in the way it took place, by profound forces, or that accidents or men did not have an effect, or that their effect was quickly erased or compensated for. One confines oneself to ignoring the possibilities that were not realized in order to uncover sufficient causes for what did happen. This is a deterministic view that does not a priori enjoy the presumption of a truth higher than the complementary and opposite view that would stress contingency. The structure of the history of events holds by definition the possibility of these two interpretations—it being well understood that depending on the period and area one or the other seems to come closer to the truth.

This complementarity of necessity and contingency in causal interpretation is enough to define the limits of the various theories that seek to pinpoint, for a society or for the whole of history, a decisive or primordial cause or the various categories of causes and their relationships. It is possible to assert, provided it has first been documented, that certain phenomena—techniques of production, the status of property, or the class struggle—have a dominant influence on all aspects of collective life, including the most subtle creations of human intelligence. When history is seen as a series or totality of human acts, no barrier is raised between the physical and the spiritual, the crude and the refined, the economic and the political, the infrastructure and the superstructure, or reality and consciousness. On this level, there is incessant and undefined action and reaction between the different terms, and it would be impossible to find one that would be either a cause without being also an effect or the very beginning of a series.

Relative and, so to speak, pragmatic distinctions between these fully legitimate terms seem naturally called for. The tools that a society possesses to insure its subsistence have perhaps more important results (who determines importance?) than the conceptions men in this same society have of the origin of the gods or of the powers that be. General propositions, concerning the comparative importance of various categories of causes, should not be excluded in advance. However, as soon as one is dealing with complex civilizations, the interaction among principal causes—tools; the organization of production; the type of power; religious, mythical, or political conceptions—becomes such that one doubts the weight of these general propositions. Does not the relative importance of all these causes vary with each society?

Besides these a posteriori judgments, setting up comparative criteria, one can think of two other kinds of propositions relative to sociohistorical causes. The first, more characteristic of sociology than of history, would be inclined to reconstruct in a comprehensible manner the structure of different societies with a view to determining the different types and, within each type, the *margin of variation*. One might attempt, for instance, to establish the degree to which a given economic organization brings about a particular kind of state or ideology. Perhaps a certain category of phenomena offers the best starting place for this intelligible reconstruction of social reality, though experience seems to indicate that specific techniques of production or types of property status can coexist with different forms of the state or of ideology.

The second kind of general proposition related to causes transcends causal thought itself. If the historian holds social groups, opponents or enemies within complex societies, to be the morally or humanly decisive factors, then he believes in the primacy of class struggle and the economic phenomena that determine or condition it. Such a primacy is no longer causal but philosophical or political. History is *essentially* class struggle not because that struggle entails all the phenomena characteristic of human societies and not because it explains them all but because in the eyes of a person motivated by the hope of suppressing classes, these appear legitimately as primary or fundamental. Let us not say that the goal of a future without classes creates a past dominated by class struggle. Let us say, rather, that from contemporary experience through a constant oscillation between what is and what has been, a historical philosophy of class struggle emerges little by little, along with the present will to transcend that struggle.

*   *   *

The history of events is neither progress nor decadence, neither the movement toward a final end nor the endless repetition of the same facts or the same cycles. It is pure continuity, diversity aligned along the flow of time. There is no reason why the historian of events should not note the life and death of empires, the massive increase in our time of the number of men or machines, of the quantity of raw materials consumed. There is no reason why the partial chains of events of which we have observed certain portions should not continue. On this level, predictions with the same probabilistic character as explanations prove possible and legitimate. The meaning of history, in the framework of causal thought, merges with the direction in which partial chains of events seem to be heading. These predictions contain a greater or lesser coefficient of uncertainty: a given chain of events does not always continue in the same direction. The state takeover of the economy witnessed in the twentieth century could be reversed in the twenty-first century by an opposite trend; progress in productivity might give way to regression consequent upon military catastrophe or limitless extension of bureaucracy. The consequences of a series of events whose prolongation seems probable are usually not to be identified with the precision that those who rely on historical providence may imagine. In fact, no one has ever been able to demonstrate that the development of productive forces (whether one means thereby technical equipment or productivity in general) necessarily implies a certain property status. The formula, repeated so often, of the contradiction between the forces and the relations of production has never been subjected to a rigorous analysis or really proved. More generally, the direction in which certain historical sequences seem headed—sequences concerning the more material aspects of societies, human acts most closely related to the natural environment, the more constraining forms of human relationships—does not seem sufficient to determine in a univocal manner the nature of other forms of human relationships. That which in the development of the economy seems predictable for the very near future leaves to politics and human existence a margin of indeterminacy into which extreme values, positive or negative, eventually infiltrate themselves.

A succession of works, as distinguished from a succession of acts, has a meaning philosophically antecedent to empirical observation. The discoveries or conquests of science are organized into a present whole wherein, rectified and made more precise, previous discoveries and conquests have their place. Scientific truth, to its own degree of approximation, remains as pertinent today as the day it was first conceived. By what term should one designate this history of science considered as truth? Accumulation, elaboration, progress? To what extent has the history of truth been necessarily what it was? All these questions go beyond the framework of this brief study.

It is enough to note here a few propositions. Only exploration of the past allows us to determine how, *in fact,* science—mathematics or physics—developed, at what date, through what thinker; how this or that theory was thought out for the first time; how this or that demonstration was perfected; and within what philosophy or theory this or that law was formulated mathematically. The history of science as a succession of acts enjoys no superiority vis-à-vis other types of histories of acts. But the relation between truths discovered yesterday and today's system, or the relation between past science in its intrinsic relation to truth and contemporary science, depends on the very nature of science and is in the domain of philosophic analysis, not historical inquiry.

At the level of acts, as we have seen, there is no rigorous separation or barrier, and the interaction of men and institutions, consciousness and economic structures can contribute to the reciprocal elucidation of consciousness and acts crystallized into a sort of social fabric. When the question is science, one can perhaps perceive that the direction taken by research, philosophical interpretations, and the errors of scientists could be made intelligible by outside influences. But the environmental explanation could never exhaust or even reach the true meaning of the work as such. Circumstances explain the search for, or the failure to find, the true solution. One need not appeal to circumstances to explain the discovery of truth since the latter derives from a capacity to form judgments, which cannot be an effect or a reflection of the subject and which the historian, like the historical personage, possesses within himself.

The relationship between works thus depends on the intrinsic meaning of the works, on the immanent end of the activity that creates them and that they express. This meaning can be revealed as the past is explored but, transcending the given historical fact, it can legitimately appear from simple inspection of the works themselves.

Is there an equivalent, for other works, of the distinction between the practical history of scientific development and the history of scientific truth? What are the relationships between art and its history and between philosophy and its history? The equivalent for the art of truth is beauty, or, if you like, artistic quality: the historian uses the milieu to explain the work in its particular details, he does not thus explain the masterpiece as such. The relevance of the masterpiece can be contrasted with that of truth. The masterpiece has meaning throughout the centuries because its meaning is inexhaustible, because it reveals to each generation another aspect of itself; truth has meaning throughout the centuries because it somehow has a unique meaning, acquired definitively. This antithesis is overly simplified: the masterpiece carries within itself certain elements that the spectators of succeeding centuries recognize and that are as intrinsically tied to it as the demonstration to the theorem. The Parthenon appears in a different light in each period, yet the technician finds in it a solution to a problem facing all architects, just as in a great canvas the painter finds an echo or a symbol of his own creative effort.

The identity of research and methods creates between periods of painting and sculpture a deep bond as well as the possibility of multiple meanings, from that bestowed by artists or their contemporaries to that of art historians or visitors to museums. Furthermore, any specific work—sculpture, architecture, philosophy—appears in retrospect as the expression of a community devoted to a particular task. This artistic community in which each creator continues the work of another creator, whether by opposition or by conscious imitation, sometimes becomes conscious of itself. It is not isolated from the society whose desires and contradictions it reflects, but neither is it completely merged with it. The artist as a man belongs to a political society rather than to the community of painting. Picasso, as a creator, is totally unaffected by the political declarations to which he subscribes.

Between the history of works considered as acts and integrated into the whole social fabric and the interpretation of a work in its imperishable significance falls the history of works as works, in other words, specialized histories that seek to grasp the relationships between works, considered as such, while at the same time relating the various moments of this history with the milieu. The history of works in their meaning as works introduces a form of intelligibility that we did not find apropos of the history of acts: a properly rational necessity.

Relating an act to an actor, an institution to a system of beliefs or a society, allows us to understand the act and the institution but not to assert that the relationship could not have been other than it was. Whether this relationship goes back to the psychology of moral philosophers, psychoanalysts, or the disciples of Pavlov, whether it is part of a total attitude toward the world, or whether it belongs to a psychological type, the historian cannot demonstrate that the particular act he is studying had necessarily to be what it was. Max Weber was right, it seems to me, in stating that most of the time the comprehensive relation must be validated in a particular case by a retrospective reckoning of probabilities. Let us say that at least in general the comprehensive relation, whether it connects two acts to each other or a single act to a whole group of them, in no way appears as necessary. It does not imply that the interpretation offered is the only one or that the relation, in the terms in which it is expressed, was necessary in either the deterministic or the rational sense.

The relation between two moments of science does not have to be necessary in the deterministic sense to appear as having inevitably to be what it is. Obviously, one cannot prove that Newton *had* to formulate the law of gravity at the time and in the form in which he did. One can even, strictly speaking, see in this law the characteristics of an invention rather than a discovery and ascribe to it a certain contingency. Nevertheless, with hindsight the historian of science is tempted to see rational development between the known facts and the law that governs them. In any case, one can see that the progress of science does not involve the two categories of necessity and contingency, in the meaning we chose to give these words in the theory of probabilistic determinism, and that it is subsequently intelligible in itself without having to be deduced from a general relation or integrated into a significant social context.

In the history of works, even in that of the arts or philosophy, we find not the counterpart to the necessity of truth but a specific intelligibility—neither that of determinism nor that of the comprehension of acts. The development of a doctrine or school and the transition from one style to another have their own intelligibility perceptible only to those who grasp the specific meaning of the works. At most, this specific intelligibility finds its way to the rational necessity of truth. What occurs could not have been otherwise not because profound forces or weighty facts alone acted and excluded or limited the intervention of individuals or accidents but because it constitutes the projection through time of the stages of a single demonstration or the moments of a demonstration.

The philosophy of history as the interpretation of the whole of history asks two fundamental questions: is it possible to grasp the totality of history at each moment by overcoming the duality of acts and works, the multiplicity of one and the other? What is the texture of this total history, the kind of intelligibility to which it might aspire? Is it closer to the intelligibility of acts or of works? If the latter, does it belong to the category of art or of science?

A philosophy of history assumes in fact that human history is not a simple sum of juxtaposed facts—individual decisions and adventures, ideas, interests, and institutions—but that it is, at the moment and in what follows, a totality in movement toward a priviliged state that gives meaning to the whole. History has meaning only if there is a logic of human coexistence that precludes no adventure but that at least, as if by natural selection, finally eliminates those that act as a diversion in relation to the permanent needs of humanity.

It is thus that Maurice Merleau-Ponty defines the fundamental requirements of what he calls the philosophy of history.

Merleau-Ponty takes as a model a philosophy of the Hegelian type and holds that type to be compelling to the point that any other interpretation would not be a philosophy of history in the meaning he reserves for this term. We will limit ourselves to observing that in that case the philosophy of history, a recent phenomenon foreign to most periods, requires an act of faith, more religious than rational: why must we postulate a priori a natural selection, the elimination of adventures that divert us from the fundamental needs of human coexistence? How can we define or even recognize the privileged state that gives meaning to the whole? Let us leave these questions for later and look again at the decisive concept, that of totality. Under what conditions would a moment of history be a totality? To what point can this be so?

The analysis of historical actions or of history as an aggregate or succession of actions has shown us that one cannot set up barriers between the various areas of social reality, between the various activities of men. But it allows us even less to assert that economic and other problems are really only a single large problem. The unity of historical actions precludes strict separations; it does not imply totalization or reduction to unity. The historian seeks to organize the various aspects of a society or civilization in such a manner as to make them appear as different expressions of one and the same existence. We cannot state to what point he accomplishes this organization. Philosophical analysis reminds us that there are limits to the unity of human lives.

I have no trouble admitting that Cézanne's life was both that of a French petit bourgeois of the nineteenth century and that of a painter and creator of new forms revealing a universe unseen before him and that would have remained unseen without him; likewise, I agree not to draw a rigid line between the petit bourgeois and the painter. But who will restore this life to an intelligible whole, unify the problem or the meaning? The specific meaning of Cézanne's painting falls within the history of painting, which has its own particular nature; reducing a work to a historical whole would kill the quality inherent in the works as such. A fortiori, the collective life of a society or civilization does not and could not form a single whole at any moment now or later. Human creations, each having its immanent goal, its own purpose, are linked to each other because in the end the same human being is expressed in any one of them. But when the historian tries to explain the diverse works of a period by reducing them to the social man of a specific time, he explains many features of these works but not the features characteristic of their unique quality as works.

This does not mean that the claim to seize the whole at any moment or later should be condemned as such. It means only that existence as a principle of synthesis between the act and the work cannot be defined empirically. Thus, in this case, existence would be but a combination of acts in the sense in which this term was used in the first part of the study. And combinations of acts always remain precarious, relative, heavy with internal multiplicity. Existence can build into a whole only on condition that it in itself possesses unity. The existence of the human person, human coexistence, do they present a unity, providing foundations for a totality at any given moment or in time?

This unity could not, of itself, suppress the plurality of works and meanings. Comparable to the unity that the problem of salvation gives to the life of a believer, it would involve values, not facts; or again comparable to the will that Kant or Jean-Paul Sartre finds in the origin of the choice that each of us makes of himself. Any unity of existence capable of subsuming the whole of history has to be connected with a problem (salvation) or a principle (freedom) that one recognizes as decisive (in value) or fundamental (as a metaphysical cause behind scattered appearances). Even so, one can doubt that the second hypothesis leads to wholeness either at a given moment or later. Even if we each conceive of ourselves in relation to a constant problem, these choices, Kantian or Sartrean, would more likely distribute themselves in a pure and simple succession or in a dispersal through time rather than in a series oriented toward a goal.

On the other hand, wholeness within the moment obtained by reference to a single problem becomes wholeness through time as soon as the problem involves successive solutions, each necessary in itself and as a stage toward the next solution. When the final stage is reached, the observer recognizes that all the stages have fulfilled an indispensable function. If one grants a parallel between the dialectics of the categories, the development of philosophy and the history of societies confer on a total interpretation the rational necessity characteristic of the movement of concepts, without alienating the plurality of works or leaving out contingencies at the level of secular history.

The philosophy of history thus described, the one postulating that unity at the moment or in time is a privileged state toward which the whole of the human past is moving, logically defines itself with reference to a single problem, basic to human existence, and by the assertion that a radical solution to this problem is in sight. To the extent, indeed, to which historical truth can be revealed only by hindsight, any philosophy of history sees itself as situated at the end of the adventure, for otherwise it would exclude the possibility of its own truth.

Thus defined, a philosophy of history appears as clearly religious not only in its origin but also in its structure. A philosophy of history that connects the whole of the past with a privileged condition and that gives its own meaning to what came before is the equivalent of a camouflaged theology of history (or to one interpretation among others that illegitimately asks to be recognized as universally valid). From theology it retains the notion of a final state whereby both to judge and to reveal meanings and human lives, as well as the distinction between sacred and profane history—the first retaining only events that lead to the final state, the second embodying those diversions and accidents whose traces are erased in the eyes of the supreme arbiter, who stands at the end of the adventure. When defined by one basic concept (for example, freedom), sacred history can take on the character of rational necessity, appropriate to the development of concepts.

Does such a construction go beyond the means or ambitions of rational thought? Let us look again at the elements of this construction. Is it possible to determine "the single great problem" in relation to which totalities can be explained? A philosophy that does not imply any transcendent absolutes can nevertheless seize the secular equivalent of the problem of salvation, but if the determination of this problem must be universally valid, it has to be formalized, and how to imagine therefore a single solution? What sort of man represents the fulfillment of man? The sage? Perhaps, but only if he has understood the totality of human experience. Otherwise, how can one choose between him and other exemplars of humanity? Let us assume that this problem has been elucidated. Its solution must be incarnated in a certain order of coexistence. Again, one can conceive abstractly a privileged state—mutual human respect, freedom, consciousness of the world and of oneself—but the passage from abstract conception to concrete representation, necessary to arrive at a philosophy of history of the Hegelian type, brings to the fore opinion and controversy, not rational certitude.

Let us choose the recognition of man by man, outcome of the master-slave dialectic, as the privileged condition. Historical conflicts will end when all men recognize each other. But to determine this privileged condition on the basis of social or historical reality, one must be able to judge different institutions in relation to this privileged condition or, if you prefer, to be specific about the institutions that would faithfully translate it into reality. Now, as soon as the philosopher pretends to judge the merits of private or collective property, the mechanisms of the market or of planning in relation to mutual human respect, he leaves philosophy and rational certitude to enter into political debate and its uncertainties. What form of property favors a humanization of society? What are the strengths and weaknesses of each institution? I do not say that one cannot decide *reasonably,* but certainly one cannot decide *rationally.* There is no institution that does not entail negative features for certain men and in relation to certain values connected with the particular problem in such a way that men of good will arrive, with the same sincerity, at opposite choices even when they share more or less the same universe and the same hierarchy of values.

The idea of reason, the goal of History as conceived by critical philosophy, cannot be identified with a coming period or with particular institutions without creating fanaticism and unreason. The search for an intelligibility higher than comprehension or probabilistic determinism, equivalent at the most generalized level to the intelligibility inherent in the development of works of art, remains legitimate. But this properly spiritual intelligibility does not require the act of faith by which a chain of events *necessarily* comes to realize the decrees of reason. We have no more reason to trust collective history than individual history. Humanity can be carried away by a cosmic catastrophe as can our child by illness. We must desire and hope that our collective adventure will lead to the humanization of society. Nothing compels us to hold this belief. The Christian is not sure of his salvation, humanity without God has even less reason to be sure of its collective salvation.

The intelligibility of the whole preserves distinct forms of intelligibility, each linked to the structure of reality and to the question that has been raised and analyzed in the preceeding pages. It does not do away with the contrast between act and creation, or with that between underlying forces and accidents, or with that between comprehension and causality, but it puts each in its place.

The intelligibility of probabilistic determinism characterizes the world in which the life of the man of action unfolds; the intelligibility of psycho-existential comprehension is born of a meeting with others, a discovery and an enrichment of oneself. The intelligibility of works reveals both the meaning immanent in each of them and the law according to which they follow one from the other; meanings that express one aspect of man and his creative capacity, a law that reveals the essence of the search and its progress. Historical totality preserves this plurality, of which the philosopher takes note, an awareness to which is added, with the always provisional discovery of the unique and essential problem, the effort to make sense of a diversity of periods within human society in a drive toward a goal vaguely outlined by reason.

2

The Intelligibility of History in the Twentieth Century

The Technical Surprise

Frederick the Great left to his legal apologists the justification of his conquests after they had taken place. Public opinion played hardly any part in the limited warfare of the eighteenth century; the professional soldiers, recruited from the lower classes of society, felt no need to know why they were fighting. In the twentieth century, the soldier and citizen have become interchangeable; and the general public, believing itself peacefully disposed, demands an accounting from its leaders. To prove the enemy responsible for a war has become each government's duty. On each side, historians and intellectuals strive not so much to maintain the morale of the fighting forces alone as to clear the conscience of the whole nation.

The analysis of the origins of the First World War, originally based upon the need for propaganda between 1914 and 1918, was carried on, even after the Allied victory, by a sort of revolt against what had happened. Middle-class Europe, proud of its civilization and sure of its progressiveness, regarded war as a monstrosity out of another age. The authors of the Treaty of Versailles demanded reparations, invoking not the defeat in arms, which the vanquished Germans (well aware of what they themselves would have done had they been victorious) would have accepted without demur, but the fact of aggression. The study of the causes of the war was inspired not as much by historical curiosity as by that spirit of moral righteousness. Who were the criminals who had plunged Europe into the abyss of violence? What fortuitous elements had revived the horrors of the past?

From *The Century of Total War*, by Raymond Aron (Garden City, N.Y.: Doubleday), pp. 9–55. © 1954 by Raymond Aron. Reprinted by permission of Doubleday & Company, Inc.

Historical research yielded inconclusive results. It did not make an end of uncertainties. Inevitably it disappointed both the pacifists and those who sat in judgment.

The historian, concerned to show the causes of an event, puts two questions, both legitimate, but which must be carefully distinguished. First of all, why did war come at that particular time; and, given the situation, who were the men, or what were the circumstances, that precipitated war? Secondly, how was the situation which led to war created? The first question refers to what are generally called the immediate causes, the second to what are called the remote origins. Historians attribute to the former more or less importance according to their philosophy and also to the results of their inquiry. If they come to the conclusion that the situation led inevitably to war, the immediate causes obviously lose importance.

In their study of the First World War, historians were deeply interested in the immediate causes. The actual events marshaled themselves in a highly orderly fashion. Before the assassination of the Archduke Francis Ferdinand, Europe was living in a state of preparedness, but no one expected an outbreak from one day to the next. Following the assassination, and especially after the Austrian ultimatum to Serbia, chancelleries and populations alike felt the dread of approaching disaster.

A multitude of books and commentaries have attempted to explain the week that passed between July 23, when Austria dispatched her ultimatum to Serbia, and the thirtieth, the day on which Russian mobilization was decreed. Archives have been exhausted, responsible leaders have published their memoirs, and historians have reconstituted the conversations, negotiations, and interviews that had taken place in Vienna, Berlin, St. Petersburg, and Paris. The very accumulation of documents seemed to result in confusion.

More apparent than real, the confusion is based upon three interrelated questions: What were the actions that rendered war not only possible, but probable, and finally inevitable? Up to what point were those actions morally or politically legitimate? What were the intentions of those responsible for them?

No one denies today, as no one doubted then, that the Austrian ultimatum introduced the possibility not only of war, but of general war. The statesmen at Vienna were aware of that risk, just as the German statesmen had recognized it at the discussions in Berlin at the beginning of July. Russia, who regarded herself as protectress of the European Slavs in the Balkans, would not allow Serbia to be crushed or permit her to be transformed from an independent kingdom into a sort of protectorate of the Dual Monarchy. The ultimatum was a challenge to Russia. All Europe realized that the initiative, heavy with menace, had come from Vienna, and that it would not have been taken without the promise of support given in Berlin.

The Serbian reply was moderate in its terms, though it rejected the proposal that Austrian officials participate in an inquiry. If we add to the ultimatum the refusal to accept Serbia's reply, and then the severance of diplomatic relations and the bombardment of Belgrade, we have a succession of acts for which Austrian diplomacy (and indirectly German diplomacy) may be held responsible. This, then, was the European situation in 1914, which made likely the advent of a general war.

Controversy has centered mainly on the legitimacy of the Austrian policy. To what extent did the conduct of the Serbian Government justify what were exorbitant demands under international law? Whatever particular Serbian officials or private politicians might have had to do with the preparation of the Archduke's assassination, the facts known at the time gave no ground for holding the Belgrade Government responsible, and consequently gave the Vienna Government no authority to make demands incompatible with Serbian sovereignty. For the rest, there is little doubt that the Austrian diplomats neither desired nor expected a simple acceptance of their ultimatum. They wanted to "teach a lesson" to the little country that was disturbing its powerful neighbor by supporting or tolerating the "liberation" propaganda of the European Slavs. The men who had determined at Vienna to "teach the lesson" resolutely accepted the possible consequences, including general war.

Thus the real issue is whether we may consider these consequences to have been possible, probable, or inevitable. There is little likelihood of a unanimous conclusion. The historian may ponder the influence of one event on another but his conclusions can never be final. In the present case, one must at least say that the Central Powers had created conditions which rendered war probable. Would its avoidance have required a miracle, or merely more diplomatic patience and imagination in the opposite camp? Speculations on what *might* have happened are endless.

The same sort of controversy was carried on over the Russian general mobilization, the first in date (though, before it became known, the Austrian mobilization had been decided on). Was not that mobilization politically legitimate as a reply to the first operations against Serbia? The German military leaders themselves regarded the Russian

mobilization as different in nature from all the other ones because of the time that it required. When that mobilization took place, had not the die been cast, and were not the general staffs in the different capitals impatient to set going a mechanism which left diplomacy no further room for action?

As long as we consider only the two questions of causality and legitimacy, careful inquiry compels us to qualify, but without fundamentally modifying, the Allied contention. It was the Vienna Cabinet that took the initiatives which all Europe has held to be bellicose. It was that Cabinet which threw down the glove to Serbia, and therefore to Russia; it was that Cabinet which wanted a *succès de prestige,* even at the risk of general war. Germany, in giving Vienna a free hand, shared the responsibility, whatever may have been the secret thoughts of her rulers. Even though it were shown that the Entente, and Russia in particular, was too prompt in taking up the challenge, the burden of guilt in the diplomatic sequence of actions and rejoinders would remain with the "initiators."

But such guilt, positive and limited—diplomatic, so to speak—is incommensurable with that imagined by popular passion. Search was made, not for this or that Minister bent on extirpating the Irredentist propaganda of the European Slavs, but for the men who had knowingly embarked on aggression. They were not discovered or, in any case, they were not discovered in the simple guise of storybook villains.

The search for motives or incentives leads to unending controversies. It is possible on the basis of certain testimony to represent German policy as inspired by the desire to launch as soon as possible a war considered to be inevitable. The proposals of Wilhelm II to the King of the Belgians may be adduced, for example. In certain military quarters it was obviously thought that the reorganization of the Russian Army would not be completed until 1917, and that the French forces were short of machine guns and heavy artillery. Such considerations, reinforcing the confidence of the general staff, must have influenced the generals in the discussions at the beginning of July. But the study of archives has revealed a German policy less sure of itself and less definite in its aim. Berlin accepted general war, but it could not be said that the responsible statesmen deliberately set out to provoke it over the Austro-Serbian dispute. That idea certainly crossed the minds of some persons at some moments, but it did not constantly determine the action of the Chancellor, the Emperor, or the Ambassadors.

In other words, when we search for motives the simple picture of aggressors and victims does not stand up to rigorous analysis.

The French statesmen certainly desired war even less. The Tsar and a good many (but not all) of the Russian leaders were afraid of war, perhaps more out of concern for the regime than for the war itself. But the Allies were determined not to tolerate the Austrians' resorting to force in the Balkans, while Viennese diplomacy was no less determined to use force if necessary to gain a *succès de prestige* at the expense of Serbia. On both sides the will to peace was conditional, not absolute. The European situation in 1914 made the localization of the conflict extremely improbable, but both Berlin and Vienna would have been satisfied to attain the immediate objective without starting a general war.

The European scene was not occupied by "sheep and wolf" states, but by sovereign states equally determined to maintain their power and prestige. In Britain and France there was no equivalent of the Pan-Germans or the romantic theorists of violence. Both countries were inclined to be conservative and to renounce dreams of conquest. The Germany of Wilhelm II, actively expansionist, was more inclined to the call of arms than the middle-class democracies. For all that, the explosion in 1914 was the result of diplomatic failure.

For a century Europe had enjoyed relative stability. Neither the Crimean War nor the Franco-Prussian War became general. With greater effort the Balkan Wars were brought to an end without irreparable injury to the European equilibrium. The "war monster" that had shaken the Continent from 1792 to 1815 had been chained up. It broke loose again in August 1914.

As soon as we leave the narrow limits of our inquiry into the assassination of the Archduke and the Austrian declaration of war, going back before the crisis of June and July 1914, there is no longer any date that can be regarded as marking the origin of the historical situation that produced the First World War. The Franco-German hostility leads us back at least to the Treaty of Frankfurt, the Russo-German hostility at least to the abandonment of the Reinsurance Treaty by the young Emperor Wilhelm II. But rather than retrace a half century of European diplomatic history, our critical inquiry must restrict itself to the formulation of definite questions.

Any student of the crisis was bound to be struck by the rapidity with which an incident involving an individual prince set all Europe ablaze. Why had the situation become so explosive? Why did so many statesmen and common men alike vaguely sense the rising storm?

The replies of the historians, although differing in detail, are on the whole irresistibly simple, disconcerting to those who want to penetrate beyond the superficial facts and root out the deepseated forces of which the very participants themselves had no knowledge.

In accordance with an unwritten law of European diplomacy, the very fact of Germany's growth in power provoked a grouping of nations to make a stand against her. The course of the war proved abundantly that the Triple Entente had no surplus of strength over the German-Austrian alliance. But the fact that the Entente was necessary for equilibrium does not explain why it was formed. It had not yet been formed at the end of the last century, though the same considerations had already made it necessary. We must therefore remember simply that the grouping of the great European nations into more or less close alliances was something neither novel nor monstrous that required a special explanation or implied the existence of a culprit.

France, once she had surmounted the consequences of defeat, would normally, in accordance with an old tradition, seek support in the East. It may be that the Franco-Russian rapprochement was facilitated or accelerated by the mistakes of the Wilhelmstrasse. But it would have been difficult, in the long run, for Germany to remain very friendly with both Russia and Austria-Hungary. In preferring the latter she inevitably brought about a rapprochement between Paris and St. Petersburg. As for Great Britain, she was bound to fear a German victory that would eliminate France as a major power and give the conqueror almost unlimited hegemony over the Continent. British diplomacy would perhaps not have heeded the peril to its own profound interests had not the Second Reich, by building a military fleet, delivered a challenge which the British Empire could not refuse.

For the rest, from the beginning of the century there was a lack of definition in the diplomatic "fronts." Contacts between the courts of Berlin and St. Petersburg were frequent until the eve of the rupture. Wilhelm II tried several times to take advantage of his personal ascendancy over Nicholas II for purposes of high diplomacy. The treaty signed by the two Emperors at Björkö in July 1905, although subsequently rejected by the Tsar's Ministers, must not be forgotten. Until the eve of the catastrophe the relations between London and Berlin, quite apart from dynastic ties, were not those of irreconcilable enemies. As late as 1914 British Ministers had the idea of appeasing German ambitions by negotiating a partition of the Portuguese colonies. In spite of the efforts of French diplomacy, no British Government had entered into any formal engagement: discussions between the general staffs did not interfere with the freedom of decision of the London Cabinet.

The division of the principal nations of Europe into two camps did not necessarily make for war. It only made it inevitable that any conflict involving two great powers would bring general war. From the moment when there was formed in the center of Europe a German empire, industrially foremost in Europe, with a population exceeding that of France by more than fifty per cent, and allied to the Dual Monarchy, a war on the small scale of that of 1870 had become impossible. Neither Russia nor Great Britain would have tolerated a new German victory which would have made of the Reich no longer merely the dominant European state, but a claimant to empire over the Continent.

The two camps were not condemned to mortal combat by any mysterious fatality. The relations between the coalitions had simply deteriorated until clear-sighted observers foresaw the inescapable outcome of armed peace. Who was to blame? The issue has been passionately argued. One side denounced the intolerable manners of Teutonic diplomacy, the demand for Delcassé's dismissal, the spectacular visit to Tangier, the dispatch of a gunboat to Agadir, the annexation of Bosnia-Herzegovina; on the other side it was pointed out that in the course of the half century during which she had been the foremost power on the Continent, Germany had added less to her overseas possessions and profited less by arms or negotiation than weakened France. Germany had made herself intolerable by her brutality, by her arrogance, and by the ambitions of which she was suspected. But under the rules of diplomacy she was not wrong in demanding compensation when France established her protectorate over Morocco. She could not fail to notice that the international conferences were not turning out to her advantage.

The growing tension centered about three principal difficulties: the rivalry between Austria and Russia in the Balkans, the Franco-German conflict over Morocco, and the arms race—on sea between Britain and Germany, and on land between all the powers. The two last causes had produced the situation, the first one kindled the spark.

There are doubtless those who contend that the immediate cause matters little, and that war might have broken out just as easily in 1911 as in 1914. The contention readily suggests itself and is not easily disproven. The fact remains that the Balkan quarrels brought about the actual rupture, just as they had helped to dissolve the pact of conservation which, despite divergent alliances, still united the sovereigns of Russia and Germany. For one thing, the clash between Russia and Austria-Hungary had a diplomatic cause. Repulsed in Asia after her defeat by Japan in 1905, Russia conformed to tradition and redirected her attention and her ambitions to Europe. But, apart from diplomacy, the clash had a deeper cause in the movement of ideas and passions. For two supranational empires still existed in an age of nationalism. The Ottoman Empire had not yet been liquidated, and already diplomats were anxiously anticipating the time when they would have to face the problem of the succession to Austria-Hungary.

Henceforth Viennese diplomacy is more understandable. It was no longer so much a question of avenging the assassination of an Archduke who had favored trialism and whose disappearance pleased many persons in high places. It was a matter of ending once and for all the nationalist propaganda that challenged the existence of Austria-Hungary. Obviously, Russia could not allow the Vienna Government a free hand.

The quarrel between chancelleries interested also the general public in each country. Diplomacy had succeeded in integrating into the Europe which followed the Congress of Vienna a united Germany and a united Italy without a general war. It was unable to perform such a feat again in the twentieth century. The national conflicts in Eastern Europe unleashed general war.

The inquiry into political responsibility carries with it no authority to banish as criminals either men or nations. But inquiry does clarify the significance and the origins of the war. The immediate occasion and the deeper cause largely coincide; for, as we have seen, the reasons for hostility among the various nations of Europe were manifold. The relative strengths and the relationships of alliance excluded partial conflicts. The rise of Germany, whose hegemony France dreaded and whose Navy menaced England, had created an opposition that claimed to be defensive but was denounced by German propaganda as an attempt at encirclement. The two camps alarmed each other, and each tried to soothe its own fears by piling up defensive armaments. The atmosphere grew heavy with multiplied incidents, which spread the conviction of approaching disaster. The explosion finally came in the East, where Russia and Austria were advancing contradictory claims, and where the principle of national sovereignty had ruined the Ottoman Empire and was beginning to undermine the still imposing edifice of the Austro-Hungarian Empire.

Wars are essentially unpredictable. But the wars of the twentieth century have been much more so than were those of the past. The very situations that bring about a modern war are destroyed in its wake. It is the battle in and for itself, and not the origin of the conflict or the peace treaty, that constitutes the major fact and produces the most far-reaching consequences.

It is impossible to recall without a smile the plans drawn up by the French general staff in the period before hostilities began in 1914. They anticipated a daily supply of 13,600 rounds for 75 mm. guns, 465 for 155 mm. guns, and 2,470,000 cartridges for the infantry; a daily production of 24 tons of B powder; 50,000 workers to be employed in 30 factories. The estimated production was to be attained on the eighty-first day after general mobilization. On September 19, instead of 13,600 rounds the general staff asked the Ministry of Armament for 50,000. It obtained that quantity in March 1915, but meanwhile, in January, it had demanded 80,000. This last figure was reached in September 1915, but by then the general staff was demanding 150,000—more than ten times the prewar estimate. This increasing demand for artillery ammunition had its parallel in all other military supplies.

Both in France and in Germany it was expected that the decisive battles would be fought and won within a few weeks. Peacetime reserves of equipment and munitions would suffice, it was thought, for the operational needs requisite to victory. The result, in France, of this remarkable optimism was that on September 15, after thirty days of operations, stocks were half depleted, and the arsenals held no more than 120,000 rounds for 75 mm. guns. If in October the peacetime reserves had not been exhausted virtually at the same moment on both sides, lack of ammunition might have brought to one or the other the decision vainly sought in the field. During the first two years, guns of one caliber were kept supplied only at the expense of guns of other calibers. Not until 1917 did production more or less fulfill the constantly increasing requirements of the battlefield. Instead of 50,000 employees, 1,600,000 were engaged in defense plants, and to these workers should be added those in the United States employed directly or indirectly in the Allied war effort. Ministers and their military advisers thought they were undertaking a war "like any other," expecting its issue to be determined by a few battles of annihilation. Instead, they had committed the people of their countries to a long trial by attrition. Between the aspiration and its fulfillment there intervened what I propose to call the "technical surprise."

In the last century the American Civil War had offered a fairly good preview of what we call total war, with regard particularly to the relentless mobilization of national resources and the competition over new inventions.[1] The period of European peace between 1871 and the

---

1. "In the Civil War in America the rifled gun came more and more to the fore. Yet, from the armament point of view, the main characteristic of this war was the extraordinary inventiveness displayed throughout it. During it the magazine-loading rifle and a

Balkan Wars had been marked by rapid progress in armaments. The underwater mine, the torpedo, and the submarine revolutionized naval tactics. On land, the universal use of the semiautomatic rifle and of the carbine, the perfecting of the machine gun, and the adoption of rapid-fire artillery gave unprecedented firepower to armies of greatly increased manpower.

Finally "technical surprise" came as the climactic element of an evolution in which the wars of the French Revolution and Empire represent an important stage, if not actually the beginning. National wars are fought by the people as a whole, and no longer by professional armies; the stakes are no longer dynastic interests or the fate of a province, but the future of the collective society or its ideals. In the epoch of democracy (that is to say, of compulsory military service) and of industry (i.e., of mass production and destruction), national wars naturally tend to expand into total wars. What needs to be explained is not how the war of 1914 spread across the Continent and became "hyperbolic,"[2] but the fact that the nineteenth century was able to escape a similar outcome to the French Revolution and the industrial revolution.

Europe had been spared in the nineteenth century by a streak of good fortune. Diplomacy was able to localize the conflicts because none of them definitely threatened the general balance of power. Neither the victory of Great Britain and France over Russia, nor that of France over Austria, nor that of Germany over Austria and, subsequently, over France, appeared to endanger seriously the onlooking powers. These events modified the balance established at Vienna, but did not destroy it. And none of them threatened the economic or social regime of any of the warring countries. The wars were limited both in regard to the resources employed and to the issue at stake, and they did not arouse ungovernable popular passion. They were fought mainly by professional armies (except for the second phase of the Franco-Prussian War). The general staffs, wedded to their habitual methods, were slow in making use of new weapons. The superiority of infantry

---

machine gun were invented. Torpedoes, land mines, submarine mines, the field telegraph, lamp and flag signalling, wire entanglements, wooden wire-bound mortars, hand-grenades, winged grenades, rockets and many forms of booby traps were tried out. Armoured trains were used; balloons were employed on both sides. Explosive bullets are mentioned, searchlights for 'stinkshells' to cause 'suffocating effects' were asked for. The use of flame-projectors was proposed and the U.S.S. Housatonic was sunk on February 17, 1864, by a small man-propelled Confederate submarine." J. F. C. Fuller, *Armament and History* (New York: Scribner, 1945), pp. 118–19.

2. The term "hyperbolic" war was first used by Pareto.

weapons contributed largely to the Prussian victory in 1866, as did the superiority of artillery (breech-loading instead of muzzle-loading guns) to that of 1870. The brutality of the initial successes in 1866 and in 1870, due to the disparity of military organization, armament, and fighting strength, prevented any resort to a strategy of attrition and the progressive mobilization that is its normal result. But such good fortune could not be repeated indefinitely.

After 1815 the principal European powers, whether out of wisdom, fear of the "monster," or obedience to tradition, had returned to the professional army. Only Prussia had maintained conscription, and she had won the foremost place in Europe. No one could fail to learn the lesson. All the nations, beginning with France, bitter in her defeat, conformed to the logic of democracy and re-established compulsory military service. The general staffs remained, on the whole, conservative. Obliged to modernize rifles and machine guns and field artillery, they made mistakes, especially the French staff, as to the strategic and tactical implications of the new weapons. They failed to grasp certain lessons of the Russo-Japanese War and the Balkan Wars, underestimated the machine gun, and almost entirely ignored the air arm and the role of the internal combustion engine. But in spite of all of this, in 1914 the nations rose in arms supplied by modern industry and went out to do battle. Hyperbolic war could have been averted only by a lightning victory of one side or the other. That possibility was removed by the Battle of the Marne, and the die was cast.

It is often contended that decisive results are impossible because of the democratic and industrial structure of modern armies. Nothing can be more mistaken, as we now know, than to imagine armies of millions of men to be essentially incapable of dealing a mortal blow, to be doomed to clash and wear each other away where they stand. The events of June 1940 dissipated that illusion. If the German Army had had the tactical and organizational superiority over the French in August 1914 that it had in June 1940, it would have gained the day as quickly; and for some years or decades the potentialities of total war would have remained unknown in Europe. Greater numerical strength, which the German general staff could have obtained by further drafts from the Eastern front, might very well have been sufficient. In short, the conditions for total war were present: all that was needed for its development was an opportunity, which in this case was offered by the approximately equal strength of the opposing forces.

Through an accidental and transient condition of warfare, which affected the West especially, total war, for four years, limited itself to the trenches. Defensive techniques were superior to offensive, so that by accumulating formidable firing power, it became possible to pulverize the enemy's front lines without too much difficulty; but the terrain won was so broken up that it became in itself an obstacle. Enemy defenses, improvised by hastily assembled reinforcements, halted the attack, which could not be supported by an artillery paralyzed by its lack of mobility and the effects of its own fire.

Until 1917 the intensification of warfare was mainly quantitative. The cry "More guns, more shells!" had a meaning that went beyond propaganda. Month after month, in offensive after offensive, more and more guns were massed and more and more rounds were fired. When there were not enough guns at the front, the artillery preparation went on for several days—giving the enemy time to prepare his resistance. Later the duration was reduced and the intensity increased. In the Somme offensive in 1916, there were 900 heavy guns and 1,100 light guns massed along 10 miles of front.[3] Neither side was able to win a decisive battle. Every breach in the line was more or less quickly filled. After initial success, the offensive petered out. Even during the latter months of 1918, when the Allies were considerably superior in men and matériel, they were able to strike heavy blows against the German Army, but there was no victory of annihilation.

Quantitative extension of warfare obviously does not prevent what might be called qualitative extension, recourse to new arms and new tactics. The French Army possessed about one hundred airplanes in August 1914, and several thousand by 1918. The use of motor vehicles for transport, of wireless communication, of armored tanks, gradually transformed the methods of operation, especially after 1917. But whatever share in the successes of the Allies may be attributed to tanks, essentially the war was brought to an end by means of the same arms with which it began. Machine guns and artillery, partly in improved models but mostly in larger numbers, completed the task they had begun. The new arms—aircraft and tanks—were not yet dominant, but they had shown that they would be in the next war.

Total war, as it took place in 1914–18, with problems of supply, strategy of attrition, stable fronts, and field fortifications, left the public with a horrifying memory of tens of thousands of soldiers sacrificed to conquer a few square miles, the inhuman life of the trenches, the crushing and startling technical superiority of arms, organization, and production over personal qualities—all of which helped dissipate the traditional romanticism of warfare and nourish revolt. Or rather, re-

---

3. At Stalingrad, in January 1943, the Russians massed 4,000 guns along 4 kilometers of front, i.e., 1 gun per meter of front.

volt against war, as old as humanity, was to be reinforced by revolt against war machines, a revolt comparable with the first revolt of craftsmen against industrial machines. But as long as the struggle continued, that latent revolt had to be repressed and enthusiasm maintained.

Thus the "technical surprise" is among the main causes of the geographical extension of war and the growth of wartime passions.

The extension of the war in Europe took a classical form. In the event of a conflict between great powers, said Machiavelli, the small ones generally have no chance to remain neutral, and nothing to gain by doing so, for their attitude arouses the enmity of the conqueror, whoever he may be; whereas if they take sides they may get into the good graces of the distributors of booty. The successive interventions of Turkey, Italy, Bulgaria, and Rumania were preceded by negotiations in conformity with tradition. Each of the major opponents exerted itself to secure a fresh ally by offering gains which ordinarily neither owned. The result of these competitive promises was usually determined in advance. Italy's aspirations could only be satisfied at Austria's expense. Great Britain and France had no difficulty in parading a generosity that Germany could match only by sacrificing her comrade in arms. On the other side, the Central Powers rallied Bulgaria, who coveted Serbian territory, whereas it was in Serbia's defense that the Allies had drawn their sword. Needless to say everyone's choice was determined by other considerations as well—a gamble on the result of the fighting, moral affinities, popular feeling, and so on.

In any case, none of these European interventions greatly increased the initial scale of hostilities or decisively modified the balance of power. Japan seized the opportunity to appropriate some strategic positions held by the Germans. Only the American intervention represents an unprecedented fact and marks a historic date, whose retrospective significance is very clear. That intervention was essentially due to the technical amplification of the war. The provocation was, of course, the German Government's declaration of unrestricted submarine warfare in violation of an agreement made several months earlier in Washington. The new technique of naval warfare, contrary to international law as understood at the time[4] (as was the British long-

---

4. When the United States entered the Second World War, the naval staff ordered unrestricted submarine warfare. The war technique that had aroused indignation twenty-five years earlier was now accepted as normal.

range blockade), precipitated the decision of the United States and thereby assured the defeat of the Second Reich.

There has subsequently been an attempt to minimize the validity of the provocation. During the isolationist period there was criticism of the bankers and industrialists who had supplied the Allies with credit, equipment, or raw material and who were now afraid, it was alleged, of losing their money or their customers. But such an interpretation, implying capitalist machinations, would, even if true, refer us back to the same reality. Even the Anglo-French alliance lacked the means to bring the total war to an end. The United States had been involved economically in the struggle before becoming militarily involved, because the joint resources of the British and French empires were insufficient to maintain the monstrous lethal machine.

Still other commentators claim that the submarine warfare was merely a pretext, and that the American leaders simply recognized at the time of that menace that British control of the seas was indispensable to the United States. American security would be endangered if Great Britain were defeated; a virtually hostile power would rule the Old World and be free to extend its domination, or at least its enterprises, across the oceans. But one may very well ask if the Americans would have recognized their solidarity with Great Britain had submarine warfare not shaken the ascendancy of the Home Fleet, revealed the German naval potential, and produced a general apprehension of a peace dictated on the scale of the war itself, that is to say, a Carthaginian peace.

At the same time we must not overlook the part played by sentiment or ideology. In critical moments the kinship of Britons and Americans dissipates mutual misunderstandings, resentments, and irritations. By inscribing on its banners the sacred words Democracy and Freedom, the Entente aroused general sympathy in America. Since it was universally inspired, the language used by the Allied representatives was understood in every continent. A crusade to make the world "safe for democracy" was, so it seemed, of world-wide concern. What meaning had the defense of German *Kultur* outside of Germany itself?

It was ideology that won over American opinion to participation in the war, arousing and maintaining the enthusiasm of a young nation. The fundamental consideration, nevertheless, was primarily materialistic. The Allies had sought American aid to help support the burden of the hyperbolic war. Economic participation became military partnership when the submarines tried to break the bond already existing between the European and American democracies, and so threatened to leave a navy regarded as hostile ruling the oceans and separating ancient Europe from the New World.

There has been incessant inquiry into the origin of the First World War, but no one has ever asked why it became hyperbolic. Did the people of different countries fight to the death because they detested each other, or did they detest each other because they fought so furiously? Did the belligerents set themselves unlimited objectives from the outset, or did they acquire those objectives in proportion to the increase in violence? Was it passion that produced the technical excess, or technical excess that fomented passion? Not unreservedly or without qualification, and fully recognizing the interaction of the two phenomena, I would maintain that the motive force of the evolution at that time was technical. Technique it was that imposed the organization of enthusiasm, condemned to failure the efforts at conciliation, drove out the old diplomatic wisdom, and contributed to the spread of the crusading spirit, finally producing a peace that created the situation from which the second war started.

The start of the first war was marked in all countries by an explosion of national fervor. Patriotism overrode social resentments and revolutionary aspirations. In a few days, sometimes in a few hours, the socialists, who had been pitiless critics of the diplomacy of both the Wilhelmstrasse and the Quai d'Orsay, were carried away by the collective enthusiasm and embraced the popular sentiment. National unity was established at once in France against German aggression, and in Germany against the Russian peril.

The German victories during the first weeks redoubled the fighting spirit of the Germans and steeled the resolution of the French. German terrorism and atrocities (which Allied propaganda exaggerated but did not invent), far from depressing the morale of the French, aroused a sort of fury, nourished by both military tradition and the "pacifist" revolt against the horrors of war.

As the sterile process of slaughter continued with no sign of an early end, enthusiasm waned and social claims, repressed by the sudden surge of ancestral passions, disrupted this national unity. Though neither side would give way, resolution was succeeded by resigned persistence, fervor gave place to reluctant acceptance. Propaganda and ideology usurped the place of genuine feeling.

At first both were adapted mainly to the needs of the country behind the lines. As a rule the combatants were killing one another without contempt or hatred. At times they felt bound together by a mystical communion of fate. Even when they hated, they hated a being of flesh and blood, the enemy whom it was necessary to kill so as not to be killed. The abstract hatreds that are ravaging our century are the work of urban masses, not of soldiers at the front. What Elie Halévy called "organized enthusiasm" forms a chapter in the history of civil mobilization. The need was desperately obvious: it was essential to maintain the nation's unity and will to fight. Defeat must be made to appear catastrophic, victory an unmixed blessing. In other words, the stake at issue escaped definition by the rules and regulations of diplomacy. It was no longer a question of shifting frontier posts a few miles. Only sublime—and vague—principles, such as the right of peoples to self-determination or "the war to end war," seemed commensurate with such violence, sacrifice, and heroism. It was technical excess that gradually introduced ideologies in place of war aims. Both sides claimed to know what they were fighting *about*, but neither said what it was fighting *for*.

Once general war had started, its provocation was bound to be forgotten, and the stake no longer had anything in common with the cause. All past relations between the European powers were reviewed and challenged. The chancelleries discovered forgotten grievances and ambitions in their files, the people in their memories.

Secret diplomacy was given free play. The British Ministers accepted Russia's claim to Constantinople, the French secured recognition of their claims in Alsace-Lorraine. The great powers signed with Italy, Rumania, and Serbia secret agreements that were not all indefensible but promised a sharing of booty rather than a peace in conformity with principles. It was easier to proclaim that the war was being fought in defense of freedom than to publish the results of such negotiations, which were interconnected and sometimes contradictory.

The same is true of the other side. At the time of its first victories, the German Government had not made known the conditions it would impose on the vanquished. But influential private associations, from the industrial groups to the Pan-German League, broadcast the most grandiose projects. Should they annex Belgium or merely require guarantees? Should they appropriate only France's colonial empire or part of her continental territory as well? The leaders of the Central Powers were also hoping for total victory; they, too, refused to bind themselves in advance by any formal announcement of their war aims. They, too, left it to the intellectuals to define the "ideas of 1914" in whose name Germany was carrying on the war for the defense and glory of her unique *Kultur*.

After two years of war, it may be that some of the German leaders, and even those of Austria-Hungary, would have been glad to return from "war ideologies" to "war aims," to silence the tumult of propaganda and allow the diplomats to speak again. But it was too late. A vague note was dispatched on December 1916 to which the Entente replied on January 10, 1917, with a note that was not precise on every point but which, by suggesting the liberation of the Czechs, seemed to imply the disintegration of Austria-Hungary. In July 1917, the German Parliament adopted a motion in favor of a peace without annexations or indemnities, but the Entente was not prepared to accept. The secret negotiations with the Emperor Charles of Austria for a separate peace collapsed, and everyone turned again to await the outcome of the battle.

From 1914 to 1918 there were special obstacles to a compromise peace. The strategic situation was temporarily favorable to the side that had the lesser chance of final victory. A war can be cut short when the side whose superiority is established on the battlefields shows moderation and renounces some of the gains that might come from victory, in order to save itself the trouble of bringing the enemy to his knees. Germany had won the first successes, and the fighting had taken place outside her territory. For all that, as the fighting went on she became the probable loser, so greatly did the resources of the Entente, which was mistress of the seas, come to exceed those of the Reich, suffocated by the blockade. In other words, according to the actual battle maps, Germany had the advantage; but according to the soundest predictions, the Entente would win in the end. In such a case, neither side could afford to make any important concessions.

Yet, quite apart from what might be called this element of chance, it was peculiarly difficult to end by negotiation in the traditional way a war that had become a war of peoples and of ideas. Nobody had started a crusade in 1914, nobody then was out to liberate oppressed nationalities, to make an end of secret diplomacy, or to spread democracy. To win sympathy in the world, and to maintain the morale of their suffering nations, governments resorted to ideology, and that element played an important part in the Allied conduct of the war from the time of the American intervention and the Russian Revolution. The war had not been started in order to bring about the triumph of particular views of life and society; but as the cost of operations mounted these views were felt to be essential to inflate the prospective profits of victory. It was declared that the peace would be durable only if it were dictated unconditionally after crushing the enemy. The demand for total victory was not so much the expression of a political philosophy as a reflex reaction to total war.

The Treaty of Versailles was far more the logical consequence of the war than its critics have admitted, both in view of the war's origins and of the ideological meaning which it progressively acquired in the course of the fighting. The Austro-Serbian diplomatic dispute had symbolized the quarrels of nationalities in Southeastern Europe. It had assumed exceptional gravity in proportion as it compromised the existence of Austria-Hungary. From 1917 onward, by proclaiming the principle of the liberation of nationalities (which often had no desire for liberation), the statesmen of the Entente gave to their enterprise a revolutionary character. They did so without calculating the consequences, and without strong convictions, so far were they carried away by the force of events. Austria-Hungary was not destroyed by the negotiations at Versailles. The recognition of the Masaryk Committee dealt the Dual Monarchy a first blow. The rejection of Emperor Charles' peace offers struck the deathblow, and all that had to be done at Versailles was to sign the death certificate. In essence, it was the acceptance of a *de facto* situation which was not so much the result of human activities or intentions as of the war itself and its irresistible dynamism.

Some of the Ministers at Vienna had believed that a sharp lesson for Serbia was indispensable to the survival of the Dual Monarchy: very likely they were wrong. Federalism, as conceived by the assassinated Archduke, offered the best method of reinforcing the old Hapsburg edifice, which the war showed to be rather solid. For two years desertions were rare; most of the South Slavs and even many of the Czechs fought to the end. Masaryk had as much difficulty in persuading his compatriots as in persuading Allied Ministers. In the end Austria-Hungary succumbed to the ideology that had been provoked by the length of the war. The effect rejoined the cause: the Europe of nationalities emerged from a war that had been kindled by a quarrel of nationalities.

But the logic of ideas did not accord with the logic of forces. It had been demonstrated that national states no longer possessed the resources needed for total war. Even Britain and France had sustained their effort only with the aid of the New World. If there was to be some sort of balance between the size of military and political units, the technique of twentieth-century warfare clearly demanded larger political units. The "Balkanization" of Europe, though probably in harmony with European passions and ideas, ran counter to the economic and military tendency toward giantism.

Nor is that all. As soon as the guns began to thunder, there appeared the critical problem of counterbalancing Germany's power. The treaty would solve nothing if it did not solve the "German problem." Would the Weimar Reich be integrated in a peaceful Europe more easily and more permanently than that of Wilhelm II?

Everything depended on Germany's acceptance of or conversion to a conservative attitude. That sort of acceptance would require, at least during a first phase of two or three decades, a mixture of contentment and impotence. The Treaty of Versailles created a maximum of discontent and an impotence that was only transitory. Whichever way she turned her eyes, toward Poland or Czechoslovakia or Austria, Germany saw grievances which she could only consider legitimate. The disarmament clauses, the demilitarization of the Rhineland, and the Little Entente made her temporarily helpless; but they did not weaken her for good and all. Having saved her unity and her industry, she had thereby kept intact the means of recovery. As Jacques Bainville put it in a famous phrase, "The treaty was too harsh for its softer elements, and too soft for the harsher ones."

The small and medium-sized states that surrounded the Reich feared her above all else. But each of them had interests, grievances, and ambitions of its own. Poland and Czechoslovakia, for example, never settled their difference over Teschen.

So long as Germany was disarmed, the French system held together with apparent solidity. As soon as the Reich recovered its sovereignty and began once more to brandish its arms, each nation sought its own safety, until all were dragged into common disaster.

That evolution had not been inescapable. France should have regrouped her allies, putting a stop to the Hitlerian enterprise at the outset. But the very consequences of the preceding war made that attitude unlikely on her part.

As soon as Russia was eliminated from the European concert by her revolution and the United States had withdrawn into isolationism, the once victorious group was potentially weaker than the vanquished. The sacrifice of a million and a half Frenchmen weighed more heavily in the balance of history than that of two million Germans. By a vital reflex France, apprehensive of the future and satisfied with her own "place in the sun," was bound to be more pacifist than the powerful but shackled Germany.

Clear-sighted calculation would have shown that the best way for France to maintain both peace and her position would have been for her to force Germany to respect the disarmament clauses, or at least the demilitarization of the Rhineland. Concern for peace should have encouraged France to resist German rearmament. Instead, by a psychological contradiction, it inspired her to appease the formidable neighbor. Unluckily that undeliberated effort was entered into with a Germany that could be appeased by nothing short of slavery.

The First World War had shown that the alliance of the Western democracies with Russia was the only means of creating a force that could hold its own against Germany. Without the Russian front, without the shifting of two German army corps to East Prussia, the Battle of the Marne would probably not have been won. The Third Reich, rearmed and adventurous, could be deterred only by enrolling Russia in the conservative camp. But Communist Russia, on its emergence from the world war, was no more interested than Germany in maintaining the status quo and the peace.

Whether we consider the international balance of power or the internal structure of each country, to say nothing of its economic organization, the Europe of Versailles was less stable than that of 1914. Territorial partition had not put an end to international quarrels, it had replaced the old quarrels by new ones. The nationalism of the new states encouraged trade barriers and became a cause of impoverishment for all. Germany was more bitter, virtually more revolutionary, and in the long run not without means of action.

It is clearly impossible to say what would have happened had a compromise peace been concluded late in 1916 or early in 1917. Speculation on what might have been the outcome of a different policy would be a waste of time. Yet the principal causes of the Second World War resulted from prolongation of the first war and, above all, of the Russian Revolution and the Fascist reactions to it in Italy and Germany.

The war destroyed those traditional institutions that might have checked the tendency in Western societies toward social leveling and other forms of collectivism. The monarchies that had crumbled in defeat would not have prevented the "democratization" of the regimes of Central Europe, but they would have reduced the risk of mass passions, secular religions, and totalitarian parties. Parliaments are soundly established only insofar as they are self-imposed by the majority, and not by violence.

Everything happened as if at a certain point violence became self-supporting. In war, as with fissionable materials, there is a critical mass. Since 1914, Europe has been shaken by wars in "chain reaction."

Dynamism of Total War

Like the first, the second war of the twentieth century originated and centered in Germany. Like the first, it grew out of all proportion, extending from its European origins until in the end it covered the planet, unleashing monstrous cruelties and passions until the atomic bomb finally brought the technique of destruction to a ghastly perfection that was, and still is, scarcely imaginable. The second war, like the first, was lost by the aggressor; but this time again after the ordeal, the world remains unconverted to the values for which the West has fought. European democracy and freedom and civilization are the victims, even more than Germany, of a victory won in their name.

Leaving aside these fundamental analogies, the second war was nearly a replica of the first. Everything happened differently but the final outcome is much the same. No one disagrees over the immediate causes of the Second World War, for Hitler signed his own works. This time there was not the approximate balance of power, as in 1914, but German superiority that brought into play the "law of amplification." The stake was still the principle of the formation of political units, but one camp at least proclaimed that the era of national sovereignty was ended. Twenty years after its triumph, the idea of nationalism belonged already to the past: the age of empires had begun. The material consequences of the war created the threat of a new conflict, not because the defeated power, powerful still and embittered, was dreaming of retaliation, but because in Europe and Asia, vanquished and victors, alike overwhelmed, were now caught between two peripheral superstates.

Public opinion and the chancelleries had learned from the much discussed events of July 1914 certain lessons which Anglo-French diplomacy did its best to apply. The statesmen made the same mistake as the French general staff. The latter, regretting the follies of the all-out offensive, placed blind faith in firepower and in the continuous front line; so that, in trying to avoid the preceding war, they precipitated the Hitlerian adventure.

British statesmen were convinced that there might have been no war if, on July 25, 1914, Downing Street had taken a definite stand and made it known to Berlin. Hence the touchingly ineffectual energy of Mr. Neville Chamberlain during the crises of 1938–39 when he made it unmistakably clear to the world and to the Führer that this time the British Empire would not remain neutral if France had again to face the Reich.

His word was not doubted in Berlin, but the times had changed. In

1939 the equivalent of the British warning of 1914 could only have come from Washington.[5] Roosevelt and most clear-sighted Americans were convinced in advance that the United States would be drawn into the war, but the backwardness of public opinion and the bonds of democracy condemned them to pass a bill, not for rearmament, which might have impressed Hitler, but for neutrality, which seemed to prohibit supplies to the belligerents on either side. Roosevelt was reduced to the prediction of a catastrophe which he might have been able to prevent.

Even apart from the American defection, the British warning would have carried more weight if it had been accompanied by additional military preparations. Hitler did not expect the British to remain neutral either in 1938 or 1939, but he was equally unconvinced that the Empire would engage in a life-and-death struggle. It was no longer enough to sever diplomatic relations (which Berlin anticipated calmly); practical proof should have been given of unshakable resolve. The Labour Party was opposed to appeasement, but also opposed to compulsory military service.

The British and French were still obsessed by the horrors of war. Even the leaders sincerely believed that no one, and certainly not a former solider, could take the initiative in cold blood. Hence they developed a series of theories attempting to explain how wars broke out, without either side wanting them, by an enigmatical chain of circumstances. The admission that war is inevitable helps, it was said, to make it so. The widespread diplomatic opinion in 1914, that war was bound to come sooner or later, may indeed have paralyzed the efforts towards a peaceful settlement of the Austro-Serbian crisis. But faced with such a regime as that of the Nazis, with their almost unlimited ambitions, such considerations were anachronistic. Was it possible to satisfy Hitler? Could he not be stopped except by force? These were the only questions. The Western democracies tried first to satisfy Hitler, and then in 1939 to stop him, when the superior strength, in the short run at least, was no longer theirs.

Other observers had been impressed by the German accusations of encirclement. Seen from Berlin, had not the alliances seemed before 1914 to threaten the security of the Reich? Had they not given the impression beyond the Rhine of a conspiracy against an actively expansionist power? Hence the British concern to declare at every mo-

---

5. The statesmen are making the same mistake today. An undertaking by Washington in 1939 might have prevented the last war. But will it suffice to prevent the next one?

ment that the London Government had no thought of encirclement, whereas, in fact, the so-called encirclement had been no more than an alliance to counterbalance Germanic force. To renounce that alliance would have increased the risk of war: the weaker the victims, the stronger the aggressor's temptation.

Finally, other observers recalled that, as of a certain day in 1914, perhaps July 29, and in any case the thirtieth, the automatism of the mobilizations had tied the hands of the diplomats. The generals had assumed control and the civil leaders had abdicated. In September 1938 and in August 1939, quite comic efforts were made to escape from that supposed automatism. It was declared again and again that mobilization was not war: true, but an essential fact was forgotten. In July 1914 the Central Powers may have wanted only a diplomatic success established by local operations at Serbia's expense, so that the peace might have been saved by allowing them that satisfaction. But there was no such situation in 1938 or 1939. In 1938 the aggressor intended to annex the Sudetenland, which amounted to the destruction of Czechoslovakia. Then, after the seizure of Prague, Poland's existence was at stake. It was reasonable to hesitate over the decision to be adopted, but not to be guided by a completely irrelevant precedent.

In retrospect the essential aspects of the situation seem remarkably simple. The arrival of the Nazis in power heralded a new diplomatic initiative. The new regime would rearm and seek a revision of the territorial clauses in the Treaty of Versailles. What would be the extent of its ambitions? Would it pursue objectives obtainable by peaceful means, or did it intend to go so far that the other nations must either resist or concede? Although some discussion was possible in 1933, one thing was certain: Hitler should never have been allowed advantages which prevented his being stopped without general war.

So long as the Rhineland remained demilitarized, France was able, even alone, to impose her will. After March 1936, not even Britain and France together could intervene locally to prevent Hitler in his enterprise. The decisive capitulation, dividing the period 1933–39, was agreed to not at Munich in 1938, but at London and Paris in March 1936. From that date, war was not inevitable (what, indeed, is the meaning of inevitability, applied to a chain of historical events?), but it had become probable. To avoid it, it would have been necessary for the conservative coalition to possess at every moment forces superior to those of the revolutionary coalition. But that superiority would have demanded the steady cooperation of one or the other of the two great powers whose intervention did in the end bring victory, the

United States or Soviet Russia. Roosevelt, however, while encouraging the Western democracies to resist, permitted the Congress to take precautions against the chain of events that had brought about intervention in 1917. (The New World, too, was moving into the future with its eyes on the past.) As for the Soviet Union, it was more afraid of being exposed alone to German aggression than of a possible world war, which could assist its subversive plans.

Western diplomacy might have rallied Soviet Russia to its side had it not hesitated so much, thereby giving the master of the Kremlin the impression that there would be no objection to German expansion eastward. (So I thought at the time; I no longer think so today, and will refrain from speculating as to what might have happened.) It was Stalin who, in March 1939, took the initiative towards an agreement with Hitler. In 1938, in the absence of a common frontier, he would not have had to enter a total war, at least in its first phase. After the elimination of Czechoslovakia as a bastion, the perspectives changed and Stalin maneuvered subtly to redirect the mounting war to the West. Britain and France, moreover, had already promised, for nothing in return from Poland and Rumania, to intervene in case of German aggression in the East—a promise for which Stalin would have eventually paid dearly. From then on, he had everything to gain (or so, at least, he thought, for his calculations were upset by the quick French defeat) from securing, through a pact with Hitler, a respite while the others would be fighting and he would be reserving his strength for the final decision.

Apart from an alliance between the Western democracies and the Soviet Union, which would have been almost impossible in view of mutual suspicion and divergence of interests, was there no chance of peace after 1936? There are those who still claim that Hitler could have been appeased; but such a hypothesis is unlikely. Germany, after establishing her protectorate over Bohemia and after destroying or bringing Poland to heel, would have so enlarged her territory and increased her resources that a less ambitious leader than Hitler could hardly have resisted temptation. There was no longer any equilibrium possible in Europe. By what miracle could a regime dedicated to unlimited dynamism stop halfway?

The truth is that in 1939 there was only one card left to play, that of "national" opposition within the Third Reich. Hitler's opponents were amazed by his successes, and wondered desperately what would come next. It is known that on the eve of Munich certain generals had decided to overthrow the Führer rather than precipitate general war. What would have happened had the democracies stood firm? What were really the chances of General Halder and the other conspirators? We shall never know. The truth is that only the replacement of the Nazis by a nationalist but not revolutionary regime would still have offered a chance of peace after 1936. A traditionalist Germany, either authoritarian or democratic, might have been appeased, but not Hitler's Germany.

It is easy to understand that the immediate causes of the second war should have provoked fewer and less passionate controversies. The first war had arisen from a "diplomatic failure." There is room for unending argument as to the likelihood of an ultimate explosion if the Sarajevo crisis had been peacefully overcome. The second war arose from Hitler's schemes of conquest. It might have broken out a year earlier if the democracies had decided to fight for Czechoslovakia; it might have been delayed had the democracies not come to the aid of Poland. But it is impossible to see how Hitler could have stopped of his own accord, or how Great Britain and France could have saved themselves without stopping him, that is to say, without fighting. Thus, what really matter are the remote origins. What were the sources of Hitler's rise to power and Germany's imperial desires? Why did the conservative states give the Teuton Caesar time to accumulate enough arms, not for victory, but for his own burial beneath the ruins of a civilization?

Western thinkers had concluded from the tragic events of 1914–18 that modern war could not pay. It would no longer leave the victors and the vanquished, but death and ruin everywhere. The spoils of victory could no longer be commensurate with the cost of battle. The only road to victory would be the avoidance of war. An irreproachable conclusion: from the point of view of England and France, the only victory would indeed have consisted in avoiding war. But it was a sterile conclusion, for if other nations have not the same opinion, how can that peaceful victory be secured?

Certain English theorists had pictured another conclusion. They thought that what was absurd was not war in itself, but total war. The 185 men who died at Trafalgar had won more for their country than the 800,000 who died in 1914–18. Wisdom would counsel that, instead of madly throwing men and wealth into the furnace, some limit should be set. War, yes, if necessary but, as Captain Liddell Hart put it, "with limited liability."

The Germans drew quite another lesson from their earlier experience. Hyperbolic war would not develop inevitably from industrial societies; it was due to a combination of chance circumstances: the approximate balance between the warning coalitions, the temporary superiority of the defensive over the offensive, and the difficulty of demolishing field fortifications. By isolating its adversaries on the principle of plucking the artichoke of its leaves, one by one, German diplomacy would provide the *Wehrmacht* with campaigns that could be brought quickly and economically to an end. The weapons tested in the last stages of the preceeding war, tanks and aircraft, would restore to the offensive its chances of success. In Spengler's famous phrase, mechanical power had reopened the era of great invasions that had ended with the supremacy of the Mongol cavalry. Finally, the cost of the fighting, even if high, would not be excessive if the yield of victory were lasting. The irrationality of the war of 1914–18 had lain in the impossibility of reconciling a life-and-death struggle with the maintenance of sovereign states. A system of independent states is compatible with limited war, but not with total war. This last consideration must inevitably herald the peace of the empires.

In 1939–40 the German calculations seemed at first to be confirmed. The campaigns in Poland and France gave a relation between output and yield that reversed the experience of 1914–18, fulfilling the most optimistic forecasts. Germany lost fewer than 40,000 dead between May 10 and June 25, 1940, and no more than 66,000 in the West up to June 6, 1944. The total casualties (killed, wounded, and prisoners) in the campaign in France were less than 100,000; and the victor added, on paper, some 30 to 40 per cent to his industrial potential, and still more if we include the gains in Czechoslovokia, Poland, and France.

Aware that the stalemate in the mud in Flanders and Lorraine had prolonged the fighting and increased its violence, Hitler—master of Europe from the Vistula to the Atlantic, but the prisoner of his conquests—was driven to extend his field of operations immeasurably, and to rush headlong from victory to victory on his way to ultimate disaster. The democracies were loath to negotiate between 1914 and 1918, though thousands of men were falling every day—but how could Great Britain have negotiated with a Caesar more powerful than Napoleon?

In his eastward drive in June 1941, Hitler was trying to secure a permanent hold on his continental empire. Henceforth, events conspired to forge the coalition which he had exerted himself to prevent. Japan, whose enterprise in the Far East was parallel to his own, but quite different in origin and significance, challenged the American giant. At once the war became no longer merely European like the first war, with extra-European prolongations, but truly global. The conflagration steadily spread. The extent and intensity of the fighting increased without limit. The successive stages of that amplification illustrate the irrepressible dynamism of modern war with its strategic bombing, guerrilla warfare, deportation of civilians, and death camps.

The theorists had conceived in advance the idea of reducing a nation by systematically bombing its towns. The Italian General, Douhet, had been the promoter of the doctrine, and its test was anticipated in a conflict between the great powers. It was, however, uncertain how much destruction could be wreaked from the air and what effect bombing would have on popular resistance. The German Air Force had been established and trained with a view to coordinated action with the Army; it did not include the equivalent of the British heavy bombers, and it had not expected important night attacks. In the course of the campaign in the West it attacked lines of communication, headquarters, strategic points in the front lines, and as far as thirty miles to the rear. It did, however, undertake "terror raids" in Holland (an entire section of Rotterdam was destroyed) and in France; these raids over inhabited districts aimed at reducing the enemy morale. The German general staff seemed to believe in the material efficacy of bombing in support of the Army and in the psychological efficacy of certain forms of bombing in full daylight, where it had the mastery of the air against a weak enemy, as in Holland, or a discouraged one, as in France.

The effect of this strategy in 1940 was to tempt the British, and then the Americans, to resort to strategic bombing on a scale unknown till then. Besieged in their island, with no likelihood of an early landing in Europe, the British had only the choice between inaction and air attacks. Daylight bombings were possible only with fighter escort. Technical resources were scarcely sufficient to enable a distinction to be made between zone bombing and the bombing of targets. Accordingly British and Germans engaged in a rivalry in more or less "indiscriminate" night bombings. Blind destruction entered into the habits of combat.

Already in the preceding war the distinction between combatants and noncombatants had been narrowed if not destroyed by firepower. In this respect the Germans had largely taken the initiative, from poison gas to the heavy artillery that shelled Paris. Bombing had added to the risks run by civilians; open cities, which in principle were spared, had become difficult to define, so greatly had the number of military objectives increased in the epoch of industrial warfare; and badly aimed bombs made it impossible for populations to distinguish between an attack on a railway station and an attack on a town. With the enormous increase in the number, tonnage, and flying range of bombers, what in 1914–18 had been a spectacular but relatively harmless episode assumed between 1939 and 1945 the dimensions of a major operation, whose military efficacy is still doubtful but whose destructive effects remain to this day.

Ten thousand tons of bombs were dropped over Germany in 1940; 30,000 in 1941; 40,000 in 1942; 120,000 in 1943; 600,000 in 1944; and 500,000 during the five first months of 1945. According to the figures of a British economist, the annual loss of production in the Reich was estimated at 2.5 per cent in 1942, 9 per cent in 1943, 17 per cent in 1944. No doubt these figures are only approximate. The losses indirectly attributable to the Allied air offensive must have been considerable. Four and a half million people were employed in clearing away ruins and in air-raid precautions, including the production of anti-aircraft weapons. But, above all, 61 cities of more than 100,000 inhabitants, on which some 500,000 tons of bombs were dropped, had 70 per cent of their dwellings (3,600,000) destroyed. Strategic bombing seems to have played a smaller part in the victory than in the postwar difficulties.

The Germans had given their enemies the right to resort to this horrible process. But two questions might have been asked: What was its military usefulness, and what would be its long-term consequences? When strategic bombing was concentrated on certain works (synthetic fuels, ball bearings), or on transportation, the military results were incomparably greater. The generals apparently miscalculated, even from their own point of view. The civilian war leaders in the democracies might have measured their responsibility toward the common civilization they claimed to be defending, but they seem to be as incapable of thinking about peace once war has started as of preparing for war before the first shot has been fired.

The strategic bombing followed a British tradition—to use as few men as possible with costly equipment in a situation where with limited losses a decision can be forced. Each nation has its cherished military memories. The French like to recall pitched battles or cavalry charges, even vain ones. The British idolize the "stalwart few" of Trafalgar or of the Battle of Britain. Millions of workers in the factories, hundreds of thousands of underlings (squires, as it were, to the modern knights), and a few thousands or tens of thousands of airmen—were not these the rejoinder to the sterile butcheries of Flanders? Apart from that, will the side with superiority in any one means of destruction ever have the wisdom to restrict the employment of that superiority when the national existence is at stake? And is anything more unlikely than a complete equilibrium in all forms of weapons?

By another departure from tradition, Hitler's conquests helped to confuse the distinction between combatants and noncombatants and to universalize violence. Wars with limited stakes, between nations whose frontiers, but not their structures, will be modified can be fought entirely by soldiers in uniform. An imperial war, whose outcome would be the installation of a higher sovereignty (*de facto,* if not *de jure*) over those of the belligerent states, almost inevitably becomes a war between whole populations. A country that passively accepted the yoke of the occupying state might be acting reasonably (in military terms, the cost of resistance might exceed the "yield"), but would it not have renounced nationhood? The enemy presence reanimates that national feeling. Total mobilization by the occupying power incites revolt; the recruitment of factory workers strengthens the underground resistance.

One of the most frequent consequences of imperialism is the conqueror's reinforcement through his conquests. The army with which Alexander set out for the East was half composed of Greeks who had fought against Philip. Less than half the army with which Napoleon crossed the Russian frontiers on June 21, 1812, was composed of Frenchmen. Hitler, too, had added to the *Wehrmacht* Finnish, Italian, Hungarian, and Rumanian divisions, to say nothing of the Spanish contingents or the League of French Volunteers.

In our time the contribution of combatants is the most spectacular but the most superficial form of mobilization of the vanquished. The German factories needed manpower: whence should it be drawn if not from occupied Europe? In 1945 the prisoners of war and foreign workers in Germany numbered between 5 and 10 millions. Applied over a wide region, the technique of total mobilization carried civilized Europe back to the time of the great migrations, whose rigors, however, were softened by administrative experience.

Centuries earlier, when armies lived on the invaded countries for lack of organized supply, their pillage provoked guerrilla fighting as soon as normal poverty became widespread, unbearable destitution, as in Spain and Russia during the Napoleonic invasions. In our age, guerrilla warfare on a grand scale was provoked, at least in the West, by incidental consequences of total war—food requisitions that merely exasperated the populations by reducing the ration below the habitual, if not the physiological, minimum; and transfers of workers, inciting tens of thousands of young men to flee conscription and swell the ranks of the Resistance.

In the East, guerrilla warfare was organized either by the government or by a revolutionary party. National resistance arose in Yugoslavia immediately following the disaster. But General

Mikhailovitch, who had witnessed the atrocities committed by Croats against Serbs, had been struck by the disproportionate losses inflicted on populations by active guerrilla warfare so long as liberating armies were unable to intervene, and wanted to spare his forces. Tito did not hesitate to carry on partisan warfare for years, but his aim was as much to secure power after Germany's defeat as to hasten that defeat.

In Russia, group leaders were parachuted behind the enemy lines with precise instructions. Filling the enemy rear with a sense of insecurity was conceived as a military task, among others, that the general staff had to carry out by arousing and exploiting popular passion. In fact, the ferocity of the occupying forces contributed quite as much to the spread of revolt as the patriotism of the population and the threats of reprisals published by the Soviet authorities. In 1941 the Ukrainians had no thought of rising against the invaders—what really happened has been carefully dissimulated. The atmosphere of a national war was largely created by the very methods of biological warfare, conceived by certain German theorists, and applied by the S.S., under the orders of some Gauleiters. On the pretext that Russia was not a signatory of the Geneva Convention, hundreds of thousands of Russian prisoners of war were allowed to starve to death during the winter of 1941–42. In the West, the German armies had behaved "correctly" to the populations and refrained from deliberately increasing the burden of occupation; but in the East, the Government General of Poland had subjected that unhappy country to a pitiless regime, and the occupied territories in Russia soon suffered a reign of terror. Among the follies committed by Hitler's representatives, none had more disastrous repercussions for the criminals themselves. The Germans finally became victims of the fury they had aroused.

Strategic bombing, deportations of workers, guerrilla warfare, terrorism, the police state—this multiplication of violence proceeds logically from an imperialist war conducted with the aid of modern industry. But there was nothing yet to imply the extermination, deliberated in cold blood and scientifically organized, of 6 million Jews; nothing to imply the concentration camps, or at least their sadistic methods of degradation and slow murder. We cannot deny Hitler's henchmen the unhappy merit of having foreseen and exceeded the requirements of total war. They have precipitated those zoological wars to which Renan, in 1871, predicted that racial passions would lead humanity.

Hitler's venture considered as a whole in 1940 gave the impression of a plan elaborated in advance and methodically carried out. In a first

phase, Germany rearmed, perhaps more ostentatiously than effectively, in order to deter France from any military rejoinder. Even before
the *Wehrmacht* had attained fighting strength, contingents were sent
into the Rhineland, a tactic based upon the accurate foresight of British blindness, French pacifism, and the diplomatic imbroglio of the
sanctions against Italy. From that moment the Western democracies
had repeatedly no other choice than to capitulate or to risk general
war. In February 1938 the Nazi regime proceeded, in perfect safety, to
annex Austria. Czechoslovakia, encircled and isolated, fell in September 1938 after a simulacrum of resistance from Great Britain and
France. The Siegfried line was hastily set up to discourage any French
inclination to an offensive; then Germany turned against Poland,
which the day before had been its accomplice in the partition of
Czechoslovakia and now suffered in its turn. At the last moment the
Western democracies made a serious effort to form a common front
with Soviet Russia. But Hitler had more to offer: Stalin could have half
of Poland; a second world war was a virtual certainty, and he would
be able to remain neutral during its first phase. What advantages for
an empire, still insecure, but always hoping to extend its revolution! In
the spring of 1940 France, herself isolated, succumbed in a few weeks.
Hitler's empire, extending from the Vistula to the Atlantic, had been
created.

The imperialistic theories that fill German literature seemed to have
been miraculously confirmed. *Militarily,* the internal combustion engine, supplying power to tanks and aircraft, seemed to have recreated
the superiority of force needed for a break-through and its exploita-
tions; railways and trucks seemed to have given land armies a mobility
comparable with that of the naval powers. *Economically,* the wide
territory of the new empire would restore the unrestricted trade that
had been lost in Europe in the first third of the twentieth century.
Politically, national states would belong to the past because they
would no longer possess either the resources needed for total war or
the dimensions needed for economic rationalization. Popular feeling,
though it had not kept up with events, seemed already to be influenced
by that irresistible evolution. The external threat no longer sufficed to
unite the French or to steel their national spirit. The country that had
given to Europe the perfect example of the national state revealed the
irremediable decline of that political unit.

The fifth column is a typical element of the age of empires. It is
recruited mainly among three sorts of men: pacifists, revolted by the
material and moral cost of total war who, at the bottom of their

hearts, prefer the triumph of an empire to the independent sovereignty of bellicose states; defeatists, who despair of their own country; and ideologues, who set their political faith above their patriotism and submit to the Caesar whose regime and ideology they admire. The elements of the German fifth column, though much less influential and numerous than has been alleged, were recruited mainly from the two first categories. Quisling in Norway, Mussert in Holland, probably belonged to the third category. In Britain and France there were scarcely any convinced Nazis who paved the way for Germany's victory because they adhered to the credo of National Socialism. Certain reactionaries saw compensation for defeat in the chance that it offered for a national revolution. Others, with Fascistic tendencies, bowed, not without satisfaction perhaps, before a military decision which they thought would be final. Obviously there could not be many genuine Nazis outside Germany.

As an imperialist ideology, in fact, Hitlerism was a challenge to common sense. Any empire that is imposed upon old nations proud of their civilization can be stabilized only by inducing the vanquished to accept their lot. The Roman Empire could not have existed if Italians, Gauls, and Africans had not been able to become Roman citizens. Once the Jews had been exterminated (a few more months would have sufficed), racialism would have lost its only international appeal. Of what use would have been the slogan "Anti-Semites of the world, unite!" when there were no longer any Jews for the gas chambers? Racialism had either to disappear or remain for the Germans to profit by. Subject peoples are not to be won over by proclaiming the superiority of the master race.

Europe in 1940 offered an approximate picture of what the empire of the immediate future might have been. Carefully plotted gradations of popular subjection were making their appearance. Poland was ruled by Germans, the Czech territory protected; nonoccupied France had the right to diplomatic representation abroad. Warsaw would have received a Governor, Prague a Protector, Paris a Nazi Ambassador. The degree of autonomy and the methods of rule were to vary. In the occupied half of France, for example, the Germans had already shown how they would "legally" control the French economy. Political assimilation would be guaranteed by the military impotence of the French. For the rest, the visible forms of independence would be respected.

The real difficulties remained. It is easy to start an imperial enterprise, but difficult to end it. Hitler, with the unsolicited, unwanted collaboration of Japan, provoked the alliance of the three greatest powers in the world: the British Commonwealth, the Soviet Union, and the United States. With this alliance, Hitler's calculated plan of conquest dissolved. We no longer witness the realization of a plan but the improvisations of an adventurer.

Even the opening phase of the enterprise, which at first glance seemed the result of imperialistic theory and technique, was really marked by constant good fortune rather than by any close attention to strategy. Hitler was deliberately following the old rule of warfare by disposing of his adversaries one by one. He tried, and almost succeeded, to make sure of being ahead with the mobilization of his troops and even of his factories. Confident of the efficacy of modern offensive weapons, he calculated that his more rapid mobilization would enable him to win a decisive victory over adversaries who had not had time to assemble their forces. This conception, based as usual on past experience, seemed to assure his success in an operation almost identical with that which had so nearly succeeded in September 1914. Thus the master of the Third Reich, to the stupefaction of his generals, eliminated Austria and Czechoslovakia without firing a shot, and liquidated at small cost Poland, Holland, Belgium, and France.[6] But the secret of these triumphs was not as much military or political as psychological. When, in 1935, Hitler proclaimed that he no longer recognized the military clauses of the Treaty of Versailles, Germany was defenseless. Hitler's superiority over his generals lay in his intuitive understanding of crowds and of peoples. He was convinced that France would not move, and he was right. The *Wehrmacht* contingents that occupied the demilitarized zone in March 1936 had orders to retire if the French Army crossed the frontiers of the Reich. The Führer was obliged to make that concession to G.H.Q., but he had accurately gauged the French state of mind. In 1938, General Beck resigned when Hitler revealed his projects in regard to Austria and Czechoslovakia. Such projects, declared the old-style generals, would inevitably lead to a world war. They were nationalists, but they were also Christians, and feared for Germany especially, but also for European civilization.

At Munich in 1938, Hitler judged correctly and achieved a peaceful success for the last time. Events had belied the fears of his professional advisers and had justified the amateur's optimism. The Führer believed more than ever in his mission and his manifest destiny. He went

---

6. In the West the superiority of the German armies, except in aircraft, was not so much quantitative as qualitative. Even in tanks the French were outclassed more because of inferior tactics and organization than numbers.

on to make his fatal mistake. The generals' objections seemed to be contradicted by the facts in September 1938, again in March 1939, and even in September 1939 and June 1940. The military victories of 1939 and 1940 exceeded the always cautious anticipations of the experts. But their pessimism as to the ultimate outcome was well founded. Peaceful triumphs and lightning victories made inevitable a war to the uttermost, in a chain of events which Hitler had refused to foresee and refused almost up to the end to recognize.

When he ordered his troops to cross the Polish frontier, he had no doubt that the result would be an Anglo-French declaration of war. But he did not think that their symbolic gesture implied fierce determination to fight to the bitter end and destroy the Third Reich. After the Polish campaign and during the campaign in France, Hitler seems still to have been unconvinced that the British would prove irreconcilable. It may be that he spread the British army at Dunkirk by holding up his armored divisions for forty-eight hours so as not to offend the *amour-propre* of the British and to leave open the opportunity of negotiating with them.

From that point onward, one searches in vain for any trace in Hitler's successive decisions of a plan elaborated in advance. For several months, without any strong conviction, he played with the idea of a landing in England; but the defeat of his aircraft led him to renounce the attempt, for which the general staffs were unenthusiastic, and in which he himself had been unable to put faith. He thought of attacking Gibraltar, and of sending his armored divisions to Alexandria and Suez. Finally, in the autumn of 1940, after the interview with Molotov, he decided on Operation Barbarossa—the invasion of Russia.

There is no lack of historical precedent to suggest that this decision followed inevitably in the wake of conquests in the West and the Battle of Britain. Hitler, like Napoleon, was pursuing the elusive Albion into the snows of Russia. For how could he strike a mortal blow at the British Commonwealth so long as the Russian Army and Air Force were intact, compelling him to keep part of the *Luftwaffe* and the *Wehrmacht* in the East, or at least in reserve? If the war of attrition continued in the West for years, would not the Soviet Union inevitably become the arbiter of the situation? Such arguments are easily mustered—as are those to the contrary. The Soviet Union was carrying out the clauses of the Russo-German Pact with scrupulous loyalty; it delivered all the promised supplies, and offered still more. There had been nothing to suggest that it would, in the near future, have to turn against the Third Reich. Thus, in concentrating its forces against the British Commonwealth in 1941, had not Germany a chance of weak-

ening England to the point of inducing her not to capitulate, but to
negotiate? During the first months of 1941, Great Britain was losing
500,000 tons of merchant shipping every month. If the submarine war
had been accompanied by the bombing of ports, and if the German
Army had utilized some of its "unemployed" divisions against
Gibraltar and Suez, it is questionable whether Roosevelt would have
been able to bring about American intervention before Great Britain
had been overcome by discouragement.[7]

There is little need to answer these questions. Our purpose is not to
speculate on what might have happened, but to arrive at a simple
statement of fact. The master of the Third Reich wanted to be an
empire builder, and probably would never have reached the limit of
his ambitions. But his own mind was not made up as to the order of
the various operations. The pact with Stalin seemed to him at the time
to be a masterpiece of diplomacy. He then hesitated before the prospect of a life-and-death struggle with the British Commonwealth, either because from a racialist point of view he deplored the reciprocal
extermination of the higher peoples, or because he had not abandoned
hope of a reconciliation.

The industrial mobilization of the Reich bears the marks of this
indecision. In 1940, after the collapse of France, the general output
was reduced. Similarly, in October 1941, when it was firmly believed
that the Russian Army had been destroyed (as the communiqués from
the Führer's headquarters declared), production was again slowed
down. Not until Stalingrad and the first Eastern defeats did the Third
Reich seem at last to be filled with a sense of urgency. At that point
total mobilization ceased to be a subject for declamations. Even then,
subsequent study has shown that industrial mobilization was less complete in Nazi Germany than in democratic Britain.

Improvisation and amateurishness mark the last phase of Hitler's
adventure. His fundamental mistake was the counterpart of the accurate intuitions of the first phase. He refused to admit that, in spite of
his theories, he had repeated the Kaiser's error in launching a war on
two fronts, against the Russians and the Anglo-Saxons. When he
could no longer deny the facts, he clung to an argument that seemed to
him unanswerable: How could the capitalist democracies and the Soviet empire co-operate to the extent of jointly crushing Germany?
Would it not be the height of folly for the British and Americans to

7. It is true that such a compromise peace in 1941 or 1942 would have been only a
truce, and would have settled nothing. So long as Great Britain subsisted on one side,
supported by the United States and the Soviet Union on the other side, Hitler's empire,
regarded as an enemy by both, would remain in a precarious situation.

lend a hand in the destruction of the only barrier that could protect Europe from the Communist flood? It may have been folly, but it was a folly that he himself had led the Anglo-Saxons to commit.

The Allies of 1914–18 were united against Germany. It was to be expected that on the day of victory the normal difficulties of victorious coalitions—divergencies of interest and competition for shares in the spoil—would show themselves. But after the elimination of Russia from the alliance, Great Britain, France, Italy, and the United States belonged to one world. They had similar national policies; none of them nurtured unlimited ambitions, and none of them regarded its Allies as possible future enemies.

Between 1939 and 1945 the United Nations, whose common hostility to Germany formed the only bond that held them together, were divided into two groups—the Soviet Union on one side and the bourgeois democracies on the other—which were bound to oppose each other when the Third Reich foundered. Rarely can hostility have been so predictable. The Germans never ceased to proclaim the fact, and Goebbels was unable to understand that the more he insisted the more he forced the Americans to camouflage it. Not for a moment, of course, did the Russian authorities forget, but the Anglo-Saxons, and particularly the Americans, often acted as if they did not regard the hostility as fundamental.

On the very day when the German armies invaded Russia Churchill delivered a speech that automatically created an Anglo-Russian alliance. The British war leader passed over the German-Soviet pact, ignored the fact that the U.S.S.R. had been guilty of aggression against Poland, and laid down the principle that the enemies of our enemies were our friends. It was a normal decision, ratified by the President of the United States and public opinion in both countries. It had been decided to destroy the Third Reich: the Soviet Union brought to the struggle its hundreds of divisions and was destined to offer millions of lives in the common cause.

The material aid sent by Great Britain and then by the United States to Russia, who had suffered heavily from the first blows of the *Wehrmacht,* was no less logical. Because there were fears in London and Washington that the Red Army might collapse, it was sent unconditionally all available equipment. But in 1943, after Stalingrad, the strategic situation changed radically: the balance of power had become favorable to the Allies, and German defeat had become only a question of time. Postwar problems appeared on the horizon. What were the ambitions of Soviet Russia? Was the army that was about to liberate Eastern Europe still a revolutionary army? Would it spread Communism, or respect the independence of sovereign nations and the rules of bourgeois democracy? The fate of the Continent depended on the reply to those questions. If the liberating army brought Soviets with it, one tyranny would have been replaced by another. The Anglo-Saxon leaders may have foreseen the danger, but they did nothing to forestall it.

As long as the war lasted, pressure could be applied by means of lend-lease. But, as General Deane has told in his book *The Strange Alliance,* Washington refused to take advantage of its position. Until 1945 the Russians' demands were met without qualification and without demanding anything in return, even when they requested material that could only be of service after the war. The Lublin Committee, composed almost exclusively of Communists, was accepted as the provisional Polish government and the only precaution taken was to send a few representatives of the British Government, who found themselves impotent hostages. The principle of distinct zones of occupation in Germany was accepted, and the Soviet zone, about a third of the Reich, was pushed forward into the heart of Western Europe. The Curzon line was recognized as the Russo-Polish frontier, and, at least provisionally, the Oder-Neisse line as the Polish-German frontier. At once the transfer was begun of 5 to 6 millions of Germans, who were expelled from the territories annexed by Poland and sent to swell the population of the Reich, 70 millions crowded in a territory smaller than that of France. To induce the Russians to participate in the war against Japan, they were granted the Kurile Islands, the southern half of Sakhalin, Port Arthur, and the restoration of special rights in Manchuria (i.e., the port of Darien, and joint administration of the railway sold to Japan). Everything happened as if the Soviet Union, which had been ravaged by invasion, were the stronger party, and as if the Anglo-Saxon powers, in spite of their inexhaustible resources, had to give in to the stiff demands of their partner.

The British and American leaders seem to have been obsessed by the fear of a new Russo-German pact. Stalin had once lent a hand to Hitler: why should he not do so again if he found it to his interest? Roosevelt and Churchill, determined to crush Hitler at the least possible expense, felt themselves to be in a weaker position than Stalin,[8] whose armies were bearing the main burden of the war, and whose

8. At the time of the Yalta Conference, the Anglo-American armies were hard pressed by the last offensive of the *Wehrmacht,* the so-called Ardennes offensive.

defection would have imposed on the Anglo-Saxons either a negotiated peace or a considerably greater sacrifice of lives.

Some of the German leaders (Goebbels, for example), if not Hitler himself, were inclined to come to terms with Stalin; but their proposals never materialized. Early in 1942 Hitler would not have offered terms acceptable to Stalin, and after Stalingrad, the Kremlin would have demanded still more. The Allies' fears were probably excessive. It was not easy, even for a despot, to forget the bloodshed, the atrocities, and the mutual invectives. Stalin was also credited with the intention of halting his troops at the frontiers and leaving it to the Anglo-Saxons to finish the job; but here again the profits that Stalin was expecting from victory were grossly underestimated.

It is striking, in any case, that Western statesmen never were aware that they had the means of countering Soviet pressure with pressure of their own. After all, if there had been a race for a separate peace, they were in the better position. (Or, rather, they would have been if such a proceeding were permissible for democracies: probably it is not.)

Modern war cannot be carried on without propaganda. This propaganda, apart from its more directly military aspects (convincing the enemy of his inevitable defeat, and maintaining civilian and military morale at home), tends more and more to assume a political character. By importing Nazism into the occupied countries, the Germans compelled the democracies to broadcast to Europe an ideology of liberation. In the sense given to the term during and after the war, the Soviet regime was no less totalitarian than that of Hitler. Was it possible to exalt the valor and the sacrifices of the Russian people and at the same time dissociate them from the Soviet regime? What seemed the easiest solution was chosen: a theoretical democracy was invented whose two related expressions were the parliamentary regime and Sovietism—a theory which brought the foreign policy of the Allies into precise agreement with Communist propaganda of the popular-front period.

Were the Western statesmen themselves prisoners of this propaganda? Did they really think that the directory of the Big Three was going to assure world peace? Roosevelt and some of his entourage, some State Department officials and New Dealers in sympathy with the Communists, seemed to have been genuinely convinced that Stalin was no longer the prophet of world revolution but the head of a national state. They believed that Stalin's war aims were not in opposition to the permanent interests of the United States and of democratic Europe. In any case, Roosevelt considered that the best means of realizing these optimistic views was to deal frankly with the master of the Kremlin: to show him constant good will, agree to everything that he could legitimately request, and treat him as a friend in order to make him one. It may be, as William C. Bullitt claims, that Roosevelt hoped to win over Stalin as he had won over so many others. Let us not forget, too, that at Yalta Mr. Roosevelt was a dying man. He was sustaining at all costs the coalition that was to crush Hitler and the Third Reich, and he had scarcely begun to think about the conflicts to follow.

There was no need of Soviet aid in defeating Japan: by 1944 probably, and in any case by early 1945, the Mikado was ready to negotiate for peace. But in order to secure capitulation without having to land on the Japanese islands, a promise of Russian intervention in the Far East was asked for and secured at Yalta. Even in Europe, the Anglo-Saxons were afraid that Stalin might leave them to complete alone the destruction of the German armies. They felt weak in Stalin's presence because they envisaged an objective difficult to attain without him. But why had they fixed on that objective?

The Westerners were interested in weakening Germany, but not in destroying her. They wanted to re-establish conservative regimes, and they could not want the Reich to resist to the death. Yet they did nothing to detach and encourage those elements in Germany that opposed the Nazis, nothing to allow the generals or the men in the ranks to anticipate anything but unconditional surrender. They acted as if their purpose were to drive the National Socialists and the nation to defend a common cause; in other words, their actions were completely unreasonable.

Even apart from the rivalry to be expected between the great powers, their attitude toward Germany was hardly justifiable. If the victors really intended to suppress Germany as an independent state and to incorporate her in an empire or a federation, the crushing of the vanquished might have passed as necessary. But nothing of the sort was envisaged. There was no question of re-establishing a federation, as in the time of the American Civil War. There was no national state in Europe that could have kept Germany permanently in subjection. The truth was that the nonrevolutionary powers, even if a new imperial enterprise had not been outlined on the horizon, should for their own sake have spared an enemy that was an indispensable member of the European community. The fact that the Westerners actually encouraged the Germans to continue a hopeless struggle can only be explained by the apparently irresistible momentum of total war. So that it should be the "war to end wars," it was carried to its limit. Because it was carried to its limit, it gave rise to a successor.

It is not known what influence the formula of "unconditional surrender" actually had on the course of events. No one can show that by a different policy the Allies would have avoided the nine last months of war, which have so heavily burdened the peace. It is possible that the conspiracy of July 20 would have failed as it did regardless of the threat of "unconditional surrender." It is possible that, whatever happened, Hitler would have remained faithful to his insistent determination never to surrender. But at least it should have been possible to foment internal opposition in Germany, instead of discouraging it.

It is suggested today that no other policy would have made any difference. Certain promises had been obtained from Stalin in regard to the liberated countries: he did not keep them. In return for lend-lease, it might have been possible to accumulate some additional promises; but how would they have protected Poland or Rumania from Sovietization? Similarly it is conceded that the high American military commanders were mistaken as to the prospects of the campaign against Japan. They feared fierce resistance from an army which was virtually intact, and they estimated losses among invading troops at some hundreds of thousands. They had not taken account of the atomic bomb, which at the time of Yalta was no more than a project, nor of the Emperor, who, faced by his cities in ruins, his Navy almost annihilated, and his islands cut off from all maritime communication, had the power to impose unconditional capitulation even on those who wanted to fight to the bitter end. But, it is added, admitting that miscalculation, what difference could it have made? At the first sign of Japanese surrender, would not the Russian Army still have invaded Manchuria, transferred the Chinese factories to Russia, and handed over the Japanese arms to the local Communists?

It is quite clear that, with or without the assent of the West, the masters of the Kremlin would have attempted to play the game they did play. But they would not have been able to play it in the Far East if Japan had conceded her defeat before the hostilities had ended in Europe. In any case, would not their game have been more difficult if they had not been allowed to camouflage it behind the unity of the Big Three? Would not the diplomatic and moral position of the Western powers have been much stronger if the Sovietization of Poland and Rumania had made its appearance from the beginning as the violation of an agreement and as a proof of imperialism? Finally, if the peril had been realized, why should there not have been an attempt to prevent the arrival of Soviet troops in Eastern Europe by planning an invasion through the Balkans?

The only justification of the Western statesmen is that their conduct of the war was characteristic of democracies in our age: they submitted passively to the dynamism of hyperbolic war. They propagated the simplest and most convincing of myths: the United Nations were the harbingers of Justice, the enemy was the incarnation of Evil. Incapable of thinking about peace, which comes after war and is its real purpose, until the end of the destruction, they made no effort to alienate the German people from the Hitler clique and took no precautions against their ally, whose ambitions were hardly more of a mystery than those of Hitler. By the time the illusions of propaganda were dissipated and the governments in London and Washington had the support of public opinion in their will to resist, the rewards of victory had been lost: Eastern Europe was Sovietized, Germany divided, and the Chinese Communists armed by courtesy of the Russian Army. The Second World War had laid the foundations for the third.

Here as earlier, it could not be said that the outcome did not logically follow the causes. In 1914 the quarrels of nationalism had set fire to Europe: out of the furnace came the Europe of nationalists. In 1939, the German will to empire had plunged Europe anew into a war between irreconcilable opponents. Patriotism was reawakened in resistance to occupation, and the victors re-established the sovereignty of the national states. That restoration was more apparent than real. In the East, the liberated states were subjected to the law of the Soviet Union and its agents, the Communist parties. In the West, they are paying for isolation by impotence and are groping their way towards a supranational organization that will not infringe on their national pride.

Europe today, divided internally and caught between two hostile empires, haunted by the memories of past grandeurs and by resentments—can it live?

Since, under a July sun, bourgeois Europe entered into the century of total war, men have lost control of their history and have been dragged along by the contradictory promptings of techniques and passions. Out of national war came a first imperial war. How far will we be dragged by the chain reactions of violence?

Part Two

The Modern World and the Meaning of History

The ideas expressed in this part are, in a way, a continuation of the problems of the intelligibility of history. In these texts, however, Aron elaborates his own philosophical attitude toward history through polemics against false theories of historical intelligibility. Taking aim primarily at Marxist targets, he attacks fanaticism and an ungrounded faith in politics.

3

On False Historical Consciousness

Two errors, apparently contradictory but in fact connected, lie at the origin of the idolatry of History. 'Churchmen' and 'faithful' both allow themselves to fall into the trap of absolutism, and then proceed to indulge in a limitless relativism.

They conjure up for themselves an imaginary moment in history, which one group christens 'the classless society', the other 'the mutual recognition of man and man'. Neither has any doubt as to the absolute finality, the unconditional validity, the radical originality of this moment to come, in relation to everything that has preceded it. This 'privileged state' will give a meaning to the whole. Assured of knowing in advance the secret of the unfinished historical adventure, they observe the confusion of the events of yesterday and today with the pomposity of the judge who looks down on the quarrels of others and dispenses praise and blame with autocratic impartiality.

Historical existence, as authentically experienced, brings into conflict individuals, groups and nations for the defence of incompatible interests or ideas. Neither the contemporary nor the historian is in a position to decide unreservedly for or against one or the other. Not that we are incapable of distinguishing good from evil, but we do not know the future and every historical cause carries its share of iniquities.

All crusaders transfigure the cause for which they risk their lives, and they have the right to ignore the ambiguities of our human condition. But the doctrinaires who try to justify this transfiguration at the

From *The Opium of the Intellectuals*, by Raymond Aron, translated by Terence Kilmartin (Garden City, N.Y.: Doubleday), pp. 135–60. © 1957 by Raymond Aron. Reprinted by permission of Doubleday & Company, Inc., and Martin Secker & Warburg, Ltd. First published in French in 1955.

same time justify, willy-nilly, the ravings of fanaticism and of terror. The socialist crusader interprets the conduct of others according to his own idea of History and, by the same token, can find no adversaries worthy of him: only reactionaries or cynics would oppose the future which he represents. Because he proclaims the universal truth of a single view of History, he reserves the right to interpret the past as he pleases.

The twin errors of absolutism and of relativism are both refuted by a logic of the retrospective knowledge and understanding of human facts. The historian, the sociologist or the jurist can bring out the *meanings* of actions, institutions and laws. They cannot discover *the* meaning of the whole. History is not absurd, but no living being can grasp its one, final meaning.

Plurality of Meanings

Human actions are always intelligible. When they cease to be so, their authors are put outside the pale of humanity, they are regarded as lunatics, strangers to the species. But intelligibility does not come under a single heading and does not guarantee that the whole, each single element of which is in itself intelligible, makes sense to the observer.

Why did Caesar cross the Rubicon? Why did Napoleon withdraw his right wing at the battle of Austerlitz? Why did Hitler invade Russia in 1941? Why did the speculator sell francs after the 1936 election? Why did the Soviet Government decide on the collectivisation of agriculture in 1930? In each of these cases, the answer is given by relating the decision to the aim envisaged: to seize power in Rome, to lure the left wing of the Austro-Russian army, to destroy the Soviet régime, to make a profit out of a devaluation, to destroy the kulaks and to increase the proportion of crops available for the market. Caesar aspired to dictatorship or royalty, Napoleon or Hitler to victory; the speculator wanted to accumulate financial profits and the Russian Government food stocks to supply the towns. But this last example shows the inadequacy of the means-end relationship. One can say, at a pinch, 'a single aim: victory' or 'a single aim: profit'. The planner must always choose between a diversity of aims: the highest possible production might perhaps in the short run have been provided by peasant owners, but the latter would have constituted a class hostile to the Soviet régime and consumed an important part of the harvest.

Even when the end is determined, historical interpretation is never exclusively confined to a consideration of the means. How can one understand the conduct of a war leader if one does not interpret each of his decisions in the light of the knowledge at his disposal, the presumed reactions of the enemy, a calculation of their respective chances—if one does not examine the organisation of their armies and their techniques of warfare? When one passes from the art of warfare to that of politics, the complexity increases. The decision of the politician, like that of the soldier, can only be understood if one has analysed all the contingencies: Caesar's, Napoleon's, or Hitler's decision reveals its significance only in a context which covers a whole epoch, a whole nation, perhaps a whole civilisation.

The inquiry can be undertaken in three directions, or it might be said to comprise three dimensions:

1. The determination of means and ends sends one back to the knowledge at the disposal of the protagonist and to the structure of his society. One goal achieved is never more than a step towards an ulterior objective. Even if power were the sole aim in politics, it would still be necessary to ascertain the kind of power to which the ambitious politician aspires. The technique of attaining power in a parliamentary régime has little in common with the one likely to be most effective in a totalitarian régime. The ambitions of Caesar, Napoleon or Hitler, each of which has its own special characteristics, are explicable only in and through the crises of the Roman Republic, the French Revolution and the Weimar Republic.

2. The determination of values is essential to the understanding of human conduct, because the latter is never strictly utilitarian. The rational calculations of speculators represent an activity, more or less widespread in different civilisations, which is always limited by a conception of the good life. The warrior and the worker, *homo politicus* and *homo œconomicus,* are bound alike by religious, moral or customary beliefs; their actions express a scale of preferences. A social régime is always the reflection of an attitude towards the cosmos, the commonwealth or God. No society has ever reduced values to a common denominator—wealth or power. The prestige of men or of professions has never been measured exclusively by money.

3. We consider it pointless to speculate on the factors that determined Napoleon's behaviour at Austerlitz, but the same Napoleon's defeats at Moscow or Waterloo are often attributed to fatigue or illness. When one observes the failure of an individual, or a series of actions by a historical personality, or the conduct of a group, one is inclined to dismiss the notion of voluntary attitudes or actions in favour of a belief in compulsive forces arising from education and environment.

Of these three dimensions, the historian is more preoccupied with the first, the sociologist with the second and the cultural anthropologist with the third, but each of these specialists depends on the others. The historian must try to free himself from his own preconceptions, and, so to speak, get under the skin of his subject. But this presupposes a certain community between the historian and the historical object. If the universe in which the men of the past lived and had their being had nothing in common with mine, if these two universes did not appear, on a certain level of abstraction, as variations on a similar theme, the other's universe would become radically foreign to me and would lose all meaning. For history as a whole to be intelligible to me, the living must be able to trace some kinship with the dead. The search for a meaning, at this stage of the analysis, is tantamount to determining the abstract constituents of the human community—compulsions, categories, typical situations, symbols or values—which produce the conditions necessary to an understanding of actions by those who witnessed them, and of past civilisations by the historians.

That there should be several dimensions open to the would-be interpreter of the past does not mean that understanding is impossible; what it suggests is the richness of reality. In a certain sense, each and every fragment of history is inexhaustible. 'Each man carries in himself the whole structure of the human condition'. Perhaps a single society, providing it was totally understood, might reveal the essence of all societies. The exhaustive analysis of a single war campaign might permit a genius to establish the perennial rules of strategy, the study of a single political entity to discover the principles common to all constitutions. But it is doubtful; after all, one never plumbs the mystery even of one's nearest and dearest.

There is also a plurality within each of these human dimensions: the placing of events is an essential step towards historical understanding, but neither the elements nor the whole provide any defined limits within which it can operate. The meaning, therefore, is ambiguous, elusive and different according to the 'whole' which one is considering.

The decision taken by Hitler at the end of 1940 to attack the Soviet Union can be explained by a strategic conception—to conquer the Red Army before Great Britain was in a position to make a landing in the West—and a political intention—to destroy the Bolshevik régime, to reduce the Slavs to the status of an inferior people, etc. This intention in its turn sends one back to Hitler's intellectual training, to the literature he had superficially studied concerning the vicissitudes of the age-long conflict between Slavs and Teutons. From a single act one is carried back willy-nilly over the whole course of European history—from the Franco-German war of 1939 to the Treaty of Verdun, from the Carolingian Empire to the Gallo-Roman kingdoms, from these to the Roman Empire, and so on.

Nor is it possible to grasp a historical atom through documents or by direct experience. Each one of the thousands or millions of men engaged in a battle lives through it in a different way. The text of a treaty is, physically, a single thing. In its meaning it is manifold: for those who draft it, it is not the same as for those who apply it; it is different again, perhaps, for the enemy who signs it with contradictory mental reservations. A conglomeration of meanings, it acquires a unity, like the battle, only in the mind which rethinks it, the mind of a historian or of a historical personality.

This indefinite, two-fold, regression does not imply that the matter under discussion was originally formless. The historian does not merely accumulate specks of dust. The element and the whole are complementary. Nothing could be more erroneous than to imagine that the one is matter and the other form, the first a datum, the second a construct. The battle of Austerlitz is a 'whole' in relation to the action of a grenadier or to the charge of the cavalry in the centre of the battlefield; it is an event in relation to the campaign of 1805, just as the latter is an event in relation to the Napoleonic wars.

There is no fundamental difference between the battle of Austerlitz, the campaign of 1805 and the Napoleonic wars. But, it will be pointed out, the battle of Austerlitz can be taken in at a single glance, it *has* been taken in by a single man, but not the campaign of 1805 or the Napoleonic wars. If this were the case, the battle of the Marne would belong to the same category as the campaign of 1805 rather than to that of the battle of Austerlitz. In fact, every event involves duration and range, in exactly the same way as a whole complex of events. For there to be any essential antithesis, the event would have to be instantaneous or individual. And this is not so.

This homogeneity of historical reconstructions does not exclude differences which appear striking when one observes the limits to which they can extend. As a complex of events grows larger, the less clear become its outlines, the less obvious its internal unity. The spatio-temporal unity of the battle of Austerlitz, the interconnection between the various actions subsumed under this title, were evident to contemporaries and remain so to the historian. On a higher level, this unity was not grasped by those who lived through the event; the link between the various elements is indirect, ambiguous. With the widening of the gap between men's experiences and their reconstruction by the historian, the risk of arbitrary judgment increases.

Individual behaviour within armies is determined by the system of organisation and discipline and, ultimately, by the plan of the commander. Individual behaviour on the field of battle is the result of the clash between opposing aims—the aims of the commanders who determine global movements, the aims of the combatants, each of whom wants to kill the other. The first type of behaviour is explained by reference to a set of rules or laws which are themselves determined by beliefs or pragmatic necessities. The second type of behaviour does not only cover the clash of swords or the exchange of shells. It belongs to the category of accidental encounters, but it is also, in certain respects, 'ordained.' A battle is rarely independent of all convention; organisation, however strict, always leaves room for rivalries. A constitution fixes the method by which rulers and legislators are chosen. It incites competition between individuals and groups for the distribution of places or functions; it strives to forestall violence by imposing rules.

The essential distinction is between ideal entities and real entities rather than between categories of behaviour. The entity formed by a constitution or a doctrine is ideal, the entity created by the men who govern themselves according to this constitution or who live according to this doctrine is real. The historian or the sociologist directs himself sometimes to the specific meaning of a text in the ideal system of the constitution or the doctrine, sometimes to the meaning as experienced by the individual consciousness. The jurist or the philosopher tends towards the apprehension of history and its works in their specific meaning, the historian according to their psychic or social manifestations.

These two interpretations are neither contradictory nor mutually exclusive. The link between the stages of a philosophical deduction or of a juridical argument is by definition incompatible with the relationship established by the psychologist or the sociologist. It reveals its meaning only to those who are prepared to penetrate the universe of the metaphysician or the jurist.

Specific meanings have been experienced by men in a given epoch in societies which adhered to certain beliefs. No philosopher has ever been a 'pure spirit', completely detached from his own time and his own country. Critical reflection should not be allowed to restrict in advance the rights of historical or sociological interpretation, without pointing out the fundamental incongruity between specific meanings and 'experienced' meanings. By its very essence, the study of origins cannot arrive at the strictly philosophical meaning or the strictly artistic quality of a creation. The state of societies explains the manifold characteristics of different creations, never the secret of the masterpiece.

The plurality of meaning which results from the indefiniteness of historical entities and the distinction between 'specific' meanings and 'experienced' meanings involves the *renewal* of historical interpretation; it offers at once a protection against the worst form of relativism; that which is combined with dogmatism. Specific meanings are first of all ignored, efforts are made to reduce philosophical works to the meaning they assume in the consciousness of the non-philosopher, 'experienced' meanings are interpreted on the basis of what is known as a dominant fact, such as the class struggle, and, finally, a single meaning, decreed by the historian, is given to the world of man, reduced to a single dimension. The multiplicity of historical entities, real and ideal, should preclude the fanaticism which refuses to recognise the diversity of roles played by individuals in a complex society, the interlacing of the systems within which human activity revolves. Historical reconstruction must inevitably retain an unfinished character, because it never succeeds in unravelling all relationships or exhausting all possible meanings.

This renewal of interpretation involves a sort of relativity: the curiosity of the interpreter affects the determining of historical entities and specific meanings. The nature of this relativity is different according to whether it is events or institutions that are in question. Events in relation to their authors are eternally what they were, even if the progress of sociological knowledge, the enriching of categories or a widened experience permit a new understanding of them. The relativity of specific meanings depends on the nature of the relationship between the creations of history, in other words, the historicity proper to each spiritual universe. It is by reaching beyond this multiplicity, but without destroying it, that unity of meaning will eventually reveal itself.

Historical Units

"A philosophy of History presupposes that human history is not a simple sum of juxtaposed facts—individual decisions and adventures, ideas, interests, institutions—but that it is, instantaneously and sequentially, a totality moving towards a privileged state which will give meaning to the whole."[1] History is certainly not a 'simple sum of

1. Maurice Merleau-Ponty, *Humanisme et Terreur* (Paris, 1947), pp. 165, 166.

juxtaposed facts'; is it an 'instantaneous totality'? The elements of a society are interdependent; they influence one another reciprocally; but they do not constitute a totality.

The separation between economic, political and religious facts is introduced by the concepts of the scientist or the necessity for the division of labour. What first strikes the unprejudiced observer is their interdependence. The historian begins not by juxtaposition or by totality, but by the intermingling of entities and relationships. Tools, the organisation of labour, the juridical forms of ownership or of exchange, the institutions which belong to ecnomic history, on the one side touch on science, which has slowly emerged from philosophy and religion, and on the other side the State, which guarantees the laws. The man who buys and sells, cultivates the soil, handles machines, remains, at bottom, the man who believes, thinks and prays. Through the interdependence of the different sectors of human activity, which entails collaboration between the different disciplines, one may discern a sort of unity on the horizon of scientific labour. It is doubtful whether, even in primitive societies, one will succeed in bringing to light a single principle from which every possible way of living and thinking could be said to derive. (The same doubt remains when it comes to a single human existence.) Complex societies appear at once coherent and multifarious; no single part of them is isolated, no historical entity constitutes a totality of meaning unambiguously defined.

How is it possible to transcend the unity of interdependence? There is the hypothesis according to which one sector of reality or one human activity could be said to *determine* the other sectors and other activities—the relations of production constituting the substructure on which political and ideological institutions are based.

On the level of the theory of knowledge, such a hypothesis would be unthinkable if it implied that economics *determined* politics or ideas without being influenced by them in return. It would, so to speak, be contradictory, or in any case incompatible with straightforward observation. Economic facts cannot be isolated as such, either materially or conceptually. They embody the means of production, and therefore science and technology, the relations of production, that is to say the organisation of labour, property laws, class distinctions (which are also controlled by the size of the population and by the modalities of hierarchy and prestige). The interaction of the elements inside the economic fact makes it impossible to conceive of the latter being able to determine without being partially determined itself. The interdependence of the social sectors or of human activities is incontrovertible.

It is therefore impossible to attach any philosophical significance to the distinction between substructure and superstructure. Where is the precise frontier between them? It may perhaps be convenient, in the study of societies, to take the organisation of labour rather than religious beliefs as one's point of departure. But how can it be affirmed *a priori* or *a posteriori* that a man's view of the world is determined by the form of his labour, but that the latter is not affected by the idea of the world which man has formed for himself?

In order to survive, the individual or the group must struggle against Nature and draw their livelihood from it. By virtue of this, the economic function acquires a sort of priority. But since even the most primitive societies never fulfil this function without organising themselves in the light of beliefs which cannot be judged in terms of efficiency, this priority does not amount to a unilateral causality or a *primum movens*.

What is the empirical significance of this priority? What are the traits common to societies which have reached a certain economico-technical maturity? What are the differences between societies anterior to and those subsequent to the discovery of the steam engine, electricity or atomic energy? Such queries belong to the realm of sociology, not philosophy.

It may not be impossible to explain social types in terms of the available means of production. Specialists in proto-history or pre-history are only too ready to subscribe to a conception of this kind, since they classify periods and groups according to the tools employed and the principal forms of activity. As regards complex societies, all one could do would be to establish the inevitable consequences of a given state of technology and then trace the framework within which political and ideological variations play their part.

In any case, there is no proof that the economic factor predominates during every period of history. Max Scheler has suggested that the primacy of blood, the primacy of power, the primacy of economics characterise the three great periods of human history. The bonds of blood cemented small, confined communities, before the advent of nations and empires. Granted that the means of production remain more or less constant, events are mainly controlled by politics. Power raises up or casts down States; it dictates the chronicle of blood and glory in which warriors take pride of place. In the modern age, economic considerations have become decisive because technology, perpetually changing and developing, is the measure of the wealth of individuals and groups.

Such propositions do not constitute philosophical truths, but merely hypothetical generalisations. They are not incompatible with the idea that the volume of collective resources determines the limits of possible variations in social organisation.

Theories relating to the efficacy of the various elements in history lead only to rather vague formulae, rarely proved and never capable of exhausting the complexity of relationships.

No single type of phenomenon can be charged with responsibility either for changes in or for the existing state of the social structure. No-one could state categorically that the invention of electrical or electronic machines or the harnessing of atomic energy may not have an influence even on literature or painting. But neither could anyone affirm that the *essentials* of literature, painting or political institutions are *determined* by technology, by the property laws or by the relations between the classes. Limits cannot be pre-imposed on the possible effects of a cause, not because the latter is exclusive or irresistible but because everything is intermingled: a society expresses itself in its literature as well as in its productivity; the microcosm reflects the whole. But the whole will only be grasped by reference to a multiplicity of viewpoints as long as man refuses to be defined entirely by a single question, as long as societies are not planned in accordance with a global system.

Thus the historian, unlike the sociologist or the philosopher, seeks unity not so much in a privileged cause as in the singularity of the historical unit—epoch, nation or culture. What are the historical units? Can one grasp unity through time and the individuality of the unit?

No-one denies the reality of the European nations in the twentieth century. But this reality is ambiguous. The homogeneity of language and culture in Great Britain, France or Spain is far from being complete. Many nationalities, defined by a language, a way of life or a culture, do not possess, in the middle of the twentieth century, a State which is their own exclusive property. In the national States which are sovereign in their rights, the life of the citizen and the decisions of his rulers are influenced by external events. To borrow a phrase of Arnold Toynbee's, the nation does not constitute an intelligible field of study. The development of France cannot be separated from that of England or Germany; it is not the expression of a unique soul, or at least the latter reveals itself gradually and progressively through cultural and economic exchanges. In abstract terms there are three questions to be considered in connection with historical entities—relating to their degree of *independence,* of *coherence* and of *originality.* The last two questions chiefly concern entities of the national type; the first has a decisive significance when it comes to Toynbee's 'intelligible fields'.

To these three questions Oswald Spengler gives a positive answer. According to him, every culture is comparable to an organism which develops according to its own inner laws and proceeds inexorably towards its end, closed in on itself, incapable of receiving anything from outside which might modify its essence; each, from its birth until its death, expresses a 'soul' which is incomparable with any other. These affirmations far transcend the facts. The assimilation of cultures to an organism, unless it can be reduced to a vague comparison, derives from a false metaphysic. To stress the originality, in every culture, of the sciences, even the mathematical sciences, and to disregard completely the accumulation or the progress of knowledge, is simply to ignore self-evident facts. The denial of the influence that cultures exercise on one another is quite arbitrary, seeing that exchanges of machines, ideas and institutions are incontestable. Taken literally, Spengler's central thesis is self-contradictory.

Arnold Toynbee's replies to the three questions express slight differences of emphasis and meaning. At the beginning of the *Study of History,* civilisations are presented as intelligible fields of study, but not nations. As the book progresses, the contacts between civilisations reveal themselves in such a way that finally the distinction between nations and civilisations, at least as regards autonomy of development, seems to be one of degree rather than kind. The internal coherence of civilisations is stated rather than proved. Toynbee continually tells us that the various elements in a civilisation harmonise with one another and that one element could not be modified without affecting the others. But he shows their interdependence rather than their harmony. At any given period, a civilisation retains elements borrowed from the past and not contemporaneous with the spirit of the time. A civilisation accumulates institutions or creations begotten by others. Where, for example, is the frontier between the civilisation of the ancients and that of Western or Eastern Christianity? What are the links between Christianity and the age of technology?

Toynbee has some difficulty in establishing the internal coherence of civilisations, because he does not express himself clearly on the singularity of each civilisation. What in fact is the basis of, what defines the originality of a civilisation? According to Toynbee, the answer would be religion. But in certain cases it is difficult to discern this special religion: what transcendent beliefs were exclusive to Japan, making it different from China? When one does see it clearly, for example in the case of the two European civilisations of Western and Eastern Christianity, Toynbee never manages to establish the peculiar essence of the faith and to infer therefrom the special characteristics of the historical entity. One does not know whether the apparent primacy of religion is causal or whether it simply reflects the hierarchy of values established by the interpreter among the various human activities. When, in the last volume of his book, Toynbee presages an eventual fusion of civilisations and a universal Church, the disciple of Spengler transforms himself into the great-grandson of Bossuet.

Once one has discarded the two metaphysical postulates of Spengler—the organicist metaphysic of cultures and the dogmatic negation of the universality of spirit and truth—there remains no further obstacle on the path to human unity. Autonomy of development, internal cohesion and the originality of civilisations subsist, outlined in reality, but not to the point of revealing a universal meaning. Civilisations do not differ in kind from other historical entities; they are more autonomous and probably less coherent than smaller entities—more than a juxtaposition and less than a totality.

This negative conclusion tallies with a proposition which might have been directly affirmed. History, like individual existence, presents no empirically observable unity, either real or significant. The actions of the individual are dove-tailed into innumerable entities. Our thoughts, far from being self-contained, reflect the heritage of the centuries. Something unique and irreplaceable, easier to grasp intuitively than to define, is discernible from one end of a human existence to the other. Biographies, by relating events to the person involved, suggest the relative constancy of a character or, in more neutral terms, of a way of reacting, and create an aesthetic impression of unity, just as psychologists or psycho-analysts suggest the ambiguous unity of a human destiny which is created as much as it is endured by each individual. That the little bourgeois of Aix was also the painter Cézanne is an incontrovertible fact; the unity of the man and the artist is not illusory, but it is almost undecipherable.

The elements of a collective history are related to one another in the same way as the episodes in an individual destiny, though to a lesser degree. One understands a society on the basis of its infrastructure: from the organisation of labour to the edifice of beliefs, the process of understanding may not meet with any insurmountable obstacles, but neither does it reveal, from one stage to the next, any essential sequence.

In other words, unity of meaning cannot be conceived without determining the values or the hierarchy of human activities. Marxists who imagine that the 'economic factor' is the unifying force are mixing up a causal primacy and a primacy of interest; implicitly they invoke the latter whenever one shows them the limitations of the former. Spengler imagines this unity of meaning, but he can only give it verisimilitude by means of a biological metaphysic. And Toynbee aims to find the equivalent of the Spenglerian doctrine through the path of empiricism, but in fact the autonomy, the coherence and the originality of civilisations gradually dissolve during the course of his studies. If the history he retraces does retain a certain structure, this is because the historian has gradually given way to the philosopher and the dialectic of empires and churches, the earthly city and the city of God, has taken over the reins of the narrative.

In the eyes of God, every existence does present a unified meaning, because everything, that is to say everything that matters, is brought into play in the dialogue between the creature and the creator, the drama in which the salvation of a soul is at stake. Existential psychoanalysis postulates an analogous unity in the choice each consciousness makes for itself: this unity is not the unity of a single act—the consciousness always remains free to go back on its decision—it is that of the meaning assumed by existence as a whole, re-thought by the observer with reference to a unique problem which is the equivalent, in an atheistic philosophy, of the problem of salvation. The adventure of mankind through time has *one* meaning to the extent that all men are collectively seeking to achieve salvation.

Logic confirms what successive doctrines suggest: philosophies of history are secularised theologies.

The End of History

The social sciences fulfil the first requirement of philosophy: to substitute for the brute facts, for the numberless acts which can be observed directly or through documents, a view of reality defined by a problem which itself constitutes a certain activity—either economic, as with all activities directed against Nature which tend to provide the collectivity with the means of subsistence and to overcome essential poverty, or political, as with all activities which tend to the formation of a collectivity or which aim at organising the lives of men in common and therefore establishing rules of co-operation and command.

Such a distinction is not *real*. Any activity which aims to create or increase the resources of the group involves politics since it demands the co-operation of individuals. In the same way, a political order involves an economic aspect since it distributes goods among the members of the collectivity and adapts itself to a communal method of work.

The formulas which the philosophies of history have made fashionable—the mastery of man over Nature, or the reconciliation of mankind—take one back to the original problems of economics and politics. Defined in political and economic terms, the 'privileged State which gives meaning to the whole' becomes identical with the radical solution to the problem of communal life or with the end of history.

Societies are never rational in the sense in which technology, deduced from science, is rational. 'Culture' gives to social behaviour and institutions—family, work, the distribution of power and prestige—innumerable forms which are bound up with metaphysical beliefs or customs sanctioned by tradition. The distinction between the different types of phenomenon is introduced, in the case of primitive societies, by the philosophy of the observer, but it is virtually there already, since the family is always subject to strict and complex rules, daily habits are never entirely arbitrary, and the hierarchy is always supported by a certain conception of the world.

On the level of *mores,* diversity asserts itself as a fact of experience and it is difficult to see how one could define a 'privileged state'. The multifarious forms of the family do not condemn the idea of a natural law, but they make it necessary to place the latter on such a level of abstraction that the empirically observed diversity will appear normal. The ultimate end of history would be not a new and concrete definition of the family, but a diversity which would not contradict the rules inseparable from man's essential humanity.

Beliefs relating to plants, animals and gods have just as much bearing on the forces and the relations of productions as the structure of the family and the State. The 'privileged state' which would mark the end of the economic adventure would have to be stripped of all 'cultural' traits, of everything that related it to a particular collectivity. In the same way, the universally true faith expresses itself in a historical language and is mixed with accidental elements.

What would this 'privileged state' consist of, and how could it differ from the abstract values which govern institutions but do not represent a predetermined institutional order?

The new fact which has caused the theological notion of the end of history to be taken up again in a rational context is technological progress. Not all philosophers evoke, after the fashion of Trotsky, the coming reign of plenty when the problem of distribution will have resolved itself, when education and the certainty of the morrow will suffice to curb human greed, but all are bound to consider that the development of science and of the means of production will change one of the essential data of existence: collective wealth will make it possible to give to one without taking away from the other, the poverty of the many will no longer be the condition of the luxury of the few.

The reign of plenty is not unthinkable or absurd. Economic progress, such as we have been able to observe it over the past two or three centuries, can be measured, roughly speaking, by increased productivity. In one hour of work a man produces an increasing quantity of goods. This progress is fastest in the secondary or industrial sector, slowest in the tertiary sector—transport, commerce and services. In the primary sector, it seems destined to slow down after a certain point is reached, at least if one admits that the law of diminishing returns operates in agriculture. The advent of the reign of plenty thus requires a limitation in the size of the population. Assuming a stationary population and an agricultural production which meets every need, total prosperity would still require that all demands for manufactured products were satisfied. Many people will be tempted to reply that these demands are by nature illimitable. But supposing they are wrong and that one can reach a saturation point as regards secondary needs. In this case the notion of demands that are by nature illimitable would have to be reserved for the tertiary sector, and here the question arises as to how these demands could be completely satisfied since they include the desire for leisure.

However many hypotheses one can think of—a stationary population, the saturation point in secondary needs, and so on—the curse of work would still not be abolished. It would still be necessary to divide essential work and to share out equitably incomes which, as regards luxury articles, would still remain unequal.

But to return to earth and to the present day. The satisfaction of primary needs and of an important part of secondary needs has never yet been achieved in any historically known society, though this objective is not beyond the bounds of possibility in the United States, which disposes of a greater cultivable area per head of population than any other country. Short of inventions which at present would be considered revolutionary or, on the other hand, atomic disasters, technological progress promises to ensure decent conditions of life for all and thereby the possibility of participating in cultural life. The manufacture of synthetic food by chemists and of synthetic raw materials by physicists, the substitution of electronic machines for human labour, are advances which will have to be paid for. Technological gains must be set against the liabilities of industrial society: economic progress so far has created proportionally more clerks than workers, and a society of employees is not necessarily 'reconciled' with itself.

The static society evoked by certain sociologists, such as Jean Fourastié, corresponds more or less to the ultimate end of economic progress such as one can imagine on the basis of present-day experience. It would not modify the essence of the 'economic problem' faced by collectivities: the need to take away from the workers a fraction of the product of their labour for the purpose of investment, the need for a fair distribution of jobs which are not all equally interesting and remunerative, the need to maintain a strict discipline and to ensure the respect of the techno-bureaucratic hierarchy. Pushing Utopia even further, one can conceive that manual labour might cease to be imposed on a minority only, but that everyone should spend part of his day or part of his life in a factory. In this way we transcend the limits of the historical horizon without transcending those of human possibilities. Even on the basis of this extreme hypothesis, certain of the exigencies to which economic life is subject today would be relaxed (in the static society there would no longer be any question of speeding up productivity but merely of maintaining the present level), but none would be completely eliminated.

In contrast to what would happen in a régime of absolute plenty, the 'economic problem' would not be radically resolved. Incomes would be distributed in cash, there would be no freedom for the individual to help himself to his share of the collective output; pay would be related to needs, though production bonuses would remain necessary to a certain extent; no one would be refused a technico-intellectual training, but inequality would continue to exist between individuals according to their abilities and according to the employment they were given in the collectivity.

The static society would not bring about a radical solution to the 'political problem', which boils down to the reconciliation between the equality of men as men and the inequality of their functions in the collectivity. The essential task, therefore, would not be very different from what it is today: to persuade men to acknowledge the superiority of others without any feeling of constraint and without any surrender of dignity. The attenuation of the rivalry between individuals and groups for the distribution of the national income would help to remove some of the bitterness of the struggle. Here again, experience should advocate caution: the claims of the semi-rich are often the most ardent. People fight for luxuries, for power or for ideas with just as much passion as they fight for money. Interests may be reconciled, but not philosophies.

Supposing the subsistence of each and everyone to be assured, collectivities would no longer appear as spheres of exploitation, continually threatened by their rivals. Inequalities of living standards between nations—the decisive fact of the twentieth century—would have been eliminated. But would the frontier posts have been pulled down? Would the peoples of the world regard one another as brothers? One must adopt a second hypothesis, whereby humanity would no longer be divided into sovereign nations but into groups living peacefully together thanks to the death of States or the advent of a universal empire. This hypothesis does not necessarily follow from the first, that of relative or absolute plenty. The quarrels of tribes, of nations or of empires have been linked in a multiplicity of ways with those of classes; they have not been mere manifestations of the class struggle. Race hatreds will survive class distinctions. Collectivities will not cease to clash with one another as soon as they have become indifferent to the taste for booty. The desire for power is no less basic than the desire for wealth.

One can *conceive* the 'radical solution' of the political problem as well as that of the economic problem. One can even establish a political equivalent to the distinction between the 'static society' and 'absolute plenty'. In the political static society, inside each collectivity all would play their part in the body politic, the rulers would rule without resorting to force and the ruled would obey without any feeling of humiliation. Between collectivities, peace would annihilate frontiers and guarantee the rights of individuals. Absolute plenty would be matched by the universality of the State and the homogeneity of the citizens—concepts which are not contradictory but which are well beyond the historical horizon, for they presuppose a fundamental change in the facts of communal life.

Technological progress depends on the development of science, that is to say of reason applied to the study of nature. It could not bring relative plenty unless one assumed a constant population level, which implies the domination of instinct by reason. It could not guarantee peace between individuals, classes or nations unless one postulated acknowledgment by men everywhere of their common essence and their social diversity, in other words the predominance of reason, in each individual, over the temptation towards revolt and violence. Humanity could never be reconciled with itself on this earth as long as the luxury of the few continued to insult the poverty of the many. Unfortunately, the growth of collective resources and the reduction of inequalities do not change the nature of men and societies: the former remain unstable, the latter hierarchical. Victory over Nature would allow but would not guarantee the rule of reason over the passions.

Thus defined, the concept of the end of history becomes identified not with an abstract ideal (liberty or equality) or with a concrete order. Human customs, in the widest sense of the word, do not represent a problem or comprise a solution. Any régime will always be characterised by historical contingencies. Between the abstraction of isolated, formal values and the characteristics peculiar to each collectivity, the concept of the end of history helps to establish the conditions on which one might succeed in satisfying simultaneously the innumerable demands we impose on society. The end of history is an idea formed by reason; it characterises not the individual man but the struggle of men collectively through the course of time. It is the 'project' of humanity in so far as the latter claims to be rational.

History and Fanaticism

In following the stages of historical interpretation, we have arrived at the concept of the end of history (or of pre-history) of which expressions such as 'the privileged state which gives a meaning to the whole' are the more or less formalised equivalents. The preceding analysis will allow us to go more deeply into the criticism sketched out in the previous chapters concerning the philosophy of the 'Churchmen' and the 'faithful'.

One can *conceive* the radical solution of the problem of communal life, whether or not one regards its realisation as possible. But there is a permanent temptation to substitute for the concept of resolved contradictions either an abstract formula—equality or fraternity—or a reality that is at once exceptional and commonplace.

M. Merleau-Ponty, as we have seen, commits these two errors each in turn. Left to itself, the idea of 'recognition' or 'acknowledgment' is as empty as that of liberty or fraternity, unless it assumes a social homogeneity among those who recognise or acknowledge one another: in this case, mutual acknowledgment would be impossible between officers and private soldiers, managers and workers, and society as such would be inhuman.

In order to give some substance to the notion of 'recognition', the same author has recourse to criteria some of which—for example public ownership—are too concrete, and others—for example, the spontaneity of the masses, or internationalism—too vague.

In Stalinist philosophy, the 'privileged' or 'final' state does not resolve itself into an ideal, but declines into a commonplace event. In the eyes of the orthodox, as soon as a Communist party has seized power the essential rupture is accomplished and one is on the way to the classless society. In fact, nothing is settled and the same necessities of accumulation, inequalities of pay, incentives and discipline subsist after the revolution. But, in the eyes of the orthodox, all these curses of industrial civilisation have changed their meaning, since the proletariat reigns and socialism is being built up.

Having confused an ideal or an episode with an objective that is at once imminent and sacred, 'Churchmen' and 'faithful' reject, with indifference or contempt, the rules of wisdom that statesmen have elaborated in order to harness for the good of the collectivity the egoism and the passions of individuals. Constitutional government, the balance of power, legal guarantees, the whole edifice of political civilisation slowly built up over the course of the ages and always incomplete, is calmly pushed aside. They accept an absolute State, allegedly in the service of the Revolution; they are not interested in the plurality of parties and the autonomy of working-class organisations. They do not protest against lawyers bullying their clients and accused persons confessing to imaginary crimes. After all, is not revolutionary justice directed towards the 'radical solution of the problem of coexistence', whilst 'liberal justice' applies unjust laws?

Statesmen who do not claim to know history's last word sometimes hesitate before embarking on an enterprise, however attractive, the cost of which would be too high. 'Churchmen' and 'faithful' ignore such scruples. The sublime end excuses the revolting means. Profoundly moralistic in regard to the present, the revolutionary is cynical in action. He protests against police brutality, the inhuman rhythm of industrial production, the severity of bourgeois courts, the execution of prisoners whose guilt has not been proved beyond doubt. Nothing, short of a total 'humanisation', can appease his hunger for justice. But as soon as he decides to give his allegiance to a party which is as implacably hostile as he is himself to the established disorder, we find him forgiving, in the name of the Revolution, everything he has hitherto relentlessly denounced. The revolutionary myth bridges the gap between moral intransigence and terrorism.

There is nothing more commonplace than this double game of inflexibility and tolerance, of which, in our day, the idolatry of history is the manifestation if not the intellectual origin. On the pretext of discovering the meaning of history, the unavoidable constraints of thought and action are totally disregarded.

The plurality of meanings which we ascribe to an act reveals not our incapacity but the limits of our knowledge and the complexity of reality. Only when we recognise that the world is essentially equivocal have we any chance of reaching the truth. Our understanding is not incomplete because we lack omniscience, but because the plurality of meanings is implicit in the object of our understanding.

The plurality of values on which any judgment of a social order must be based does not call for a definitive choice. Economic or political systems are neither infinitely variable, like human customs, nor incapable of modification, like the principles of an ideal law. They forbid acquiescence in anarchical scepticism, whereby all societies are regarded as equally detestable and in the long run everyone decides as his fancy dictates; they also discourage all claims to the possession of the key to human destiny.

A solution of the 'economic problem' and of the 'political problem' is conceivable because one can succeed in establishing the constant data of both of them. But this constancy does not permit us to imagine that one can ever make a sudden jump from the realm of necessity to that of freedom.

The end of history, according to revealed religion, can result from the conversion of souls or from a decree of the deity. Relative or absolute plenty, peaceful relations between collectivities, the voluntary submission of men to their freely chosen rulers—all these are not beyond the bounds of human possibility. In measuring the distance between what is and what should be, we compare the realities which meet our eyes with these ultimate aims, and by means of this comparison we have a chance of choosing rationally, but only on condition that we never assimilate the object of our historical choice with the idea of a radical solution.

This idea rightly challenges the cynical or naturalistic ideologies which regard man as an animal and teach one to treat him as such. It enables us to condemn institutions which by their very nature deny men's humanity. But it has not the power to determine concretely what the social order should be, or what our obligations should be, at any given moment.

The essential historicity of political choices is founded not on the rejection of the natural law, nor on the opposition of facts and values, nor on the mutual incongruity of the great civilisations, nor on the impossibility of arguing with those who refuse to argue. Even if we assumed that there were principles of law superior to the course of history, even if we eliminated from the discussion the power-hungry fanatic who does not care a fig if he is caught out in a blatant contradiction, even if we ignored the peculiarities of cultures which are incapable of communicating, political choice would still remain inseparable from particular circumstances, sometimes rational but never finally proved and never of the same nature as scientific truths or moral imperatives.

The impossibility of proof is due to the intractable laws of social existence and the plurality of values. Incentives are needed in order to increase productivity; an edifice of authority must be built up in order to persuade quarrelsome and recalcitrant individuals to co-operate; these ineluctable necessities symbolise the gap between the history which we live and the end of history which we conceive. Not that work or obedience as such are contrary to man's predestined lot, but they become so if they are born of constraint. And violence has never ceased to play a part in any known society. In this sense, politics have always been based on the notion of the lesser evil, and they will continue to be so as long as men are what they are.

What passes for optimism is most often the effect of an intellectual error. It is permissible and quite reasonable to prefer planning to the free market, but anyone who expects planning to usher in the reign of plenty misjudges the efficiency of bureaucrats and the extent of available resources. It is not absurd to prefer the authority of a single party to the slow deliberations of the parliamentary system, but anyone who counts on the dictatorship of the proletariat to accomplish freedom misjudges human nature and ignores the inevitable results of the concentration of power in a few hands. It is possible to transform writers into engineers of the soul and to recruit artists into the service of propaganda, but anyone who wonders why philosophers who are prisoners of dialectical materialism or novelists enslaved by socialist realism are lacking in genius misjudges the very essence of the creative process. The idolators of history cause more and more intellectual and moral havoc, not because they are inspired by good or bad sentiments, but because they have wrong ideas.

Human reality in process of development has a structure; every action has a place in a complex of actions; individuals are bound up with régimes; ideas organise themselves into doctrines. One cannot ascribe to the conduct or the thoughts of others a meaning arbitrarily deduced from one's own interpretation of events. The last word is never said and one must not judge one's adversaries as if one's own cause were identified with the ultimate truth.

A true understanding of the past recalls us to the duty of tolerance; a false philosophy of history breeds only fantacism.

*   *   *

What, then, in the last analysis, is the significance of the question so often asked: has history a meaning? In one sense, it can be answered immediately. History is as intelligible as the acts and the works of men, as long as one discovers therein a common mode of thinking and reacting.

In another sense, history is also quite obviously meaningful. One understands an event by placing it in a context, and an achievement by establishing either the inspiration of the creator or the significance of the creation for the near or distant spectator. Meanings are as manifold as the orientations of curiosity or the dimensions of reality. The real question turns on the singular. Since every moment of history has several meanings, how can history as a whole have only one?

There is a three-fold plurality to overcome: that of civilisations, that of régimes and that of activities—art, science, religion.

The plurality of civilisations would be mastered if and when it could be said that all men belonged to a single vast society; the plurality of régimes if and when the collective order was organised in accordance with the 'project' of Humanity; and the plurality of activities if and when a universally valid philosophy established the destination of mankind.

Will a universal State consistent with men's perennial demands be finally established? The question turns on events to come and we cannot answer dogmatically yes or no. For *political* development to have a single meaning it would suffice for humanity to have a single vocation, for societies, instead of being strangers to one another, to appear as successive stages in a quest.

Would this universal State solve the riddle of history? Yes, in the eyes of those who see no other end but the rational exploitation of the planet. No, in the eyes of those who decline to confuse existence in society with the salvation of the soul. Whatever the answer, it will be formulated by philosophy and not by knowledge of the past.

In the last analysis, history has the meaning which our philosophy ascribes to it—an imaginary museum if man is essentially the builder of monuments, the creator of sublime forms and images for their own sake—or Progress if the indefinite exploration of Nature alone raises the human above the level of animality. The meaning given by philosophy to the historic adventure determines the structure of essential development, but it does not determine the future.

The philosopher, not the historian, knows what man seeks. The historian, not the philosopher, tells us what man has found and what, perhaps, he will find tomorrow.

4

Fanaticism, Prudence, and Faith

Many critics, even some of those who were sympathetic to the book, criticized *The Opium of the Intellectuals* for being negative, for abounding in refutations without providing anything constructive. I earned this reproach by writing the last sentence—"Let us all pray for the coming of the skeptics if they will put an end to fanaticism"— although the whole of the last page means exactly the opposite of what hurried readers found there. As a matter of fact, I expressed the fear, not the hope, that the loss of so-called absolute truths might incline intellectuals toward skepticism: "Yet man, who does not expect a miraculous change either from revolution or from reform, is not obliged to resign himself to the unjustifiable. He does not give his soul to an abstract humanity, a tyrannical party, an absurd scholasticism, because he loves people, participates in living communities, respects the truth."

Many of the writings that are termed "constructive" are just as futile as plans for a universal state or a new organization of business. The term "constructive" is applied even to projects that are unrealizable, and the term "negative" to analyses which tend to delimit what is possible and to form political judgment—a judgment which is essentially historical in nature and which must focus on the real or set itself an attainable objective. One is sometimes tempted to invert the hierarchy of values and to take the term "negative" as a compliment.

The only criticism that would deserve to be classified as negative

From *Marxism and the Existentialists*, by Raymond Aron, translated by Helen Weaver (New York: Harper & Row), pp. 91–108. Volume 40, World Perspectives, planned and edited by Ruth Nanda Anshen. English translation © 1969 by Raymond Aron. Reprinted by permission of Harper & Row, Publishers, Inc. First published in French in 1956.

would be one which, while dispelling illusions, did not help to discover or judge the present or permanent reality.

Before 1917, no Marxist[1] believed a socialist revolution to be possible in a country where the industrial proletariat numbered only three million workers and represented only a paltry minority. Of course it is always possible to reconcile an interpretation with reality by introducing a supplementary hypothesis: Russia, because economic development had been retarded there, constituted the weakest link in the capitalist chain; the industry there was concentrated, largely financed by foreign capital, and for this reason it aroused greater rebelliousness in the masses than the national industry of the countries of western Europe, although it had arrived at a later phase.

All these hypotheses do not explain away certain major facts which we would not need to recall if certain left-wing intellectuals did not go out of their way to forget them: The revolutions which call themselves Marxist have succeeded only in countries where the development typical of capitalism has not occurred; the strength of the Communist parties in the West is in inverse ratio to the development of capitalism; it is not the capitalist dynamism which swells the ranks of the revolutionary parties in France or Italy, but the paralysis of this dynamism.

From these major facts two conclusions may immediately be drawn. The first of these, which is theoretical, involves one of the classic versions of historical materialism, which is found in the Introduction to the *Contribution to the Critique of Political Economy*. It is manifestly false that humanity sets itself only problems that it is capable of solving, false that the relations of production correspond to the development of the forces of production, false that the state of ownership corresponds to the state of the forces of production, false that the movement of the economy is autonomous or obeys a determinism of its own. The rise of the Bolshevik party preceded the expansion of the proletariat and of capitalism, due to exceptional circumstances (war, difficulties of food control, the collapse of the traditional regime). The Bolshevik party was able to seize the power and so prove that the form of the state and the conceptions of the governors could determine, as well as reflect, the economic organization.

The second conclusion, which is historical, is that there is no paral-

---

1. One can find passages in which Marx foresaw that the revolution would break out in Russia, whose social and political structure was more fragile than that of the West. But this idea is difficult to reconcile with the classic theory in the Introduction to the *Contribution to the Critique of Political Economy*.

lelism or correspondence between the development of the forces of production and the shift from capitalism to socialism. One cannot dogmatically decree that a country with a so-called capitalist regime (individual ownership of the means of production, mechanisms of the market) will not someday arrive at a so-called socialist regime (collective ownership, curtailment or elimination of the mechanisms of the market). In this sense a non-Stalinist Marxist could say that General Motors is no longer an example of individual ownership since the shares are divided among hundreds of thousands of persons. One would need only subordinate the board of directors to the state or to a mixed committee of shareholders, workers, and employees to arrive at a state which certain Marxists would not hesitate to call socialist. Similar observations might be made in regard to the mechanisms of the market, whose sphere of influence is shrinking, and the planned economy, which is gradually gaining.

However valid these conclusions may be in the long run, if by socialism one means the Soviet regime and by capitalism the regime of the Western countries, the present rivalry between socialism and capitalism has nothing in common with the struggle between the future and the past, between two stages in the development of industrial society. For the moment we are witnessing a rivalry between two methods of industrialization, and there is no reason why the most effective way of running the American economy must necessarily be the best way of initiating or accelerating industrialization in India or China.

In other words, there is a Marxist critique of the Stalinist interpretation of the world situation. If one refers to the phases of economic growth, a planned economy of the Soviet type is a crude technique for catching up with more advanced countries at the price of imposing sacrifices on populations even more severe than those imposed by industrialization in western Europe during the first half of the nineteenth century.

A Marxist critique of this kind which adopted the primacy of the forces of production would arrange the various economic regimes in an order which would culminate in the regime of the Western type, and in which the liberalism of nineteenth-century Europe and the sovietism of the twentieth century would be two modalities of an outmoded stage. Even if one does not subscribe to this critique, the fact remains that one cannot discuss a socialism which has built an enormous industry by reducing the standard of living of the masses and a capitalism which has raised the standard of living, reduced working hours, and permitted the consolidation of labor unions, as if these were the same realities that Marx considered a century ago or that he anticipated according to a system which has since been refuted by events.

We must therefore distinguish the choice between socialism and capitalism from the choice between sovietism and a society of the Western type, and raise separately the question of reforms to be introduced to Western societies characterized by rapid expansion (United States), societies characterized by slower expansion (France), and the various underdeveloped societies. To force the Chinese, Russian, North Korean, and Czech regimes into the same category of socialism, and the French, American, Egyptian, and Indian regimes into the same category of capitalism, is to be sure of understanding nothing and confusing everything. Reference to the theory of economic growth and the phases of growth at least enables one to avoid an error which we whom old-timers call revolutionaries have been denouncing for ten years and which Merleau-Ponty condemns today: the error of defining the Soviet Union by public enterprise and the United States by free enterprise.

In criticizing this historical error we thereby eliminate the philosophical error which consisted in attributing a suprahistoric value to the Marxist dialectic of alienation, as identified with the capitalism-socialism dialectic. Not that there is not a suprahistorical truth in the dialectic of alienation. Man creates institutions and loses himself in his creations. The challenging of institutions by man, who feels a stranger to himself in his own existence, is the source of the historical movement. The origin of doctrinarism is the implicit or explicit assumption that economic alienation is the primary cause of all alienations and that individual ownership of the means of production the primary cause of all economic alienation. Once this monism has been eliminated one can proceed to a reasonable comparison of the economic, social, and political advantages and disadvantages of the various regimes in themselves and according to the phases of growth.

The two economic values most commonly invoked in our time are increase of the gross national product and equalitarian distribution of income. It is not certain that a concern for increase inspires the same measures as a concern for equality. Nor has it been proved that industrial societies are capable of the same measure of equalization of income at various phases of their development. It is possible that the broadening of the salary range is favorable to productivity. Generally speaking, one can say that the two objectives—wealth and equalitarian justice—are not contradictory, since the facts suggest a reduction of inequalities with an increase of wealth. But at a given moment these two points of reference may compel one not to a radical choice, but to an ambiguous compromise.

However, the two criteria which we have just indicated are not the only ones. Limitation of the powers vested in the administrators of collective labor seems consistent with a fundamental requirement of a political nature. But the rigor of discipline and the authority of the leaders may be favorable to productivity. A comparison of the yield from private ownership and collective ownership, from public ownership where an absolute power reigns and democratized public ownership, may reveal contradictions between efficiency and a human ideal.

This way of raising the problems is imposed by a double critique: a sociological critique of a causal monism in which a *single* element (regime of ownership, a procedure for the establishment of equilibrium) determines the principle traits of an economic regime, and a philosophical critique of the use to which the existentialists have put the dialectic of alienation, a dialectic which acquires concrete value in the sociological translation which Marx gave it but which without this translation remains formal and applicable to all regimes.

This plurality of considerations does not prevent one from grasping wholes, from comprehending a political and economic regime such as the Soviet regime or the American regime in its unity or essence. This procedure, however precarious, is scientifically legitimate and politically inevitable. It must be prefaced by an analysis which has revealed the traits common to all regimes and the advantages or disadvantages peculiar to each.

Every modern economic regime is characterized by factory workers, and the proportion of skilled workers to non-skilled workers depends more on technology than on the state of ownership. The factory workers will be embedded in a collective organization of administration and labor without being capable of grasping fully the meaning of the tasks that are entrusted to them. The condition of the workers nevertheless varies greatly according to size of salaries, breadth of salary range, relations within the factory or business, relations between labor unions and leaders, private or public, and according to their sense of participation or alienation, a sense that is partially determined by the ideology to which the workers subscribe and the idea they have of the society. To declare flatly that a worker in a capitalist factory in France or the United States is by definition exploited and that a worker in a Soviet factory is not, is not an example of synthetic thought, it is pure nonsense. It is merely a convenient way of substituting verbal gymnastics for a painstaking investigation of reality.

From Criticism to Reasonable Action

Politics is action: political theory is either the comprehension of action crystallized in events or the determination of what action is possible or advisable in a given situation. Since to my way of thinking completed action has not obeyed laws or a dialectic, I cannot offer the equivalent of the Marxist doctrine in which past and future, knowledge and practice are united in a single system. Since the present situation of the world, considered in the context of an economic interpretation, gives rise to different problems in underdeveloped countries, Western countries of retarded growth, and Western countries of accelerated growth,[2] the true doctrine can only be one which shows the diversity of solutions.

To be sure, I have not explicitly indicated either the objectives to be aimed at or the hierarchy to be established among the objectives—I have deliberately refrained from discussing objectives—but these, in fact, are imperatively suggested by modern civilization. They are the objectives of the left, henceforth victorious—a left which runs the risk of being defeated by its own victory. I have not challenged the values of the left; one need only define clearly *all* of these values to reveal their possible contradiction and consequently the partial truth of the men and doctrines of the right.

The major fact of our age is neither socialism, nor capitalism, nor the intervention of the state, nor free enterprise: it is the monstrous development of technology and industry, of which the massive concentrations of workers in Detroit, Billancourt, Moscow, and Coventry are the consequence and symbol. Industiral society is the genus of which Soviet and Western societies are the species.

No nation and no party rejects or can consciously reject industrial civilization, which is the foundation not only of the living standard of the masses, but of military strength. It is conceivable that the ruling classes of certain Islamic or Asiatic countries would tolerate the poverty of their populations (even with Western technology, they cannot be sure of remedying this poverty if the birth rate remains too high); they would not tolerate a position of subservience to which they would be condemned by the absence of industry. In the native land of Gandhi the rulers are impressed by the Soviet example, which is an example of power much more than an example of abundance.

The imperative of economic progress forces right-wing thinkers to

---

2. It goes without saying that these three types of countries are not the only ones: I am presenting a simplified typology.

accept the instability of the conditions of existence from one generation to another.[3] This same imperative obliges left-wing thinkers to
consider the compatibility or incompatibility of their various ends.

It has been established that the standard of living of the workers
depends more on the productivity of work than on the form of
ownership of businesses, that the distribution of income is not necessarily less equitable under a regime of private ownership and competition than under a regime of planned economy. If the two major
objectives of the left in the economic realm are growth and fair distribution, experimental proof exists to the effect that public ownership
and planned economy are not necessary means. Socialist doctrinarism
is born of a devotion to anachronistic ideologies. The critique of myths
leads directly not to a choice, but to a reasonable consideration of the
regimes in which nations have to live.

But why should I have brought up the matter of choice? Neither the
Americans nor the British nor the French nor the Soviets have to
choose from among different regimes. The Americans and the British
are satisfied with their regime and will modify it in accordance with
events. If a crisis should arise they will not hesitate to intervene, even if
it becomes necessary to move, without admitting it or while insisting
on the contrary, toward a kind of planned economy. One need only
show that the economic objectives of the left may be attained within
the context of the Western regimes to dispel the prestige of the revolutionary mythology and encourage men to use reason to solve problems
which are more technological than ideological.

The case of France is unusual. It would seem that the French economy suffers from an insufficiency of dynamism. Her geographical situation and the sentiments of the people rule out the imitation or
importation of the Soviet regime, not to speak of the repugnance that
would be felt by the vast majority of Frenchmen (including most of
those who vote for the Communist party) for Soviet methods as soon
as they had any direct experience of them. So criticism, by dispelling
nostalgia for the beneficial upheaval, clears the way for the effort of
construction.

There is not so much difference, in France, between a so-called leftist economist like Mr. Sauvy and a so-called rightist economist like
myself. To be sure, Mr. Sauvy sometimes suggests that the feudal
powers are the principal persons responsible for stagnation. He is not
unaware that resistance to change comes from the small at least as

---

3. It would be worth reflecting on the significance of conservatism in an economically progressive society.

much as from the great and that workers' unions or unions of civil servants or agricultural producers are just as given to Malthusianism as employers' unions. He sometimes promotes the legend of an expansionist left against a Malthusian right, although he has shown better than anyone to what a degree the government of the Popular Front of 1936 had been Malthusian out of ignorance.

To me loyalty to one party has never been a decision of fundamental importance. To join the Communist party is to accept a theory of the world and of history. To join the Socialist party or the MRP (*Mouvement républicain populaire*) is to demonstrate one's loyalty to or at least sympathy for a representation of society, a spiritual family. I do not believe in the validity of a system comparable to that of the Communists; I feel detached from the preferences or *Weltanschauung* of the left or the right, the socialists or radicals, the MRP or the independents. According to the circumstances I am in agreement or disagreement with the action of a given movement or a given party. In 1941 or 1942 I disapproved of the passion with which the Gaullists, from the outside, denounced the "treason" of Vichy. In 1947 I favored a revision of the Constitution or of constitutional procedure which the *Rassemblement du peuple français* professed to want. When the attempt of the RPF failed, the social republicans aggravated the faults of the regime, and I could neither associate myself with their action nor keep silent about its disastrous consequences. Perhaps such an attitude is contrary to the morality (or immorality) of political action; it is not contrary to the obligations of the writer.

If my criticisms seem to be directed primarily against the left, the fault may lie with the desire which motivates me to convince my friends. The fault also lies with the attitude adopted by the majority of leftists today, an attitude which I see as a betrayal of the "eternal" left.

The left came out of the movement of the Enlightenment. It places intellectual freedom above all else, it wants to tear down all Bastilles, it aspires to the simultaneous flowering of wealth, through the exploitation of natural resources, and justice, through the decline of superstition and the reign of Reason. That prejudice in favor of the tyranny of a single party which elevates a pseudo-rationalist superstition into an official ideology is, in my opinion, the shame of the intellectuals of the left. Not only are they sacrificing the best part of the legacy of the Enlightenment—respect for reason, liberalism—but they are sacrificing it in an age when there is no reason for the sacrifice, at least in the West, since economic expansion in no sense requires the suppression of parliaments, parties, or the free discussion of ideas.

Here again, the criticism of myth has an immediate positive function. How have the intellectuals been drawn into this denial?[4] Through the *monist* error: ultimately, the Marxist ignores politics; he decrees that the economically dominant class is by definition in possession of the power. The arrival of the proletariat to the rank of ruling class will be tantamount to the liberation of the masses. Having traced the origin of economic alienation to private ownership of the instruments of production, we arrive at the ludicrous conclusion that public ownership of the instruments of production and the omnipotence of one party are tantamount to the classless society, by a series of verbal equivalences (power of the party = power of the proletariat = abolition of private ownership = abolition of classes = human liberation).

Economic expansion, whether pursued by the Soviet method or the Western method, never guarantees a respect for political values. The increase of total wealth or even the reduction of economic inequalities implies neither the safeguarding of personal or intellectual freedom nor the maintaining of representative institutions. Indeed, as Tocqueville and Burckhardt saw clearly a century ago, societies without an aristocracy, motivated by the spirit of commerce and the boundless desire for wealth, are susceptible to the conformist tyranny of majorities and the concentration of power in a monstrous state. Whatever tensions may be created by the retardation of economic progress in France, the most difficult task from a long-range historical point of view is not to assure the increase of collective resources, but to avoid falling into the tyranny of mass societies.

I do not oppose those leftist intellectuals who demand the acceleration of economic growth in France. Although I am probably more aware than they are of the cost of growth, I am nevertheless in agreement with them in principle, as long as they are not fascinated by the Soviet model. I do condemn them for the partiality that prompts them always to take sides against the Westerners: though ready to accept Communism in the underdeveloped countries to promote industrialization, they nevertheless remain hostile to the United States, which can give lessons in industrialization to all of us. When it is a question of the Soviet Union, economic progress justifies the destruction of national independence in Asia or even in Europe. When it is a

---

4. I shall omit the psychological reasons, conscious or unconscious, to which I alluded in *The Opium of the Intellectuals* and which provoked so much criticism. An intellectual of the left has the right to regard all businessmen and all right-wing writers as bigots or cynics. It is high treason to suggest that "interests" are not confined to one side, and Mr. Duverger does not hesitate to draw an idealized portrait of the intellectual whose sole concern is to defend the oppressed and combat injustice. The picture is edifying.

question of European colonies, the right of peoples to self-determination is invoked in all its rigor. The semi-violent repression practiced by the Westerners in Cyprus or Africa is denounced ruthlessly, while the radical repression in the Soviet Union, with transfers of populations, is ignored or pardoned. The democratic freedoms are invoked against the democratic governments of the West, but their disappearance is excused when it is the work of a regime that calls itself proletarian.

Skepticism and Faith

Have I fully explained why *The Opium of the Intellectuals* is regarded as a negative book? Certainly not, and I see other reasons myself.

Many readers are irritated by what one of my adversaries at the *Centre des Intellectuels catholiques* has called "my dramatic dryness." I must confess to an extreme repugnance to reply to this type of argument. Those who let it be known that their own sentiments are noble and those of their adversaries selfish or base strike me as exhibitionists. I have never considered that there was any merit or difficulty in suffering or that sympathy for the misery of others was the prerogative of those who write for *Le Monde, Les Temps modernes, L'Esprit,* or *La Vie intellectuelle.* Political analysis gains by divesting itself of all sentimentality. Lucidity demands effort: passion automatically goes at a gallop.

I reproach Merleau-Ponty, to whom I feel so close, for having written against Sartre that "one doesn't get rid of poverty simply by hailing the revolution from afar." Of course one does not get rid of it so cheaply, but how are we privileged persons to discharge our debt? All my life I have only known one person whom the misery of others prevented from living: Simone Weil. She followed her path and ended in quest of sainthood. We whom the misery of men does not prevent from living—at least let it not prevent us from thinking. Let us not believe ourselves obliged to talk nonsense to bear witness to our noble sentiments.

Also, I refuse to pass those hasty judgments to which so many of my adversaries and even friends invite me. I refuse to say, with Mr. Duverger, that "the left is the party of the weak, the oppressed and the victims," for that party, the party of Simone Weil, is neither to the right nor to the left; it is eternally on the side of the vanquished, and as everybody knows, Mr. Duverger does not belong to it. I refuse to say that "at the present time Marxism provides the only comprehensive theory of social injustice," for in that case the biologists would have to say that Darwinism as expounded by Darwin provides the only comprehensive theory of the evolution of the species. I refuse to denounce capitalism as such, or the bourgeoisie as such, to hold the "feudal lords" (which ones?) responsible for the errors committed in France over the past fifty years. Every society has a ruling class, and the party which is volunteering today to take over brings with it a society worse than the existing one. I consent to denounce social injustices but not social injustice itself, of which private ownership is alleged to be the major cause and Marxism the theory.

I am quite aware that Etienne Borne, who only wishes me well, reproaches me in a friendly way for "deploying an immense talent in order to explain with irrefutable reasons why things cannot be otherwise than what they are." It is true that I argue against utopianism more often than against conservatism. In France at the present time, the criticism of ideologies is one way of hastening reforms. On the level of philosophy, not of the daily paper, Etienne Borne as well as Father Leblond reproach me for not indicating in the foreseeable future the reconciliation of values which are temporarily incompatible. A strange reproach coming from Catholics who believe the world to be corrupted by sin!

It seems to me essential to reveal the plurality of considerations on which political or economic action must depend. I do not regard this plurality as incoherent. In the economic realm the concern for production and the concern for equitable distribution are not in the long run either contradictory or concordant. The reconciliation of justice with growth requires a compromise between equality and the adjustment of retribution to merit. The economic objective of a better living standard often comes into conflict with the political objective of power.

In the political realm it seems to me that the fundamental problem is to reconcile the participation of all men in the community with the diversity of tasks. Men have sought the solution to this antinomy in two ways. The first way is to proclaim the social and political equality of individuals in spite of the prestige of the functions performed by each. No doubt modern societies are the only ones to have extended universally the principle of equality which the ancient city states limited to citizens alone and which even the Roman Empire did not extend either to slaves or to all conquered peoples. But the more democracy tries to restore to complex societies that economic and social equality which small, non-literate populations maintained with difficulty, the more apparent becomes the contrast between justice and reality. Democratic societies and Soviet societies are doomed, albeit to different degrees, to hypocrisy, because the weight of things does not permit them to effectively realize their ideal.

The second solution consists in sanctioning the inequality of conditions and rendering it acceptable by convincing all non-privileged persons that the hierarchy reflects a higher cosmic or religious order and that it does not impair the dignity or opportunity of the individual. The caste system is the extreme form of the unequalitarian solution which has, at its worst, given rise to horrors, but whose principle was not inherently hateful. Or at least if the unequalitarian solution is inherently imperfect, the other solution is too, at least as long as circumstances do not make it possible to realize it effectively.

Indeed, the religion of salvation has, throughout history, oscillated between two extremes. Either it has sanctioned or accepted the temporal inequalities by devaluating them: in comparison to the sole essential, the salvation of the soul, what importance have the things of this world, wealth and power? Or else it has denounced social and economic inequalities in the name of evangelical truth and solemnly called upon men to reorganize institutions in accordance with the precepts of Christ and the Church. Each of these two attitudes involves a danger to the authenticity of religion. The first runs the risk of leading to a kind of quietism, a complacent acceptance of injustices, and even the sanctification of the established order. The second, carried to its conclusion, would sustain the revolutionary impulse, since societies have, up to the present, been so incapable of giving their citizens that equality of condition or opportunity which is solemnly granted to souls.

The Christian socialists (and by inspiration, the progressists belong to this tradition) often have the conviction that they alone are capable of saving the Church from compromising itself with the established injustice, that they and they alone are faithful to the teachings of Christ. Churches, even churches of salvation, never entirely avoid relapsing into what Bergson called static religion. They are inclined to justify the powers which accord them a monopoly (or, in our time, certain privileges) in the realm of the administration of sacraments or the education of the young. The Christian, whose opinions are politically conservative, and the clergy, concerned about schools or convents, tend, in order to excuse a lack of concern for social inequalities, to invoke the idea that the real match is not played in the political arena. At the other extreme the progressist carries historical hope—i.e., temporal hope—as far as it will go.

I shall refrain from choosing between these two attitudes: either, in its authentic expression, may legitimately call itself Christian. Perhaps the most profoundly Christian citizen would be one who experienced at every moment the tension between these two exigencies. He would never have the sense of having done enough for human justice, and yet he would feel that the results of this tireless effort were negligible and must appear as such in comparison with the only thing really at stake. He would be neither resigned to human misery nor forgetful of sin.

In our day in France the pendulum is swinging toward evangelical socialism, at least in the intellectual Catholic circles of the capital. The "hierarchy" is criticized for taking an exaggerated interest in the schools and for compromising itself with the "established disorder," to quote E. Mounier, in a vain effort to collect a few subsidies from the state. I have not taken sides in this debate, and there was no reason why I should. It makes no difference to me whether the Catholics vote for the left or for the right. What interests me is the fact that some Catholics are so attracted by the parties that promise the kingdom of God on earth that they forgive them for persecutions inflicted on Christians in China and eastern Europe.

I was quite surprised, at the *Centre des Intellectuels catholiques,* to hear a Jesuit father, as far as possible from progressism, present the anticipation of the kingdom of God on earth as a hope, if not a belief, that was necessary. What is the definition of this kingdom of God? I am astonished at the facility with which Catholic thinkers are adopting the optimism of the age of Enlightenment, amplified and vulgarized by Marxism. The attempt to outflank the Communists on the left strikes me as politically futile and, in terms of doctrine, if not of dogma, questionable. Besides, this technological optimism belongs to the avant-garde of yesterday rather than to that of today.

I have not even criticized this optimism as such; I have confined myself to tracing the steps by which one passes from the classless society—the materialist version of the kingdom of God on earth—to a theory of historical evolution, to one class, then to one party as the agent of salvation.

Finally, the stages of profane history—the succession of social regimes—are confused with the moments of sacred history, the dialogue of men (and of each man) with God. It is necessary and easy to mark the separation between these two histories and to remember that anyone who believes totally in the first ceases for that very reason to believe in the second.

My friend Father Dubarle, in an intelligent article, begins by agreeing with me so closely that he considers the point too obvious to require proof. "Surely, then, history, the real and concrete history which presents itself at the level of human experience and reason, is not that secular substitute for divinity which has fascinated so many contemporary minds with its dream. All these things are very well said, and one feels, moreover, when one reflects, a certain surprise (a surprise which is shared by Mr. Aron) to find that there is such a need for them to be said in our day. . . ." Then he suggests by means of subtle questions that the rigorous separations between temporal and eternal, profane and sacred may provide more apparent clarity than real light. I shall try, however, to reply to these questions which I am not sure I really understand.

"A Christian," he writes, "would therefore ask Mr. Aron whether he can accept the idea that a sermon about eternity tries also to confer, albeit in a subordinate and relative fashion, a humanly important significance to the temporal history of the human race." I have never dreamed of refusing "a humanly important significance to the temporal history of the human race." Not being a believer in the ordinary sense of the term, how could I have denied this importance without falling into out-and-out nihilism? The discussion does not concern "the importance of the temporal history"; the discussion concerns the truth of an interpretation of history that shows humanity advancing toward the classless society, with one class and one party playing the role of savior in this adventure. Once this mythology has been eliminated, temporal history remains important, but it ceases to obey either a pre-established determinism or a dialectic; it imposes on men tasks that are constantly being renewed and fundamentally permanent. Never will men finish subjecting the weight of institutions to the desire for justice.

Let us not go into the problem of clericalism or the role of the church in societies that reject a state religion: I have not dealt with this problem, to which Father Dubarle for some reason alludes. In twentieth-century France the Church accepts the fact that the state declares religion to be a "private affair." It no longer demands that the state impose by force the universal truth to which it continues, legitimately from its point of view, to lay claim; it consents to civic and political equality being accorded to nonbelievers. I do not believe that Father Dubarle is any less a partisan of secularity than myself.

Secularity does not reduce the Church to the administration of the sacraments or condemn her to silence in the realm of politics or economics. The Church wants to imbue the organization of the City with the Christian spirit. In this sense all Christians, and not progressist Christians alone, want to "introduce the eternal into the temporal." But they do not all think that this introduction leads, according to a deterministic or dialectical order, to the kingdom of God on earth. But when I deny that the evolution is orderly or that the vision is ever total, I am immediately suspected of denying all significance to history and all commerce between the eternal and the temporal. Strange misunderstanding, or rather, one that reveals so much! Anyone who has understood the nature of men and societies knows that "Christianity" involves a secular effort and the acceptance of a role in the game of history. He also knows that this game is never entirely won, or in any case that profane history, economic or social history, will have no final fulfillment. Neither the Christian nor the rationalist therefore turns away from the temporal drama, for even if they know nothing about the future they do know something about the principles of a human society. If so many Catholics are afraid to renounce the historical dialectic it is because they too have lost their principles and, like the existentialists, look to myths for the certainties they lack.

The progressist Christians play among believers a role analogous to that of the existentialists among unbelievers. The latter incorporate fragments of Marxism into a philosophy of extreme individualism and quasi-nihilism because, denying any permanence to human nature, they oscillate between a lawless voluntarism and a doctrinarism based on myths. The progressist Christians refuse to judge regimes according to the conditions imposed on churches and are ready to attribute an almost sacred value to an economic technique, the class struggle, or a method of action. When I denounce the conversion of Kierkegaard's descendants to doctrinarism or the oscillation of the progressists between "revolutionarism" toward the liberal societies and "secular clericalism" favoring the Communist societies, I am accused of skepticism, as if my skepticism were aimed at authentic faith when in fact it is aimed at schemes, models, and utopias.

This skepticism is useful or harmful according to whether fanaticism or indifference is more to be feared; in any case it is philosophically necessary insofar as it will put an end to the ravages of abstract passions and bring men back to the elementary distinction between principles and judgments based on expediency. For want of principles both existentialists and progressist Christians count on a class or a historical dialectic to provide them with conviction. Dogmatic when they should be cautious, the existentialists have begun by denying what they should have affirmed. They have no use for prudence, "the god of this world below"; they invest the historical movement with reason after having divested it of man. The progressists attribute to Revolution that sacred quality which they are afraid of no longer finding in the life of the Church and the adventures of souls.

Is it, then, so difficult to see that I have less against fanaticism than I have against skepticism, which is its ultimate origin?

Part Three

The Failure of Marxism

While the first and second parts of this volume could be conceived of as a refutation of the intellectual basis of Marxist ideology, part 3 refers to the failure of Marxism on the historical level. Aron states that the Marxist prophecy not only has failed its fulfillment but, even worse, has become the theoretical support of totalitarianism and oppression in our time.

By reflecting on the historical misadventures of Marxism, Aron reveals the historical lucidity of Tocqueville.

5

Marx's Messianism and Its Misadventures

Prophetism and Reality

Of all the socialist doctrines current in the last century, only Marx's became an official doctrine of the workers' parties. Historians have made many attempts to understand the posthumous fame of a writer whose lifework contains not only propaganda masterpieces such as the *Communist Manifesto*, but also works beyond the grasp of the ordinary reader. Perhaps it is the combination of simple ideas and difficult theories (the latter based upon the former) that explains Marxism's success. Everyone can understand the basic message, and the scholars, in their comments on the text of *Capital*, must temper the messianic faith of the activists with some words of caution.

The basic message is the *prophetism* that emerges from Marx's critique of capitalism. Each era of Marxism is defined by a particular version of the prophetism, ever at odds with the facts (which, as Lenin remarked, are stubborn). The first, the era of the Second International, extending to World War I, was marked by Bernstein's *revisionism*, which was a testimony of the contradiction between the prophetism and the actual course of development of European capitalism. The second era (which began in 1914 or 1917 and ended with the victory of Mao Tse-tung in China) demonstrated the fact that developed capitalism does not lead to revolution: it is Marxism-Leninism that brings revolutions about. But are they in the image of the one prophesied by Marx? Do they lead to socialism?

The third era tends to furnish negative responses to these questions.

From *In Defense of Decadent Europe*, by Raymond Aron, translated by Stephen Cox (South Bend, Ind.: Regnery/Gateway, 1979), pp. 3–27. Reprinted by permission of the publisher. First published in French in 1977.

Khrushchev's Twentieth Congress speech and the split between the Soviet Union and the People's Republic of China have shaken Marxism-Leninism, in much the same way the improvement of the standards of living in Europe and in the United States had done, and as World War I had shaken the Marxism of the Second International.

None of the three Marxisms—that of Kautsky, of Lenin-Stalin-Mao, or of the present day—have been able to reconcile the prophetism with historical reality. But none of them have completely disappeared.

The Major Themes

Marxism, *as interpreted by those who declare themselves Marxists,* presents itself first and foremost as a *philosophy of history,* an overall view of the "human adventure" from so-called primitive societies right up to the socialist society of the future. The capitalism immediately preceding socialism is the last "antagonistic" régime, torn as it is by contradictions and by man's exploitation of man. After capitalism, progress will continue, but social progress will no longer require political revolution. If this sort of interpretation of history can be called *historicism,* and if the expectation of a future society in which mankind will achieve its essential purpose can be referred to as *humanism,* then Marxism cannot be other than a kind of historicism and a kind of humanism.

For some years now, of course, there have been learned scholars with their own learned and esoteric languages who have stated, repeatedly, that Marxism is not a kind of historicism and not a kind of humanism. If the custodians of the faith do not interdict these new scholars' assertions, it is because they are addressed to only a limited public and do not disturb the pillars of the temple. Who would pardon the crimes of Stalin, who would fall under the spell of a bureaucrat like Brezhnev unless both of them—the monster and the Mister Average—bore within themselves the hope of mankind? It matters very little whether or not it is called historicist; Marxism remains a *prophetism.*

This prophetism is draped in scientific, or rather scientistic, fancy dress. In order for the prophecy of socialism—the end of prehistory; a classless society with no exploitation of man by man—to be different in nature from the various forms of Judeo-Christian millenarianism, history has to obey laws (this word, common in the scientific vocabulary, especially that of the nineteenth century, confers a sort of guarantee of scientific rigor). In other words, in one shape or another, the prophetism of the Marxist Vulgate is based on the laws of historical development, on the laws that determine the succession of the modes of production and of economic and social systems.

We are dealing here with macro-historical laws which apply to a society or civilization as a whole, not with laws such as the law of falling bodies, or Boyle's or even Gresham's Law. Take the latter, for instance: "Bad money drives out the good." It does not require the transformation of the entire economic system: it states that when two different coins are in circulation, the good one—the one which inspires people's confidence—will become rare because they will hold onto it, whereas the bad one, the one seen as likely to lose its value, will circulate in abundance.

Of the laws of historical development, one and only one is of intense concern to Marxists—the one which enables them to assert the necessity of a passage from capitalism to socialism. This law in its turn is subdivided into two propositions: that capitalism will give way to a different mode of production (just as capitalism itself took over from feudalism); and that the succeeding mode of production will be socialist—in other words, it will put an end not only to the particular form of exploitation implied by capitalism, but the exploitation of man by man.

To assure a proper mixture of prophecy and historical law, it is required that the capitalist system suffer a dual condemnation: it must be intrinsically unjust and, as such, it must be incapable of surviving. (Marx regularly expected its collapse, a century ago, with each new crisis of the cotton industry.)

Marx's stroke of genius was in having found a way of uniting these two condemnations and of basing one upon the other. Why is capitalism *per se* unjust? It is because of the surplus value which is basic to capitalism, and the mainspring of entrepreneurial activity. Why does capitalism proceed to its downfall of its own accord, like the sorcerer's apprentice? Because the frantic quest for surplus value tends of its own accord, toward paralysis: the quest for surplus value through the accumulation of capital finishes with the destruction of the conditions necessary to the creation of surplus value.

For the benefit of readers unfamiliar with the Marxist texts, let us recapitulate the principal stages of the proof. Starting point or *major premise: the theory of work value.* The value of each commodity (or object exchanged) is equal to the quantity of average human labor required to produce it.

Second stage or *minor premise: the theory of wages.* First of all, the capitalist mode of production is fixed by the private ownership of the means of production; the capitalist buys the workers' labor power in order to operate instruments of production which he himself owns. He does not buy labor but labor power; the wage is the price of labor power for a given time. What is the value of this labor power? Like any commodity, labor power has a value equal to the quantity of average human labor necessary to produce it. And producing labor power signifies providing worker and family with the indispensable means of subsistence. Is it possible to determine the *indispensable* level of these means? Marx replies that the level varies in relation to the "social conscience," but the working wage of his time was so close to the physiological minimum that he did not bother much about the oscillations around rock bottom.

Third stage and *conclusion: the theory of surplus value.* Given that the value of the commodity is measurable by the quantity of average human labor it embodies, and given that the value of the commodity (labor power) is measurable by the value of the commodities needed for the maintenance of worker and family, it is enough to assert that the labor power—the worker—produces more value than it receives in its wages, so that there exists a *margin* between the value of the wage (or buying power of labor power) and the value produced by this same labor power. This margin is called surplus value (profit).

This proof, which is an integral part both of Marx's Marxism and of the *vulgar* Marxisms, contains the same ambivalence as does the prophetism/historical laws combination: it joins scientific analysis and moral condemnation. Labor power is paid according to its value but, in a system of private ownership, this leaves the surplus value to the owner of the means of production. And what is more obnoxious than a régime which treats human work as a commodity?[1]

How does one make the transition from the theory of surplus value, which brings to light the "intrinsic injustice" of a capitalist régime, to the confirmation of the historical law that guarantees the passage from capitalism to socialism? On this point, Marx and the Marxists offer several answers.

The simplest is that of pauperization. Let us suppose that, in their thirst for profit, the capitalists constantly increase productive capacity

---

1. This argument illustrates the shift from the economic critique to the moral. Although this argument still impresses some people, it is meaningless. Any modern economy, whether socialist or capitalist, has to calculate the cost of labor.

and that they distribute the lowest possible buying power to the wage earners. There will then be a growing contradiction between the development of productive forces and the return on production (whatever the precise meaning of the German expression *Produktionsver-hältnisse* may be). And if the masses become poorer and poorer as society becomes richer and richer (or more and more capable of producing riches), the revolution that breaks out will no longer be that of a minority for the benefit of a minority, but of the majority for the benefit of all.

Another, more subtle, approach to the problem is derived from the law of diminishing returns. The rate of surplus value (e.g., the profit rate) is defined as the ratio between labor and surplus labor or between the wage (or variable capital) and surplus value.[2] On the other hand, profit is calculated in relation to the entire capital—not just the wages paid to the workers but the wages plus the fraction of the value of the machinery which is incorporated in the commodity. The profit rate will therefore be the ratio between surplus value and the total of the constant capital and the variable capital. Let us postulate that surplus value is levied exclusively on the variable capital (or labor power). The value of the machinery is incorporated in the commodity; each commodity incorporates a fraction of that value equal to the decrease in value (or depreciation) of the machinery. Therefore, the denominator of the "profit rate" fraction increases as the constant capital (or plant) represents a greater part of the total capital. Hence, by definition, the profit rate tends to diminish. (The idea that the profit rate has a long-term tendency to decline does not belong to Marx alone, but is borrowed from the economists of his time. His own special contribution is the explanation of the law by the *theory of surplus value.*)[3]

Besides pauperization and the law of the declining rate of profit, Marx and the Marxists afford other, more complex versions of the "law of the transition from capitalism to socialism." Without going into technical expositions, let us say that the Marxist schema of surplus value taken in combination with the agent of a free market, raises the question: How is surplus value realized? How are buyers found for

---

2. In the numerical examples which he gives in illustration of his proof, Marx always assumes equality between the variable capital (or cost of labor power) and surplus value ($v = s$). This gives a rate of exploitation (the ratio between labor and surplus labor) of 100%—a rate which is implied but never proven.

3. The profit rate is written as follows: $s/(c + v)$. Since the surplus value (s) is levied exclusively on v (variable capital or labor power), the growth of c (constant capital or plant) in its relation to v inevitably involves the decline of the profit rate.

consumer products? How is capital accumulated? What are the conditions under which surplus value is levied on the workers' labor so that more surplus value can be realized, ensuring, in other words, the perpetuation of the cycle? Rosa Luxemburg and Lenin (who, however, very strongly opposed Luxemburg's theory) both attempted to prove that a capitalist society cannot dispense with virgin territories to exploit. They located in the need for capital the root source of imperialism.

The theory of surplus value which is at the center of the Marxists' condemnation—moral and historical—of capitalism serves as a preface to a general Marxist theory of human development. In one of his most famous texts, the introduction to his *Contribution to the Critique of Political Economy*, Marx first of all distinguishes the three modes of production: slavery, serfdom, and wage labor; then an Asiatic mode, outside the West; and finally, in the future: socialism.

Marx's notions about slavery, serfdom, and wage labor suggest three ways of obtaining surplus value. The slave owner puts to work the labor power belonging to him, and he gains because it produces more value than it consumes in the form of the food provided by the master. In like manner, the feudal lord, owner of the land, keeps for himself the whole share of the crop except for what the serf uses for sowing and for consumption. Wage labor is revealed as the *ultimate form* of exploitation: the proletarian is free, but forced to sell his labor power; for this, he receives the proper price, the value, in other words, of his own reproduction. But this free economy—in which the owner exchanges the worker's labor power for wages—remains based, under capitalism, upon the exploitation of man by man: the surplus value, once levied by slavery and later by the military strength of the feudal lords, is obtained and accumulated with no open violence or violation of laws, but through the supply-and-demand relationship between a seller who possesses nothing and a buyer who possesses capital.

In the dim past, imagines Marx, there existed a primitive community; on the horizon ahead: a non-antagonistic society. Between the two, three modes of levying surplus value represent not so much three ages of history as three models of the relationship between owner and worker. In the Asiatic mode of production, it is the state bureaucracy—playing the part performed by the owners, in the West—which exploits the village communities.

The opposition between owners of the means of production and workers is all the more central a theme because it provides a "scientific" basis for class struggle and because it also characterizes all of society:

... a certain mode of production, or industrial stage, is always combined with a certain mode of cooperation, or social stage, and this mode of cooperation is itself a "productive force"; further, ... the multitude of productive forces accessible to men determines the nature of society; hence, the "history of humanity" must always be studied and treated in relation to the history of industry and exchange.[4]

Productive forces, social relations, classes, and class struggle belong to what Marxists call the "infrastructure," although without ever clarifying the position of the state, of law, or of science within the infra- and superstructure. If science counts as a productive force, does it not belong to the infrastructure? And where are the ideas, which are inseparable from science? The state which maintains the "antagonistic" society is *ipso facto* in the service of the class that exploits the other classes. But the state, which controls the "instruments of violence," possesses, hence, a certain autonomy with respect to the owners of the means of production. It does not have the same function as the owners nor does it exercise its function in the same way, in the various modes of production.

I have presented the themes of Marxist prophetism, commencing with its overall view of history. I might have done as Marx does in the *Communist Manifesto* and taken classes and their struggles as the starting point:

The history of all hitherto existing society is the history of class struggles. Freeman and slave, patrician and plebeian, lord and serf, guild-master and journeyman, in a word, oppressor and oppressed, stood in constant opposition to one another, carried on an interrupted, now hidden, now open fight, a fight that each time ended, either in a revolutionary reconstitution of society at large, or in the common ruin of the contending classes. . . . The modern bourgeois society that has sprouted from the ruins of feudal society has not done away with class antagonisms. . . . Our epoch, the epoch of the bourgeoisie, possesses, however, this distinctive feature: it has simplified the class antagonisms. Society as a whole is more and more splitting up into two great hostile camps, into two great classes directly facing each other: Bourgeoisie and Proletariat.

4. Marx/Engels, *The German Ideology,* pt. I (London: Lawrence and Wishart, 1977), p. 50.

This famous text suggests an historical issue: What classes composed a particular historical society? It also raises other questions. Is it true that capitalist societies tend towards a simplified dualistic structure with "the bourgeoisie" on one side and "the proletariat" on the other? On a higher level of analysis, how does the analysis of the development of capitalist society as described in *Capital* fit in with the vision of history in terms of class struggle?

The historic task of overthrowing "the last antagonistic society," the last one to contain classes in struggle, falls to the proletariat. Why? The slaves did not overthrow ancient society, nor the serfs feudal society. In the works of his youth, when he had not yet studied political economy, Marx uses philosophical arguments to justify proletarian messianism:

> Where, then, is the *positive* possibility of a German emancipation? In the formation of a class with *radical chains,* a class of civil society which is not a class of civil society, an estate which is the dissolution of all estates, a sphere which has a universal character by its universal suffering and claims no *particular right* because no *particular wrong* but *wrong generally* is perpetrated against it; which can no longer invoke a *historical* but only a *human* title; which does not stand in any one-sided antithesis to the premises of the German state; a sphere, finally, which cannot emancipate itself without emancipating itself from all other spheres of society, which, in a word, is the *complete loss* of man and hence can win itself only through the *complete rewinning of man.*[5]

I repeat that this is a text of Marx's youth, predating his research into economics. But it is no less interesting to note that proletarian messianism and the historic mission of a proletariat responsible for revolution and for human liberation were already in the mind of Marx the philosopher before he consulted reality to prove them. A revolution that puts an end to all antagonisms is a radical innovation compared to past revolutions, just as the proletariat viewed as an *emancipating class* resembles none of the classes which in past times have made mankind progress from one mode of production to another.

Between the two modes of production, capitalist and socialist,

5. This famous text dates from 1844, in the *Introduction to the Critique of Hegel's Philosophy of Law.* How might this class, with no position in society, become the ruling class? The question has no answer except for the Leninist or Stalinist solution which substitutes the party for the proletariat, and a mythical proletariat for the real one.

Marx mentions an intermediary and indispensable link—the *dictatorship of the proletariat,* an expression which recurs several times in his work, from the letter to Weydemeyer of 1852 to the days of the Commune in 1871, and later still in the *Critique of the Gotha Program.* What meaning did Marx himself assign to this expression? All polemics aside, there are grounds for various interpretations.

According to one interpretation, which certainly contains an element of truth, Marx starts from the revolutionary experience. In light of the French Revolution, he reaches the conclusion that absolute power—the only power capable of achieving the transformations involved in the shift from one mode of production to another—must inevitably undergo a transition. And capitalist societies *may* have a democratic type of state, with formal freedoms, with governmental representatives elected by universal suffrage: need it be said, nevertheless, that the bourgeoisie is "exercising its own dictatorship"? If the answer is yes, the form of the state which would assume the dictatorship of the proletariat is not fixed, particularly since the proletariat must not take possession of the bourgeois state in order to manage it for its own benefit, but in order to bring it down, the final goal being the "withering away" of the state.

Similarly, in the economic area, Marx visualized successive phases. The passage which is most often cited as the standard authority on the subject occurs in his *Critique of the Gotha Program.* During the first phase, that of socialism, each individual producer is to receive a quantity of value proportional to the value created by his work. Equality will consequently not prevail, because not all individuals can contribute in equal measure to the common wealth. It is only in the second phase, that of communism, that each individual receives an income proportional to his needs.

Yet beginning with the phase of socialism, Marx seems to imagine that, generally speaking, the market—the sale and purchase of goods—will disappear. Everyone is to receive not money but purchasing certificates. The "associated producers" are to manage the economy, determining the share of the national product to be devoted to public expenditure, the upkeep and replacement of the means of production, and the investments necessary to expand those means. As for the allocation of the share of the national product destined for consumption among the various spheres of industry and agriculture, Marx seems to look on this as a simple matter corresponding to known and pre-established needs.

Whatever the nature of his profound cogitations on the working—firstly of the socialist, then of the communist—economy, it seems to me that Marx never did renounce his *prophetism,* namely, his radical cleavage between the antagonistic régimes and the future, nonantagonistic, régime of mankind. Certainly there are any number of texts by Marx, and especially by Engels after Marx's death, which condone a reformist version of the doctrine. But there remains in my view a contradiction between Marx's prophetism and the candid adherence to a reformist, nonrevolutionary line of action. (It is to me a revealing fact that a socialist so typically social-democratic as Léon Blum, who only felt at ease in a parliamentary society little prone to violence, should never—except perhaps after 1945—have given up the theme of the definitive split. I can still hear him telling an audience of students, fifty years ago, that the day would come when the creaking, worm-eaten old tree of capitalism would have to be brutally cut down or uprooted. Between the wars he stubbornly clung to the distinction between the *exercise of power* in a capitalist society and the *seizure of power* that would symbolize the revolutionary split. Unlike the Bolsheviks, he refused to admit the contradiction between professing a revolutionary outlook and temporarily being at the head of a capitalist society. And unlike revisionists of the Bernstein variety or today's social democrats, he would not resign himself to defining socialism as the sum of the reforms achievable without abrogating legality.)

All Marxists proclaim the unity of theory and practice. This equivocal attitude is, in at least two ways, significant: as adherents of a prophetic system, they set their actions in the framework of a "vision of history" and do their utmost, for better or for worse, to avoid sacrificing the future to the contingencies of the present; theirs is long-term thinking. In addition, they model their world after their theory; the world they see, and in which their actions take place, fits into their theory: hence their practice fits, of its own accord, into their theory.

The Marxism of the Second International

The Marxism of the Second International—by which I mean the ideology proclaimed by the Marxist parties, especially German social democracy—has its origin in the prophetic themes as I have summarized them. The books of Friedrich Engels, in particular the most famous of them, *Anti-Dühring,* simplified and popularized the thinking of Marx in order to facilitate its use as a doctrine of action and as the ideology of a mass movement.

The economic interpretation of history is transformed, first, into historical materialism and becomes an integral part of a metaphysical materialism, with the movement of matter and history alike obeying laws baptized as "dialectical." The simplest or, if you like, the crudest expression of these laws is to be found in *Anti-Dühring*. Reality, both inorganic and organic, is a state of constant flux, of transformation. Echoing Heraclitus, we might say that "no one bathes twice in the same river." But if the cosmos, life, and mankind are in a state of *becoming*, this does not occur as a series of infinitesimal changes but by sudden mutations. Between matter and life, plants and animals, animals and mankind, feudalism and capitalism, there subsists a homogeneity of substance—the basis of materialism—but, from one level or one type of reality to another, there appears a discontinuity.

The discontinuity or rupture implied by the shift from one species or one economic system to another is in harmony with a Hegelian idea adopted by Engels as a law of the dialectic: the transition from quantity into quality. After a certain point, quantitative change brings about a qualitative mutation. This law could lead toward an evolutionary or reformist interpretation of history. In fact, in Friedrich Engels's writings the law of the transition from quantity to quality and the law of mutation are mutually supportive. Taken in tandem, they confirm the revolutionary, prophetic interpretation of Marx's thinking. Capitalism will not give rise to socialism by gradually reforming itself; at some point there must be a break, a revolution.

The second contribution of Engels, which I call the *schema of the historical development of our epoch*, tends to overcome the possible contradictions between the various laws of history. On the one hand, that which fixes the direction of capitalist development is the development of the forces of production—which signifies, in the Marxists' analysis, both capital accumulation and the rising productivity of labor. On the other hand, within the capitalist society, the working class organizes, creating its own institutions and wringing advantages out of the capitalist class. So it must be supposed, firstly, that the development of the productive forces matures the process of mutation (or revolution), and secondly that the working class, by organizing itself within the capitalist régime, prepares itself for revolution and the seizure of power.

Unfortunately for the orthodoxy of the Second International, these two visions are incompatible: the first assumes that the productive forces can no longer fit into the structure of the "relations of capitalist production"—a dictum lacking in precision, but which suggests either that the creation of enterprises vast enough to ensure the necessary capital accumulation is impossible,[6] or else that the purchasing power distributed to the masses is inadequate. Neither idea lends itself to serious discussion. The first disagrees with the Marxist polemic against monopolies; the second disagrees with the facts. The pauperization theory was contradicted toward the end of the nineteenth century by the rise in the living standard of the working class, the power of the German trade unions, and the creation of cooperatives and other socialist-inspired institutions. Did the proletarians of Wilhelmine Germany have nothing to lose but their chains? Anyone who would believe that particular proposition would believe anything.

Friedrich Engels—unlike Marx, who died too early—took an active part, both personally and through the medium of his direct disciples, Karl Kautsky in particular, in the "Marxifying" of the socialist parties and of the workers' movement in the continent of Europe. By this I mean he caused the leaders of the socialist parties and, to a lesser extent, the trade union leaders to adhere to Marxism (as interpreted by Friedrich Engels). Engels retained, in essence, Marx's prophetic themes; positing them within a materialist metaphysic, he proclaimed the dialectic to be both a method and a doctrine, he combined Marx's economic interpretation of history with materialism and—using the *schema of historical development*—he linked reformism and revolution: revolution ripens as a consequence of the development of the productive forces; the socialist parties and the working-class movement, in becoming stronger, play a part in bringing about the "creative split" leading to Marx's vision of a new world order.

The last quarter of the nineteenth century, during Marx's own lifetime and after his death, posed a number of problems which, although theoretical at first, later came to dominate the practice of Marxism. How far can the analysis of capitalist society undertaken by Marx in *Capital* be regarded as universally valid? Will all societies follow the path of England and the Western European countries? Marx had too great a sense of history to categorically deny the possibility of different roads to socialism. But the question did arise: What is left of the prophetism, the schema of historical development, what is left, even of the economic interpretation of history, if just any professedly Marxist party—no matter what the degree of development of the productive forces—can build socialism?

In Wilhelmine Germany, the great Marxist debate matched Karl

6. The Soviet taste for giantism seems to derive from this idea that private ownership is incapable of accommodating the necessary concentrations of productive forces.

Kautsky against Eduard Bernstein (later, they both wound up in the same "revisionist" camp). Friedrich Engels and his disciple Kautsky had "Marxified" the Social Democratic party of Wilhelmine Germany, which resulted not only in the party's adherence to a few ideas stemming from (or declared valid by) Marx, but in the establishment of a philosophical-historical doctrine into which the members of the party were initiated. Every party congress proclaimed, in its final motions, *not so much the immutable truth* of the theory *as the correct interpretation* of the events or, rather, of history-in-the-making. In this respect, the Bolsheviks and the parties of the Third International continued the practice of the Second. The congresses of the Second could pronounce excommunication (although this did not mean execution or even necessarily expulsion). They followed the same procedure, the same political-intellectual routine. Due to its historic mission, the party did not confine itself to setting immediate goals but set its duties in the framework of a broad interpretation of history. Practice—the party line defined at every congress—was not separated from theory—the diagnosis, bearing on the circumstances, and in relation always to the class struggle and the socialism of the future. Eduard Bernstein and the revisionists were condemned for doctrinal reasons, not because they were suggesting a practice significantly different from the one actually being followed by the Social Democratic party, but because they cast doubt on the cardinal feature of the prophetism: the radical disjunction between capitalism and socialism and the revolutionary hiatus that divided the two.

In this debate, Kautsky remained in the prophetic camp and believed himself faithful (and probably was so) to the teachings of Friedrich Engels. The major argument against the trade unionists and revisionists—an argument which salves the conscience of socialists whenever they act against the apparent will of the majority—was formulated by Kautsky before Lenin made it the foundation of bolshevism in *What Is To Be Done?* It holds that, left to themselves, the workers do not get beyond trade unionism: they aspire to improving their own condition in the here and now, and overlook their duty toward mankind, namely, the destruction of capitalism and the building of socialism, the classless society. Who reminds the workers of their destiny? Who holds onto the awareness of the historic mission of the proletariat in the face of the temptations of "bourgeoisification"? It is the *intellectuals*. Marxism, a doctrine of intellectuals, attracts intellectuals because of the historic role it confers on them, which heightens their status in their own eyes. The intellectuals go to the proletariat to provide guidance, not to learn.

Marxism-Leninism

What did Lenin add to the Marxism of the Second International? Four books, each of which contained one or two of the essential ideas (or ideological themes) marking the shift from the original Marxism to the succeeding version (or, if one prefers, from Marxism to Marxism-Leninism): *What Is To Be Done?*; *Materialism and Empiriocriticism*; *Imperialism, the Final Stage of Capitalism*; and, lastly, *The State and Revolution*.

The first book is basically a reply to the objections put forward by working-class reformism against Marxism. The idea that the workers, left to themselves, lean toward trade unionism (the wish to improve their life in the here and now) and that Marxism is brought to them from the outside, by intellectuals, comes from Kautsky, but in *What Is To Be Done?* Lenin gives it what in retrospect appears to be an altogether different application by joining it to a principle of organization—democratic centralism—whose outcome is only too well known.

After citing with approval an article by Kautsky in *Die Neue Zeit*, Lenin goes on to say that, as soon as the working masses are incapable, in the course of their movement, of working out an independent ideology for themselves, the *sole* question is whether to choose a bourgeois ideology or a socialist ideology. There is no middle ground (because mankind has not forged a "third" ideology; besides, in a society torn by class antagonisms it is impossible for there to be any ideology outside or above the classes).

> Hence, to belittle the socialist ideology *in any way*, to *turn away from it, in the slightest degree*, means to strengthen bourgeois ideology. There is a lot of talk about spontaneity, but the *spontaneous* development of the working-class movement leads to its becoming subordinated to the bourgeois ideology, *leads to its developing according to the program of the Credo*,[7] for the spontaneous working-class movement is trade unionism . . . and trade unionism means the ideological enslavement of the workers by the bourgeoisie. Hence, our task, the task of Social Democracy, is to *combat spontaneity, to divert* the working-class movement from this spontaneous, trade-unionist striving to come under the wing of the bourgeoisie, and to bring it under the wing of revolutionary Social Democracy.[8]

7. This was a text by the so-called economist group, to which Lenin was opposed.
8. Lenin, *What Is To Be Done?* (Peking: Foreign Languages Press, 1975), pp. 48–49.

Lenin, in contrast with any number of French sociologists, never thought that his own Marxism was the spontaneous ideology of the working class. On the other hand, he did stress the idea, which goes back to Marx, of the simplification of the class struggle to a contest between the proletariat and the bourgeoisie. Hence, unless trade union action binds itself to revolutionary social democracy (in today's terms to Marxism-Leninism), according to Lenin it drifts into the camp of the bourgeoisie. Thus, at the beginning of this century, the foundation was laid for the polemic against the social democratic parties.

> Class political consciousness can be brought to the workers *only from without,* that is, only from outside of the sphere of relations betwen workers and employers. The sphere from which alone it is possible to obtain this knowledge is the sphere of relationships between *all* the classes and strata and the state and the government, the sphere of the interrelations between *all* the classes.[9]

The clash between working-class trade unionists (or "economists") and social democrats gave rise to the role of the professional revolutionaries.

> A workers' organization must, in the first place, be a trade organization; secondly, it must be as broad as possible; and thirdly, it must be as little clandestine as possible (here, and further on, of course, I have only autocratic Russia in mind). On the other hand, the organizations or revolutionaries must consist first, foremost, and mainly of people who make revolutionary action their profession (that is why I speak of organizations of *revolutionaries,* meaning revolutionary Social Democrats). In view of this common feature of the members of such an organization, *all distinctions as between workers and intellectuals,* and certainly distinctions of trade and profession, must be *utterly obliterated.* Such an organization must of necessity be not too extensive and as secret as possible.[10]

Lenin sees this secret organization of professional revolutionaries as "a small, compact core of the most reliable, experienced, and hardened workers."[11] It is the core of professionals that runs the specifically

9. Ibid., p. 98.
10. Ibid., p. 138.
11. Ibid., p. 146.

political struggle and controls the local sections and mass organizations, and it is this same core, armed with the Marxist prophecy and armored against working-class spontaneity (always inclined toward trade unionism), that will lead the revolution. As Rosa Luxemburg wrote, criticizing Lenin's *One Step Forward, Two Steps Back,* he is defending the ideas of the *ultracentralist* tendency:

> . . . on the one hand, the selection and constitution as a separate body of the most eminent active revolutionaries, as distinct from the unorganized, though revolutionary, mass around them; on the other, severe discipline in whose name the other leaders of the Party intervene directly and resolutely in all the affairs of the Party's local organizations.[12]

Democratic centralism (the first example of the institutionalized lie) means the opposite of democracy, the absolute power of the Central Committee over the party as a whole.

It was a structure adapted to clandestine action but conceived, also, as a continuing prerequisite of effective action. The critique formulated by Trotsky at that time—that the Central Committee takes the place of the party, the Politburo of the Central Committee and, in the last analysis, the secretary-general of the Politburo—found shattering and tragic confirmation in reality. By a chain of serial delegation, the first link was the substitution of party for proletariat in the name of the Marxism of the intellectuals, and the final link was the substitution of one man for the party. In those days, the thesis made no stir: although German social democracy respected a democratic constitution, Kautsky himself, the leading thinker of the Second International, assigned intellectuals a prominent role vis-à-vis the workers and the trade unions.

Lenin made a second contribution to the body of belief known as Marxism-Leninism in the short book called *Imperialism, the Final Stage of Capitalism,* written at the start of World War I. Like other theorists of the Second International, he had referred, long before 1914, to colonial exploitation by the capitalist countries as a way of explaining history's apparent contradiction. He denied the rising standards of living in the capitalist countries and introduced the notion of a working-class aristocracy which took the bourgeoisie's thirty pieces of silver—in other words, relatively higher wages—as the price of its

---

12. Rosa Luxemburg in *Iskra,* July 10, 1904, quoted by K. Papaioannou in the anthology *Marx et les Marxistes* (Paris: Flammarion, 1972), pp. 269–71.

own betrayal (meaning the rejection of the class struggle in favor of class collaboration). According to him, it was this that explained revisionism, the inclination of some social democrats to rely on economic progress and piecemeal reforms to improve the life of the proletariat without a break with capitalism. The attitude of the different socialist parties at the moment when the European war broke out caused him more indignation than surprise: the whole of the Second International was treasonous, not just the revisionists alone. He and his followers became, finally, the sole embodiment of the world proletariat and of socialism.

Marx himself was not unaware of the tendency of capitalist societies toward external expansion; he saw that the capitalist mode of production—the most advanced mode—would overthrow traditional societies and cover the entire globe. Nor did he at all regret the expansion of capitalism and of Europe hand in hand: while he denounced its cruelties, he also discerned the promise inherent in the "looting" of the planet by the colonialists. In India, the British would break up the remnants of an Asiatic mode of production, the age-old organization of the villages under the arbitrary power of an inefficient and predatory bureaucracy. Marx, too, has an occasional tendency not to distinguish between the *concept of capitalism*—an economic system defined by private ownership of the means of production and by commercial exchange—and the *concrete historical entity* constituted by those countries in which a system of this order is more or less imperfectly realized.

On the other hand, he did not systematically account for the causes of European wars in terms of economic rivalries between countries but usually explained them, following the ordinary method of historians, in terms of clashes of national interest and the ambitions of great powers. He was exceptionally strong in his condemnation of the imperialism—in the commonplace sense of the urge for conquest or for territorial expansion—of tsarist Russia.[13]

In his judgments of the wars of the nineteenth century, Marx took sides according to 1) the type of domestic system maintained by the states concerned, 2) the foreseeable consequences of the victory of one side or the other, and 3) the accountability of the belligerents—he sided with Prussia in 1870 until the fall of the empire, and then with France once it had turned republican. Lenin started with the simple assumption that Marx's subtle analyses belonged to a bygone era: Marx

---

13. See also Miklos Molnar's book, *Marx, Engels et la politique internationale* (Paris: Gallimard, 1975).

was compelled to choose from *among* various imperialisms, whereas he himself was at liberty to choose *against all* imperialisms—the socialist movement, newly come to power being their successor and grave digger. Lenin counted on a revolution which would emerge from war itself and which he would lead. The Bolshevik party would deal with the behavior of the working masses—misled by traitors or other surviving groups—by proclaiming the truth of history to them.

Lenin could have interpreted the war of 1914 as Marx had interpreted the war of 1870. The European states had warred among themselves for centuries before they acquired capitalist economies, as Lenin knew quite well. But the authors R. Hilferding and, in particular, J. A. Hobson provided him with another possible way to interpret the war: to demonstrate not only that the French, British, and Germans who had carved up Africa among themselves all deserved to be called *imperialists* (as was undoubtedly the case), but that they were destroying each other in an unforgivable struggle *because of their imperialism*. The establishing of a link between the monopolistic structure of the capitalist economy, the role of the banks, and the concentration of capital on the one hand and colonial conquests on the other, and then decreeing that the competing expansionism of national capitalistic systems did not allow any friendly division was all it would require.

He decreed that the war was imperialistic on both sides, a diagnosis he supported by referring to Clausewitz's classic description of war as the "continuation of state policy by other means." All the states involved had carried on imperialist policies before 1914; the war through which they had been pursuing their policies had not changed in nature: it remained imperialistic. Socialists who did not use all possible means, each in his own country, to oppose imperialism (and thus also the war) were betraying their faith and their earlier commitments.

The theory of imperialism accomplished several objectives: it enabled Lenin to explain the rising living standards of the working aristocracy without casting doubt on the Marxist interpretation of the development of capitalism; it placed wars within the historical framework of capitalism; it accounted for working-class revisionism and the social democratic betrayal; it made plausible the eventuality of revolution even in Russia, in spite of Russia's lagging so far behind the more advanced capitalist areas. The theory had everything—it lacked only truth.

It can be said therefore that Lenin awaited and expected a worldwide revolution, from 1914 on, with no concern for the specific conditions prevailing in this or that given country. Before 1914, loyal to the historical schema of Engels, he had discounted any hypothesis of a socialist revolution in tsarist Russia or of permanent revolution. It was events—World War I—that led him to renew his historic vision and to judge possible and necessary—*because of the combination of world events*—what had seemed to him in the Russian context incompatible with Marxism and, therefore, impossible.

Before 1914, Lenin's Marxism did not differ visibly from the Marxism of the Second International. Or, at any rate, the book that revealed the underlying originality of Leninism, *Materialism and Empiriocriticism*, had not been read with attention—nor did it deserve to be, except for documentary purposes. In one sense, Lenin confined himself to pursuing the thinking of Friedrich Engels in *Anti-Dühring*. The economic interpretation of history as outlined, without systematic interpretation, in the writings of Marx, becomes inseparable from a metaphysical materialism. Man and human societies form part of natural reality and are subject to its laws, as are all inorganic and organic phenomena. Lenin presents Engels's metaphysical system by referring to the alternative of realism (or materialism) and idealism. External reality exists, it is primary in relation to awareness or thought; knowledge *reflects* this reality and, by its progress, comes closer and closer to the truth, to a faithful reproduction of reality.

No one attached any special importance to Lenin's philosophy, to his junction of objective laws and dialectics—which resulted in the dialectical laws of development by mutation, the transformation from quantity to quality, and the negation of the negation. In retrospect, what is striking when one rereads *Materialism and Empiriocriticism* is the presence, throughout, of the thesis that *any metaphysical deviation implies political deviation*.

German social democracy, although deeply inspired by Marx's atheism, imposed no philosophical orthodoxy; it tolerated Kantians, Hegelians, positivists. Before he came to power, Lenin was unable to impose orthodoxy, but he excommunicated deviationists with the pen before expelling them if the opportunity presented itself. His system of thought established in advance the system of total discipline he later practiced.

The fourth book mentioned above, *The State and Revolution*, makes no original contribution to the thinking of Marx himself, but it combines realism and utopianism in a style made all the more striking by Lenin's apparent unawareness of the contradiction. The subject is: the conception of the state guiding the Bolshevik party's plan of action in July 1917, some months before its victory.

Lenin comments on Marx's letter to Weydemeyer of March 3, 1852.[14] Marx borrowed the thesis of the class struggle from the bourgeois historians, but he himself showed that it is linked only to certain phases of the historical development of production, that it leads necessarily to the dictatorship of the proletariat, and that this in turn leads to the abolition of all classes and to a classless society. The proletariat wants to seize the state, but only in order to destroy it:

> ... the next attempt of the French revolution will be no longer, as before, to transfer the bureaucratic-military machine from one to another, but to *smash* it. ... And this is what our heroic Party comrades in Paris are attempting.[15]

Thus, two ideas are brought together: the substitution of the dictatorship of the proletariat for the dictatorship of the bourgeoisie; and the commencement of the dismantling of the state's administrative, military, and police machinery with a view toward hastening its withering away and eventual extinction. By what ideological trick can the dictatorship of the proletariat simultaneously constitute the first phase of the withering away of the state? In a primary sense, this "hocus-pocus" is a built-in part of the definition of the state, considered as an instrument utilized by the ruling class to preserve its own power and to exploit the masses. Political or parliamentary democracy makes no essential difference in the application of the trick.

> Democracy is a *state* which recognizes the subordination of the minority to the majority, i.e., an organization for the systematic use of *force* by one class against another, by one section of the population against another.[16]

The dictatorship of the proletariat would also constitute a kind of force, but the fact that this force would be exercised by the vast majority against the tiny exploiting minority would already represent a "democratic step forward."

Lenin offers the Paris Commune as the model of a state in transition, with the standing army replaced by the people under arms, all officials elected, subject to recall, and never paid more than workmen's wages. He quotes from Marx's *The Civil War in France*:

14. Lenin, *The State and Revolution: The Marxist Theory of the State and the Tasks of the Proletariat in the Revolution,* written in 1917, (Moscow: Progress Publishers, 1977), pp. 34–35.
15. Letter to Kugelmann, April 12, 1871.
16. Lenin, *The State and Revolution,* p. 79.

> The judicial functionaries lost that sham indepen-
> dence . . . ; they were thenceforward to be elective, re-
> sponsible, and revocable.[17]

These are some of the reforms which Lenin says would alter the nature
of the state created by the dictatorship of the proletariat, and would
reveal its transitory character.

Looking beyond this mutation, Lenin proceeds to offer a truly utopian account of the state apparatus of the future:

> Capitalist culture has created large-scale production, facto-
> ries, railways, the postal service, telephones, etc., and *on
> this basis* the great majority of the functions of the old
> "state power" have become so simplified and can be re-
> duced to such exceedingly simple operations of registra-
> tion, filing and checking that they can be easily performed
> by every literate person. . . .[18]

Incredible as the statement may seem, Lenin really believed that capitalism would bequeath to the proletariat an economy comparable
with a public service, and that the armed proletariat would take this
over by using the few necessary experts, since the jobs of the vast
majority of officials would have been so simplified that anyone could
do them. He had given no greater consideration than did Marx himself
to the radical difference between managing a business and managing
an entire economy.

> *All* citizens become employees and workers of a *single*
> country-wide State "syndicate." All that is required is that
> they should work equally, do their proper share of work,
> and get equal pay.[19]

In this utopia, memories of Saint-Simon (the administration of
things replacing the government of people) mingle with the Jacobin
myth (the people in arms under the guidance of its vanguard) and the
radical misappreciation of the economy and the state. Dialectical
sleight of hand enables the ruthless dictatorship of the proletariat to be
announced as preceding the withering away of the state itself, by
switching the pros and cons from extreme dictatorship against a tiny

17. Ibid., p. 42.
18. Ibid., p. 44.
19. Ibid., p. 96.

minority to total freedom for everyone. The world is still waiting for the realization of that switch.

Of course, Lenin also takes up the distinction between the two phases which are to succeed the revolution: the phase of socialism, during which everyone will receive a reward equal in value to the amount of labor produced (in the form of a noncirculating certificate), and then the phase of communism, when everyone will receive a share of the social revenue proportional to each person's needs. Reading *The State and Revolution* and recalling the prophecy of socialism and communism after the proletarian revolution, one cannot doubt that the Bolsheviks really were convinced that eliminating private ownership of the means of production, along with the market—and thus abolishing surplus value and exploitation—would be of incomparable benefit to mankind.

Here again, history—the supreme tribunal, according to the Marxists themselves has given its verdict. Just as the development of capitalism before 1914 had refuted the *schema of historical development,* so the experience not only of the Soviet Union but of all the socialist economies has refuted the Marxist-Leninist utopia.

We can leave the economists to argue over the merits of Marxist conceptualization—the distinction between surplus value and profit, and the origin of profit only in living labor (variable capital). What reality makes crystal-clear is that the meaning currently assigned to the theory of surplus value, namely, that of an immense reserve of wealth "stolen" from the workers and available immediately after the revolution, does not hold up to experience any more than it does to reason.

After the 1917 Revolution: The Present Situation

What is left of those two pseudoscientific myths: Marxism (the destruction of capitalism by its internal contradictions) and Marxism-Leninism (the transfiguration of society—or even *la condition humaine*—by the abolishment of private ownership of the means of production)? At the risk of inciting the irony of Parisian Marxists, why not quote here the passage from Solzhenitsyn's *Letter to Soviet Leaders* in which he shows the bankruptcy of Marxism (or of Marxism-Leninism)—a "decrepit" and "hopelessly antiquated" doctrine which

... even during its best decades ... was totally mistaken in its predictions and was never a science. . . .[20]

20. This and the following excerpts are from Alexander Solzhenitsyn, *Letter to Soviet Leaders* (London: Index on Censorship/Fontana, 1974), pp. 42–43.

> [Ideology] was mistaken when it forecast that the pro-
> letariat would be endlessly oppressed and would never
> achieve anything in a bourgeois democracy—if only we
> could shower people with as much food, clothing and lei-
> sure as they have gained under capitalism!

It obviously cannot be argued, except absurdly, that the working class
did not gain benefit from the economic development in capitalist
societies.

> [Ideology] missed the point when it asserted that the
> prosperity of the European countries depended on their
> colonies—it was only after they had shaken the colonies
> off that they began to accomplish their "economic mir-
> acles."

There again, contrary to all sophistry and false subtlety, Solzhenitsyn
is right. The thesis put forth by the Marxists, particularly by Lenin,
that the rise in living standards of the upper level of the proletariat
came as a result of exploitation of colonies is untenable when compared, for example, with the experience of a country such as the
Netherlands, which drew considerable revenues from Indonesia and
which nonetheless has succeeded in raising the living standards of its
population after the loss of its empire.

> [Ideology] was mistaken through and through in its pre-
> diction that socialists could only ever come to power by an
> armed uprising.

Marx did not say this explicitly, and it may be that he did not always
think it. All the same, the Marxist-Leninists the author has in mind
protect their dogmatism by decreeing that the socialist parties which
have come to power peacefully have "betrayed socialism" and "re-
formed capitalism without destroying it." Their messianism causes
them to make that judgment: if it is postulated that the transition to
socialism requires a violent break, it follows that, without such a rupture, the socialists in power have not fulfilled the socialist mission.

> [Ideology] miscalculated in thinking that the first upris-
> ings would take place in the advanced industrial coun-
> tries—quite the reverse. And the picture of how the whole
> world would rapidly be overtaken by revolutions. . . ?

A classical argument, impossible to refute by what I have called
Marx's *schema of historical development*. Certainly it is possible to

find texts by Marx or Engels stating that other countries will not re-produce the English experience as such, or envisaging revolution else-where than in the most industrially advanced countries. The fact remains that in neither Great Britain nor the United States is the en-dogenous development of capitalism leading toward révolution. Yet capitalism's self-destruction as "the victim of its own contradictions" was one of Marx's central theses, one which his disciples always held onto until events proved it wrong.

> And the picture of how . . . states would soon wither away was sheer delusion, sheer ignorance of human nature. And as for wars being characteristic of capitalism alone and coming to an end when capitalism did—we have already witnessed the longest war of the twentieth century so far, and it was not capitalism that rejected negotiations and a truce for fifteen to twenty years; and God forbid that we should witness the bloodiest and most brutal of all mankind's wars—a war between two communist super-powers. Then there was nationalism, which this theory also buried in 1848 as a "survival"—but find a stronger force in the world today!

This text contains a debatable proposition: ought the fifteen or twenty years of Cold War to be referred to as war? Was it only the Soviet Union that refused negotiations and a truce? For the rest, socialism did not curb nationalism, but always reinforced it. The rivalry between the Soviet Union and People's China has proven, if proof be required, that inter-state conflicts which existed *before* capitalism did, will continue to endure after capitalism's demise.

The Marxism of Marx and Engels ceased, after 1914, to fulfill its function as the ideology of the Second International and the various socialist movements. After 1917 it became the justification of "the Soviet experience." Its subsequent destiny was determined, all in all, by the Marxist-Leninist faith and by a society wanting to conform to that faith. There exists a country, according to the sacred phrase, where capitalism has disappeared because the proletariat—through the medium of the Communist party—has taken over the state and its means of production.

Between the two world wars, the exponents of Marxist ideology fell into two camps: the Bolsheviks and all those who adhered to the Third International, and the socialists or social democrats who refused to see in the Soviet Union the fulfillment of the prophecy. The debate be-tween Lenin and Karl Kautsky, on looking back, is symbolically significant to this day. It was Kautsky who pointed out the disparity between the labor movement and the socialist vision; it was also he who conferred on the intellectuals the task of bringing socialist doctrine to the proletariat and imparting to it the sense of historic mission. On the other hand, German social democracy retained democratic procedures within the party, and it called for democratization of the institutions of Prussia and of Wilhelmine Germany.

The period which opened in 1929 was at the same time that of the Great Depression, the Great Purge, and the Great Temptation. In the West, millions were unemployed, as everybody knew; in the East, millions of *kulaks* were being deported or exterminated during the years of agricultural collectivization, as no one knew—or wanted to know. Moscow triumphantly published bulletins of victory, of unrivalled growth-rates; in the West, even after recovery of the economy, production was not going at full capacity. In 1933, Hitler moved into the Chancellery and, in the face of liberalism and socialism, he established the Third Reich, the Nazi hierarchy, and Aryan racial supremacy. He brought the universities and the press to heel and connected the state with a single party. "Fascism" as a political genre and "National Socialism" as a particular example came to represent absolute evil in the eyes of the Left (which grew to include liberals and moderates).

The Great Purge—the liquidation of the Leninist Old Guard after what were witchcraft trials, and the imprisonment of millions of Soviet citizens, deported or liquidated—all this the majority of the Western intelligentsia refused to see and, sometimes, even when seeing it, refused to mention. Hitler gave Stalin an all-absolving excuse. To question the guilt of Zinoviev or Bukharin was to accuse Stalin, thus to act in the same way as Hitler, thus to become his "objective ally," and thus to act as an "agent" of the Gestapo. Out of the Great Depression there came *la grande tentation*—the temptation of the Soviet Union as model and promise. And only the Big Lie, which concealed the Soviet archipelago of concentration camps, made the Great Temptation possible.

The socialist parties, all of them more or less compromised in the management of capitalist society in time of crisis, no longer held out any transcendent hope. Even if they still kept references to "socialization of the means of production" and to the "dictatorship of the proletariat" in their statutes, they acted in accordance with Eduard Bernstein's revisionism, inasmuch as they were integrated in capitalist society as well as in representative democracy. Crisis was affecting both of these institutions: the democratic system lacked majority government, the capitalist system was faced with hundreds of thousands of unemployed. Most of those who still called themselves "Marxists" without going over to Marxism-Leninism were not unaware of some of the features of Soviet despotism and, if they wanted to base their actions on history, they could no longer seem to find a place for themselves.

The third epoch of Marxist ideology started after 1945 and, for the first time, it was no longer Germany but France that became its center and home. In Paris, philosophers—and first among them Jean-Paul Sartre—declared themselves Marxists, but without endorsing the dogmatism (which should more properly be called Soviet than Marxist-Leninist).

During the Cold War years, from 1946 until Nikita Khrushchev's speech in 1956, the historical circumstances were radically different from those previous to 1939. The German *Reich* no longer existed, the British empire was tottering. When the fighting ended, the division of the Old Continent was being drawn on the map. By the summer of 1945, the expression "Iron Curtain" was coming into common usage. The Soviet Union was not so much *une expérience socialiste*, be it dreadful or glorious; rather it was the Red Army, bringing with it occupation régimes together with revolutions sanctioned by the authority of the state.

A good many intellectuals who had belonged to the Communist party or had worked with it in the struggle against fascism, aligned themselves now with the opposite camp. The socialists of the old tradition, and even the liberals, had detested fascism more than communism, and had supported, if not applauded, the Popular Front. With fascism eliminated and conservatism weakened, they found themselves willy-nilly in the anti-Communist coalition. It was a coalition which, embracing as it did all non-Communists, from the socialists to the Right (only ex-Fascists were excluded, out of hostility), was now best defined by its hostility toward Marxism-Leninism and in particular toward its ideological claim of being the exclusive guardian of the Absolute Truth. Hence the spread of the concept of *pluralism:* acceptance of *several* parties and of *rival* doctrines became the hallmark of liberal Europe. Yet this identification of pluralism with liberalism is not free of risk. Should the same rights be granted to parties who do not abide by the rules of the game as to constitutional parties? What a swindle to fall for, if the loss of one battle meant losing the war.

We all know now—and the Communists themselves do not deny it—that in the Soviet Union the years 1945–53 were no less stern and cruel than the years of Collectivization and of the Great Purge. The concentration camps were filled with civilians and prisoners, handed over to the Soviet authorities by the Allies. Never, except in the days of the Great Purge, was Stalinist terror so omnipresent, never did it stretch out so far, nor strike with more apparent irrationality. The state, appointing itself as the judge of truth in biology, excommunicated genetics. In the satellite countries, resistance fighters with democratic convictions soon were returned to the camps they had just left.

Yet, in those days, Communists and their fellow travelers were passionately defending the "achievements of the first socialist revolution in history." If one were to believe them, there was not a single concentration camp, but only camps for "reeducation through labor." Maurice Thorez proclaimed that the French people would never fight against the Red Army. Political-ideological debate tended to come down to a duel between the Communists, flanked by their fellow travelers, and the rest, which included the socialists. The elimination of the socialist parties in the countries of Eastern Europe fueled the anticommunism of socialists of the Jean Jaurès and Léon Blum persuasions.

Khrushchev's Secret Speech put an end to this delirium. No question now of a socialist paradise: millions of innocent people had died in the camps, and millions of innocent people had confessed under torture to crimes they had not committed. Collective property, planning, economic power, the Red Army—these remained. But what remained of the essential link, according to Marxism or Marxism-Leninism, between the social restructuring of the economy and the communist prophecy? Was it the proletariat that wielded power, or was it the party? If the proletariat, then how could it tyrannize itself, dispatch millions of its own to the camps? When had the "deviation" begun? With Lenin? With Stalin? What was the Marxist explanation for the "cult of personality"?

The events of 1956—Khrushchev's speech, the Hungarian Uprising—caused the desertion of a section of the intelligentsia and weakened the Western Communists' unconditional devotion to the Soviet Union. They also had the effect of restoring some vitality to Communist parties, by provoking them to criticize themselves and compelling them to stop blindly repeating the orders from Moscow. The Soviet Union after Stalin—under Khrushchev and, after him, Brezhnev—appeared more and more "normalized" (i.e., authoritarian and bureaucratic), and minus its revolutionary aura. The specter of the Red Army had taken over from the specter of communism.

Twenty-three years later, where do we stand? One is tempted to answer, Back where we started. The revelation of the crimes of Stalinism has made no lasting impression on the *apparatchiks* in the Soviet Union, nor even on bureaucrats beyond the Russian borders. Quite a few of them, especially in the USSR, had little to learn from what Khrushchev made public. The condemnation of Stalinism by the Marxist-Leninists remains partial and equivocal. Khrushchev regretted the excessive repression which had *accompanied* collectivization, not collectivization itself. He blamed Stalin for having turned terrorist methods against the party; he did not criticize their use against other elements and classes.

At the same time, the condemnation of Stalinism favored the diffusion of divers brands of Marxism (which I call the Marxist Vulgate). With a good conscience, intellectuals and activists again took up Marx's messianism and one or the other of his arguments, at the same time dissociating themselves from the Soviet experience. And, swearing by all they hold sacred that their own Marxism has nothing to do with the one which Solzhenitsyn attacks, they continue to "Marxify" the universities, the social sciences, and the political and literary magazines—naively convinced that *their* revolution will not end in the same despotism, too eagerly bent on destroying capitalist-liberal society to ask themselves what society they would build on the ruins.

In the Soviet Union, Marxism (Marxism-Leninism) is still the official ideology of a bureaucratic despotism of totalitarian character. In the West, various kinds of (more or less imaginary) Marxism abound, building up prejudices in favor of state planning and collective ownership of property, and condemning the "imperialism" of a West which no longer has any colonies.

6

Tocqueville and Marx

Tocqueville's vocabulary is not unambiguous and the two words he is most apt to use are neither rigorously defined nor always taken in the same sense. His thought, however, seems to me easily grasped.

In the majority of cases, Tocqueville uses the term democracy to signify a *state of society* and not a *form of government*. Democracy is opposed to aristocracy. The Ancien Régime was founded on the inequality of social conditions, on a nobility rooted in the soil; all true aristocracy is ultimately territorial because only the ownership of land assures the necessary continuity. It is true that in *Democracy in America* (vol. II, 2, chap. XX), Tocqueville conjures up an aristocracy that might arise out of industry: "Thus, as the bulk of the nation turns to democracy, the particular class that is engaged in industry becomes more aristocratic. Men become more and more similar in the one and different in the other, and inequality increases in the little society in proportion to its decrease in the larger one." But if it is true that, in the world of industry, a few very rich men are set against a very wretched multitude, Tocqueville scarcely believed that very rich men were capable of forming a true aristocracy or that the contrasts visible in the small manufacturing classes were the sign or symbol of what society as a whole would become. There are rich men, he wrote, but the class of rich men does not exist,

> for these rich men have no common spirit or aims, no common traditions or hopes. There are thus individual members but no body of membership. . . . Not only are the rich

From *Politics and History: Selected Essays by Raymond Aron*, edited and translated by Miriam Bernheim Conant, pp. 139–65. © 1978 by The Free Press. Reprinted with permission of The Free Press, a Division of Macmillan, Inc. Originally presented as one of the 1963 Jefferson Lectures at the University of California—Berkeley.

> not solidly united among themselves, but one can say that
> there is no real link between the poor and the rich. . . . The
> manufacturer asks nothing of the worker but his labor, and
> the worker expects nothing from him but his wages. . . .
> The territorial aristocracy of past centuries was committed
> by law, or felt the obligation through tradition, to come to
> the rescue of its servants and alleviate their misery. . . . Be-
> tween the worker and the master there are frequent rela-
> tions but no true association. I believe that, all things
> considered, the manufacturing aristocracy that we see ris-
> ing before our eyes is one of the harshest that has ever ap-
> peared on earth; but it is at the same time one of the most
> restricted and least dangerous.

Democracy, as it is usually conceived by Tocqueville, is thus essentially a negation of aristocracy, the disappearance of privileged orders,
the elimination of distinctions between estates, and, little by little, a
tendency toward economic equality, a uniformity in ways of living.
The master-servant relationship disappears along with the aristocracy,
as does the authority to command combined with an obligation to
protect those who obey. Power and wealth tend to become dissoci-
ated. Work becomes a normal, honorable activity for each and all.
Aristocracies disdain profit motivated work. In democratic societies
the two ideas of work and gain are visibly united. Servants and the
president both receive a salary. "He is paid to command as they are to
serve."

If this is the most usual, as well as the most obvious, meaning that
the term democracy takes on in Tocqueville, he is nevertheless conscious of the distance between the definition of democracy as a *state of
society* and the traditional definition of democracy as a *type of regime.*
Monarchy, aristocracy, democracy—according to the age-old classification, do they not mean the sovereignty of one, a few, and all? A text,
discovered in Tocqueville's papers and published by J. P. Mayer in the
second volume of *L'Ancien Régime et la Révolution,* reveals how hesi-
tant Tocqueville was to break the link between the *social* and the *political* definition of democracy.

> It will be claimed that a country governed by an absolute
> prince is a democracy because he will govern through laws
> and amid institutions that are favorable to the condition of
> the people. His government will be a democratic govern-
> ment. He will form a democratic monarchy. Now the

words democracy, monarchy, democratic government can mean only one thing according to the real meaning of the words: a government in which the people play a more or less significant role. Its meaning is intimately linked to the idea of political freedom. To give the title of democratic government to a government in which there is no political freedom is a palpable absurdity in terms of the natural meaning of the words. What has brought about the adoption of false or in any case obscure expressions is: (1) the wish to provide the multitude with illusions, the words democratic government having always enjoyed a certain success with it; (2) the genuine difficulty of finding a word to express an idea as complex as the following: an absolute government, in which the people have no part in running affairs but in which the upper classes enjoy no privileges and laws are drawn up in such a way as to favor as much as possible the people's well-being.[1]

This fragment appears in the chapter that Tocqueville had planned to devote to the work of the Constituent Assembly. And, he writes, "I never examine the system of laws of the Constituent Assembly without finding the twin characteristics of *liberalism* and *democracy,* which brings me back bitterly to the present." At the time he wrote these lines, he was self-exiled from French officialdom because of the coup d'état by which Louis Napoleon restored the empire. An imperial regime is neither aristocratic nor democratic. It is a despotism superimposed on a society with democratic tendencies. Ernest Renan as well, after the defeat of 1870, was to raise the issue of democracy or of a false conception of democracy. As against the abuse of the word democracy by spokesmen of a despotic regime, Tocqueville recalls that the society to which the Constituent Assembly aspired would have been free as well as democratic, "not a military society but a civilian one." The chapter entitled "Les Idées de 1789," on the Constituent Assembly, exalts "the soundness of its general views, the true grandeur of its purposes, the generosity, the loftiness of its sentiments, *the admirable union of a taste for freedom and for equality that it revealed.*" Thus, the fragment itself is integrated into Tocqueville's general scheme of things.

In any case, yesterday's aristocracy is condemned and, even in a despotic regime, laws could be made in such a way as to favor as much

---

1. *Oeuvres complètes,* vol. II, 2, p. 199; hereafter cited O.C.

as possible the well-being of the people. But if modern societies, even despotic ones, preserve certain democratic traits, the profound inspiration of the French Revolution as well as the American is to join *democracy* and *liberalism, equality* and *freedom*.

But what meaning does Tocqueville give to the word freedom, a word so widely used and so equivocal, since in the name of freedom men in every period have claimed powers they feel unjustly deprived of and have protested against real oppression? The clearest definition of freedom that Tocqueville provides can be found, it seems to me, in his essay "L'Etat social et politique de la France," published in 1836.

> According to the modern notion, the democratic notion, and I dare say the correct notion of freedom, it is assumed that each man has received from nature the gifts necessary to conduct his affairs and carries at birth an equal and indefeasible right to live independently from his peers in everything that relates only to himself and to regulate his own destiny as he sees fit.[2]

Thus defined, freedom is both negative and undetermined—negative in the sense that it is expressed through independence, the choice by each of his own destiny; undetermined in the sense that it remains to be seen how far that which "relates only to himself" goes for each. This freedom with relation to others—what, in English, is called *freedom* from—also has, according to other texts, a possible content: it is *freedom in view of* or *freedom to*. Independence-freedom, what Montesquieu would have called security or absence of the arbitrary, can be genuinely realized only in properly political freedom, that is, participation by the citizen in the administration of local affairs and the care of public matters. Now, political freedom, which despotism, even when it claims to be democratic, eliminates, is in Tocqueville's eyes the supreme value. This passionate attachment to political freedom can certainly be seen as personally motivated. But he himself gives a properly sociological justification to the value he attaches to political freedom, specifically in democratic societies.

In democratic societies,

> the desire to become rich at any cost, the taste for business, the love of profit, the quest for well-being and material joys are thus the most common passions. These passions easily spread to all classes, penetrate into those very ones that

2. O.C., vol. II, 1, p. 62.

had hitherto been most inhospitable to them, and would soon enervate and degrade the whole nation if nothing were to stand in their way. Now it is of the essence of despotism to encourage and extend them.

And, a little further, in this same preface to *L'Ancien Régime et la Révolution,* he writes again:

> Only freedom is capable of tearing them away from the cult of money and the petty daily cares of their personal affairs to make them aware at all times of the nation above and beside them; it alone replaces from time to time the love of comfort with higher and more energetic passions, gives ambition greater goals than the acquisition of wealth, and creates the light that makes it possible to perceive and judge the vices and virtues of men.

And finally:

> I am not afraid to state that the common level of hearts and minds will never cease to degenerate as long as equality and despotism are joined in them.

Though Tocqueville speaks of freedom in the singular, and not freedoms in the manner of the counterrevolutionaries, he clearly enumerates, here and there, the various aspects of freedom: "the ability of a nation to govern itself, the guarantees of the law, freedom of thought, speech, and writing"—in other words, intellectual and personal freedoms, the protection the law provides against the arbitrary, and finally the participation of citizens, through their elected representatives, in public life. It is the sum total of these freedoms that constitutes, in his eyes, *freedom,* alone capable of raising egalitarian societies, mainly concerned with material well-being, to greatness.

In this passion for freedom, it is not only the sociologist who is speaking, it is also the man, and if I may say so, the aristocrat, the descendant of a great family. In the essay "L'Etat social et politique de la France avant et depuis 1789," from which we took his definition of the modern notion of freedom, Tocqueville also analyzes the aristocratic notion of freedom:

> One can see in it the use of a common right or enjoyment of a privilege. To seek to be free in one's actions or in some of one's actions not because all men have a general right to

independence but because one possesses in oneself a particular right to remain independent, such was the manner in
which freedom was understood in the Middle Ages and the
way in which it has nearly always been understood in aristocratic societies. . . . This aristocratic notion of freedom
produces in those who have inherited it an exalted opinion
of their individual value, a passionate taste for independence. It gives to selfishness a singular power and energy.
Held by individuals, it has often led men to the most extraordinary actions; adopted by a whole nation, it has created the greatest peoples that have ever existed. The
Romans believed that they alone of the whole human race
had the right to enjoy independence, and it was much less
from nature than from Rome that they believed they derived the right to be free.[3]

This freedom, privilege of the aristocracy, belongs to an irretrieva-
ble past, and in 1836 Tocqueville used the word *juste* for the modern
notion of freedom—the rights of all. In 1856, twenty years later, without going back on his historic judgment, he permitted the nostalgia for
aristocratic freedom that survived in his soul to appear[4] and in addition revealed the link, in his very person, between the aristocratic tradition and a passionate attachment to democratic freedom.

Nearly all the guarantees against abuses of power that we
possessed during the thirty-seven years of representative
government are highly prized by [the aristocracy]. One
feels, in reading its *cahiers*, amid its prejudices and failings,
the spirit and a few of the great qualities of the aristocracy.
It is forever to be regretted that instead of bending this
nobility to the service of the law, it was lopped off and
uprooted. By this action the nation was deprived of a necessary part of its substance and a wound was inflicted on
freedom that will never be healed.

This text should not be interpreted as an admission of fidelity to his
class, inadvertently made by the sociologist of democracy. It is the
sociologist who adds to independence-freedom and participation-freedom a third term, more difficult to define in depth, perhaps, but still

---

3. O.C., vol. II, 1, p. 62.
4. In chapter XI of Book II of *L'Ancien Régime et la Révolution*, entitled "De l'es-
pèce de liberté qui se rencontrait sous l'ancien régime et de son influence sur la Révolution," O.C., vol. II, 1.

more indispensable to the precise understanding of freedom: the nature of the relations between he who commands and he who obeys.

> However subservient the men of the Ancien Régime were to the will of the king, there was a sort of obedience that was unknown to them: they did not know what it was to submit to an illegitimate and contested power, one scarcely honored, often despised, but accepted because it is useful or can inflict harm. This degrading form of servitude was always unknown to them.

And a little later:

> For them, the worst evil of obedience was constraint; for us, this is the least. The worst is the servile feeling that creates obedience.

One can speculate, reading this text, about the foundation of freedom in America, where society was so to speak spontaneously democratic. In fact, there is no contradiction. The privilege-freedom known to the Ancien Régime gave rise to "profound audacious geniuses," but it was in itself "unregulated and unhealthy, it prepared the French to topple despotism, but it made them less capable than any other people, perhaps, to form in its place the free and peaceful empire of laws." On the contrary, in America, free institutions were born with society itself and had as a foundation not the privileged and arrogant spirit of the aristocracy, but a religious spirit. Accepting the laws, the citizen obeys a power he respects, whoever may hold it temporarily. If he opportunistically obeys an illegitimate regime, the citizen is degraded into a subject. Or again, as we would say today, he is a consumer, anxious about his well-being, not a citizen, concerned about and responsible for public affairs.

Between the obedience of the aristocrat to a sovereign he venerates and the obedience of the citizen to laws he has helped make, the gap is enormous. Each of these two kinds of obedience characterizes a society. But both are compatible with freedom because they are consistent with recognized legitimacy. Obedience is servitude when power is illegitimate and despised and has no other principle,[5] as Montesquieu would have said, than fear or conformity.

Thus emerges the theory of liberal democracy, in many respects

---

5. In Montesquieu's sense, that is to say, the sentiment by which a particular regime is able to prosper.

different from the ancient republic that Montesquieu had taken as a model of democracy. Work, commerce, industry, the desire for profit and well-being, and the pursuit of happiness are thus no longer in contradiction with the principle of democracy.

> The Americans are not a virtuous people, and yet they are free. This does not prove absolutely that virtue, as Montesquieu believed, is not essential to the existence of the republic. Montesquieu's idea must not be construed narrowly. What this great man meant is that republics could continue only by society acting upon itself. What he meant by virtue is the moral power that each individual exercises upon himself and that prevents him from violating the rights of others. When the triumph of a man over temptations is the result of the weakness of the temptation and calculated self-interest, it does not constitute virtue in the eyes of the moralist; but it enters into the idea of Montesquieu, who was speaking of the effect much more than of the cause. In America, it is not virtue that is great, but temptation that is small, and this comes to the same thing. It is not altruism that is great, it is self-interest that is well understood, and this again comes nearly to the same thing. Montesquieu was thus right though he was speaking of ancient virtue, and what he says of the Greeks and Romans applies to the Americans.[6]

Perhaps a few passages, borrowed from the second part of *Democracy,* will serve as a useful commentary on this analysis of American virtue:

> The passion for material well-being is essentially a middle-class passion and grows and spreads with this class; it becomes preponderant with it. It is from there that it enters the upper reaches of society and descends to the mass of the people.[7]

And, in the following chapter, the thought is completed:

> This particular taste that men of democratic times have for material joys is not naturally opposed to order; on the con-

---

6. This fragment, found in Tocqueville's notes, was published by J. P. Mayer in the *Nouvelle Revue française* of April 1, 1959, and in the *Revue internationale de philosophie* (1959), number 49.

7. O.C., vol. I, 2, part 1, chap. X, p. 135.

trary, it often needs order to be gratified. Neither is it an enemy of regular habits since good habits are useful to public tranquility and encourage industry. Often it even comes to be combined with a kind of religious morality. One wants to be as well off as possible in this world, without renouncing one's chances in the other.[8]

This middle-class society, opulent, democratic in spite or because of a universal concern for work and well-being, inspired mixed feelings in the descendant of the old nobility. But he saw in it the inevitable future, and it remained in his eyes worthy of respect as long as it respected freedom, which was its origin, its foundation, its very soul, not

> the sort of corrupted freedom whose use is common to animals and man and that consists in doing whatever one pleases. This freedom is the enemy of all authority; it cannot accept any rules; with it we become inferior to ourselves; it is the enemy of truth and peace; and God felt it necessary to rise against it! But there is a civic and moral freedom that finds its strength in unity and that the mission of power itself is to protect: it is the freedom to do without fear everything that is right and good.[9]

Logically, this definition is so to speak a "vicious circle." We must be free to do what is "right and good." But who determines what is right and good? These formulas take on precise meaning only in the historical context in which each person knows what the state has a right to demand or forbid and, by the same token, what the individual has a right to claim as the private sphere that he alone rules.

Among sociologists of the past century—for he deserves this title as much as Auguste Comte—Tocqueville offers a triple originality. He defines modern society not by industry, in the manner of Auguste Comte, or by capitalism, in the manner of Marx, but by *equality of conditions,* that is, by democracy in the social sense of the term. On the other hand, in contrast to Comte and Marx, he is, with regard to history and the future, a *probabilist.* He does not predict an irresistible movement toward a specific regime, positivist or socialist. Tocqueville states, as obvious, that certain movements will prolong themselves,

8. O.C., vol. 1, 2, part 1, chap. XI, p. 138.

9. Speech by the magistrate Winthrop, as cited by Tocqueville, O.C., vol. I, 1, part 1, chap. II, p. 41.

that certain institutions are dead (the landed aristocracy), others inevitable (the equalization of conditions). But there is no adequate way of determining, in Max Weber's words, the political regime from the democratic state of society. The political superstructure may be despotic or liberal; multiple circumstances, traditions, and living men determine which of the two alternatives will carry the day. Finally—and he has been criticized many times for this originality—*he refuses to subordinate politics to economics,* either to prophesy, in the manner of the Saint-Simonians, that the administration of things will replace the rule of men or, in the manner of Marx, to confuse the socially privileged class with the politically dominant one. Not that Tocqueville was unaware of social classes. It is enough to reread *L'Ancien Régime et la Révolution* to discover a class analysis of French society on the eve of the revolution: "One can no doubt object to what I am saying by bringing up individuals; I am speaking of classes; they alone must occupy history."[10] And, just as clearly, in a fragment from the second part of *L'Ancien Régime,* this description of the Third Estate that could well illustrate the Marxist conception of classes:

> We see in this entire first part that a complete unity exists in the whole body of the Third Estate because class interests, class relations, conformity of position, uniformity of grievances in the past, and the discipline of the guild hold strongly together and carry forward in unison the most dissimilar minds, those very ones who least of all agree on the further road to follow and on the goal to achieve in the future. One is first and foremost of one's class before being of one's own opinion.[11]

But these texts relate to the France of the Ancien Régime, whose tragedy, in Tocqueville's eyes, was precisely the separation and inequality of classes.

> The division into classes was the crime of the old monarchy and became later its excuse. . . . When the different classes that formed the society of ancient France came into contact, sixty years ago, after having been isolated so long by so many barriers, they touched at first only at their most sensitive spots and met only to tear each other to pieces. Even in our day, their jealousies and hatreds survive.[12]

10. O.C., vol. II, 1, chap. XII, p. 170.
11. O.C., vol. II, 2, chap. I, text note 8.
12. O.C., vol. II, 1, chap. X, pp. 166–167.

In other words, it is the Ancien Régime rather than modern society that appears to Tocqueville to be divided into classes. The rich, in the United States, do not constitute the equivalent of an aristocracy; a manufacturing aristocracy will never be a true aristocracy. It is to the extent that the distinctions of the Ancien Régime survive that inequalities of wealth take on the appearance of classes in modern society. In this sense, Tocqueville had, it seems to me, a premonition of the ambivalence in the Marxist conception of classes, the synthesis between the orders of the Ancien Régime and the inequalities characteristic of any industrial society. The middle-class society of prosperity is assuredly stratified. But is it divided into classes as the capitalist society observed by Marx at the start of the last century seemed to be and in which inequalities in economic functions and income reproduced, while accentuating them, the distinctions between the former estates?

*   *   *

Tocqueville elaborated his system of thought between 1830 and 1840, if one dares apply the term system to an author whose fundamental ideas were few, simple, and profound and who multiplied their illustrations and applications by the observation of facts. It is in the following decade, 1840–1850, that Karl Marx went through the stages of an intellectual journey that was to lead him to a doctrine today hailed by a third of mankind—a billion human beings—a doctrine that it is fair to say has shaken up the world, inflicting on itself a glaring contradiction inasmuch as it has denied the influence of ideas, an influence of which its own destiny offers a shining example.

Marx himself was convinced, from the start, that democracy is the truth of our time and even the definitive truth, one that illuminates itself just as it illuminates whatever is opposed to it.

> Democracy is the solved *riddle* of all constitutions. Here, not merely *implicitly* and in essence but *existing* in reality, the constitution is constantly brought back to its actual basis, the *actual human being, the actual people,* and established as the people's *own work.* The constitution appears as what it is, a free product of man.[13]

13. Karl Marx, "Contribution to the Critique of Hegel's Philosophy of Law," Karl Marx and Frederick Engels, *Collected Works* (London: Lawrence & Wishart, 1975), vol. 3, p. 29; hereafter C.W. Aron's French quotation is from the French translation of Karl Marx, "Kritik des Hegelschen Staatsrechts," MEGA I 1/1 *Oeuvres philosophiques* (Paris: Costes, 1935), vol. 4, p. 67; hereafter O.P.

Outlining a comparison that holds a primary place in his thought during his formative years, Marx wrote:

> Just as it is not religion which creates man but man who creates religion, so it is not the constitution which creates the people but the people which creates the constitution. In a certain respect the relation of democracy to all other forms of State is like the relation of Christianity to all other religions. Christianity is *the* religion, the *essence* of religion, deified man as a *particular* religion. Similarly, democracy is the *essence of all state* constitutions—socialised man as a *particular* state constitution. Democracy stands to the other constitutions as the genus stands to its species; except that here the genus itself appears as an existent, and therefore as one *particular* species over against the others whose existence does not correspond to their essence.[14]

Is there any need to underscore the difference in style between Tocqueville and Marx and also the difference in meaning given by the one and the other to the same word, democracy? Equality of conditions, representative government, personal and intellectual freedoms, this is liberal democracy, the full realization of modern society according to Tocqueville. Democracy, according to Marx, is the secret truth, the resolved enigma of all constitutions because the people are the source, the creators of all political superstructures, and because man arrives at the truth about himself, at a consciousness of that truth, only by seeing himself as master and possessor of all the institutions within which he has, over the centuries, allowed himself to become alienated. But if the end of history is, in this sense, democracy, the sovereignty of the entire people, it is also the end of the duality between society and the state, between private and public life. Real democracy, true democracy, will not exhaust itself in episodic participation in public life through elections or elected representatives; it will be achieved only when the worker and the citizens are one, when the life of the people and the political empyrean come together.

> Up till now the *political constitution* has been the *religious* sphere, the *religion* of national life, the heaven of its generality over against the *earthly existence* of its actuality. . . . *Political life* in the modern sense is the *scholasticism* of national life.[15]

---

14. *C.W.*, vol. 3, pp. 29–30; *O.P.*, pp. 67–68.
15. *C.W.*, vol. 3, p. 31; *O.P.*, pp. 70–71.

Let us try to translate this Hegelian language into a language accessible to nonphilosophers. The man of civil society, involved in work, industry, and commerce, remains locked in himself, in his particularity. As a citizen he participates in the universality of the state, but this participation remains marginal to his private, concrete life as a worker. Political citizenship is, in relation to the activity of the worker, like the destiny of the immortal soul in Christianity in relation to our miserable life on this earth. These two separations, these two alienations are parallel: the duality of the profane and sacred, like that of the private and the public, has as its origin man's failure to accomplish his humanity.

Two famous texts, taken from Marx's youthful works, will illustrate the theme of these two dualities, this double alienation:

> The *political revolution* resolves civil life into its component parts, without *revolutionizing* these components themselves or subjecting them to criticism. It regards civil society, the world of needs, labour, private interests, civil law, as the *basis of its existence,* as a *pre-condition* not requiring further substantiation and therefore as its natural basis. Finally, man as a member of civil society is held to be man in *the proper sense, homme,* as distinct from the *citoyen,* because he is man in his sensous, individual, *immediate* existance, whereas *political* man is only abstract, artificial man, man as an *allegorical, juridical* person. The real man is recognised only in the shape of the *egoistic* individual, the *true* man is recognised only in the shape of the *abstract citizen.*[16]

In other words, a purely political revolution, one that does not modify the social infrastructure, does not allow man to realize himself because it confuses the genuine man with the worker locked into his particularity and because man is in conformity with his essence; that is to say, socialized man, a participant in universality, appears only in the form of an abstract citizen. The *civil society*[17] of workers will never be reconciled to the empyrean of politics as long as it is given over to the arbitrariness of desires, the anarchy of selfishness, the struggle of all against all. Similarly, the duality of the profane and the sacred, of society and religion, will last as long as man, failing to realize his essence on this earth, projects it into an illusory transcendence.

16. Marx, "On the Jewish Question," *C.W.,* vol. 3, p. 167 ("Zur Judenfrage," *O.P.,* pp. 200–201).
17. In German, *bürgerliche Gesellschaft.*

> This state, this society, produce religion, an *inverted world consciousness,* because they are an inverted world. . . . It is the *fantastic realisation* of the human essence because *human essence* has no true reality. The struggle against religion is therefore indirectly a fight against *the world* of which religion is the spiritual *aroma.*[18]

To free man from religious illusion, to free man from the separation between the worker and the citizen, this double liberation is impossible as long as the "weapon of criticism" and the "criticism of weapons" do not reach to the roots, that is to say, to the economy. Religion is the image of a topsy-turvy world and politics is separated from the real life of one and all because work itself is alienated since the private ownership of the means of production makes the worker the slave of a master and the master himself the slave of things, of merchandise and the market. Human emancipation, beyond religion and politics, can be accomplished only by an economic and social revolution thanks to which

> the real, individual man re-absorbs in himself the abstract citizen, and as an individual human being has become a *species being* in his everyday life, in his particular work, and in his particular situation, only when man has recognized and organized his *"forces propres"* as *social* forces, and consequently no longer separates social power from himself in the shape of political power.[19]

That Marx does invoke freedom and is truly intent on the liberation of man is beyond dispute. He radically criticizes religion but

> the criticism of religion ends with the teaching that *man is the highest being for man,* hence with the *categorical imperative to overthrow all relations* in which man is a debased, enslaved, forsaken, despicable being.[20]

The young Marx did not renounce the aspirations and ideals of the liberal movement, of which the Revolution of 1848 was both expression and failure. But the radicalism of his critique and the goals

---

18. Marx, "Contributions to the Critique of Hegel's Philosophy of Law," p. 175 ("Zur Kritik der Hegelschen Rechtsphilosophie," *O.P.,* p. 84).

19. Marx, "On the Jewish Question," p. 168.

20. Marx, "Contributions to the Critique of Hegel's Philosophy of Law," p. 182; *O.P.,* p. 97.

proposed by this radical critique take us into a world profoundly foreign to that of liberal democracy. Wherein lies the originality of the revolution dreamed by the young Marx?

> Communism differs from all previous movements in that it overturns the basis of all earlier relations of production and intercourse, and for the first time consciously treats all naturally evolved premises as the creations of hitherto existing men, strips them of their natural character and subjugates them to the power of the united individuals.[21]

What is new is not so much the idea of an upheaval of economic conditions, of the means of production and exchange, as the refusal *to hold any of the given facts of the social order as fatal, eluding human control.* It is through Promethean arrogance, through confidence in the capacity of united men to become masters of nature and society, that Marxist inspiration differs in essence from liberal inspiration and that it is still today, as much or more than the latter, the soul of industrial societies, on one side or the other of the Iron Curtain.

From the very start, Marx did not want to return to the conquests of the French revolution; he wanted to complete them. Democracy, freedom, equality—these values appeared obvious to him. What made him indignant was that democracy should be exclusively political; that equality should go no further than the voting booth; that freedom, proclaimed by the constitution, should not prevent the enslavement of the proletariat or the twelve-hour workday for women and children. Though the texts we have cited are written in a philosophic idiom, their meaning is as precise as the indignation is sincere. If Marx dubbed political and personal freedoms "formal," it was not that he despised them, it was because they seemed to him ludicrous as long as the real conditions of life barred most men from the authentic enjoyment of these subjective rights. To create a society in which *all* men would be in a position, for *their entire life,* to accomplish *effectively* the democratic ideal, this assuredly was the utopia toward which the thought of the young Marx tended.

But what, concretely, is the significance of inserting the democratic ideal into civil society or, to state it more clearly, how can the worker reach a freedom comparable to the formal freedom of the citizen? One interpretation, rather trite, has long been adopted. The worker is deprived of his freedom because he is under the orders of an entrepre-

---

21. Marx, "The German Ideology," *C.W.,* vol. 5, p. 81 ("Die deutsche Ideologie," *O.P.,* p. 231).

neur, just as the latter is enslaved to the anonymous mechanisms of the market. In this case, it is through the suppression of private ownership of the means of production that civil society—or the socioeconomic infrastructure—will be "democratized," brought under control of the combined producers. According to another interpretation, which can also be based on a number of Marx's texts, the first condition for liberation is the development of the productive forces, the making available of all the resources necessary for a decent life, in the end, a reduction of the working day. A famous passage in the third volume of *Capital* points out that work will always be in the realm of necessity. It is outside, beyond work, that the realm of freedom begins.

These two interpretations, both of them valid, do not take into account certain essential elements of Marx's thought. It is easy to expose the contrast between the servitude of the proletarian and the abstract freedom of the citizen: in England in the first half of the last century this contrast was glaring and scandalous. But through what actual institutions could civil and political society, economic and political activity, be merged? And what would be the outcome of this merger? The day the worker is directly at the service of the community and no longer at the service of the owner of the means of production, he is a citizen in the manner of a civil servant who, in his very work, participates in the public realm. But does this politicization of economic life, the public character given to an activity today private, spell liberation or servitude for individuals? It will be liberation if one decrees, by definition, that freedom is obedience to necessity and that, in a humanity in control of its destiny, each accomplishes the part that universal reason attributes to him. But if freedom begins beyond necessity and is realized in the margin of choice and autonomy reserved to the individual, what Marx calls emancipation can, in fact, become degraded into servitude.

Let us not forget: Marx himself always recognized the risk of servitude involved in the refusal to discriminate between civil society and political society. After all, in the Middle Ages this nondiscrimination existed:

> In the Middle Ages there were serfs, feudal estates, merchant and trade guilds, corporations of scholars, etc.: that is to say, in the Middle Ages property, trade, society, men are *political*; the material content of the state is given by its form; every private sphere has a political character or is a political sphere; that is, politics is a characteristic of the private sphere too. In the Middle Ages the political con-

stitution is the constitution of private property, but only because the constitution of private property is a political constitution. In the Middle Ages the life of the nation and the life of the state are identical. Man is the actual principle of the state—but *unfree* man. It is thus the democracy of *unfreedom*.[22]

Certainly, Marx, when he wrote these lines, did not doubt that the return to a merging of society and state would be realized in the democracy of freedom: men would be equal and not, as in the Middle Ages, locked up in a class or corporation: the state would be the business of all and not a few. At the limit, according to the Saint-Simonian formula, the administration of things would replace the government of men and, by the same token, in a merged society and state, it is society that would survive and the state that would wither away. But on what is this liberal optimism founded if not on a utopian picture of "administration by the combined producers"?

Later, having replaced philosophic language with socioeconomic language, Marx gave another expression to this same danger of total emancipation degenerating into total servitude. The Marxist classification of economic regimes is based on a unique criterion, in his eyes, decisive: the relation between men at work, which determines the method of extracting and distributing surplus value. The slave is the property of his master, who takes care of him but keeps for himself all value produced beyond the cost of upkeep. Similarly, the serf is bound to the soil and the lord owns the means of production and keeps for himself the value produced beyond what the worker and his family need to survive. Capitalism conceals exploitation under the appearance of freedom (the proletarian is neither a slave nor a serf; he offers himself on a labor market where he negotiates with the buyer of his labor power) and the appearance of equality (wages are the apparently equitable counterpart of labor furnished by the worker). But the exploitation has not disappeared; it has, so to speak, realized itself by camouflage: wages are but the equivalent of the goods necessary to the life of the worker and his family. The rest—that is to say, surplus value—belongs to the owner of the means of production.

The elimination of the capitalist class opens up the way for an economy without exploitation, or an economy in which the community itself would distribute, according to needs and justice, the resources

22. Marx, "Critique of Hegel's Philosophy of the State," *C.W.*, vol. 3, p. 32 ("Kritik des Hegelschen Staatsrechts," *O.P.*, vol. 4).

necessary to the development of the means of production and incomes for consumption. But this elimination of private exploiters could also restore what Marx called the *Asian mode of production,* in other words, the separation of society into two parts (that it is best not to call classes): the huge majority of workers on one side, the state apparatus on the other, with its army of civil servants organized according to a strict hierarchy, surplus value being extracted by the state apparatus and distributed according to the will of the masters of this apparatus. From this angle also, Marx had a premonition of the potential for enslavement contained within the drive to overcome the duality characteristic of liberal democracy between the worker and the citizen, between society and the state, between the private sphere and the public realm.

Marx, it is true, from 1848 on, once he had reached the end of the intellectual journey that had led the young Hegelian to the materialist conception of history, no longer stressed the will for radical revolution but the inevitable character of that revolution. The Promethean ambition was no longer that of an individual or of all humanity or even of the proletarian class to the extent that its only mission was to realize a destiny determined in advance. Capitalism is condemned by its internal contradictions and, if the timing and form of the catastrophe remain unknown and perhaps undetermined, the catastrophe itself, terrible and beneficial, is inevitable. Thus, it would seem that Tocqueville left men the responsibility of choice, within the democratic world, between freedom and despotism, whereas Marx condemned that world either to submit passively to the dialectic, or to try to oppose it in vain, or finally to accelerate its development.

In fact, the dialogue of the two men is the opposite of what it seems. Marx invoked historical determinism not as an alibi for cowardly resignation but as both justification and dissimulation of a truly demiurgic will. To reconstruct society, from its socioeconomic foundations, so that freedom and equality would be given to all at all times, such will be the revolution of the *fourth estate,* a continuation and a completion of the French Revolution, which was the revolution of the third estate. Thus, when Lenin and the Bolsheviks, at the beginning of the century, tired of leaving to recalcitrant history the task of crushing capitalism and building socialism, placed their trust in the party to replace the dialectic and the proletariat itself, they assuredly betrayed the doctrine that had become official in the Second International and sacrificed certain elements of the Marxist heritage, but they rediscovered one element, and an original and vital one: faith in the capacity of united men to liquidate the relics of past centuries and with supreme authority to construct a social order upon new foundations.

* * *

It would be easy to analyze the dialogue between Tocqueville and Marx that we have just sketched according to a sociological and so to speak Marxist method. One was an aristocrat, who rallied to democracy by reason and not sentiment, but who, though sometimes demonstrating the coming of a radically different order, remained the defender of the existing structure and was passionately hostile to socialism. The other was by origin a bourgeois but, in revolt against a bourgeoisie that betrayed its own values, became the representative of the working class, denouncing the injustices it was subjected to and announcing the revenge the future would bring. One, out of social conservatism, made himself, against his private preferences, the theoretician of liberal democracy, that is to say, bourgeois democracy; the other wanted to be, with total commitment, the theoretician as well as the leader of an organized working class.

Though they were contemporaries, they so to speak ignored each other. I doubt whether Tocqueville even knew of the *Communist Manifesto*. Marx had certainly read *Democracy in America,* but if he suspected and sometimes suggested that the course of history could be different in the Old and New Worlds, the example of American democracy did not suffice to modify the picture he had formed, once and for all, of the inevitable and catastrophic future of capitalist societies. One explicitly placed above all else the safeguarding of individual and political freedoms, but liberal democracy also seemed to Tocqueville the most effective protection of the social hierarchy and of economic inequalities. The other judged ridiculous any reforms that allowed the survival, along with private ownership of the means of production, of the ultimate cause of social contradictions and the plight of the workers.

The two men shared a distaste for opportunism, a total fidelity to themselves and their ideas. Tocqueville retired from politics the day Louis Napoleon violated the constitution and reestablished the empire. Karl Marx, until the end of his life, remained a rebel, committed to the struggle against a cruel society and for a class that bore the whole brunt of social injustice. Both believed in freedom, both had as a goal a just society, but one would leave industry and commerce to themselves, to be spontaneously run by individuals under the control of laws, and feared that the individual might come to lose independence-freedom and participation-freedom all at once. The other held the free activity of individuals in industry and commerce to be the cause of the servitude of all. Thus, for one the major condition of freedom was representative government and for the other, economic revolution.

This contrast can easily be explained by the origins, careers, and temperaments of the two men, yet not without a paradox that deserves to be stressed: it was a Norman aristocrat who became the doctrinaire of liberal democracy, the son of a Rhenish bourgeois who became the prophet of the fourth estate. It was in the United States that the descendant of European nobility studied the model of the future society. It was in Victorian England that the young Hegelian completed his economic studies and borrowed from Ricardo concepts and methods thanks to which he tried to give scientific form to his hopes and indignation.

Whatever the partial truth of these sociobiographical interpretations, the fact remains that, at a decisive point, the contrast turns on a fact or an evolutionary tendency. Does an economy founded on the private ownership of the means of production set up a trench between the rich and the poor or not? Does it create enemy classes, incapable of cooperation and by this very fact doomed to fight each other mercilessly until the death of one and the triumph of the other? It is possible to contend that Tocqueville guaranteed himself a certain intellectual comfort by predicting that the society of the future would be dominated by the middle class. This peaceful waiting and optimistic prediction absolved him from the effort to struggle against present injustices. What he had in mind for a future Europe was a society as mobile as the American one, and he was easily resigned to the persistence on the old continent of class discrimination and the powerlessness of the poor. But, this said, his vision in the long run was nonetheless true and Marx's false, without the latter's short-term view being correct either, since from the middle of the last century on, he counted on the salvationist upheaval from year to year.

Why was it that the man who reasoned in political terms and not the one who had read all the economic books foresaw the diffusion of prosperity? One answer would be to claim the superiority of naive observation and historical experience over the unilateral and imperfect arguments of specialists. Tocqueville, as we have seen, reasoned from social equality to political equality and from political equality to an egalitarian tendency in the distribution of income. The passage from the one to the other seemed to him likely in the long run and governed by the deep forces that determine the destiny of societies. As for the development of productive capacity and technical revolutions, he knew no more and said no more than any other educated man of his time. But he believed in all simplicity that the combination of increased resources and a democratic climate would probably lead to an improvement in the destiny of most and not to the contrast between an excess of misery at one extreme and an excess of wealth at the other.

As an economist Marx questioned, and to a certain extent rightly, this complacence. In an economy founded on private ownership of the means of production, it was not inconceivable that wealth would be concentrated in the hands of a minority without the masses profiting from it (as has happened many times). Nevertheless, a paradox remains. No economist of his time was as attentive as Marx to the dynamism of the modern economy; none repeated so stubbornly that a static model is remote from reality and that capitalism is defined by the accumulation of capital, therefore by the development of productive forces, and indirectly by greater productivity. Now, why does Marx draw the conclusion that a dynamic model with strong capital accumulation will lead to the impoverishment of the masses in spite of growing productivity?

A complete answer would require a detailed study of Ricardo's system and the manner in which Marx used it for his own ends. But a few elementary observations will suffice. Having taken work as the unit of measure for value, and for measuring wages (or the value of the labor force) the goods necessary for the life of the worker and his family, Marx could arrive at one of two conclusions. If, thanks to the rise in productivity, the hours necessary to produce goods representing the value of wages go down, then either the rate of exploitation increases or wages, without representing added value, must represent a greater quantity of goods. Marx did not assert that the rate of exploitation would rise; he said that the rate would remain stable. He should have recognized that with the same part of the day being devoted to producing a value equal to wages, and with productivity having risen, the standard of living would tend to rise or poverty to diminish. To avoid this conclusion, Marx, unlike many economists of his day, did not introduce the effect on the birthrate, and therefore on the supply of work, of an increase in wages, but cited instead the industrial reserve army, in other words, the pressure permanently exerted on wage scales by the availability of unemployed workers, unemployed because of changes in technology.

If Marx had approached the study of the economy as a pure observer without knowing in advance what he wanted to demonstrate, he would not have insisted with so much force on *absolute pauperiza-*

tion, which does not obviously result from his analysis of capitalism, any more than he would have concluded from the increase in constant capital in relation to variable capital—therefore, of the fall of the rate of profit[23]—the progressive paralysis of an economy whose driving power is private investment.

In the prosperous West of 1963, Marx seems to have been wrong in economic matters, precisely an area in which he was one of the most learned and erudite men of his times, and Tocqueville seems to have divined the future despite his ignorance (a relative ignorance, of course) and perhaps thanks to it. Propelled by his common sense or by his intuition, he admitted without solid proof or deep analysis that a society obsessed by the concern for material well-being will assure to the majority the moral status and economic conditions of the middle class. Such a society will be agitated by incessant demands and conflicts of interest, but little prone to revolutions. Too many individuals will have something to lose for endemic dissatisfaction to result in revolt: "What if I don't own today, I may own tomorrow, and my children will own it if I don't." Thus, without too great a paradox, one can credit Tocqueville with having had a premonition of the anxious and peaceful society in which Westeners live fifteen years after the second world war.

At the same time it is impossible not to attribute to Marx a cardinal error: that in a regime of private property and a market economy the condition of the masses would worsen fatally and that, paralyzed by its contradictions and torn by class war, capitalism, incapable of self-reform, would perish. It is tempting to proceed still further in this line of thought and see, in the very successes achieved by Marx's doctrine, the confirmation of Tocqueville's alternative.

A probabilistic thinker, the latter left two roads open to mankind's future: liberal democracy or despotic democracy. Do not the Soviet regimes represent one of the alternative terms and the Western regimes the other, so that the persistence of capitalism in the West would refute Marxist prophecies whereas despotisms claiming to be Marxist confirm rather than refute Tocqueville's thought? Did he not, in a passage we quoted earlier, conceive of despotisms without aristocracies, in which the laws would aim at the well-being of the masses?

Let us take care, however, not to be carried away by an interpretation that is both easy and seductive. If in the course of these past years

---

23. Surplus value (s) being drawn exclusively from variabie capital (v), the increase in constant capital (c) in relation to variable capital (v) obviously entails a decrease in the ratio $s/(v + c)$.

sociologists have paid more attention to politics, to constitutions in the wider meaning of the term (ways of selecting leaders, methods of exercising authority), it is assuredly because of the striking contrast between the two greatest powers in the world, both committed to industrial growth, one claiming to be liberal democratic (in Tocqueville's sense of the term), the other having as its ideal the suppression of classes, the merging of society and state, according to the dream of the young Marx. We call Soviet society despotic but the spokesmen of this society return the accusation and denounce the enslavement of Western proletarians to the private owners of the means of production, the enslavement of the state itself to the monopolists, that is to say, to the socially dominant minority, which is consequently capable of manipulating those representatives whom the citizens have the illusion of having chosen to govern in their name.

Is this exchange of accusations the symbol of an irreducible dialogue? Does the same word have two different meanings depending on which side of the Iron Curtain it is uttered? Or do the facts themselves allow us to decide between rival claims?

Marx's cardinal error, as we have said, was to believe, or to write as though he believed, that only radical revolution can liberate the worker, in the double sense of improving his standard of living and allowing him to participate in collective life. The other cardinal error, not of Marx but of the Marxists, was to draw a false conclusion from fair criticism. The personal freedoms or subjective (political) rights to which Tocqueville was passionately committed are not sufficient to give a feeling of freedom, much less a freedom that will effectively create a future for those who live miserably on ever uncertain wages. This critique is true but the conclusion—that formal freedoms are a luxury for the privileged—is false. For the Soviet experience is a glaring demonstration that the "combined producers," under the direction of the proletariat organized as a ruling class, can be experienced by individuals not as the architects of total liberation but as those responsible for total servitude.

I am thinking of the Hungarian revolution of 1956, the only antitotalitarian revolution of the century that could be called victorious even though the intervention of a foreign army finally "reestablished order in Budapest." Now this revolution is the one, to my knowledge, that most resembles the one Marx dreamed about in 1843 in the name of revolution. "Philsophy," he wrote, "is the head of this emancipation, the proletariat its heart." In Hungary, it was the intellectuals, united in the Petöfi circle, who launched the popular revolt, by taking a stand against established lies, against the mystification of which they themselves had been victims. The workers went into the street and overthrew the Rakosi regime, in their eyes the incarnation of despotism, at the appeal of writers or artists, in order to realize the values of which intellectuals are the custodians: the right to truth, the simplest and deepest of subjective rights that liberals, in the nineteenth-century European meaning of the word, hold to be the essence of freedom.

Let us reflect a moment on the meaning of this inversion, this paradox that conceals an authentic logic. What do formal freedoms mean? cried Marx—the right to speak, to write, to choose one's representatives, and to adhere to one's god—if real life, the everyday life of work, is imprisoned by the ruthless necessity created by the power of the boss and the tyranny of need? Against a certain complacency of the privileged, who are disposed to accommodate themselves to the misery of the majority as long as formal freedoms are respected. Marx's protest has lost none of its freshness. But the day when, under the pretext of real freedom, the authority of the state spreads to the whole of society and no longer tends to recognize a private sphere, it is formal freedoms that intellectuals and the masses themselves demand.

No revolution, in its aspirations and watchwords, is as close to the Revolution of 1848 as the Hungarian revolution of 1956. And yet it confronts not a traditional despotism but a regime claiming to be one of the proletariat and intellectuals, a regime of the future, and which to hide from itself the true nature of its adversaries attempts to disqualify them by labeling them counterrevolutionaries. Nothing could be a greater lie. Neither the Petöfi circle nor Imre Nagy is counterrevolutionary or aims at bringing back the dead Hungary of the Ancien Régime or returning to the large landowners their former holdings, to the capitalists their banks and factories. They do not question the public ownership of the means of production and in a certain way this subject interests no one (at least if it is a question of vast concentrations of capital: the peasant remains interested in his land, and nationalization of trade and handicrafts cannot be justified on the level of technique). In brief, intellectuals and popular masses, in 1956 as in 1848, cry "freedom" and they are thinking of subjective rights, of participation-freedom through elections and many parties, and finally of national, collective freedom, of which each one feels the lack since the citizen has the sense of being reduced to a ridiculous role if those he chooses to govern are themselves the toys of an outside and all-powerful force.

One could object that the Hungarian revolution was above all a national one and that we falsify its meaning by interpreting it as a dialectic between formal and real freedoms: formal freedoms, despised by the Marxists, are from now on the stake of popular movements in a country wherein, with the whole of society submissive and seemingly integrated with the state, protest can become only immediately political. But the case of Hungary is an extreme case. Even in the Soviet Union, what is constantly at issue is how much (formal) freedom it is appropriate to allow intellectuals. During the years of monolithic Stalinism, the question apparently did not arise. The discipline imposed from above, by one man alone ruling through terror, was such that speech itself was in bondage and the changing version of the ideology was at each moment repeated by millions of voices and echoed to the four corners of the universe. When men in white jackets were decreed to be assassins, the apparatus of all parties and all propaganda machines echoed the master's decree, and the indignation spread to Parisian doctors, ignorant of everything but won over, sometimes by humanitarianism, to Marxism-Leninism. Since Stalin's death the discipline of lying has disintegrated and the regime seeks a compromise between respect for state orthodoxy and the freedom of expression to which writers and artists aspire.

Why refuse to painters the right to formalism and to musicians the right to dodecaphony? But if art is no longer at the service of the party and socialist growth, if ideology no longer dominates the whole of social existence, then the unity of a classless society, the merging of this nonantagonistic society and the state that wills itself the expression of the whole, is in turn compromised. A distinction emerges between the public sphere and the private ones, between the area in which public will rules and those in which the individual can be left to himself. But then, on that day, on what will the monopoly of the party be based? How can it justify its claim to absolute power? Why would it alone have the right to proclaim absolute truth and to interpret it, at every moment, against the constant perils of dogmatism and revisionism? It is not chance but logic that causes Marxist-Leninist regimes, in search of real socioeconomic freedoms, to experience the opposition of the heirs of all those who throughout the centuries have fought orthodoxies and refused not to obey Caesar but to worship him—the eternal protesters who have never definitely won the game but have never resigned themselves to considering it lost.

It will be objected that the dialogue of Khrushchev and the intellectuals, and the Hungarian revolution of 1956, has nothing to do with Marx's Marxism and that the latter did not aim at suppressing but completing the formal freedoms of the bourgeoisie. I do not deny this point. But a doctrine of action such as Marx's is responsible not only for its intentions but also for its implications even if they are contrary to its values and goals. Now I agree that an all-powerful party, such as the Bolshevik party, does not conform to Marx's thought; as early as 1917, a great number of Marxists refused to allow that public owner- ship of the means of production and a planned economy constitute the achievement of socialism in the absence of political freedom; it nev- ertheless remains difficult to conceive the elimination of class antag- onisms, the end of the duality between society and state, without an absolute authority, without something like what is called the dic- tatorship of the proletariat. The proletariat, that is to say, millions of workers, cannot itself exercise a dictatorship. Thus, it is not histor- ically surprising that Marxism—rejecting the method of progressive reforms, refusing to admit the permanence of distinct economic and political spheres, and aiming at a liberation of all through mastery by the combined producers over their destiny—should end up with the total enslavement of all to one party, even to one man. Because how could the "combined producers" reorganize society from its founda- tions if their "combination" does not show itself capable of command, in other words, if the combination of producers itself does not form a party, with a hierarchy, a general staff, a chief?

Must one say that, by an irony of history, the governed are seeking formal freedoms there where the philosophy of real freedoms rules? And that, on the other hand, formal freedoms are being belittled in favor of real freedoms there where the former are guaranteed, at least for the most part, but where there continue to exist, along with private ownership of the means of production, social power and perhaps po- litical power among a minority in the private sphere? This dialectic, which contains a part of the truth, expresses despite everything an otherwise complex historical reality.

In Hungary the revolutionary élan came from intellectuals, but the popular masses would not have followed if they had not felt them- selves to be downtrodden and thus exploited. And since there were no more private exploiters, only the Hungarian Communist party or the Soviet Union could be responsible for the exploitation. In any case, economic policy, as practiced throughout Eastern Europe in the post- war years, resembled on one essential point what Marx considered typical of capitalism: "Accummulate, accumulate, that is the law and the prophets." This famous formula can be translated, in the language of socialist construction, by the primacy of investment, in particular, in heavy industry over consumption. A revolution against poverty, despite the development of the means of production—is this not the revolution that Marx anticipated and that the rise in living standards in the West has forestalled?

On the other hand, it would be a mistake to believe that in the West formal freedoms can be considered assured or that real freedoms are the only ones demanded. What characterizes Western regimes, as compared to those of the Soviet bloc, is pluralism—a plurality of spheres, private and public, a plurality of social groups among which certain form classes by becoming conscious of their own mission and their opposition to the existing order, a plurality of parties in competition for the exercise of power. Depending on countries and circumstances, it is formal freedoms—as during the McCarthy period—or real freedoms—as in the eyes of workers devoted to the Marxist-Leninist doctrine—that seem in peril and constitute the stake in conflicts. Sometimes it is society that seems tyrannical rather than the state (in the eyes of American blacks, for example); sometimes it is the state that, by refusing wage increases or being thought to be under the influence of plutocratic minorities or a conspiracy of the military or the industrialists, seems to escape the will of those who, according to the law of democracy, should provide its inspiration if not its management.

The dialectic of formal and real freedoms, of Soviet regimes and Western ones, thus cannot be reduced to an ironic reversal of for or against, with men setting out on the conquest of real freedoms having destroyed formal ones without increasing the standard of living or broadening people's participation in the community, which would have been the authentic content of real freedom, while the masses, in societies faithful to formal freedoms, continue to aspire to more real freedom, that is to say, to more material well-being and to increased participation in the administration of industry or the state. For this oversimplified antithesis, I would substitute the following one: wherever a single party maintains a despotic regime and forbids intellectuals, writers, or artists to work according to their talent, the demand for formal freedom, silent or public, regains luster and in certain cases its past virulence. As for the masses, they do not seem, even if dissatisfied, to question the dogmas of the government, that is to say, public ownership of the means of production and planning. But, at least in the countries of Eastern Europe, they do question the one-party state, and left to themselves, Poles, Czechs, and Hungarians would reestablish party rivalry and parliamentary deliberations. In other words, economic and social grievances, on the other side of the Iron Curtain, are of course multiple and diverse but they do not become organized into a rival ideology when in the political sphere a substitute ideology or even institutions are available.

In the West, the principles of formal freedoms and liberal democracy are not seriously challenged, except by minorities devoted to the doctrine of Marxism-Leninism or again in circumstances in which the regime reveals itself incapable of resolving urgent problems. As for social and economic dissatisfactions or demands, they are many and diverse, but they no more readily become organized in an ideology, or a system or doctrine of substitution, than on the other side of the Iron Curtain. Depending on the case, the protesters blame the state or the monopolies, the big corporations that spearhead technical progress or the small firms that are prisoners of anachronistic methods. Setting aside once again the minority that puts its faith in a Soviet-type regime, the intellectuals in the West, like the masses, are neither contented nor revolutionary, neither free nor enslaved.

The prevailing mood is such that dissatisfaction is incapable of inspiring a revolutionary will, liberation is incomplete, but the causes of this semiservitude are so numerous and so obscure that no total theory can encompass them all, no action eliminate them. Western dissatisfaction rejects both despair and hope.

*   *   *

If these analyses are correct, what answer should we give the question raised earlier: are today's industrial societies the heirs of *liberalism*, concerned primarily with subjective rights and representative institutions, or of the *Promethean ambition* of the Marxists, concerned with freedom in their own way but with a freedom that would come about through the fundamental reorganization of society beginning with its existing socioeconomic infrastructure?

One answer is that, from one perspective, all industrial societies are heirs of the Promethean ambition in the sense that they all lay such trust in the mastery achieved through the technological control of nature and the organization of social phenomena that no government, no theorist, would admit as inevitable certain forms of human misery, and none would accept passively the undeserved disasters that here and there befall individuals. Among the freedoms proclaimed by the Atlantic Charter there are two that would have been ignored by traditional liberalism—*freedom from want* and *freedom from fear*—because want and fear, hunger and war, were inherent to human existence throughout the centuries. That poverty and violence have been as of now eliminated, no one believes: that one day they might be, why not hope? That the ambition to eliminate them is new and shows an arrogance that the founding fathers as well as Tocqueville would not have shared or approved is beyond doubt. For this ambition emerges from equating the tyranny of things with the tyranny of men or, again, to put it perhaps more precisely, from the assertion that a man deprived of bread and education is not a victim of things but of men. Only men can deprive other men of the right to select a government and worship a god. But what men are responsible for, and what men can conquer want and fear? *No social condition must be accepted as independent of the rational will of men.* This is nearly a textually Marxist formula but it expresses the *common faith* or *universal illusion of modern societies.*

From the moment this equivalence is raised or this ambition asserted, industrial societies, even of the Western type, even if they continue to quote Madison or Jefferson and to reject Marx and Marxism, even if they in fact remain liberal democracies, are permeated with a spirit fundamentally different from the one that inspired the framers of the American Constitution or the actors in the French Revolution. As long as the only despotism one fears is that of a government without checks or a man corrupted by excess power, it is against the power of the state or the arbitrariness of governments that one multiplies one's precautions. From the day when poverty and misfortune are no less imputable to society itself than abuse by the police or the injustice of kings, must the major concern be to limit the government or, quite the contrary, to give it means commensurate with the tasks that one expects of it, that is to say, almost unlimited means? Liberalism, because it was suspicious of men, was stingy in granting them authority to govern. The confidence we feel in science, technology, and organization becomes as irritated with the slow pace of deliberations as it does with the paralysis that can be created by checks and balances, in which the drafters of constitutions once saw the supreme art and guarantee of freedom. What was yesterday the pride of legislators is today the despair of technicians.

Let there be no mistake: Western type industrial societies and, more than all others, the more advanced among them, remain liberal democracies in Tocqueville's sense. The author of *Democracy in America* saw correctly. The union has endured, having been threatened only once and, as he predicted, by slavery. Institutions that in his eyes were the expression and guarantee of freedom—the role of citizens in local administration, voluntary associations, the mutual support between the democratic and religious spirit—have survived, in spite of the advance of centralization and the strengthening of the presidency, a strengthening that Tocqueville had furthermore declared to be inevitable from the day when the republic would have to face enemies and be engaged in an active foreign policy.

It would therefore be absurd to suggest that the effort to assure to all individuals material resources sufficient to realize themselves, that is, to be really free to determine their destiny, is contrary to the eighteenth-century ideal of liberalism, the fear of despotism and the arbitrary, and proper constitutional procedures. It is even obvious at first glance that liberal democracies have taken root and prospered today especially, if not exclusively, in countries that have reached a standard of living sufficient for the mass of the population to feel its benefits. In particular, in the United States, why should a contradiction be felt between subjective rights or formal freedoms and real freedom (distribution of material well-being and social participation) since it is within the framework of a liberal constitution that the republic raised itself to the first rank of economic power and abundance?

It is therefore not so much a matter of suggesting any sort of contradiction; but how can one not recognize that fear of the arbitrary and Promethean arrogance belong to two spiritual universes, express two very different attitudes toward society? It may be that the Americans will be the first to arrive on the moon and thus demonstrate that the endless Senate investigating committees, survivals of bourgeois traditions, in no way weaken the will that Spengler would have called Faustian and the efficiency of collective organization. I do not deny that the United States can maintain intact its original values since each nation remains, sometimes unconsciously, faithful to the ideal that presided at its birth.

Is what is true for the United States true to the same degree of the other countries of the West? Is it true for the rest of the world? Let us not try to settle the issue but to give it a radical expression. Half a century ago, a constitution and formal freedoms still represented, if not the whole, at least an essential element of modernity. Japan, whose deliberate Westernization, a conscious response to external danger, is one of the most extraordinary events of history, tried to introduce a constitution and a parliament at the same time as the science and technology of Europe and America. The young Turks, too, were no less anxious than the army to modernize politics, and political modernization was symbolized by a parliament. Today a blast furnace symbolizes modernity better than a parliament.

It is fair to object that the very opposition of Soviet and Western societies has made this ambiguity of modernity inevitable. Since the Soviet Union rose to the summit of political power and technological efficiency without a plurality of parties, without respect for formal freedoms, without even a constitutional mechanism, why should these survivals of a preindustrial age, these procedures invented by republics of landowners or the bourgeoisie, be surrounded with a halo? Why should nations desiring rapid growth, rightly anxious to give individuals the material means to live their lives, be encumbered by these subtle mechanisms, better designed to brake than to promote public action? In all of the new nations, the ambition is to construct or reconstruct the social order from its foundations, that is to say, it is the Marxist ambition, and not liberal modesty, that corresponds to the sentiments of the elites even more than to those of the masses. Even the merging of society and the state, the worker and the citizen—much protested by men on the other side of the Iron Curtain and repugnant to Westerners—seems, in the form of the single party, to be a useful method to rally a people, force it to change its traditional ways of life, and unite social and political forces in a common thrust. Liberal freedoms require the separation of spheres and respect for forms. Out of impatience and perhaps an illusion of efficiency, single parties are multiplying over the planet, even without reference to Marxism-Leninism, and denying individual freedoms in the hope that the "combined producers" will first build a new social order to free men from want, if not from fear.

＊　＊　＊

Let me repeat in conclusion: I do not doubt the compatibility of the old ideal of liberal democracy with the renewed ideal of Promethean mastery over nature and society itself. Western societies, American society, are proof not only that formal freedoms and real freedoms are not contradictory but that, in our time, it is in the same societies that both are least imperfectly realized.

What I should like to express from this historical dialogue between Tocqueville and Marx, between liberal democracy and socialist construction, is that the industrial society in which we live and which the thinkers of the past century divined is democratic in essence if one means by that, as Tocqueville does, the elimination of hereditary aristocracies; it is normally, if not necessarily, democratic if one means that no one is excluded from citizenship and the spread of material well-being. On the other hand, it is liberal only by tradition or survival if by liberalism one means respect for individual rights, personal freedoms, and constitutional procedures.

Western societies today have a triple ideal, *bourgeois citizenship, technological efficiency,* and *the right of every individual to choose the path of his salvation.* Of these three ideals, none should be sacrificed. Let us not be so naive as to believe that it is easy to achieve all three.

Part Four
A Sociology
of Modern Societies

In the first of the following pieces, both written in 1960, Aron discusses the basic questions of modern sociology—in particular, the epistemological status of sociological knowledge, and the sociologist's role and responsibility in society. In chapter 8 he develops a highly synthetic view of modern industrial and democratic society, pointing out the oligarchical tendency in modern democracies.

7

Science and Consciousness
of Society

All societies, in the past, have had a relatively precise idea of what they were and of what they wanted to be. Modern societies are those that for the first time lay claim to scientific self-awareness. The vocation of sociology is therefore to act as the conscience, but also as the measure of consciousness, of those societies that are sufficiently ambitious or venturesome to offer themselves to unbiased observation and unrestrained inquisitiveness.

Sociology, in our era, has been subject to three attitudes on the part of societies: *hostility,* even to the point of suppression; *approval,* even involving the active use of sociology; and more or less total *indifference.* The National Socialist regime suppressed sociology as most German academics understood the term before 1933. The privileged, or the rulers, in the Soviet Union as well as in the United States, patronize what they mutually call sociology. Sociologists in France, whether in the Fourth or Fifth Republic, have lacked a sense of mission: partisan or ideological disputes relative to the economic or political order continue to be waged, essentially, as if the social sciences did not exist.

Leaving aside the two extremes, hostility and indifference, let us consider instead the intermediate case of interested approval, as illustrated by the two contrasting examples of the Soviet Union and the United States. In the Soviet Union, the term *sociology* refers to a theory that justifies Soviet society and condemns Western societies. In the United States, the term refers to the empirical study and conceptual

Translated by Charles Krance from *Archives européennes de sociologie* 1 (1960): 1–30. Reproduced with permission. Charles Krance dedicates the translation of this chapter and of chapters 8 and 12 "to the memory of my father, who advised me long ago to read some Aron."

elaboration of social phenomena; a study which, judging from all appearances, entails neither justification nor condemnation but may nonetheless carry certain social implications.

The relationship between society and sociology can be considered from two points of view. One can begin with the model provided by the natural sciences, the ideal of objective knowledge, and then question, as Max Weber did do solicitously, to what degree the historian, the economist, and the sociologist are capable of approaching rigorous objectivity, which is the sole ideal that befits the profession of the scientist. In this perspective, the entrenchment of sociology in the surrounding society is considered an obstacle to be surmounted along the way toward impartiality. Alternatively, one may decide that knowledge of society is a social phenomenon and thus cannot help but exert an influence on the way society is perceived by the scientist. In this perspective, what is put in question are the possible modalities of the social function of sociology: Is sociology conservative, revolutionary, or reformist? Are sociologists, by the very condition of their work, compelled to reinforce or weaken the regime in which they live?

These two problematics, though distinct from one another, are not mutually independent. Whether it be true or false, a proposition of fact or of theory can exercise a conservative or revolutionary influence. The content of a given sociology does not alone determine the function it fulfills in a given social environment.

I

Any knowledge of society, no matter how scientific, bears social implications; it either weakens or reinforces a given institution, valorizes or devalorizes a given custom, gives weight of argument for one side or another.

In its first phase, sociology most often appeared to be destructive of the society about which it had (or claimed to have) knowledge. It is easy, indeed, to indicate the typical mechanisms by which a sociology becomes revolutionary, whether willingly or not:

1. Sociology can reveal the gap between a value adhered to by a society and the reality of collective life (for example, the inequality of opportunities at birth remains considerable).

2. Sociology can reveal that the effective means for attaining goals, whether these be individual (the technique of social success) or collective (the power of the collectivity), are in direct contradiction to the ethics preached in schools and churches.

3. Sociology can reveal that a certain organization of social life, handed down through the centuries, is destined to disappear for lack of adaptation to economic or intellectual exigencies.

A science has only to bring a few ordinarily hidden facts to light in order to *unmask;* it need only specify the conditions of success in order to lapse into *cynicism;* and it need only extend causal relations into the future in order to *prophesy.* Now what science does not have the discovery of *facts, conditions,* and *causes* as its function?

Three of the great sociological systems of the last century illustrate the three concepts by which we have qualified three contingent tendencies of sociology: Marxist sociology has unmasked capitalist-bourgeois societies; Pareto's sociology seems to have given lessons in cynicism to apprentice dictators and active minorities; Auguste Comte's sociology heralded the advent of human unity and positive religion. Of these three systems, two exercise all three functions at the same time. The Marxists have learned a lesson in cynicism from their master, at least in matters of directing the action of the proletariat, and they have not doubted that the prophecy of socialist victory will one day be fulfilled. Pareto was inclined to prophesy the rise of a violent elite that would take the place of the decadent bourgeoisie, and he was no less zealous in unmasking both than was Marx himself.

Marx avoided Pareto's cynicism inasmuch as he restricted his unmasking to capitalistic societies, and considered the cause of the proletariat as being of a different nature than that of the other classes. The prophecy of the classless society allowed for the unmasking of the enemies of the proletariat without devalorizing the values invoked by the combatants.

Pareto, for his part, wrote that he would abstain from publishing his treatise on general sociology if he thought this thick book might have a wide readership. He thus did not hesitate to stress the contradiction between scientific truth and social usefulness: he judged it impossible to scientifically analyze the functioning of society without weakening the bond of obligations and restraints that maintains social order. And, in fact, he had few readers: those writers, whether communists or fascists, who thought of themselves as his pupils were, in accordance with the teachings of their master himself, not to quote him as their authority. The doctrine prohibits the cynic from displaying cynicism. It is from this contradiction that Machiavelli drew a sizable portion of his power of fascination. Pareto's fifteen hundred pages do not enjoy a similar capacity for magical appeal.

It would be wrong, however, to attribute revolutionary action to sociology as such. Depending on the circumstances, sociology becomes conservative quite as naturally as it becomes revolutionary. Sociology need only ascertain (or believe itself to be ascertaining) that the facts are increasingly consonant with the proclaimed values, and—instead of unmasking social inequality—it proclaims the progressive disappearance of classes. It need only situate the salvational revolution behind, rather than beyond, our present situation, and—instead of triggering a revolt against bourgeois society—it indoctrinates the individual with devotion to the socialist collectivity. It need only devalorize violence or class struggle, and stress continuous progress, and—instead of giving lessons in cynicism after the manner of Pareto—it teaches morality in the manner of Auguste Comte.

One could argue against this position that it is not sociology as such that is revolutionary or conservative but, rather, the kind of systematic sociology that appears in the works of Auguste Comte or Karl Marx. In such a view, Marxist sociology, in the Soviet Union, would be said to have social implications because it claims total truth, while the empirical and analytical sociology of the United States could make no such claim. This objection, I believe, does not hold. Not that I refuse to recognize, or to attenuate, the full significance of the opposition between these two types of sociology. But they both have social implications, and both can be revolutionary or conservative.

In the last century, it is true, sociological doctrines were presented in the guise of a total form: they embodied politics and ethics alike. They had essential social implications by design rather than by accident. It was probably Auguste Comte who most clearly formulated the methodological conception that gave rise to the claims of yesterday's sociology.

According to Comte, the science of biology bore witness to a reversal in cognitive progression. Comte viewed those sciences anterior to biology as proceeding from first principles to the whole, whereas those that followed began by seizing the whole, their rudiments having no significance unless they were included in, and understood in relation to, the whole. From this primacy of the whole, Comte drew the conclusion that sociology begins by the most general laws (the law of the three stages, the transition from military activity to industrial activity, etc.). Now these laws allow for the resolution of the basic problems of all historical sociology: the relationship between first principles and the social whole, the determination of the principal types of social order, the order of succession of these types, the nature of present and future society.

In the abstract, a synthetic sociology of this kind could fall short of dictating rules of action: the inevitable future could be contrary to our wishes or to ethics. In fact, the inevitable future announced by Comte, just as that announced by Marx, is the realization of the ideal: a peaceable society blossoming with love, according to the former; a classless society, according to the latter.

Any synthetic sociology that derives its laws from historical evolution entails consequences for the course of action that those who subscribe to it are irresistibly led to take. A sociology that places present societies in a historical becoming [le devenir historique], that prophesies what the future society will be, weakens the societies for which it predicts ruin, and reinforces those whose success it proclaims as having already been inscribed.

It would be a mistake, however, to imagine that sociology ceases to be useful, as either a support or a critique of a given society or party, from the moment it renounces synthetic or prophetic ambitions. Sociology, even when analytic and empirical, is reviled by the right and the left alike, according to whether it brings to light certain facts that are judged by one side or the other to be unpleasant, or contrary to the proclaimed values or the interpretation of reality offered by either side. Inasmuch as individuals immediately judge social facts as being good or bad, objective sociology too is charged with making value judgments, for the simple reason that, when it brings facts to light, the intention of approving or criticizing is imputed to it.

This attribution to the scientist of intentional judgments—whether favorable or unfavorable—stemming from the confrontation of facts and values is a general reason why a sociology, even an empirical one, bears social implications. I see two other reasons also. First of all, such a sociology refuses to subscribe to the global interpretations of synthetic sociology. It is hostile or skeptical toward such interpretations. Those who adhere to one of these (the current trend of Marxist interpretation, for example) scarcely distinguish between skepticism and hostility: they view skepticism as a barely camouflaged form of hostility. Whether the American sociologist declares ignorance with respect to the future of Soviet socialism, or whether he declares the prophecy of the final victory of socialism to be false, the Soviet sociologist in both cases will judge him to be anti-Marxist. For it is of the essence of totalitarian ideologies to consider all those who do not accept them, regardless of the nuances of their rejection, as adversaries. In other words, just as nonideology is seen by the ideologue as the equivalent of anti-ideology, so the supporters of a synthetic sociology will accuse empirical sociology of being ideological on the grounds that it refuses to appreciate global problems and fails to take fundamental laws into account.

Second, an empirical sociology does not limit itself to establishing facts; it assembles and arranges them. There is some truth in Auguste Comte's formula, despite his sometimes abusive application of it: one can truly understand a fragment of a society only by reinstating it in the whole. An inquiry into the psychology of workers in a given factory means nothing unless certain factors are taken into account, such as the role the factory plays in the surrounding area, and in the branch of industry involved; the status of ownership of the means of production; the relations between industrial workers' organizations and employees; and so forth. Even more to the point, the interpretation of a nation may well be warped if it is made in isolation without comparison with foreign nations. Comprehensive considerations and comparisons of individual cases are indispensable to the truth of analytic sociologies.

Let us summarize. The sociologist cannot remain aloof from the conflicts of the society to which he belongs. Whether he limits himself to fractional studies or strives for a global view, he nonetheless makes judgments on the social order and thus subjects them to the use of both partisans and adversaries of this order for their own ends. Historical and synthetic sociology of the Marxist type alone condemns certain societies while exalting others. Empirical and analytic sociology identifies with none of the conflicting parties; without even invoking the ideological character that ideologues impute to the refusal of ideology, however, it nonetheless provides arguments to one party and to the other, turn and turn about. I do not intend to draw from this fact the conclusion that all sociologies are equally ideological and partisan (quite to the contrary), or that sociologists, by virtue of the fact that they cannot remain neutral, have no reason to repress their passions or practice self-imposed moderation. My conclusion is quite otherwise: the sociologist must, at the same time, be conscious of his preferences and of the social implications of his theories, and he must seek out those conditions in which knowledge of society conforms to the requirements of science.

II

Let us consider an example I find of particular interest: that of social classes. Indeed, the theory of classes is central in Marxist-Leninist sociology, and its importance is recognized by Western sociology. In the eyes of Soviet sociologists, Soviet society is made up of nonantagonistic classes, while capitalist society is seen as being torn apart by the struggle of fundamentally hostile classes. American sociologists, while not denying the existence of classes, do not view them as necessarily constituting the major differentiation in American society. Both Soviets and Americans willingly speak of a classless society (although they give different meanings to the term) with respect to their own, and a class society with respect to the other's. Polemic use of the term is obvious, both here and there. But where are the facts, the uncertainties, the interpretations?

All modern societies are heterogeneous. Let us discount, as Joseph Schumpeter has done, the distinctions between races and nationalities that exist in most nations, even in those which were formed in the most distant past. Individual members of modern societies seem to differ from one another for purely social reasons. If we say that they *seem* to differ in this way, it is not so much because the differences are questionable than because social distinctions, which are not reducible to biological and hereditary differences between individuals, may nonetheless be connected to such differences to a degree that is difficult to gauge.

Individuals exercise *different* trades and professions, they have *unequal* income, they have *different* lifestyles, they do not enjoy the same prestige. This heterogeneity tends to become hierarchical and collective. Whether it is a question of financial resources or of social esteem, it is the maxima and the minima, or the haves and the have-nots, that are noticed. These differences are such that they lead to the formation of groups within which incomes, jobs, lifestyles, and prestige are analogous and share the same relative importance. It is with this latter trait—the collective character of inequalities—that a few uncertainties begin to appear: is it the differential between incomes or the differential between degrees of prestige that accounts for their no longer occupying the same rank? To what degree do the different criteria, such as lifestyle and income, for example, coincide? (A small farmer is closer to a midsize farmer with respect to lifestyle and thought, even if his income is closer to that of a skilled laborer.)

This heterogeneity, hierarchized in groups that each admit of a certain homogeneity, can be called *stratification*. All modern industrial societies are stratified and are destined to stay that way for a long time. It is unlikely that the diversity of jobs will disappear, or that this diversity will cease to create a hierarchical heterogeneity; jobs will continue to be considered unequal in terms of dignity and prestige, thereby sanctioning the inequality of remuneration.

Given this stratified heterogeneity, what meaning can be attributed to the formula "classless society" (which amounts to looking for what is considered to be essential to a class)? I perceive at least four possible meanings.

1. If distinctions between hierarchical groups were strictly set for life—in other words, if the laborer's son had as much chance to become an entrepreneur as the entrepreneur's own son did—classes would no longer exist as a fate imposed upon the individual. By the same token they would appear strictly functional, called into being, that is, by the intrinsic needs of collective life.

In fact, such perfect mobility can never really be, because it would presuppose a perfect homogeneity: the laborer's son would have as much chance to succeed in his studies only if the modes of existence were the same at the top and at the bottom of the pyramid. Social distinctions could be called strictly functional, and could appear to be the expression of biological differences only after social mobility had placed the individuals at the same starting point. Nevertheless, application of the "classless society" formula is conceivable in proportion as social mobility increases and as the hereditary character of social conditions diminishes.

2. The distinction between hierarchized groups varies in magnitude. The tendency away from distinction can be understood in two different ways. First, the boundaries between groups become ever less distinguishable, inasmuch as the number of intermediaries between unskilled workman and entrepreneur increases, with the skilled workman, the foreman, and technical specialists constituting supplementary ranks in the hierarchy. And, second, the inequalities of income between members of different groups are reduced to the point that lifestyles, ways of thinking and feeling, are increasingly alike. This three-pronged hypothesis does not necessarily imply internal concordance: the swelling of intermediary ranks and the reduction of inequalities of income do not necessarily bring about homogeneity in lifestyles and ways of thinking. The very notion of inequality of income is equivocal: even if income inequalities remain constant, in both absolute and relative terms, they do not necessarily result in heterogeneity in the basic standard of living. It is conceivable that, in an affluent society, food and clothing may be the same at the top as at the bottom of the pyramid, even if income at the apex is more than a hundred times higher than at the base.

3. Are these objectively distinct groups self-conscious or not? Do they view themselves as intentional or tractable unities? To what extent is the bourgeois aware of being bourgeois, and to what extent does he desire to be so? Class consciousness is obviously not independent of the material phenomena that we have just considered, but nei-

ther does it derive from them as a result of an inexorable mechanism. In other words, groups can be very different, materially and psychologically, and yet not be conscious of themselves as individual units. They can be very much alike, objectively, and not lose their consciousness of being apart from one another. Is this to be regarded as inadequate consciousness vis-à-vis reality? Such a formulaic conclusion is too simple—all the more so as the terms *consciousness* and *reality* are not immediate opposites: social reality is made up of experiences undergone by the consciousness of all.

4. Finally, we cannot ignore Marx's formula, which probably expresses the essence of his thinking on classes. An approximately homogeneous social group does not, by this fact alone, constitute a class. Individuals who share the same fate must think of themselves as a unity on the national level, and they must stand in opposition to other groups in order to defend their own interest. A class has self-interest only on the condition that it is, and wills itself to be, struggling against other classes. In this sense it is doubtful that the Soviet formula of nonantagonistic classes is authentically Marxist.

Of these four meanings, more than one of which can be subdivided, the first two lend themselves to a theoretically objective study, not bound to the observer's preferences; the third designates a reality difficult to circumscribe. As for the fourth, it is by nature tied to a comprehensive interpretation of the society under consideration.

Social mobility, continuity or discontinuity of the hierarchy, presence or absence of clearly defined demarcations, heightened or diminished heterogeneity of lifestyles and modes of thought, narrow or wide differences of income—such facts are often difficult to establish with certainty or precision; in themselves, however, they are neither equivocal nor imperceptible. Nor are the evolutionary trends in modern industrial societies disputable. As long as there is progress in productivity, as long as there is a rise in the standard of living, as long as labor continues to shift from agriculture to industry and commercial or administrative sectors, all mobility increases rather than diminishes, the range of remuneration shrinks rather than expands, the intermediate ranks multiply, and the means of mass communication allow an increasing portion of the population to participate in the same forms of entertainment and culture (or nonculture). That said, the distance, both material and psychological, between manual laborers and privileged minorities (industrial leaders or professionals) remains obvious. What remains to be seen are the minute causes of this distance, the importance the sociologist must attribute to it, and the importance individuals themselves attribute to it.

The two phenomena—class-consciousness and the consciousness of antagonism—are in themselves difficult to grasp. If I try to remember what my "class-consciousness" was before my sociological training began, I can do so only with difficulty and can barely prevent the intervening years from appearing to be the cause of the indistinctiveness. To put it another way, I do not consider it a proven fact that every member of a modern society is conscious of belonging to a clearly defined group, included within the total society and dubbed a class. The reality of stratified groups is incontestable; that of self-conscious classes is not. I marvel that so many sociologists continue rigorously to define classes without further being able to tell us how many classes there are in a given society, or whether all individuals *psychologically* belong to a class.

Similarly, I am amazed that sociologists so often forget the fact that class-consciousness and consciousness of antagonism are subject to the political regime, the tenets of the state, and the persuasions of intellectuals (including sociologists themselves). Class-consciousness is the consciousness of belonging to a group that embodies a portion of the members of a national society and that sets itself against other groups, thereby occupying a determined place in the hierarchy. Leaders cannot create this consciousness if it does not exist implicitly as a result of material circumstances. The state cannot eliminate the feeling of otherness if the living conditions of different groups are too far apart. But the right or the prohibition of class propaganda, the right or the prohibition of class organization, determine, in part, the degree of reality of that evanescent phenomenon known as "class-consciousness." A sociology of classes divorced from the sociology of political and social regimes has become an absurdity in our time.

That's not all. The problem of classes is, in a sense, a modern form of the eternal problem of social unity, friendship among citizens. In this regard, modern societies distinguish themselves from historical societies by the intransigence with which they proclaim the ideal of citizens as theoretically being equal and, so to speak, alike. If we recapitulate the enumeration that appears in the opening lines of the *Communist Manifesto* (freemen and slaves, lords and serfs, guild masters and journeymen), if we call to mind the Greek city-states, in which democracy was embodied by the citizens alone, or the Middle Ages with its hierarchy of hereditarily transmitted ranks, or the ancien régime with its orders, then the originality of modern societies appears glaringly obvious: these societies are the first categorically to deny judicial and hereditary distinctions between their members. Socioeconomic heterogeneity is recognized as fact, inherited from the past, which must be surmounted along the way to a homogeneous society. If American propaganda has attempted to spread the formula of a classless society, it is not only for the purpose of satisfying the requirements of the cold war; it is also that this formula is closely connected with the proclaimed ideal of modern societies.

At the present time, experience has shown that the objective distinctions between stratified groups can be reduced but not eliminated. On the other hand, class-consciousness, especially the consciousness of antagonism, can be blunted and almost eliminated. There are thus three means of establishing that a stage of classless society has already been reached: by decreeing that classes are disappearing as a result of the increase of intermediate categories, the acceleration of mobility, and the progressive assimilation of lifestyles; by decreeing that classes are disappearing together with class-consciousness and the consciousness of antagonism; or by attributing to one of the factors of social heterogeneity an exclusive or at least predominant causality, and by stating that this factor has vanished in one type of society and not in another. Two of these means are applied in comparable fashion in the Soviet Union and the United States. The third means is reserved for Soviet or even Marxist sociologists.

Class, the Marxists say, is characterized by a particular place in the process of production. This infinitely repeated formula presents an immediately apparent ambiguity: if the "process of production" formula is taken in a purely technical sense, the working class occupies the same place in the Soviet as in the American process. On the other hand, if the formula is judicially defined, the American worker, who works on machines that are owned by capitalists, does not occupy the same place as the Soviet worker, whose instruments of production are collectively owned.

The Soviet and Marxist sociologist is therefore tempted to stress the ownership of the means of production. He is certainly free to declare: "I call classes those social groups that are defined by a determined relationship to the means of production." But, following from this, landowning farmers will be in the same class with Dupont de Nemours, Ford, or Boussac, while a manager who does not own company stock or a manager appointed by the state are mere wage earners. The consequences are so manifestly absurd that all sociologists are forced to modify the theory and add other criteria to that of ownership.

Moreover, since experience seems to show that nationalization does not appreciably modify either the organization of business firms or the material condition of workers, the sociologist tries to demonstrate the decisive importance of property and classes by another means: by assimilating every regime to a particular class. Capitalism, the regime of private ownership of the means of production, is defined as such by the political domination of capitalists. The socially privileged minority is, by virtue of this fact, the authoritative minority of the state. Whence the definition, by Soviet sociologists, of the regimes of societies behind the iron curtain as socialist or proletarian. These same sociologists see fit to agree to the idea of class-consciousness in capitalist societies because it weakens those societies; they do not agree to it in socialist regimes that emerge from the revolution.

This antithesis pertains to political regimes rather than social distinctions. Of course, the presence or absence of individual ownership of the means of production does exert some influence on the modality of social distinctions. Private ownership of business firms renders the distribution of income more complex, and creates certain additional inequalities; it can accentuate the feeling of alienation among workers in relation to their work, and the feeling of otherness vis-à-vis the organizers of collective work. But this factor is neither exclusive nor dominant. When workers (or those who speak in their name) enjoy a steadily rising standard of living, they sometimes openly prefer a private entrepreneur or corporation to an authoritative and official representative of the state as organizer of their work and remunerator of their efforts. The essential, decreed difference between capitalist and socialist societies cannot be explained in terms of business firms or social hetereogeneity; what must be considered is "the class in power," here and there.

But this set phrase, "the class in power," obviously has only mythological significance if the class is the proletariat. It may be the party that is in power, or perhaps the Central Committee, the Politburo (or Presidium), or even Stalin alone, during the period of the personality cult; the millions of workers, however, are in the factories and not in the Kremlin. Although the distinction between social class and politically ruling minority is obvious on this side of the iron curtain, it impels us to reexamine the so-called confusion between the bourgeois, or capitalist class, and the politically ruling class in Western societies. The absurdity of this confusion is not as obvious as that of the confusion between proletariat and party. The bourgeoisie, in effect, includes all of the privileged, or the equivalent of what the Soviet sociologist calls a stratum rather than a class—namely, the *intelligentsia*. The latter, in fact, includes all nonmanual workers, technical specialists, administrators, writers, members of the party apparatus, officers, etc.

If one were to suggest that in the Soviet Union it is the *intelligentsia* that is in power, the proposition would be universally derided. To suggest that in the West it is the bourgeoisie that is in power makes scarcely any more sense, unless the concept of the bourgeoisie is restricted to one of the several minorities commonly designated as bourgeois. But then it would have to be demonstrated that this minority (monopolists, directors of trusts, etc.) is in fact omnipotent.

To declare that classes are, or are not, opposed to one another is not the same thing as to state a fact; it is simply the stating of an opinion, whether sympathetic or hostile, concerning a political regime. Indeed, whatever the social heterogeneity may be, whatever may be the status of ownership, social groups have *one* interest in common with regard to economic growth, from which they all derive benefits, and *some* interests that may be in conflict with regard to the distribution of income or the sharing in investment profits, or even the distribution of authority in the running of the whole society itself. It goes without saying that a regime that prohibits professional organizations and individual demands represses rival interests. But psychologists have taught us that feelings that are repressed do not necessarily disappear.

III

At the core of the problematics of classes I perceive an antinomy between the fact of differentiation and the ideal of equality. Certainly, neither the fact nor the ideal is precisely defined. No one denies that the members of a collectivity are condemned to exercise different trades and that they are born with physical and intellectual differences. But modern societies push the egalitarian ideal much farther than any society in the past. Not only do they insist on not witholding its benefits from any individual, but, beyond formal or judicial equality, they take pride in offering to the greatest possible number of citizens similar living conditions, and in reducing the advantages that children inherit from the success of their fathers.

Social differentiation is important in itself, since it is based on a vague but compelling ideal and also because it is considered to be a curable ill, or at least a social misfortune that needs to be surmounted. It is important by virtue of its causes: it is related, as a matter of fact, to certain characteristic traits of all social orders as well as of the modern one. Only structural analysis can specify the extent to which the ideal of homogeneity is accessible. Finally, social differentiation is important by virtue of its effects: the sociologist may be interested in the precise forms that it assumes in every village or in every global society. His interest is no more ridiculous than that of the collector who busies himself looking for all the stamps of the Argentine Republic. But there is one *essentially* important consequence of differentiation: to what degree do there exist stratified groups which become self-conscious and rise up against other groups, with the will to struggle, either through peaceful or violent means? The judgment that is brought to bear on the impact of this aspect of the phenomenon is not an arbitrary one, for it is derived from the eternal requirement of *consensus*. Every society comprises conflicts between individuals or groups on the one hand, and the mutually shared acceptance of a community on the other. The sociologist, in studying modern societies, tries to answer the traditional question: to what extent, and under what conditions, can there subsist a community among stratified groups? If this, fundamentally, is the problem of classes, it explains why sociologists rarely avoid partiality, and also how they could avoid it.

There are many modes of sociological bias. The first and most common form of bias is the *arbitrary selection of facts*. Social heterogeneity appears more or less distinct, depending on one's point of view: when one is inclined to justify a social order, it is easy to stress the indications of increasing homogeneity and neglect the signs of a subsisting heterogeneity. Science implies, above all, the will to see the facts as they are and not as they ought to be according to official doctrine. In this sense, science is possible only in societies that lend themselves to "disenchantment."

The second type of sociological bias results from *confusion, at the theoretical level, between conventional definition and definitions that express the results of research.*[1] We have the right to point out dif-

---

1. For example, Gurvitch proposes the following definition of class: "Social classes are particular de facto and distanced groupings, characterized by their superfunctionality, their tendency towards advanced structuring, their resistance to penetration by the global society, and their radical incompatibility with other classes." Everyone has the right to choose his definitions; it remains to be seen if there exist, in modern societies, realities that correspond to this definition. No one will doubt that classes are "distanced groupings": we have never seen all the members of the French or German proletariat, a fortiori the worldwide proletariat, lumped together as one group. It will be admitted without too much difficulty that classes are not organized (the party that appeals to a given class is organized, the class itself is not), or that classes are neither unifunctional nor plurifunctional but, rather, suprafunctional (the distinction between pluri- and suprafunctional lends itself to controversies of a largely conceptual nature). But when it is affirmed that classes have their own values and functions, or that they resist penetration by the global society, the observer asks for proof, and maintains, in

ferences (or not to point them out) between *strata* and *classes*, but inquiry alone allows us to say that there are (or that there are not) constituent groupings on the national level, each one of which is conscious of its unity and its opposition to other groups; the same requisite holds true when one wishes to specify the character of actual antagonisms.

The third type of sociological bias consists in *claiming to know with certainty and precision those phenomena which, by their very nature, are equivocal.* A sociologist who had the courage to observe himself, or straightforwardly look around himself, would recognize the difficulty of formulating categorical propositions of a general nature concerning what has come to be called "class consciousness" or "class antagonism." Let me make myself clear: I am not advising against the study of such phenomena; on the contrary, they seem to me more interesting than the mobility rate, whether gross or net. What I do fear is that sociologists may think themselves bound, because of their obligations as scientists, to attribute to the consciousness of those who constitute their object of study a firmness it does not have. That such and such percentage of French workers votes for the Communist party is an incontestable fact; that the Communist party has for some years now been incapable of triggering strikes out of strictly political motives, and that workers in May 1958 did not have the slightest intention to take to the streets, is another fact. Do voters sincerely wish that the party they vote for should come to power? How many of them sincerely wish it? Why would the answer to such questions be any less equivocal than the notion of sincerity itself?

The fourth form of sociological bias is *the arbitrary determination of what is important or essential.* Marxist sociologists have the right to consider that the most important thing is the question of ownership of the means of production. Still, they must justify their decision, that is, they must specify what, in fact, are the consequences of the two statuses of ownership for social heterogeneity, and what are the re-

---

any case, that such a definition can only be the conclusion of empirical study, and not a mode of designating an object or a theory that prompts research.

What is more, it is doubtful that propositions such as "Classes are resistant to penetration by the global society," or "Classes create their own functions," are necessarily true or false for all the classes in all industrial societies, or for all the classes in a single industrial society. I have always been surprised that most sociologists have not drawn inferences, though it is easy to do, from the difficulties they experienced when they tried to specify the classes into which a particular society was divided. Everything, from Marx to Gurvitch, transpires as if one were assured that societies are divided into classes, without being sure of the number and identity of these classes.

ciprocally dependent relations between status of ownership and political regime.

The fifth type of sociological bias consists in *projecting, upon reality itself, the observer's judgment of the merits or defects of the social order*, a judgment that the sociologist has the right to make, but that is not inscribed in fact, whether material or psychological. The Soviet sociologists who declare that classes in Soviet society are not antagonistic, while those of capitalist society are, may mean three different things.

They may mean that the classes in Soviet society are not conscious of their antagonism, while the classes in capitalist society are conscious of having fundamentally opposed interests. This affirmation, however, is refuted by cooperation between classes such as is practiced by American labor unions, and also by labor unions and the Labour party in England.

Or they may mean that antagonism *must* exist in one case, and *must not* exist in the other. Since this having-to-be does not express a historical determinism, it expresses an ethical or political obligation. But then this obligtation, in order not to be the simple expression of a preference, whether individual or collective, must be founded on the state of class relations in one social order and the other. If pauperization were to accompany economic growth, antagonism would of course be an integral part of reality. If the increase of the standard of living and the reduction of inequalities accompany certain phases of growth, whatever the regime, there is no evidence either of peace on the one side or of antagonism on the other.

Or Soviet sociologists may mean that, *in fact*, classes clash here and cooperate there. But unless one bears in mind the incontestable antithesis between authorization and interdiction of class organizations, this third meaning sends us back to either of the first two. Either the classes, in capitalism, *are* conscious of their opposition because of the private ownership of the means of production, or they *must* be opposed to capitalism. Since capitalism does not prevent the simultaneous rise in the standard of living of all classes, the so-called reality of antagonism is based solely on the acknowledged character of competition between classes, or on the superior effectiveness of a Soviet-type regime. This superior effectiveness is not substantiated, and the very concept of effectiveness lends itself to multiple interpretations.

What is therefore required, to avoid bias, is a triple effort with respect to empirical exactitude, to theory or criticism, and finally to values, which are implicit in society as well as in science.

That the sociologist must primarily and above all explore the real is, so to speak, self-evident. But this necessary exploration inevitably reveals that society violates, here and there, the values it proclaims. All currently known societies include institutions that are incompatible with the ideal they profess. Archaic societies were probably the least unfaithful to their ideals. Modern societies, by virtue of their egalitarian aspirations and chaotic transformations, seem to forswear themselves more than all those that preceded them. Democratic principles notwithstanding, racial prejudice and single-party and state doctrine in the name of human liberation are but two examples of these innumerable contradictions between the way collectivities conduct themselves and the way their own language prescribes that they ought to conduct themselves. Sociology ceases to be faithful to its mission as a science as soon as it casts a veil over a part of reality.

But it is no less unfaithful to its mission when it limits itself to bringing to light the authentic imperfections of the society under study. The enemy of the United States finds all the arguments it needs in literary and scientific works of American writers. The enemy of the Soviet Union may have greater difficulties in finding what it is looking for in Soviet writings. Yet, there is no lack of anti-Soviet books composed almost exclusively of censored articles in the Russian press or passages of self-criticism in official books.

In order to avoid camouflage or defamation, countless facts must be gathered and ordered, and the significance of this fact or that must be measured. *The way to objectivity is through theory,* if we agree that theory should designate the determination of the problem in its diverse aspects, the elaboration of concepts, the enumeration of circumstances, determinants, and effects. It is only in relation to a theory thus conceived that we can indicate the significance both of a doctrine such as that of the Soviets (which defines class in terms of the ownership of the means of production), and of fractional inquiries performed by Western observers.

Only a theory such as this can allow for the kind of comparisons without which the interpretation of a particular society's structure will almost inevitably be warped by either excessive indulgence or severity. By means of formal and pluralistic theory, we can simultaneously grasp the phenomena of stratification that are common to all modern societies, and the specific traits of one regime and another, as concerns classes (the degree of consistency from one generation to the next; the existing awareness of constituting a unity or of being opposed to one class or another with regard to the distribution of income or the sharing of authority; the relative magnitudes of the consciousness of antagonism or of community).

Would this scientific comparison of class relations in either of these types of modern society cease to be useful for the needs of ideological controversy? Certainly not. Every sociology of classes lends itself to ideological exploitation, and it is easy to see why. As long as there is private ownership of the means of production, there will also be several categories of income; moreover, certain profits will appear to be disproportionate to the services rendered by the individuals to the collectivity. But if all private ownership of the means of production is eliminated, the state extends its functions and its powers beyond all limits, thus threatening individual liberties as well as lawful competition between parties and even the quality of economic management.

In other words, every social structure presents dangers or disadvantages, both in relation to the objective of efficacy and to the values common to modern societies.

I do not thereby conclude that the sociologist must avoid value judgments; but he must clearly clarify those which are diffuse and implicit in his social environment and, as far as possible, specify his own. When a sociologist studies social mobility, or the proportion of farmers' or laborers' sons among students, he would be wrong, in my view, to feign complete neutrality. The Soviet sociologist compares the social recruitment of students on both sides of the iron curtain, convinced that a superior mobility in the East, as revealed by statistics, would be considered a merit *on both sides.*

It is better, therefore, not to feign indifference to the ideological or political significance of facts such as these. It is better to analyze the vague aspirations toward equality and social mobility as precisely as possible and to examine the extent to which they can be satisfied; and, furthermore, to calculate what other benefits (individual freedom, pluralism of parties, representative institutions) risk being sacrificed as a result of exclusive consideration of the egalitarian objective.

The sociologist who studies classes must not ignore the value judgments made spontaneously by his readers. Their spontaneous judgments, however, are generally partial because they fail to recognize the implications of a phenomenon that may in itself be desirable, or the price that would have to be paid in order to attain a goal that appears commensurate with the shared ideal. The sociologist does not differ from the politician or the man in the street by virtue of his not having preferences or his refusal to express opinions; he should differ from them by his consideration of the whole, by his refusal systematically to exalt or denigrate, and by recognizing those defects that are inseparable from the regime he chooses to study, as well as the merits that are proper to the regime he opposes.

The sociologist strives to be scientific, not by neutrality but by fairness.

IV

It may be of some use to indicate briefly how this conception of *fairness* differs from the conception of *objectivity* developed by Max Weber. (It goes without saying that we will consider only one aspect of Weber's epistemology, the aspect that refers to the problems discussed in this article.)

Weber wanted the sociologist, whether as scientist or professor, to stay outside of the conflicts of the forum, and he thought he could guarantee neutrality by imposing a kind of asceticism, by prohibiting definite political opinions and value judgments. Critics have pointed out that Weber himself did not abide by this rule, and that his works—in particular the sociology of religion—were full of value judgments: "His work would not be merely dull but absolutely meaningless if he did not speak almost constantly of practically all intellectual and moral virtues and vices in the appropriate language, i.e., in the language of praise and blame. I have in mind expressions like these: 'grand figures,' 'incomparable grandeur,' 'perfection that is nowhere surpassed,' 'pseudo-systematics,' 'this laxity was undoubtedly a product of decline,' 'absolutely unartistic'" (Leo Strauss, *Natural Right and History* [Chicago: University of Chicago Press, 1953], p. 51).

One can respond to this criticism by saying that Max Weber, in accordance with the spirit if not the letter of his doctrine, did not proscribe value judgments from within the object under study. In reality, a sociology of art cannot disregard the quality of individual works, any more than a sociology of religion can disregard the quality of spiritual experience, because the fact under study (whether works of art or experience) is not defined unless its quality is taken into account. What a sociologist may *not* do, on the other hand, is establish a hierarchy between radically different works or experiences, as for example between the statuary art of Ellora and that of Reims, or between Buddhist and Christian saints.

Whether one agrees with the objection or with the response, or even with both, the sociology that interests us here—that of political and social institutions—does not abstain, whatever Weber may have said, from praising or blaming: "Weber, like every other man who ever discussed social matters in a relevant manner, could not avoid speaking of avarice, greed, unscrupulousness, vanity, devotion, sense of proportion, and similar things, i.e., making value judgments. . . . What would become of political science if it were not permitted to deal with phenomena like narrow party spirit, boss rule, pressure groups, statesmanship, corruption, even moral corruption, i.e., with phenomena which are, as it were, constituted by value judgments?" (Strauss, ibid., pp. 52–53).

We have added, in the preceding pages, a further argument against the forced interdiction of value judgments: sociology praises or blames, even when it affects not to, because the student or reader who inevitably interprets the facts or accounts with respect to his own values or to those of the collectivity therefore sees them as so many signs of approval or criticism. Individuals judge social phenomena spontaneously; they have a vague but strong sense of what is fair and what is not. This feeling is part of reality itself. In presenting facts or causal explanations in a neutral style, as if he were abstaining from appraising them, the sociologist affects to be a man unlike all others, and pretends to be unaware of the underlying meaning of his interpretations, as if social reality could be authentically understood without regard to the demands that citizens make upon their state.

But there is more. Falsely convinced that neutrality opens the way to objectivity, Weber left the sociologist with a wide degree of liberty in forming ideal types. What is objective and universally valid are causal events or relations. As for concepts—all of which he called ideal types because they were neither reflections of the real nor Aristotelean concepts, and because they all involved a kind of utopian rationalization—Weber considered them to be formed by the scientist as a function of the questions that the scientist puts to the object, and in terms of the scientist's interest in the society's past or present. The element of choice or arbitrariness that is included in the ideal type did not, in his view, contradict the ideal of objectivity, because the type was a mere instrument, a means of grasping reality by comparing the intellectual image with the concrete event.

Now if it is true that the concepts of the social sciences all bear some trace of utopian rationalization, it does not appear true that ideal types are mere instruments and that the object of knowledge is always situated farther beyond. In fact, the social sciences strive to substitute a more elaborate description, and one that is more clarified conceptually, for the vague consciousness that we acquire of society. The objectivity of this description is not guaranteed, whether by neutrality (for that is impossible) or by the sole truth of facts (false images can be given of true facts). It is in the arrangement of facts and the composition of intellectual images that the scientist risks partiality rather than the fairness he should be seeking. But he avoids bias and attains fairness only by denying himself the liberty that Max Weber permitted in the construction of ideal types, and by elaborating an analytic theory that would at least indicate the principal determining factors and allow for a reconstruction of the whole.

Let us note, moreover, that these remarks bear on Weber's explicit methodology and not on his practical applications. Like any other sociologist worthy of the name, Weber went to great efforts, first to reconstruct limited systems—law, economics, politics—then the total system of society, by following the natural connections between systems and by singling out those determinants which, in each system or in a particular type of social order, exercise the greatest influence on the whole. He endeavored to go back to the most abstract types that dominate historical diversity in order gradually to bring out, by a kind of progressive particularization, the diversity of distinct structures. We accept the notion that this typology, when applied to universal history, may be intimately linked to the questions of the scientist's own times or, for that matter, to the scientist's own questions. We similarly accept the fact that this typology does not claim to be the only possible one. But, for every society under consideration, sociological interpretation is objective insofar as it is "comprehensive," in the original French meaning of the term [i.e., "graspable"]: there can be no comprehension (*Verstehen*) without there being a grasp of the whole, a balance of elements, an arrangement of facts, a perception of the originality particular to one species of social order compared to the other species within the same genus.

Such a comprehension is obviously not neutral with regard to the ideologies of political parties, although it may not identify with any of these. If a party presents its ideology as a scientific truth (Marxism, for example), sociology has to subject that ideology to criticism, and the sociologist must dispassionately accept the accusation that will be leveled against him that "he is dabbling in politics." The principal propositions of Marxism (relation between powers and the scale of production, surplus value, exploitation and profit, pauperization, economic regime and social classes, economic alienation and other forms of alienation, etc.) concern facts, relations, and evolutionary tendencies. They are either true or false, probable or improbable, proved or unproved: if the sociologist does not always succeed in proving or refuting them, it is because they are expressed in such equivocal terms that they end up being devoid of meaning for want of an indispensable modicum of precision. The investigation and criticism of statements of fact which are found in all ideologies cannot help but be incumbent upon sociology; consequently, sociology cannot avoid taking a stand, whether for or against, in relation to the interpretations and programs of political parties.

What is really in question are the limits of the intervention of science in political disputes. Even if the sociologist demonstrates that Marxist propositions are, scientifically, 90 percent false, this does not imply that the other parties are right. Decisions, one way or the other, are made at singular junctures, with neither opponent being the sole spokesman for truth and really wanting the good of all. The fact that action is therefore, of a different essence than knowledge can be agreed upon without our necessarily having recourse to the radical heterogeneity of fact and value.

Aside from the question of the constraints of action, the arguments proposed by Weber (and by others as well) are to some extent valid. Most concrete actions are injurious to some interests and advantageous to others: a reasonable pro and con judgment is not of the same nature as the establishment of facts (although it is not radically different either, as Weber suggested). At a higher level, every social order entails a portion of injustice or, if you like, partial nonaccomplishment of its own objectives. Science can clarify the choice between diverse orders; it can show that a certain choice is more reasonable than others: the weighing of merits and defects is incumbent upon moral conscience rather than on scientific consciousness.

Even on this point I would hesitate today to follow Weber to the end. The weighing of advantages and shortcomings proper to each social order, as I have suggested in my analysis of social classes, is part and parcel of the comparison itself of the diverse, distinct orders (at least when it is a question of two species of the same genus, or of two forms of industrial society, for example). The results of scientific comparison spontaneously give rise to decisions of prudence. Perhaps the confrontation of radically different societies, the Greek city-state and modern democracy, for example, can result in a *neutral* intellection of essences. I doubt that the same is true when societies profess the same ideals and share a basically common structure.

Max Weber, for his part, recognized only two terms: objective science of facts and causal relations; and free, irrational commitment. Since he rightly perceived no global determinism with regard to the real, he affirmed that every position taken regarding political matters required a personal choice, and that this choice sacrificed certain values in order to satisfy other ones. This pluralistic vision was not in itself false, but it implied an incoherence of the real and an anarchy of incompatible values. If science is the comprehension of the whole, it does not supply one truth of action; but it does judge those individuals who are arbitrarily fascinated by one aspect of the real, or who are inclined, by fanaticism, to sacrifice everything to *one* value. In other words, Weber refused to recognize reasonable politics based on a balanced analysis of the social order because he wanted to reserve the rights of the ethics of conviction, to elevate the pacifist or revolutionary trade unionist who is unconcerned with the consequences of his acts to the same level of dignity as the responsible statesman; and finally, in the name of the contradiction of ultimate ends, he wanted to "save" ideologists, although science is particularly suited for unmasking ideologies.

Perhaps, at certain junctures, and beyond reasonable dialogue, one might again witness face-to-face confrontations between individuals or "conceptions of the world." But we are nowadays witnessing the end of the ideological age. Yesterday's ideologies, devalued by history itself, today look less like expressions of metaphysics or politics legitimately engaged in grand battle than like confused conglomerates of half-truths and obscure passions. Instead of laying the foundations of the legitimacy of commitment (even frenzied commitment) as Weber did, our intention is to lay the foundations of the legitimacy of scientific criticism.

This intention, as I willingly recognize and as I shall demonstrate in the next section, is tied to a historical moment (just as Weber's intention was, though it was different from mine); it is nonetheless constituent of authentic sociology.

V

If by "revolutionary" we designate those sociologies which promulgate or recommend upheavals of the social order, then the great doctrines of the nineteenth century—Auguste Comte, Marx, Pareto—were revolutionary, while modern schools, whether the empirical school in the United States or the "synthetic" school in the Soviet Union, are not. The latter two are conservative inasmuch as they deny the necessity of upheaval and endorse the existing order, as far as its principal traits are concerned.

This endorsement, in the Soviet Union, is explicitly doctrinal, since it is based on the self-interpretation that the Soviet state arrives at by referring to the inspirational theory of the regime's founders. In the United States, the endorsement is implicit: it results from the failure to recognize the possibility of revolution, and the affirmation that American society is constantly drawing nearer to its professed ideal. This progress, moreover, emphasizes contrasts rather than similarities.

American sociology is essentially *reformist*. Practiced by scholars who, for the most part, are liberals in the American sense of the word, it is almost always favorable (whether consciously or not) to so-called progressive measures, namely those that are designed to increase social mobility, to reduce inequalities, and to encourage the integration of ethnic or racial minorities in the community. Its reformist character, however, makes American sociology vulnerable to accusations, by some, of being *subversive* and, by others, of being henceforth subservient to the social powers-that-be.

The first accusation comes from extremists (McCarthyists or anti-communists). The second, far more interesting accusation is formulated by critics such as C. Wright Mills who denounce the fact that research is subordinate to those institutions that finance it, and who also denounce the conservative implications of Talcott Parsons's formalistic and superhistorical conceptualism. Research as such, whether analytic or empirical, is neither partial nor hostile to the existing order. But it is enough that researchers might be at the service of institutions and that they investigate principally the reasons for maladjusted or "devious" behavior (whether in the case of soldiers in combat or workers in the workshop), for it to appear that the ultimate goal is integration and that conservatism is the unacknowledged doctrine.

The institutional character of research and education does, assuredly, entail risks for sociologists: in the Soviet Union, the sociologist can easily become the spokesman for state-controlled orthodoxy; in the United States, the sociologist can just as easily become an adviser in human manipulation for industrial or even political enterprises. But it would be wrong, in my opinion, to explain the ideological tendencies of current sociology by its social situation alone. To a large degree, sociologists have ceased to be revolutionary because in the twentieth century none of the great modern societies carries within itself any revolutionary virtualities, except in terms of confrontation with the opposing type of modern society, or in terms of the inability to choose among possible types. In American society there continue to be multiple conflicts between individuals and groups, the stakes of which are economic and political, either in turn or simultaneously. A certain group, whether racial, ethnic, or social, will feel exploited and humiliated by the distribution of income or prestige. Those who have not climbed very high on the social ladder, whether because they lack certain skills or because of accidents of birth or competition, may develop a consciousness of belonging to a class that is lower than, and in opposition to, those who have succeeded. Groups that are relatively widespread and cohesive sometimes become conscious that they do not have a fair share of authority, and enter into a struggle to gain power, whether individual power in the case of minorities, or power of representation in the case of large groups. But whatever the stakes, economic or political, it is not easy to see what the objective of a truly revolutionary movement would be. Only the "lunatic fringe" can be revolutionary in the United States. One can legitimately ask if American sociology is still performing its function of social criticism, but how can it be blamed for not being revolutionary in a country where no one knows what a revolution ought to bring about?

Soviet sociology, on the other hand, could not be revolutionary unless it were to impugn the very basis of the Soviet *state* (whereas American sociology, in order to be revolutionary, would have to impugn the basis of American *society*)—that is, unless it denied the proletarian character of the seizing of power by the Bolshevik party in 1917, or denied that working class and party are identical. The bond between state doctrine and sociological theory does not allow Soviet sociologists the freedom of their Western colleagues. But if they were free, they too would probably be reformists rather than revolutionaries. Indeed, the Soviet economy, as it has been structured, can evolve only slowly toward the mechanisms of the market; the single-party monopoly of power is probably necessary for the functioning of current planification. The party monopoly, like the inflexibility of planification, could be relaxed only progressively, barring an upheaval from which a new despotism might emerge.

Why is it that the revolutionary spirit has shifted from dialogue within great nations to dialogue between nations, and that Soviet sociologists are no longer revolutionary except with regard to other sociologists? Twentieth-century doctrines evolved during an early phase of modernization; the relations between the development of productive forces, class struggle, and forms of political regimes were not clearly understood and gave vent to grandiose and equivocal doctrines. Once the development of productive forces reaches a certain point, the conflicts between social groups do not disappear but take on a decisive significance to the degree that their principal stakes are the power base and the ways the economy is administered. In a modern, prosperous society, the number of those who judge themselves to be unfairly treated and who despair of obtaining redress, by means of reforms, for wrongs suffered, is not of a magnitude as to make the conflicts of social groups an inexpiable struggle between classes, for or against the established regime. In the Soviet Union, the consecration of the state by the powers of ideology prohibits all challenge to the regime. In the United States, no class or party *aims* to present such a challenge.

When a state has presided over the construction of a great industry, when it has transformed the lives of millions of people who have moved from the farm to the city, it emerges, in the eyes of the masses—no matter what technique it may have used to achieve those ends—as living proof of the successful efforts of industrialization. The split of the people into two enemy classes, the one being answerable to the minority in power, the other rising up against it, does not occur. The revolt of the American proletariat against capitalist monopoly exists only in the fictitious world of Soviet ideologues.

The revolutionary polemic spills over and beyond national boundaries, or spreads within countries which, like France, are divided into partisans of one or the other of the two regimes, not to mention the partisans of a regime (never yet witnessed) that could supposedly be as organized as that of the East and as liberal as that of the West. Even in these countries torn apart by maladjusted ideologies, sociology, to the extent that it encourages empirical research, gradually weakens revolutionary passions and draws nearer to American reformism. This is not because sociologists are selling out but because the revolutionary myth is a legacy of the nineteenth century and no longer has any meaning. By converting to an "enlightened conservatism," sociologists are confining their study to the expression of historical evolution.

On the other hand, when traditional society slows down or paralyzes modernization, sociology, simply by analyzing the real, becomes revolutionary: it shows, at once, that traditional society is condemned and what the prolongation of the agony is costing. There too, the meaning that sociology acquires is imputable to society rather than to sociologists.

Perhaps we can now answer the question that we posed at the outset: to what degree has the effort scientifically to study social reality modified the extent of self-awareness on the part of modern societies?

At a fundamental level, the empirical and possibly quantitative study of social phenomena is (and will continue to be) increasingly practiced in all modern countries. It complies with both the inquisitiveness of citizens and the interests of those who govern. Whether in connection with housing or social security, the attitudes of workers in the workshop, the electorate's sectional interests, or housewives in a housing development, statistical surveys and psychological inquiries provide useful and practical information to constructors, managers, and governors alike. Soviet rulers can also profit from the knowledge of what the true state of mind of the governed is, not merely the state of mind postulated by doctrine. As concerns fractional, administrative, or technical problems, modern societies have, and will continue to have, ever more recourse to science.

This body of analytic research is not without its ideological consequences, since it helps bring to light the correspondence or contradiction between proclaimed ideal and collective existence, i.e., the narrowing or widening of the gap between principles and reality. Nevertheless, the science of sociographics can modify society's self-consciousness only insofar as it is interpreted by a theory. For the time being, at least, what the Soviets mean by theory is the survival of a doctrine from the past century, a doctrine that antedated both the flourishing of capitalism and the so-called Marxist revolutions. Scientific sociology has had little (if any) effect on the self-awareness of Soviet society; instead, the self-consciousness of the Soviet regime, by that regime's intent to implant it in the masses, hinders the progress of sociological knowledge.

Indeed, theory is scientific insofar as it maintains a critical stance. It must take into account, as far as possible, all the determining factors and all the facets of the phenomenon under consideration. It is permissible to single out a given determinant as essential, but only on the condition of *objectively* specifying the consequences that the presence or absence of this determinant would have. A theory of classes can be considered scientific to the exact degree that it does not *arbitrarily* choose among points of view and, arriving at a particular interpretation, does not neglect the facts and arguments raised by other interpretations.

In other words, where society in its entirety or political regimes are concerned, science, thus far, has not modified consciousness; for critical, comparative, and pluralistic theory barely exists. On one side it is repressed by the ideological dogmatism of the state, while on the other side it suffers setbacks because of its lack of concern with other possible structures and its exclusive concern with fractional studies within the framework of an undebated global structure.

Will the progress of critical theory shake the foundations of spontaneous self-consciousness in societies in the near future? Experience makes one rather doubt it. Sociology does not modify the social reactions of men, including sociologists, any more than psychoanalysis modifies the psychic mechanism of individuals, including psychoanalysts. Logically, a science which (in the manner of social anthropology) professes that a hierarchy cannot be established between archaic and modern societies, or between those formerly called barbarian and those we no longer dare call civilized, ought to create uncertainty and shake the faith. In point of fact, scientists, without too much difficulty, connect membership in their own society with the affirmation of theoretical equality among all societies. Likewise, the "theoreticians" of bolshevism did not hesitate to seize power when the opportunity presented itself, despite the fact that, in the actual state of productive forces, socialism according to the doctrine was impossible in Russia. Since the social order is at stake in the conflicts of our time, the bolsheviks give the name "scientific" to Marxist-Leninist ideology, which they quote as their authority in the battle of parties and states. But the function of this ideology is no different from that which non-scientific ideologies, through the ages, have performed: it vaguely sketches the traits of the good society, and justifies the present in terms of an ideal or imagined future. Actually, the bolsheviks do not teach us the art of acting according to the conclusions of science but, rather, the art of putting doctrine aside when circumstances smile upon the bold.

Belief in the power of a few, in the era of masses and technology; such is probably the supreme lesson offered to us by the bolsheviks. This lesson is contrary to their theory. The history of the Soviet Union is an epic of heroes, although its spokesmen speak only of determinism, of classes, of masses. It is in the United States that a collective epic has been enacted, and it is there that people authentically believe in the *common man*. Let the Marxists teach us not to forget famous men, and we will teach them that there are limits, fixed by social mechanisms, to the omnipotence of the founding fathers.[2]

There is no dialogue without irony: the irony of the exchange requires that each one learn from the other what his own theory ought to have taught him a long time ago. For dialogue to have been scientific and not ironic, sociology ought to have attained a state of self-consciousness. For the time being, however, sociology is more exacting in conducting research than in criticizing its own results.

---

2. Aron uses the word *bâtisseurs* here: a straightforward translation of the term yields "builder" or, from its synonym *fondateur*, "founder." The word *bâtisseur*, however, can have a figurative and pejorative connotation, as in the phrase *bâtisseurs d'utopies*. In the spirit of Aron's argument, particularly in the last section of his article, but also in the spirit of his concluding paragraph, I have therefore opted for the (self-consciously) ironic equivalent: "founding fathers."—Trans.

8

Social Class, Political Class, Ruling Class

Sociologists do not agree on the definition of the term *class:* either they do not all use it to designate the same reality, or they have differing views of the reality to which it is applied. But they all admit, at least, that the concept of class is a legitimate one, and that social groups deserve to be called classes. The very legitimacy of concepts like "political class" or "elite" class is questioned by a number of sociologists. Does the *ruling class* exist, or is it only a myth? Is the *power elite* created by the morose imagination of the sociologist, or does it in fact dominate American society?

Most American sociologists have an aversion to the concept of a ruling class, the very fact of such a class running counter to the ideology of "government of the people, by the people, for the people." Marxist sociologists like it even less, for according to Soviet ideology "monopolists" reign in the United States and "proletarians" reign in the Soviet Union. The existence of a ruling class is incompatible with the antithesis of the bourgeois regime (where it is the monopolists who govern) and the socialist regime (where the proletariat is in power): allowing for the possibility that there *is* a social reality that corresponds to the concept of a ruling class, the fact remains that in the United States it is not the monopolists, and in the USSR it is not the proletariat, who exercise the higher functions of administration and state.

This reference to official doctrines ought not suggest a polemical intention; instead, it should simply call attention to an incontestable fact: the question of the ruling class is loaded with ideological implica-

Translated by Charles Krance from *Archives européennes de sociologie* 1 (1960): 260–81. Reproduced with permission.

tions. Sociological analysis should aim to indicate the possibilities and limits of objective study.

Let us return to the first theorists of sociology at the beginning of the nineteenth century: Saint-Simon and Auguste Comte, Alexis de Tocqueville, Karl Marx. They all stress the opposition between the ancien régime and modern, postrevolutionary society. Prerevolutionary society was composed of orders or estates. Before 1789, the French were not born free and equal, they did not all have the same rights, they were not all subject to the same obligations. Social heterogeneity was considered normal, a heterogeneity of legal status and not merely one of trade or profession or, for that matter, of lifestyle. Whatever social mobility there may have been, the classes appeared to be hereditary; the legal status of the nobleman, just as that of the non-nobleman, was determined at birth. The French Revolution brought about a society whose principles were fundamentally different. All members of the collectivity became theoretically subject to the same legislation; and although a limitation on the right to vote, or a distinction between active and passive citizens, was maintained in Western Europe almost to the end of the past century, the revolutionary theoreticians had recognized and proclaimed the universal extension of citizenship. Juridically homogeneous and composed of citizens who were legally equal, modern society was nonetheless divided into groups (I am intentionally using the vaguest term) that arranged themselves into a rather clear hierarchy, the members of each group having sufficient traits in common to be discernible from members of other groups. It was a matter of interpreting the difference between the society of the ancien régime and modern society, of specifying the relations between the *estates* of yesterday and the *social groups* of today.

One interpretation is epitomized by Saint-Simon's famous parable: let us suppose that, due to a catastrophe, the elite[1] of diplomats, state councillors, ministers, parliamentarians, and generals, is suddenly eliminated; society will not be mortally stricken, the same quantity of goods will be produced, the living conditions of most will not be appreciably affected. On the other hand, let us suppose that the elite of bankers, industrialists, engineers, and technicians is eliminated; society will be paralyzed because the production of goods will cease or slow down. The central theme of this famous text is the opposition of industrial society and politico-military society. The former is the infrastructure,

---

1. I use the term *elite* here to designate the minority which, in each of the professions listed, has been most successful and occupies the highest positions.

the latter is no more than superstructure (if we translate the Saint-Simonian distinction into Marxist expressions). The two schools—Saint-Simonian and positivist on the one hand, Marxist on the other—diverge from the moment that each interprets the oppositions within industrial society. Saint-Simon and Auguste Comte, without denying the conflicts of interest between employers and employees, hold these to be secondary—the interests of both parties being fundamentally allied to one another and opposed, instead, to the interests of the survivors of the theological and military age. On the other hand, according to Karl Marx, the opposition between wage earners and capitalists, between laborers and owners of the means of production, is decisive. Each of the two parties, in this view, constitutes a class, and it is the struggle between these two classes that provides the mainspring of historical movement and finally of the the socialist revolution.

Marxism is, so to speak, an interpretation of the society of the ancien régime from the vantage point of modern society, and of modern society from the vantage point of ancien régime society. Neither judicial equality nor even political equality have appreciably modified the condition of the people. Workers are not "freed" simply because they vote every four years. The *social groups* of modern societies are no less distinguishable; their hierarchies are no less distinct than the prerevolutionary orders. But if they are comparable to the latter, despite the judicial equality of individuals, don't they cast a retrospective light on the true origin and structural basis of the ancien régime? The upper class (let us henceforth use this term in place of the term "social group") is invariably the one that possesses the means of production, yesterday the land, today the land or factories. In our time, capitalists are the equivalent of feudal barons, and the latter in their time were the equivalent of capitalists. Marx does not deny the originality of the modern society as expressed by the Saint-Simonians, but he does deny the essential solidarity of producers that the Saint-Simonian and positivist economists affirmed. It is only after the socialist revolution that social classes, both those of the ancien régime and those of modern society, will be erased, and that the promises extended by the prodigious development of productive capacities will be fulfilled.

Using an identical scheme to interpret the two societies—pre- and postrevolutionary—makes it possible, among other things, to compare the rise of the bourgeoisie with the rise of the proletariat. As the relations of capitalist production were formed in the midst of feudal society, so too the relations of socialist production will be formed in the midst of capitalist society, and the socialist revolution will give the power to the proletariat just as the bourgeois revolution gave political power to the bourgeoisie, who already possessed the reality of social power. But this rapprochement itself immediately illustrates the paradox, or rather the internal contradiction, of the Marxist interpretation.

Let us consider the world of labor: within all complex societies one can distinguish different groups according to the kind of work performed by members of each group (farmers, merchants, artisans) and, within each group, a hierarchy with regard to property, success, wealth, and income. The feudal lord and the landowning or industrial capitalist have in common the ownership of the means of production. But the function of the feudal lord was military; once the security of the peasants was assured, they had no further need of the lord. Only in the case of large farm estates, where collective labor required organizational or judicial officials, did they need the equivalent of a ground landlord. In mills or factories such organizational or managerial officials are obviously indispensable, even when they are not necessarily proprietors. In other words, eliminating capitalists cannot mean eliminating the administrators of collective labor; it only means eliminating proprietors, leaving it to nonowners to exercise the functions of organization or management.

The comparison between the rise of the third estate and that of the fourth immediately becomes doubly problematic. In the eyes of both Saint-Simon and Karl Marx, the bourgeoisie represented the working class, as opposed to the aristocracy, a military class with feudal origins. The opposition between the bourgeoisie and the proletariat, on the other hand, takes place within the context of modern society. The aristocracy could disappear as soon as it ceased to fulfill a military function, or as soon as this function was fulfilled by others. Likewise, the bourgeoisie can disappear to the extent that it is defined by the ownership of the means of production, and to the extent that individual proprietors are not necessary. But the functions fulfilled by the bourgeois—organization and management of collective labor—must then be fulfilled by others. In what respect, then, does the managerial personnel in an industrial society that does not possess the instruments of production differ from the managerial personnel in a society where individual appropriation of the means of production still exists? That is the first question to be posed in connection with the rise of the proletariat.

Within prerevolutionary society, the bourgeoisie constituted a privileged minority and held positions of command and prestige. The revolution gave the bourgeois the political power formerly exercised by the king and, in part, by the nobles. While they acceded to power, however, the bourgeois remained as they were. The proletariat, on the other hand, can delegate "representatives" to exercise political power; yet the representatives cease to live like the proletariat the minute they assume the directorship of a factory, a trust, or an administrative office. Bourgeois in power are bourgeois. Proletarians in power are no longer proletarians.

Alexis de Tocqueville, whose thoughts were no less concentrated than those of Comte or Marx on the comparison of the ancien régime and modern society, for his part considered social classes to be the principal personae of history. His book *The Old Regime and the French Revolution* includes this revealing sentence: "I am dealing here with classes as a whole, to my mind the historian's proper study" (trans. Stuart Gilbert, Garden City, N.Y.: Doubleday, 1955, p. 122).

Tocqueville does not systematically enumerate the struggling classes any more than Marx did in *The Class Struggles in France* or in *The Eighteenth Brumaire of Louis Napoleon*. But the prophet of socialism and the descendant of the old nobility, both of them equally good observers, evoke, in the course of their respective accounts or analyses, the following groups: the aristocracy (in which Marx distinguishes two fractions—legitimist landlords and Orleanist bankers); the upper bourgeoisie of business or law; the peasants (many of whom are property owners); the lower bourgeoisie of the cities (artisans or tradespeople); and the workers—a list to which Marx adds the class of the underworld, or Lumpenproletariat. All of these groups—some of them survivors of the ancien régime, others belonging to modern society—appear in person on the stage of history. In June 1848 it is the laborers, fighting alone, abandoned by their leaders. As for the national guard, it too is composed of lower bourgeois who have the feeling that they are fighting for themselves, for their class interest.

The existence of the state, and of the state apparatus, both civil and military, creates no less a difficulty for this interpretation of social and political history in terms of class. Louis-Napoleon and his circle of former Parisian bohemians seize the French state: which is the class in power? The property-owning peasants who voted, in a body, for the nephew of the great emperor? The upper, capitalist bourgeoisie whose interests were to be safeguarded and protected by the imperial regime? Is it the relation of social groups that is expressed in the imperial regime? Would this relation have allowed for another regime, and what would have been the consequences of a bourgeois republic?

Tocqueville would have had no problem in answering any of these questions. Although in his eyes classes were the principal personae of history, neither state nor government can be entirely explained in terms of classes and their struggles. Governors [i.e., rulers] are, so to speak, representatives, but neither mode of representation nor constitutional rules are rigorously determined by the social conjuncture. Modern societies do lean toward equality, but they can be either liberal or despotic.

Marx observes the enormous apparatus of state and the conquest of this apparatus by a clique of adventurers. He refuses, however, to derive the lesson from these facts—namely, the lack of direct correspondence between political conflicts and social struggles—and its implications concerning the efficacy of the state apparatus, which, although never independent of social classes, can never, on the other hand, be adequately defined by the mere power of a class. Having dogmatically affirmed that the state is the instrument of exploitation in the service of the dominant class, Marx observes, as a historian, the relative autonomy of political order. But he refuses to recognize it explicitly. He seeks refuge in utopia when he contemplates the proletarian revolution. The true revolution will consist in *destroying* the state apparatus and not in conquering it, as is the case with all revolutions which maintain a class society and the domination/exploitation of the masses by the bourgeoisie.

The utopia of a revolution that destroys the state apparatus offered an easy target to the realist theoreticians of the ruling class.

The modern theorists of *elites* or *oligarchies,* Gaetano Mosca, Vilfredo Pareto, and Robert Michels, are, in a sense, the legitimate descendants of classical political philosophy. But at the same time they are critics of parliamentary democracy and socialist utopia alike. Political philosophers have never put in doubt the inequality of men in terms of intellectual capacity, or the inequality of citizens in terms of wealth or power. The problem, in their eyes, was not to efface these inequalities, be they natural or social, but rather to ensure accession to positions of responsibility by the worthiest, and at the same time to establish reciprocal relations of authority and obedience, of benevolence and confidence, between governors and governed. Machiavelli had suggested that these relations were not always what they should have been, according to the moralists, and that the means most commonly used by rulers—force and ruse (lions and foxes)—were both blameworthy and necessary. Machiavelli's pessimism aside, however, the classical conception was prone to appear cynical as soon as it was used against democratic or socialist ideology. To say that all parties, including those that claim to have democratic roots and that comply with a democratic constitution, are in fact directed by a small number of men, by a more or less permanent governing committee, amounts to a return to the "eternal iron law"[2] of oligarchy, a law that appears deceptive or scandalous only to democrats given to believe that the power *of* the people is exercised *by* the people.

What is true for a party is true (a fortiori) for a regime. Whatever the mode of recruiting rulers, whatever the theoretical or practical functioning of the state may be, a regime is always in the hands of a small number of men. In this respect, so-called democratic regimes are no different from so-called despotic or authoritarian regimes. The *formulas* can change, that is to say the ideas or principles in the name of which the minorities reign, but the *oligarchic* fact remains. Mosca spent the first part of his life tirelessly unmasking liberal and bourgeois democracies, exposing the power of politicians, the intrigues and pressures exerted by financiers and industrialists that were germinating behind the institutional façades and appeals for popular support. Pareto pursued the same undertaking in an even more polemical tone, and, while declaring himself to be in agreement with Marx with respect to class struggle, he denounced, in advance, the so-called proletarian revolution of the future as a further example of a revolution conducted by a minority for the benefit of a minority. Marx admitted the oligarchical interpretation of all revolutions except the socialist revolution. It was easy and tempting to ignore this exception and to make the past account for the alleged revolution conducted in the name of the largest number and for the benefit of all.

Three terms were used to designate these oligarchies, which Mosca distinguished according to their respective formulas and Pareto characterized by their psychosocial attitude (the violent and the cunning, the revolutionary trade-unionists and the plutocrats): *elite, political class, ruling class.* The choice between these three terms may seem to be a free one: after all, sociologists legitimately use whatever terms they like as long as they provide their exact definitions. But a hesitance to choose between them reflects ambiguity with regard to the reality of the matter.

Pareto begins by defining the elite in an objective manner, that is, by referring to traits that are observable from the outside. Let us con-

---

2. Aron uses the expression *la loi d'airain,* the label given by Ferdinand Lassalle to the law which, in capitalist regimes, keeps the minimum wage at its lowest possible level. Marx tells us, however, "that nothing of the 'iron law of wages' is Lassalle's except the word 'iron' borrowed from Goethe's 'great, eternal iron laws.'" (From Karl Marx, "Marginal Notes to the Program of the German Workers' Party," in *The Essential Marx: The Non-Economic Writings,* ed. and trans. Saul K. Padover [New York: New American Library, 1978], p. 181.)—Trans.

sider those few who, whatever their profession—prostitutes or scholars—have succeeded, and who are thought by their peers and by the general public to be the best: the totality of those who have "made it big" constitutes what we will call the elite of society, the *best* (*hoi aristoi*), not in a moral sense but in the social and, so to speak, neutral sense. Rather than referring to the aggregate of the successful, however, when Pareto speaks of the elite, he most often refers to the small number of individuals who exercise political functions of administration or government, and also those who, while neither officials, deputies, nor ministers, influence or determine the conduct of the governing minority.

I too give these three words—*elite, political class, ruling class*— three different meanings; I designate another reality by each of them, or, if you like, with the help of each I pose another problem.

I use the term *elite* in the widest sense: the totality of those who, in diverse activities, have risen to the top of the hierarchy and occupy privileged positions that are sanctioned either by the amount of earned income or by recognized prestige. The term *political class* should be reserved for the much narrower minority, which effectively exercises the political functions of government. The ruling class should then be situated between the elite and the *political class;* it includes those among the privileged who, while they do not exercise political functions per se, cannot help but exercise influence both on those who govern and on those who obey, either by virtue of the moral authority they enjoy or because of the economic or financial power they possess.

I use the term *elite*[3] the least willingly of the three, because it has equivocal connotations. Is it possible, or even useful, to constitute a totality embodying all the successful, including the kings of thieves? Success in certain professions, such as those practiced in solitude by artisans, is not widely recognized outside of a narrow circle, and confers neither authority nor fame. It is neither very easy nor very useful to trace the circle inside which *success* assures entry into the elite. This word, fundamentally, serves no other purpose than to hark back to the eternal iron law of oligarchy, the inequality of talent and success (success not always being proportional to talent).

On the other hand, the terms *political class* and *ruling class* pose an important problem: the relations between the minority that actually exercises political power and a less narrowly defined minority that

3. On the other hand, I have no objection to the use of the term *elite* in the plural, as an equivalent of what I later call ruling classes.

exercises the functions of command or prestige in the society but not in the state. Every regime, whether democratic or soviet, comprises a political class. A society does not allow of *one* ruling class if industrial leaders, labor union leaders, and political party leaders consider each other mutual enemies, to the point of having no consciousness of solidarity.

The iron fact, or law, of oligarchy can be stressed with an aggressive intention regarding ideologies. Naïve democrats fancy that the people govern in the West, whereas the electors are in effect "manipulated" by "wily" politicians. Communists, whether believers or cynics, affirm that the proletariat is in power in the Soviet Union, whereas the central committee, the presidium, even the secretary-general "manipulate" the masses and, in the name of the proletariat, exercise a power which is more absolute than that of kings or emperors of the past. Such polemical and political argumentation is cheap. It is of no great interest to us, although it obviously includes a parcel of truth. It amounts to situating the problem without solving it. Given that, always and everywhere, a small number governs, what is this small number? What are its modes of recruitment, organization, formulation? How is authority exercised? What are the relations between the political class and the other privileged individuals, the other holders of power and prestige?

These questions are all the more unavoidable in that social differentiation, ever since the earliest sociological doctrines of the past century, has progressed over the same period of time in which claims for equality have been repeatedly affirmed. Today, equality before the law is hardly called in question on a theoretical level, and the universality of political participation by the right to vote is no longer at stake in the conflict. All members of the community are citizens. But citizens, in the sphere of what Hegel called "civil society,"[4] in the sphere of economic activity, all have professions. Whether on the level of city, region, or state, the administrative and political functions alike (the latter often being elective) are exercised by professionals or soon-to-be professionals. The political class is not hereditary either in the East or in the West. In the East, just as in the West, the holders of state authority have *ties* (which still remain to be specified) with those in a position of economic power and those who enjoy intellectual or spiritual prestige. We must analyze the various social categories that can belong to

---

4. *Bürgerliche Gesellschaft*, normally translated by "civil society."

the ruling class—or rather, as I have expressed it elsewhere—the different kinds of elite, if we want to compare societies in terms of their political class or their ruling class.

Four antitheses—*temporal power* and *spiritual power, civil power* and *military power, political power* and *administrative power, political power* and *economic power*—illustrate, it seems to me, the modern differentiation of authoritative functions, the multiplication of social groups that are capable of effectively exercising the functions of command or of substantially influencing those who exercise them.

In all societies, those individuals who establish the hierarchy of values, who formulate the ways of thinking and determine the content of beliefs, constitute what Auguste Comte called spiritual power. In our times, spiritual power is shared or disputed by three types of men: priests, the survivors of the spiritual power that the founder of positivism called *theological; intellectuals,* writers or scholars; and party *ideologues.* A quick look at both Soviet and Western regimes is enough to perceive a fundamental difference in the structural relations of *ruling categories:*[5] according to the Soviet formula, it is the party ideologues who proclaim the supreme truth and point out what is sacred. Priests are officially held in lowest esteem, and intellectuals must subscribe to the ideological truth, which is diffused to varying degrees, depending on the times and on individuals.

Power, in modern societies, proclaims itself to be civil in its origins and legitimacy, since it invokes a democratic legitimacy. But it is effective only on condition it obtains obedience from the chiefs of the army and of the police. In our time, in fact, there are many regimes which owe their accession to the participation and influence of the army. Many are the politicians who began by wearing a uniform, and who owe all or part of their moral authority, their prestige, to their military past.

The modern state is primarily an administrative state. Citizens as well as economic matters are permanently subject to the commands of officials who, in each instance, establish the rules of competition between individuals and draw inferences from the laws. This administrative power is in a sense "depersonalized" and sometimes "depoliticized": the officials order as officials, and the citizens obey both the laws and the anonymous representatives of the state. But the high officials belong nonetheless to the governing minority, both because they influence politicians' decisions and because the administrative power exercises an influence on the distribution of the social

5. Or, if you prefer, the elite.

product, a distribution that constitutes one of the stakes of the struggle between social groups.

Politicians are differentiated, in the West, from administrators, although in some regimes ministers are chosen from among the officials. They are "professionals" to a greater or lesser degree according to whether or not politics is their exclusive career and the sole source of their income; but they are always "differentiated" in the sense that their activity, as representatives or ministers, involves a network of obligations, rights, and specific actions.

This political behavior, taken as a whole, is linked to other groupings of social behavior and, more strictly, to what can be called the economic aggregate. Two categories of the privileged, holders of two kinds of power, emerge from the economic aggregate: *collective labor administrators,* owners of the means of production, managers, and engineers; and the *movers of the masses,* labor union leaders and eventually political party leaders, wanting to organize a professional group (industrial workers) on the basis of class affiliation.

These ruling categories are all present in any modern society, whether of a Soviet or a Western regime. I use the term *structure of the ruling class* or *ruling categories* for those relations that are formulaically prescribed, or imposed by law or custom, between the various types of the privileged; holders of either moral authority, legal power, or effective economic or social power. Western-type regimes are defined not by the mere differentiation of these categories but by free dialogue between them. Soviet-type regimes are defined by a lesser differentiation, especially by a lesser freedom of dialogue or of opposition between priests and intellectuals, intellectuals and ideologues, ideologues and party chiefs, and party chiefs and rulers. The officials of collective labor do not constitute a separate category from state officials. Mass leaders on the industrial level and union secretaries function as cadres rather than claimants, and are recruited accordingly.

A regime of the Soviet type, by comparison to a Western-type regime, presents two major characteristics: it strives to reestablish the fusion of state and society, while modernity has been creating or accentuating the distinction by differentiating the political functions, by tolerating professional or political organizations that are independent, and legitimately rivals, of one another. In the East, the administrators of collective labor, ranging from the industrial plant to the central planning bureau, are all officials, while in the West these administrators are divided into multiple categories (proprietors, nonproprietary managers, state officials). In the East, party chiefs are simultaneously and permanently executive heads, mass leaders, and official ideologists, whereas in the West those who govern are faced by an opposition—relatively independent heads of unions, writers, scholars, and ideologists who constantly argue about the true and the false, the sacred and the scandalous, while the temporary ruler's voice lacks the force to overpower the tumult of debate or propaganda.

These remarks are not intended to develop a theory of the ruling class, either in the East or the West, but only to indicate the type of problems posed by the study of *modern oligarchies,* or, in other words, the study of the *oligarchical fact in modern societies.* Social differentiation has not spared the *oligarchs,* but it has resulted in two extreme modes of being: the regrouping of ruling categories under the temporal and spiritual authority of the heads of a single party, and the disintegration of the ruling class in a kind of permanent cold war between the ruling categories. Most Western regimes are situated between these two extreme forms. Great Britain seems to me to be the most typical example of a country whose regime, although of a Western type, still possesses a ruling class: the upper strata of the business world, the university, the press, the church, and politics all gather in the same clubs; they often have family ties, they are conscious of constituting a community, they have a relatively well-defined picture of the higher interests of England. This class is open to individual talents; it absorbs those of modest origin and does not reject those already in its midst who have assumed the leadership of popular protest movements. The ruling categories constitute a ruling class to the very degree that the political class and the social elite overlap.

The empirical study of a ruling category includes essentially four aspects. First, from what social origins are politicians (or high officials, or intellectuals) recruited? Second, what are the qualities that seem to assure success, what forms does the career of a member of the ruling party take and from what professional backgrounds are such members drawn? Third, what manner of thinking, what conceptions of existence, are characteristic of this category? Fourth, what coherence and consciousness of solidarity is there among the members of this category?

These questions, and others that can be added to them, become decisive when we are dealing with political class and the relations between industrial leaders and leaders of state. The most serious decisions are made by one man or a few men. It is sometimes one man who must choose between peace and war. In this sense, the concentration of power is not a hypothesis but a fact. The primary task, then, is to determine the degree to which the decisions made by the president of the United States or the members of the cabinet express the interests, the will, or the ideals of a small group that can be called "the power elite," "monopolists," or "capitalists."

I shall first of all demonstrate that this question is more empirical than theoretical, that it relies on inquiry, not on doctrine or the analysis of concepts. The following remarks, therefore, will strive to circumscribe rather than deal with the subject itself. It goes without saying that in a regime founded on ownership of the means of production, the measures taken by legislators and ministers will not be fundamentally opposed to the owners' interests. The governors, in such cases, are not radically hostile to the interests of those who have succeeded on the economic plane. The rulers of Western democracies are not, and cannot be, enemies of what the Soviets call capitalist regimes on the grounds that such regimes admit of the private ownership of the means of production, and that they do not impose a totally planned economy. But this proposition is too obvious to be instructive.

To formulate truly worthwhile questions, we must go beyond this platitude. Capitalist regimes, according to such a vague definition, include extremely diverse forms, depending, in part, on the extent to which collective ownership, planification, or fiscal policy are widespread, progressive, etc. Before defining power in a given Western democracy in terms of capitalists or monopolists, one should first establish that the capitalists or monopolists are conscious of their solidarity and that they share a common notion of class and class interests. But the facts do not seem to suggest that such a consciousness exists, or that class interest is known and recognized by those it supposedly lumps together.

There would be nothing abnormal or unbelievable for a director of Standard Oil or General Motors to address himself directly to the government in order to obtain orders for production or, for that matter, to ask for government intervention against the threat of nationalization. Whether the government would yield to such pressures, of course, can only be guessed at. It would, however, be interesting if the political rulers were to make a decision on the sole basis that these pressures conformed to the interests of either such an influential and giant corporation individually, or to those of giant corporations, or "monopolies," in general. It so happens that this type of action has never been witnessed and is, indeed, improbable.

The Republican businessmen who filled the Eisenhower administration preached and applied the doctrine of sound currency and financial tight-fistedness because it satisfied their system of values; and they did so despite the fact that, in many regards, that doctrine was less favorable to the swelling of profits than the opposite one would have been. They tried to reduce military expenditures so as to balance the budget. They had no common interpretation of the international situation, and they would have had great difficulty determining what diplomacy best suited the class interest of big capitalism.

No one disputes the fact that military chiefs and leaders of industry in the United States today enjoy a very close relationship, for reasons of arms production certainly, but also because generals, when they retire, are offered positions in industry. Would foreign policy be in any way different if these ties were less firmly established? Do generals recommend a particular program in view of their future appointments? Whatever the regime, army chiefs and heads of industry in an industrial society are intimately linked. Are American diplomacy and the volume of arms production determined by these personal or social ties? In my opinion, no one has yet made credible the affirmative answer to such questions.

It remains for us to specify the relations between these ruling categories and social classes. Judging from all available evidence, the relations vary according to types of societies and regimes. We will therefore consider these relations only in the case of modern industrial society, such as has developed through the twentieth century in the United States, in the Soviet Union, and in Western Europe.

Population, as a whole, is divided into professions—agricultural cultivation, industry, services—that economic progress has multiplied and diversified. The income of each depends essentially on the place occupied in the respective production processes, this place being defined either in relation to the ownership of the means of production, or to the qualification of the work provided, or to both criteria at the same time. Soviet-type societies allow for only the second criterion, since they radically eliminate ownership of the means of production. The social organization that seems primordial to individuals is the system of production and exchange, the family community no longer being a unit of production, and the religious or ideological communities no longer furnishing, in most cases, the means of livelihood. "Civil society" (*die bürgerliche Gesellschaft*), as Hegel used the term, embodies the whole of the collectivity and constitutes, so to speak, its infrastructure. Does this give rise to opposing classes, one of which, the exploited class, is committed to the revolutionary overthrow of the established regime? Neither in the Soviet Union nor in the United States is the working class revolutionary; in other words, it does not appear to think or act as if its objective or ambition were to overthrow the economic or political regime. Nor is the working class in power; it has not transformed itself into a "universal class," whether in the East or the West. It seems revolutionary, in France and Italy, to the extent that the party to which a large number of workers give their vote models itself on a Soviet type, within a Western-type society.

Industrial workers, whether Russian or American, are consolidated with a certain organization, either administrative or technical. Empirical study establishes the magnitude of the differences in income within the working class. What is the wage scale differential between unskilled and the most highly skilled labor? Does the collective totality of workers enjoy the same lifestyle and share the same convictions? Are all workers mutually conscious of constituting a social or historical unit with its own, particular mission? In other words, when it comes down to classes—and we are using the working class as an example, for it is this class that, according to all authors, presents the most marked characteristics of class—two types of questions are raised: to what degree does class exist *objectively?* To what point is it self-conscious, and what does this consciousness contain in terms of either conservative, reformist, or revolutionary attitudes?

The first question arises in an identical manner in relation to the Soviet working class and the American working class. The second question does not arise, or call for a definite response, with regard to the Soviet working class because the structure of the ruling categories prohibits both question and answer. Let us place ourselves inside a modern industrial enterprise: the workers are subject to an authority that is neither democratically instituted (since it is nominated rather than elected), nor democratically exercised (it commands rather than discusses). If labor unions are free, they are likely to make rather vigorous claims, whether economic (wages, profit sharing), or political (participation in authority). If labor unions are directed by secretaries who are named by, or subject to, the party, certain claims will not be made. The very existence of a specific class interest, which might well be opposed to the interest of management, will be denied.

Let us now place ourselves on a higher level, that of industrial workers as a whole. The same opposition is revealed, and even more clearly. Class consciousness, the idea of a common vocation, depends more on propaganda and organization than on the degree of objective community (to what extent are the workers at the same time identical to, and different from, the other members of the total society?). Workers cannot rise to self-awareness as class if the economic and political regime prohibits autonomous organizations, or, to use another expression, if the structure of ruling categories prohibits dialogue between intellectuals, popular leaders, and politicians.

Class relations are not unilaterally determined by ruling-category relations. It would be foolish, in comparing the various Western societies, to attribute the revolutionary attitude[6] of the working class, in France or in Italy, exclusively to the actions of leaders. Do leaders determine the popular attitude? Or, to put it another way, are the masses swept along by the leaders? The answer must vary according to circumstances, and it is rarely categorical one way or another. All I have sought to demonstrate is that "class relations" in industrial societies can see the light of day only on condition that socioeconomic organizations outside of the single-party apparatus are tolerated. A comparison between the Soviet universe and the Western world reveals that it is the structure of ruling categories, and not class relations, that determines the essence of economico-political regimes.

Social groups, it is true, are formed differently, according to whether private ownership of the means of production, of land and machines, is or is not tolerated. The distribution of profits, standard of living, and lifestyle of each group are alike influenced by the rules that govern ownership and, even more, by the mode of regulation (open market versus planned economy). The major differences stem from the structure of ruling categories, from the relations established by the regime between the society and the state. For a Soviet-type regime to be installed, all that is required is that a Communist party, with or without the help of the Red Army, seize power. It is thus not the state of productive forces but the state of political forces, indeed military forces, that is the predominant cause—the cause of characteristics that are specifically those of each type of society, the cause of the rise or fall of one type of society or another.

Let us compare the results of these analyses with the sociological doctrines mentioned above, and also with the varying degrees of justification or polemics with which every regime interprets itself and other regimes.

The reality of the Soviet regime has little in common with the myth of "universal class" and "power of the proletariat." Power is exercised by the party that represents the proletariat but is no longer directed by proletarians. To be sure, a Communist-type revolution

---

6. The phrase is excessively simple, and revolutionary attitude involves many nuances. But our concerns here are limited to a theoretical analysis, and do not include description.

radically eliminates the survivors of former privileged classes (no-blemen and bourgeois-proprietors) and in this sense calls forth the ruling categories of the new society from amidst the working masses; it can thus, in theory at least, increase the chances of progress for the most talented individuals in each generation, since the handing down of privilege, though not totally precluded, is extenuated by the sup-pression of private property and accumulated family wealth.[7]

The merits of such a regime are, in part, the ones it attributes to itself; but they are also, in some measure, exactly opposite to those that are claimed by the official ideology. The struggle of groups for their share of the social product and the clash between workers and owners disappear, as the doctrine dictates, and society ceases to be the theater of a permanent cold war. Peace is restored not by suppressing the occurrence or the stakes of conflicts, however, but by preventing the organization of armies and of war propaganda. Saint-Simonians and Marxists alike deemed the cooperation of all producers to be in-dispensable, rulers and employees sharing the same basic interests. But the Saint-Simonians did not believe it necessary to abolish private ownership of the means of production for all producers to become conscious of their solidarity. Marxists, on the contrary, believed that there would be class struggle as long as there was a distinction be-tween capitalists and proletarians. They eliminated private ownership of the means of production (i.e., capitalists); then, in compliance with their doctrine, they proclaimed that there were no more classes or that the classes were no longer antagonistic; and finally, so that reality could not give the lie to their doctrine, they arrogated a monopoly to the party and its ideology. Eager to follow suit, the representatives of all groups, expressing themselves through the medium and vocabulary of the party, testified to the disappearance of classes and their struggles.

The Soviet regime is a reaction against the characteristic tendency of Western societies to differentiate functions and disperse ruling cate-gories. It reestablishes the unity of a ruling class, the spiritual and political unity of ruling categories which, in the West, is compromised by the dialogue of politicians, intellectuals, and popular leaders. In this sense, the Soviet regime is the opposite of what it claims to be; it accentuates the very oligarchy it denies, it confirms Pareto's cynicism, it is the victory of a minority that invokes the voice of history or of the proletariat as other minorities have invoked the voice of God or of the

7. The children of a Politburo member, from the very moment of birth, obviously enjoy certain advantages.

people. Pareto's theory of elites is better suited than Marxism is to the interpretation of revolutions that quote Marx as their authority. The revolutionary and creative effectiveness of the state has been gloriously illustrated by those who regarded the state as nothing else than the instrument of the economically privileged class. It is easy for those who possess military might also to secure possession of both economic means and power.

But the West, for all its "unmasking" of Soviet reality with the aid of Paretan conceptions, would be wrong in failing to recognize the historical accomplishments of the opposing regime. For the latter has, in fact, brought an end to class struggle, though admittedly not by substituting a miraculous harmony of interests for yesterday's conflicts; instead, it has simply proclaimed, and prohibited the questioning of, the very fact that such a harmony henceforth exists. The monopoly of a single party and ideology, the obedience of intellectuals and popular leaders to the party chiefs' orders, all contribute to the restoration of a ruling class. Western regimes, however, are not so much threatened by the omnipotence of monopolists as they are by the disintegration of the *social consensus* and the rivalry between ruling categories.

Those Soviet polemicists and Western critics who consider themselves to be informed Marxists "unmask" Western-type democracies by revealing the sinister roles played by monopolists or the power elite. Once again, the fact of oligarchy is unquestionable. But the characteristic trait of oligarchy, in Western-type societies, is not the secret despotism of a group of men (heads of industry or army chiefs); it is the absence of a commonly shared will and conception among those ruling groups that are thrust into a competitive relationship by the very law of democracy. The danger is all the greater as the competition between ruling groups does not necessarily give ordinary citizens a sense of freedom. Even if, as in the United States, the functioning of the economy or the conduct of diplomacy are not controlled or managed by anyone in particular—whether by one man alone, or by an association of men who are conscious of their constituting a group—the citizen still does not gain the conviction that he is capable of influencing either the course of events or the actions of the immeasurable industrial or military machinery. The mythology of a sovereign and clandestine elite will continue to prosper because it expresses the impotence felt by the majority of citizens, and identifies "those in control." The powerlessness is no less authentic in the case where "those in control" do not exist, or, better, where they are everyone and no one.

The theorists of the elite are not wrong in "unmasking" democracy. There is no government of the people by the people. Nor has it been demonstrated, however, that the desires or wishes of the greatest number have no effect on the conduct of those who govern. The question—to what extent do rulers manipulate the masses, or, conversely, to what degree do they limit themselves to translating the voters' aspirations into action?—is to a large extent a false question. In all regimes there is dialogue between those who govern and those who are governed. The plurality of parties, the regularity of elections, and the freedom of debate all reinforce public opinion and reduce the margin of maneuvering and manipulation by the ruling categories. But unbridled competition between the ruling categories, while it gives certain guarantees to the governed, does not grant them power, whether real or illusory.

Supposing that the ruling categories came down to viewing each other as mutual enemies, or that the state were no longer run by a determined minority that is conscious of its mission: the masses would not enjoy, for all that, the exaltation of freedom; on the contrary, they would imagine a mysterious elite, off in the shadows, spinning the threads of their fate. For if so many millions of men are powerless, a few must indeed be all-powerful.

The controversy, both scientific and political, surrounding the concepts of social class and ruling class has as its origin a specific trait of modern societies: the separation of social power from political authority, the differentiation of functions, particularly of political functions. The sociological theoreticians in the past century all recognized this dissociation of society and state (to use the German antithesis of *Gesellschaft und Staat*), and they all admitted that the development of industrial society would contribute to the reestablishment of unity; for the relics of the feudal system and of the ancien régime were finally disappearing, and the state was becoming the authentic manifestation of modern society. But none of the great Continental sociologists had a clear idea of what the modern state would be, as a truthful expression of modern society. Some saw it as being taken over by producers, others augured its dying out after the victory of the proletariat, and still others puzzled over the retrospective probability of a representative regime or despotism.

A principal cause of these uncertainties was the ambiguity of the notion of class, applied at one and the same time to privileged minorities (the nobility and the bourgeoisie), and to the masses (peasants and workers). The privileged classes of the ancien régime were minorities who possessed social, military, and political power alike: social power, in terms of land ownership; military strength, in that they were either combatants or officers; and political force, accrued by their exercise of judiciary and administrative functions. Before the revolution, the noble class had lost a large part of its economic power, and almost all its judiciary or administrative functions as well. Different men exercised these functions now, and these men were increasingly dependent on the state apparatus. But the nobility continued to be regarded as the model of the "dominating class," a minority characterized as being socially privileged and exercising real power, both in society and the state. This perception, to be sure, is incommensurate with regard to modern society, because the latter is characterized by a differentiation of functions that prohibits owners and managers of the means of production from themselves being either military chiefs or executive heads. Since this confusion of powers and forces is impossible in our times, the ideologues invented the myth of clandestine elites, who are said to exercise their omnipotence through intermediary individuals.

The reality of the matter is at the same time simpler and more complex. Relations of command, in modern societies, are essentially multiple: worker, citizen, taxpayer, and motorist are each of them answerable to a particular technical, administrative, legal, and political discipline. The men who direct these organizations and who preside over the various apparatuses inevitably differ from one another. On the factual level, the plurality of ruling categories is the primary datum, while in every regime the relations between the ruling categories are of a specific nature. Western regimes tolerate dialogue between these categories; Soviet regimes assign the power of monopoly to one party or ideology: they reestablish, for the benefit of the political leaders, the supremacy of a power both temporal and spiritual. The dissociation between society and state is reduced; the competition between elites is attenuated.

All modern societies claim judicial and political equality, together with a democratic principle of legitimacy, as their very foundations. At the vertex, they possess either a single party and a state ideology, or multiple parties and incessant debate. Between the base and the vertex are, first, the social groups, each one defined in terms of its participation in the production process, its standard of living and lifestyle, its ways of thinking and its system of values; then come the relations between these groups, described in terms of the attitude that the masses and the rulers in each of group assume toward the other groups. The relations between union leaders and entrepreneurs are determined, in the West, at one and the same time by the regime (which authorizes free negotiation), by the state of mind of the masses, and by the conceptions of mass leaders and administrators of labor (whether owners or managers). In the East, these relations are above all determined by the regime, which prohibits open conflict or the affirmation of opposed interests, although in certain circumstances the sentiments of the masses may influence some of the union leaders, even when the latter are state officials. In other words, the intermediate zone of intergroup relationships can be understood only by referring to the socioeconomic data, and also to the regime of the state in question, because the regime controls both the structure of ruling categories and the degrees to which social groups acquire, or fail to acquire, self-awareness.

The plurality of ruling categories is inseperable from the nature of modern societies, but these categories can, under given conditions, constitute a ruling class: when they are reduced to manageable proportions by a single party; when, in spite of competition, they keep a sense of common interest with regard to the regime and to the state; or when they continue to recruit their greatest number of members from among a narrow and, so to speak, aristocratic milieu. The two concepts of ruling categories and ruling class can and must be utilized with a view to scientific analyses, and with no partisan intention. In the eyes of some, they appear as being politically oriented, but this is a mistake. The concepts, it is true, "unmask" the mythical fusion of the proletariat and the ruling class in Soviet societies, and likewise the alleged fusion of economic might and political power in democratic societies. But they also unmask the naïveté of democratic, Lincoln-esque ideology: "by the people and for the people." In other respects, the concepts do not settle the real issues, whether in the East or in the West, of harmony or clash between the sentiments and interests of the greatest number, on the one hand, and the action of the ruling minorities, on the other. It is not impossible to advance the argument that a ruling class, when unified by a one-party discipline, is more effective for the good of society than is free competition between minorities.

After all, is it the sociologist's fault if a given regime offers a self-interpretation that is farther removed from reality than the self-interpretation that other regimes usually give of themselves?

Part Five

International Politics in the Nuclear Age

The three texts that follow include the most important aspects of Aron's theory of international relations. Since his theory is based on the concept of the state of nature, it may be considered a continuation of the classical tradition of political thought.

Aron discusses the moral and strategic problems of international politics after the Second World War. In particular, he considers the question of peace and war in the nuclear age.

9

The Anarchical Order
of Power

Men continue to belong to political units pretending to independence. Hence, there is no "planetary society" or "human society" comparable to Pueblo or French society, or to the society of the United States or the Soviet Union.

The examples just given intentionally illustrate the diversity of the "political units" or "societies" of which the state claims to be the sovereign expression. A historian of the school of Spengler or Toynbee would contrast "national societies," naïvely proud of their originality, with the "intelligible field" that makes up a whole "civilization," such as ancient civilization or Western Christian civilization.[1] An ethnologist would reply that the truly intelligible field lies below and not above politically organized society. A state such as the Soviet Union encompasses many ethnic groups or cultural communities whose past, customs, and even creeds remain different in many respects.

We shall, nonetheless, take the multiplicity of legally sovereign states (according to the Charter of the United Nations) as the characteristic trait of the "asocial society" or the "anarchical order" of mankind. The former expression goes back to Kant; the latter borrows the notion of anarchy from the banal critique of the system of rival sovereignties. Both seek to emphasize the *essential imperfection* of "human society," to assume the existence of a "society" of all mankind in the sense that the city-states and empires of the ancient world and the nation-states of Europe constituted one.

This essential imperfection is not corrected by the growth of com-

Reprinted with permission from *Britannica Perspectives,* © 1968 by Encyclopaedia Britannica, Inc. The work from which this excerpt is drawn was published under the title "The Promethean Dream: Society in Search of Itself."
  1. Toynbee prefers to use the term society in designating these "intelligible fields."

mercial transactions between countries and continents. It is in vain that telecommunication satellites transmit words and images instantaneously; it is in vain that scholars and intellectuals meet at conventions. However useful relations transcending national borders among private individuals may be—whether in the domain of sports, science, tourism, religion, or business—and whatever influence these individual relations may exert over a long term on the "reserved domain" of relations between states, international relations still remain today what they have been throughout history: they have not entirely left the state of the law of the jungle. A sovereign collectivity is one which makes its own laws and whose leaders acknowledge obedience to no one else in certain matters—those affecting so-called vital interests, which in certain circumstances involve the choice between war and peace. The state is not solely, but it is at the very least and in any case, that agency which possesses the monopoly of legitimate violence. Now this monopoly must be effective and not merely legal. What army would be capable of fulfilling for the whole of mankind the function entrusted to the police force in nation-states? All civilizations (or societies, in Toynbee's use of the word) have known a violent history whose mainspring has been the relations between states. Modern civilization, while planetary in its technico-economic dynamism, has not eliminated or even morally modified interstate relations, which, despite our individual condemnations of their cruelty and our desire to shake off their yoke, continue mercilessly in their unreasonable rationality to forge our common destiny.

"Asocial society," "anarchical order," "unreasonable rationality"—these apparently contradictory expressions are not dictated by a taste for paradox or literary affectation. The society of sovereign states is in essence asocial, since it does not outlaw the recourse to force among the "collective persons" that are its members. Order, if there be one, in this society of states is anarchical in that it rejects the authority of law, of morality, or of collective force. In an anarchical society, why would any individual entrust to someone other than himself the concern for his security? On the other hand, when one thermonuclear bomb alone has more power of destruction than all the bombs or shells used during World War II, is it not unreasonable to risk a war whose sole possible benefits would be insignificant compared to the certain costs?

It is easy to elicit enthusiasm by contrasting the spirit of science with the unenlightened parochial spirit. Jets fly at over 500 miles per hour; tomorrow supersonic planes will fly at Mach 2 or 3; ballistic missiles cover nearly 10,000 miles in an hour; and customs officials continue to guard borders; armies, incapable of protecting populations, consume resources that would be better used to combat hunger or underdevelopment. How long will the contradiction between the universal diffusion of technology and the survival of traditional diplomacy persist?

The entire planet alone is scaled to the technology of the 20th century: the conquest of outer space testifies to this even more eloquently than thermonuclear bombs. It does not necessarily follow that the continuation of traditional diplomacy is merely a "survival." Or at least—before hastening to condemn—we must attempt to understand the anarchical order of the international system, as it has been for millennia and remains today (though not without substantial modifications due to changes in thought and events).

The Social Animal

Man is *naturally* a social animal (the word nature here being understood in the meaning given to it by biologists). Human young depend on their mothers for a long period; the family by itself is weak and threatened. The species can evolve toward the full realization of its potentialities only in and through societies capable of preserving what preceding generations have acquired, and, thus, of promoting the further accumulation of knowledge and power. The so-called archaic societies that came into being with the Neolithic revolution were limited. Each placed itself spontaneously at the centre of a universe it interpreted both arbitrarily and intelligibly. Defined by a system of values, a way of life, indeed a world view, each tended to regard the others as foreign and, therefore, strange, though this strangeness did not necessarily provoke hostility. In this sense, Bergson is wrong in affirming that collectivities are like wolves to one another (*Homo homini lupus*), while members of the collectivities are like gods to one another (*Homo homini deus*). The most closed societies were not devoid of internal conflicts and were not perforce dedicated to a struggle unto death with nearby or distant societies. So long as the strictly political organization—borders, laws, central power—is imperfect, the limits of the societies themselves do not stand out clearly, and often one hesitates over the meanings of the words used to designate its groupings (family, clan, village, tribe, and so forth). But these semantic uncertainties, reflecting ambiguities inscribed in reality itself, do not eliminate the major fact: mankind began by division and not by unity. Every human society grew conscious of its originality in developing a culture—it established itself by distinction from the others, proud, rather than anxious, to discover itself different from others.

The interstate relations one observes throughout the several thousand years of major history (of so-called higher civilization) are a work of culture, and as such they may be called artificial if one equates the nature of man or of societies with their initial state. Even biologists would condemn such an equation: man is an animal species which, being organized in stable groups, has a history. This history does not mark the end of the biological evolution of the species, but it is no less evident than that evolution. The history of civilizations and the evolution of the species react upon one another, whatever interpretation one makes of this duality, according to one's metaphysical or religious beliefs.

Conflicts between states, more or less regulated by tradition, custom, or law, form an integral part of civilizations; they belong not to the biological but to the human order. This proposition is not in contradiction with the theory common among the classic philosophers, according to which the relations between states derive from the *state of nature*. The latter stood in contrast to the civil society (*l'état civil*), and both sprang from culture, not from animal nature. The concept of nature, in this sense, is ambiguous because it contrasts at times with convention, at other times with civil society, and most times with both together. In contrast to conventions, the state of nature is characteristic of man qua man, leaving aside the infinite and arbitrary diversity of mores. Hence, natural laws are universal laws—those applying to all men, irrespective of the norms to which an individual is subject by virtue of his membership in a particular society. In contrast to civil society, the state of nature excludes a supreme authority, a tribunal entitled to render verdicts, a police authorized to enforce them: therefore each man is responsible for his own security, free in his decisions, including the decision to take up arms.

The concept of the state of nature represented an interpretation of the behaviour appropriate to historical man, a pessimistic or optimistic metaphysics. Some philosophers described the state of nature as the war of all against all; others, on the contrary, depict man as peaceful and benign outside of society. Some proclaim that the state of nature knows no other law than that of might; others, claiming that man by himself tends toward the fulfillment of his reasonable nature, placed the laws of nature above civil law. But all made a distinction between the state of nature where each man, separate or sovereign, can count only on himself, and civil society where law reigns, where justice is rendered by tribunals, where the police suppress violence.

This distinction does not at all suggest that the present style of interstate relations represents the survival of a primordial situation of individuals or societies—the war of all against all: archaic societies were not all bellicose, and the struggles in which they engaged were often ritualized to the point of being closer to our competitive games than to death struggles of the industrial age. Nor does this distinction imply that interstate hostilities derive through the mysteries of the collective unconsciousness, from the enmity that primitive man spontaneously felt for the foreigner: it is simply the product of historic experience, confirmed by the study of all civilizations. City-states and empires alike were established through violence; the maintenance of peace was the first task of those in power within politically organized units, but peace among these units was never imposed by the same method. All international systems have been anarchical, in the strict sense of the term: they have not been subjected to an *arché*. Once an *arché* is recognized, the political units are deprived of their constitutive principle—auto-nomy, in-dependence, the ability of making on their own decisions involving their destiny.

This distinction in essence does not exclude a similarity in the realm of practice. Within states, too, individuals and groups rival one another, and there is a permanent danger of recourse to violence. And it is true that there is not a single state which has not been established by violence, from narrower collectivities of differing cultures. The homogeneity of a people has been the work of centuries, meaning, most often, the work of force. Only the United States of America has a slightly different history. Leaving aside the wars against the Indians, then against Mexico and Spain, U.S. nationality was forged by a constitutional law established for nearly two centuries. Millions of immigrants freely decided to join this *commonwealth*, this community.

In short, the philosophical distinction between the state of nature and civil society expresses a permanent fact of history: men live in society, but there have always been many societies and not one society. Every historic society has been distinctive and in more or less regular relation with other societies. Within each of them, the rival ambitions of individuals or groups, ethnic heterogeneity, and opposition of interests created a permanent danger of illegitimate violence. Between societies, recourse to armed force was legitimate since, in the absence of civil authority, each could count only on itself to ward off perils and to survive.

It is scarcely necessary, in order to explain the endemic character of wars, to endow man with greater aggressiveness than that of other primates: the conditions, constant throughout history, of the political organization of mankind suffice to explain the precariousness of peace and the frequency of wars. Peace could be safeguarded only, and always temporarily, by the balance of rival powers or the victory of the strongest and the establishment of an empire.

The "natural" character of the specificity of interstate relations (legitimacy of recourse to force), as confirmed by historical experience, imposes no conclusion regarding the future of human society; it merely prohibits an illusory extrapolation. The transition from *many* sovereignties to *one* sovereignty is neither logically nor materially impossible, but it would be *essentially* different from the transition from city-state to empire. Empires eliminated or integrated sovereign states; they did not eliminate all external sovereignty. United under one sovereignty, mankind would no longer have any enemy—unless it be on another planet. This would be a mutation *of* history itself and not a mutation *within* history.

A world state is not in contradiction with the biological or social nature of man, as it has been revealed throughout the centuries. If Rome was able to spread its domain to the British Isles and to Byzantium at a time when legions traveled by foot, modern techniques for movement on land, on sea, and in air make a planetary empire materially possible. What excludes such an empire today and for the foreseeable future are the historic protagonists. By historic protagonists I mean the politically organized collectivities, the minorities governing them, and perhaps the peoples themselves. Heads of state hold fast to sovereignty—that is, to their freedom of action internally and externally, of which the term sovereignty represents the juridical or ideological expression. Peoples respond to the call for "national independence," some because they have barely emerged from a colonial regime, and others because they are nostalgic for their lost grandeur, or because the official ideology depicts classes and states engaged in a death struggle.

If we use the word *nationalism* here to indicate the will of politically organized collectivities, established in a territory and subject to a state, to maintain vis-à-vis other similar collectivities a liberty theoretically total and at least equal to that of others, then we would have to say that the planetary expansion of technology and of modern economy does not result in a universal state. Peoples or states act on the stage of history like individuals who *refuse* to submit to a master and *do not know how* to submit to a common law. In seeking to establish or maintain a universal state one encounters the same obstacle. To establish a universal state, in the absence of consent, it would be necessary to break the resistance of states, as the resistance of the feudal barons was broken by the armed force of the kings, or that of the Greek city-states or of Macedonia was broken by the Roman legions. But the monarchic precedent has no value as an example so long as a universal sovereignty must encompass heterogeneous peoples; the Roman precedent might serve as a model, but it inspires terror. At what price and with what consequences would unity be arrived at through the defeat of all the pretenders to empire save one?

But let us suppose that the universal state has been established: it could survive only by the effective monopoly of legitimate violence. It would have to possess enough weapons to prevent provincial groups from resorting to force or, at least, to prevent the spread of conflicts, if these groups preserved an army. But could the army of the universal state succeed in *restraining* local armies by the threat of nuclear weapons alone (supposing that these were a monopoly of the universal state)? Or are we to imagine the estates reduced to the level of administrations, virtually disarmed? Under this hypothesis, one requires of these administrations (ex-states) a confidence in the loyalty of its people (ex-citizens) of which our period provides few examples. In both cases, one assumes that the main problem has been solved, namely, the consent of the peoples and the states to surrender to a universal state a portion of the autonomy that has been held essential over the centuries. But all indications are that they do not fear the nuclear apocalypse enough to abdicate their sovereignty.

Lord Russell gave mankind a deadline of a few decades, until the end of the century, to choose between a world-state and annihilation. But at the end of the second decade of the atomic age, a third path has appeared.

Forms of Warfare

History has thus far refused to pose the ultimate choice between collective suicide and the abdication of states. It has gradually brought a certain order out of the anarchy common to all international systems, an order favouring the limitation of armed conflicts, subject to an oligarchy camouflaged by democratic symbols.

This order results in the first place from a quasi-control of interstate violence—a control as novel as the historic conjuncture itself. There are three sorts of weapons available today, corresponding to three combat methods: let us say, symbolically, the submachine gun, the tank, and the atomic bomb—the first being adapted to guerrilla warfare, the second to regular army fighting, the third to thermonuclear exchanges (or push-button warfare, to adopt the terminology of science fiction). In terms of power of destruction, there is nothing in common between the guerrilla fighter, the tank driver, and the crew of the Minuteman missile, any more than between a wrench used by a garage mechanic, a conveyor belt in an automobile factory, and the equipment of an atomic plant. But more recent techniques, while they may be most characteristic of the present age, do not eliminate former techniques, and this is for two reasons. Automation (where it is possible and profitable) is so expensive that it can only be partial and gradual. Large sectors of the economy continue to remain refractory to the new technology, and the mechanic's wrench, even the shovel and the pick, continue to remain symbolic. Similarly, the thermonuclear bomb and the ballistic missile have eliminated neither the machine gun of the guerrilla fighter nor the coolie who transports on his back the rice and munitions of the combatants.

The individual weapon—light, effective in short-term operations, in ambushes, and in man-to-man fighting—was the response of the colonized peoples to the colonial domination of the European states. The white man imposed his domination on the peoples of Asia and Africa thanks to the superiority of his technology and science, thanks also to his prestige. Once that prestige had been eroded by familiarity, domination tended to have no basis other than force. The Vietnamese, Indonesians, or Congolese could not defeat the regular armies of France, the Netherlands, or Belgium, but they could deny the colonial regime's security. If they have the sympathy and complicity of the masses, a few thousand guerrillas can strip the rich few of the desire and ability to rule. In the twenty years since the explosions of Hiroshima and Nagasaki, the machine guns of guerrillas have changed the map of the world much more than have tanks or atomic bombs. At Dien Bien Phu, these guerrillas had become soldiers, organized in divisions, who dealt a death blow to the French expeditionary force, worn out by seven years of struggle against elusive combatants. Thus ended an empire.

Wars, all limited and local, between regular or quasi-regular armies, have all ended since 1945 in armistices that have not been followed by peace treaties. The demarcation lines give sanction to the accidental results of combat operations at the time of the cease-fire: such is the case of the border between India and Pakistan in Kashmir, between Israel and the Arab states in the Near East, and between North and South Korea after three years of fighting. The contrast is striking between the victory of the rebels over the Dutch or the French in Indonesia or Vietnam, and the stalemates or armistices without peace treaties at the conclusion of hostilities between regular forces.

Need we add that the reason for this contrast is more political than military. The guerrillas won nearly everywhere because the "imperialists," morally and materially weakened by World War II, no longer believed in their mission, and because the empire becomes too costly when it entails economic obligations toward conquered peoples. Israeli tanks could have gone on to Cairo in 1956; if there had been enough of them, American tanks could have reached the Yalu. The Great Powers of the international system wanted, above all, to arrive at a compromise when they confronted one another directly or through satellites interposed prudently between them; most times they stopped military operations between secondary states as quickly as possible; they prevented weapons from fulfilling their secular function of deciding otherwise insoluble questions. By their intervention, they have perpetuated situations that, in other times, would have been deemed absurd; the division of Jerusalem [before the Israeli military action in 1967] or of Kashmir. The limitation of hostilities has seemed to be the prime object of the Great Powers during this period, if not of the interested parties.

Is the guerrilla fighter a vestige of the past who will disappear with the disappearance of underdevelopment itself? To be sure, when one observes the relations between Israel and the Arab states, the punitive expenditures undertaken by units of the regular Israeli Army—between 1949 and 1967—in response to operations by the fedayeen, one is tempted to draw a sort of correlation between the level of development and the nature of weapons, between the type of society and the mode of combat. This correlation is indeed linked to particular circumstances, without being entirely accidental. As soon as guerrillas have won the war, driven out the colonialists, and founded a state, the state seeks to create a regular army equipped with heavy weapons, tanks, pursuit planes, and bombers. Each new state does so because other states that have preceded it in the career of independence have done so before it. Concern for prestige? Not entirely. A regular army protects the new state against other guerrillas who might be recruited among the veterans or among those who expected that the end of domination would usher in a new era, a sort of golden age. It is also useful in the border disputes that threaten to break out after the end of colonialism and hence of anticolonialist solidarity. Finally, it must not be forgotten that even in industrialized countries, during times of oppression there have been snipers and guerrillas.

In truth, the guerrilla belongs to our age as he belongs to most ages of human history; but he assumes a novel form in the industrial age. He incarnates the antitechnical to the extent to which he defies the instruments of massive destruction developed by science, but he utilizes weapons and means of communication that have also been forged by the modern age, and he has likewise developed rational methods of action. If technology refers not only to the material objects made by machines but also to a form of thought—a sort of pragmatism pushed to its extreme—guerrilla warfare, as taught by the Chinese after long experience, is henceforth conducted according to technological principles. These entail a technique of organization, a technique for the psychological manipulation of the masses, appealing to terror and to hope. To be sure, the guerrilla, more often than the soldier in uniform, is left to his own devices; he must therefore be capable of initiative, and he must retain in solitude the sense of his own responsibility, as well as the consciousness of a solidarity with his dispersed comrades. But, the more guerrilla warfare becomes organized, the more the guerrilla resembles the soldier. The discipline he is subject to will never have the same physical immediacy as in regular armies, but its distant and diffused character is compensated for by its merciless sanctions. Leaders are nowhere and everywhere. There is, so to speak, no longer any question of the *degree* of crime or punishment. The difference between guerrillas and soldiers remains; the tendency toward their rapprochement grows out of a like desire for effective techniques.

As an isolated volunteer, the guerrilla seems superior to the soldier in human qualities. Although heroic, he is not necessarily holy: all depends on the cause for which he sacrifices his peaceful existence or his life. Since 1940, the guerrilla has symbolized the struggle against the Nazis, then against the "colonialists." He has profited from the sympathy of progressivist opinion despite the often inevitable cruelty of his means. He has been David against Goliath, the Pekinese or Kabyle peasant, barehanded against planes or tanks, the soldier in the shadows destined more for martyrdom than for glory. Should this same guerrilla serve a doubtful cause, or the population for the most part be against his cause, or should his victory bring to power a detested regime, he would become again, in the eyes of all defenders of the established order, whether Occidentals or Afro-Asians, what he has been in other times—the outlaw, closer to the bandit than to the soldier, the man who kills unexpectedly and often randomly, the man who introduces a reign of suspicion and terror, who confuses the essential distinction between peace and war, between law and violence. When faced with mechanical monsters, he incarnates the grandeur of the resistant, rebel, or heretic. When faced with the norms of civilized existence, he incarnates the aggression—animal or human, primitive or permanent—that society must control in order to survive.

The triad of the submachine gun, the tank, and the ballistic missile with a thermonuclear warhead, of the guerrilla, the soldier, and the crew of the ballistic missiles buried in silos, will have tomorrow, as today, a historic significance. The complex dialectic linking each of these three types of weapons to the other two will continue symbolically, at least until mankind substitutes the rule of law for that of violence. Each of these three weapons, each of the three methods of combat will preserve its meaning. Nuclear weapons exclude a repetition of the total wars that have occupied the first half of the 20th century. Regular armies remain the guarantee of internal peace in all states that cannot do without an eventual recourse to force. At the same time, they provide strategists with a means of avoiding the alternative of all-or-nothing, of passivity or the apocalypse. States aspiring to play leading roles on the world scene can no more do without nuclear weapons than without conventional weapons. Guerrilla rebellion, the supreme and often the desperate response to injustice, poses an ironic challenge to the omnipotence of machines.

Does the dialectic of the three weapons serve to constitute an international order? During the postwar period it has been the principle of what has come to be called variously the Cold War or bellicose peace, precarious order or endemic disorder. Contemporaries have denounced this constant ambiguity; there is no outbreak of major war, but true peace is neither imposed by a victor nor arrived at together by rivals. In retrospect, the historian tends to place a more balanced judgment on the first two decades of the atomic age, and indeed he may even indulge in the secret hope that this ambiguous conjecture, this limitation of violence, should continue.

Nuclear Diplomacy

For twenty years, from 1945 to 1965, only two states were worthy of the title of nuclear power. Great Britain, while possessing nuclear weapons, has not conducted an independent diplomacy. France and Communist China have exploded atomic bombs, but do not possess the combination of bombs, missiles to carry them, and a network of alert and communication without which the weapons cannot really be effective military or diplomatic arms. At the time of the Korean War, the United States had only a limited stock of nuclear weapons, including neither thermonuclear bombs nor tactical nuclear weapons. From 1953 on, as Stalin's successors perfected and completed their new armaments, they spoke more and more willingly of peaceful coexistence. They were tempted, between 1958 and 1962, to obtain a modification of the status quo in Berlin through threat of force, under the protection of intercontinental missiles. They never risked carrying out their threat. When they were forced by a U.S. ultimatum to withdraw their ballistic missiles from Cuba, they immediately gave up their Berlin operation. The two major powers—thermonuclear duopolists—became aware of their common interest not to become involved in a war of annihilation; in other words, they understood that none of the stakes of their conflict was worth the cost of a war in which nuclear weapons would be used. Let us consider the terminology borrowed by rational strategists from economics: they compare cost and profit— that is, the losses in lives and goods that a war would entail on the one hand, and the possible fruits of victory on the other (the latter being appraised on the basis of a coefficient calculated in terms of the uncertainty of the outcome). The higher the losses, the fewer the advantages of victory, even if the risk of defeat is slight, and the more the rational strategist is inclined to prefer the drawbacks of peace to the risks of war.

On the whole, the optimistic argument based on "peace through fear" remains valid, no matter how many nuclear powers there are. States producing these weapons will discover at the same time both their power and their impotency, the capacity they have acquired to destroy and the vulnerability of their own population and cities. There is nothing to prevent us from conjecturing about the spread of wisdom that might accompany the proliferation of nuclear weapons.

It would nonetheless be imprudent to overlook the circumstances that have favoured the logical use that the two major powers have made of their nuclear weapons. In the first place and above all, both the United States and the Soviet Union were victors in the war, satisfied with the result, having neither a defeat to avenge nor territory to conquer. The Soviet Union, seizing the opportunity to exploit its victory, had subjected 100 million Europeans to its Marxist-Leninist regime. The United States, despite the call for a rollback, resigned itself to this *fait accompli* and confined itself to preventing any further advance of the Soviet forces in Europe. The success of containment was acceptable to both of the major powers, since each could interpret it as a success: the Americans because they had achieved their stated goal, and the Russians because they had never wanted to do more than consolidate their hegemony over Eastern Europe, including East Germany.

To be sure, despite the fact that the stakes of their rivalry were not *national* in the narrow sense of the term (neither begrudged the existence and the territory of the other), the two major powers still remained enemies in that each claimed their ideologies to be universally valid. In certain cases, the most inexpiable struggles are those involving the confrontation not of national interests (a province, a border line) but rather this nonmaterial good—the glory of preeminence, the power, at last uncontested, of no longer having a rival at one's side. No one can say whether, in the absence of nuclear weapons, the victors of World War II would have resolved their conflict by force. There is little doubt that possession of these weapons contributed to a preference for peaceful solutions.

In many respects, duopoly is a less unpredictable situation than one involving numerous participants. The situation was all the more stable as long as each of the duopolists exercised virtually uncontested power within its own camp. The United States and the Soviet Union avoided direct confrontation as much as possible. West Germany, the state least satisfied by the status quo, has not had an autonomous diplomacy vis-à-vis Pankow or Moscow. In Asia, until the schism between the Soviet Union and Communist China, the leaders of the Kremlin, sole possessors of a nuclear force capable of counterbalancing America's, retained, in case of crisis, the means of influencing the decisions of the North Koreans and the Chinese. Thus the two major powers imperceptibly acquired the habit of pursuing their politico-ideological rivalry while keeping the risks of an "unthinkable war" at a minimum.

Technico-strategic precautions reinforced political prudence. Analysts in institutes and universities envisioned the possibility of a war involving the use of nuclear weapons which neither side desired. U.S. statesmen, especially, did their utmost to take precautions in order to attenuate such a danger. Security mechanisms were developed to prevent the accidental explosion of a bomb and to prevent an officer, no matter what his grade, from making the decision to utilize nuclear weapons without having received an order from the President of the United States (the latter alone has the legal authority to make such a decision and, thanks to electronics, these weapons are for the most part physically impossible to use without that decision), and finally to prevent extreme escalation if, by some misfortune, in spite of every effort, an atomic bomb should be set off.

These sophisticated technico-political precautions are the expression of a strategic concept that is not so much new as renovated. The two major wars of the 20th century had been, from a certain point of view, total wars: World War I, having broken out over an obscure conflict in the Balkans and spread through the alliance system, had, to the surprise of most of the generals and statesmen, lasted over four years, thanks to improvised mobilization of all able-bodied men in combat units and factories. The close relationship between the military and industrial spheres foreseen by certain sociologists at the beginning of the 19th century was readily apparent. The diplomatic system of Old Europe, the centre of the world system, crumbled under the weight of the war and the revolutions it brought with it. World War II was still more total, since the Japanese attempt at empire building had accompanied that of the Third Reich, and the very existence of the sovereignty of the defeated states had been suspended for a period that the victors themselves reserved the right to determine.

Public opinion and the private views of statesmen were haunted by the spectre of these total wars, and tended to be limited to an absolute alternative of peace or war. Since 1945, because of thermonuclear bombs, the efforts of strategic thinking, the Cunning of Reason, those responsible for world politics have finally understood the lesson of Clausewitz: absolute war—one resulting from unlimited escalation— is not a model, but a menace that can be warded off as long as the means of force remain in the service of policy, the "intelligence of the state." It falls to this intelligence to weigh the risks that must be run, and the sacrifices that it is legitimate to accept to attain a goal.

On the one hand, the blurring of the distinction between war and peace has brought about the bellicose peace: the permanent mobilization of the nuclear apparatus, the limited use of military force here and there throughout the world, the qualitative race for armaments, with each of the major powers devoting billions and billions of dollars to the development of bombs, missiles, planes, and ever more sophisticated conventional weapons. It has also made total war less probable—that monstrous and absurd war in which thermonuclear powers heap upon one another, as in an orgy, all the means of destruction at their disposal. The strategy of the flexible response has become a fact at times of crisis—the strategy of all nuclear powers, despite the fact that in periods of calm certain states will proclaim the doctrine of massive retaliation—futile talk so long as the hour of reckoning does not sound.

For twenty years, nuclear weapons have constantly been placed at the service of a defensive strategy; in their military concept they are not a primary but a final recourse. The very term *deterrent* suggests this defensive use. To deter someone is to prevent him from taking certain action under threat of sanctions. Why would the sanction be necessarily or immediately unlimited? For ten to fifteen years, the obsession over the preceding wars, the confusion over nuclear weapons, and the strategy of deterrence was such that the weapons themselves were called a deterrent, as if any weapon were not, in certain cases, a deterrent in the hands of a determined man. Neither of the two nuclear powers has ever tried, until now, to obtain a modification of the status quo at the expense of the other or the surrender of a nonnuclear power by the threat of using these weapons. In Cuba, the United States restored the *status quo ante;* in Berlin, the Soviets finally accommodated themselves to the military presence of the West in West Berlin.

Circumstances have likewise favoured limitations on the use of conventional weapons. The nuclear powers alone possessed large stocks of these, and after the Korean campaign they feared to use them wherever there was a possibility of escalation. Elsewhere, the states involved in conflicts possessed relatively few weapons. The United Nations served as an intermediary between the two major powers and the states directly involved, standing behind the peace efforts made by one or another of the major powers, or even by the member-states as a whole.

Finally, the submachine gun has been widely used to prosecute wars of liberation, and these have, for the most part, ended in the victory of the guerrillas. There have been exceptions, however—in the Philippines and in Malaysia. But these wars have tended to result in the independence of countries formerly subject to colonial domination. Now U.S. and Soviet opinion were in agreement with Afro-Asian countries in condemning en bloc, on principle, the governing of coloured peoples by white men (even though the same condemnation did not extend to the governing of Asian peoples by the Russians). The Europeans never went the whole way in using their military force in these colonial struggles. The French, who fought from 1946 to 1954 in Indochina, from 1954 to 1962 in Algeria, never attacked the logistical bases of the guerrillas in China, in Tunisia, or in Morocco. In one case, they did not have the indispensable military resources; in the other, they were paralyzed by a guilty conscience, by the opposition of their allies and that of a segment of French opinion. Nevertheless, in 1962, thanks to the fortified lines along the borders, the isolation of Algeria had succeeded in choking out the guerrillas. The French government consented to Algerian independence not because the guerrillas had won on the battlefield but because, politically, no other solution was feasible in the long run.

From the moment that wars of liberation take on as their objective not the winning of independence from a colonial state but the installing of a regime identified by U.S. public opinion with communism, the guerrilla ceases, in the estimation of that opinion, to be a freedom fighter and becomes instead the perhaps sincere but blind militant of a despotic party, and the rules by which wars are fought are, and will be, changed. North Vietnam experienced the horrors of large-scale bombing because it supported the action of the Vietcong in the South.

The dialectic of the three weapons has, for twenty years, maintained peace among nuclear powers, favoured decolonization with minimum diplomatic upheaval, and restrained the use of conventional weapons. Will this dialectic play the same role in the decades ahead?

Dialectic of Weapons

As far as thermonuclear weapons are concerned, there are three sets of conditions necessary to the prolongation of "peace through fear": *technical*—the maintenance of the balance of terror; *strategic*—the acceptance by all heads of state of the doctrine of so-called graduated response, progressive retaliation; and *political*—the nature of the conflict and the stakes.

The concept of flexible response by a cool head during a period of crisis requires that nuclear weapons be sufficiently dispersed or protected so that a first strike cannot eliminate the capacity for retaliation by any one of the states involved. This kind of stability depends therefore on the qualitative armaments race so far as the major powers are concerned, and on the acquisition of a nuclear apparatus (weapons and delivery vehicles) by new members of the atomic club.

The two major powers of the two decades after 1945 are both opposed to the proliferation of atomic weapons—the United States, with an ostentatious passion, the Soviet Union more discreetly. According to the law of probabilities, does not the danger of an explosion increase along with the number of bombs—or even more, with the number of states possessing them? This is irrefutable reasoning on an abstract plane, but far from reality: it assumes that the problem is resolved—in other words, that other states have decided to leave to two, three, or four among them the exclusive possession of weapons that are considered decisive in any modern conflict.

In theory, according to strict Machiavellian logic, the United States and the Soviet Union could have or even should have opposed at all costs the development of Chinese nuclear capability. However, the informal Russo-American alliance against atomic proliferation does not suffice to eliminate politico-ideological enmity. Furthermore, just as the nuclear powers have never used their supreme weapons offensively to compel the surrender of a state without such arms by imposing a choice between submission and annihilation, so too they have never attempted by such a threat to prevent the development of a new atomic force. All indications are that they will continue to respect the sovereignty of states—whether out of weakness or because of their mutual political antagonism—and resign themselves to an evolution contrary to their common interest.

Proliferation probably will not stop with the fifth nuclear power (China), but this does not mean that it will be unlimited, at least in the foreseeable future. Switzerland and Sweden would use such weapons to protect their neutrality—in other words, they will not be playing for the highest stakes. India will one day follow the lead of China, Israel that of France or Switzerland. This proliferation will not be without risks: one would have to be blind or to believe in the rationality of all statesmen to deny this. But the error of too many specialists is to confuse these numerous and diverse threats with the probability of the unthinkable war. The danger is probably smaller for the superpowers of today than for less important countries, who will have joined the atomic club without sufficient resources.

Under what conditions is peace through fear most stable? Where the forces of reprisal are least vulnerable, the states have both the will and the means to apply the doctrine of graduated response, and the disproportion between the cost and the stakes, between the risk of war and the violence of enmity, is enormous. All the conditions that further peace through fear are met in the case of the relations between the United States and the Soviet Union. Short of an improbable technical breakthrough, they will persist during the decades ahead. They will not be met to the same extent elsewhere, in Asia or the Near East. But the United States and the Soviet Union will not allow themselves to be dragged unwillingly into a war of annihilation. The dissemination of nuclear weapons increases, to a degree that cannot be precisely assessed, the danger that, one day or another, nuclear weapons will be used militarily on some battlefield or other. At least for the next twenty or thirty years proliferation should not threaten the military foundation of the present order—the existence of arms so terrifying that even those who possess them keep them on reserve to be used only as an ultimate course. The greatest threat to mankind, then, is not that a few more states should come to possess nuclear weapons but that statesmen should begin to make a different use of their weapons in the diplomatic game.

The foundation of the present order of power, this anarchical order that tends toward the limitation of violence, is in the final analysis *psychological.* One reads in a report made to UNESCO that war begins in the minds of men. Such a simplistic theory is more false than true; in our times, one is tempted to state that the citizens of one state detest those of another because they have fought or are fighting them, rather than vice versa. In any event, if diplomatic conditions require a reversal of alliances, a well-designed propaganda campaign is sufficient to overcome collective passions or to direct them toward another goal. On the other hand, when some states possess means of destruction against which all the others cannot protect themselves, and to which they cannot respond, the essential focus lies predominantly in the minds of men, especially in those few who are responsible for the diplomacy or strategy of the nuclear powers.

The strictly defensive or deterrent use of atomic weapons is dictated by a certain logic. It has been rightly said that the very limitless nature of these weapons renders their effective utilization difficult. It has been rightly said that there is no common ground between the capacity to destroy and the ability to convince, between *strength* as it is measured according to strictly military potential and the *power* of a state to obtain the submission or consent of other states. It has been rightly said that never before have states so superior in strength as the United States and the Soviet Union been defied with impunity by dwarf states like Albania and Cuba. It has been rightly said that from now until the end of this century no state will even come close to attaining the economic and military potential of either of the superpowers. China and India, both larger in population, have not even gone beyond the first phase of industrialization. All the other states either have a much smaller population (and among industrialized countries, the Soviet Union and the United States have a relatively high demographic rate of growth) or a much lower per capita income. An American writer caused a scandal in 1964 by declaring that by the end of the century the two superpowers of today would outstrip their potential rivals even more decisively. The statement nonetheless was incontestable, provided two conditions prevail: that the Soviet Union and the United States maintain the same internal coherence and political will within their borders, and that potential resources be identified with military strength and diplomatic power.

In reality, what ought to have caused an outcry was not the very plausible prediction of a continued or enlarged gap between the resources at the disposal of the two major powers and those of other states, but rather the transition from resources to power and strength. At the beginning of the 1960s, observers were struck by the disintegration of the blocs, by the impunity of the smaller states, by the apparent uselessness of nuclear weapons in daily relations or even in struggles for national liberation. It is to be hoped that this disproportion between the power of destruction and the power of persuasion might be prolonged and increased, but it is not determined solely by the nature of weapons or by the dialectic of the three weapons. For the time being, happily, statesmen are paralyzed by the "atomic taboo." The atomic weapon, like the gold reserves used to back currency, is buried in the ground and accumulated in stockpiles, although always ready to be used. To paraphrase Clausewitz, one might say that nuclear weapons allow firm commitments to be honoured and credit operations to be paid in cash. But nuclear weapons are not employed physically, any more than gold is removed from the storage vaults. The crisis—with its exchanges of threats and messages, its dialogue of affirmations of will—is the equivalent of what Clausewitz called commitment.

The true question concerning the future thus involves the continuation of this fragile order, founded at once on a strategic doctrine gradually and spontaneously elaborated by the protagonists of history, and on prohibitions arising out of the depths of the human conscience—or perhaps, one might say, out of the collective unconsciousness. Will the superpowers respect the imperative of the solely deterrent use of nuclear weapons? Will not the inclusion of new members in the atomic club push them to reestablish, through defense against ballistic missiles or civil defense, the margin of superiority that the progress of the Chinese and the Europeans threatens to reduce? Will the smaller nuclear powers be capable of the same moderation if their so-called retaliatory force is vulnerable? Will not the states that have reduced their conventional weapons to a minimum in order to acquire a nuclear force be driven some day to the choice between passivity (that is, defeat) or a violation of the atomic taboo?

Finally, and above all, a question that one hesitates even to pose can hardly fail to haunt the minds of those who are concerned about the future. As long as war is and remains an act of violence in which one collective person attempts to compel another collective person, the offensive use of the nuclear threat is morally and even materially difficult: if the person one is bent on bringing to surrender remains indifferent to the warning shots, if "Ruritania" allows first one, and then two of its cities to be destroyed rather than surrender, what choice do the superpowers have in ending destruction that becomes more futile than monstrous? It may be recognized once again that man is capable of preferring his reasons for living over his very life! The order of power in the atomic age is thus founded on the *atomic taboo,* the rational strategy of the major powers, and the courage of historic man. But what might happen the day when the states involved are no longer comparable to "collective persons," each seeking to obtain the submission of the other, but to a Hitler bent on exterminating an entire race deemed to be a noxious animal species?

Heaven forbid that there should ever be a statesman who would view nuclear weapons not only as deterrent weapons—that is, instruments to be used in human dialogue—but also as arms of extermination.

The Order of Power

An anarchical order is normally inegalitarian to the extent to which, in the absence of a common law or an impartial police, the powerful prevail over the weak. Thus, Plato's Callicles deemed natural (in conformity with nature) the domination of the most powerful. According to Spinoza and Hobbes, in the absence of civil society power determines rights. Philosophers did not ignore the fact that at least a principle of equality exists between individuals. The weak man is still able, in certain circumstances, to kill the strong man. Man does not act as man when he kills his fellow as the hunter kills his prey: the essential quality of victory is lost when the defeated is no longer present to recognize his defeat.

The anarchical order of the international system has always been inegalitarian. In the most complex system, that of the Greek city-states or of the European states prior to 1914, the great powers constituted a closed club with membership reserved to sovereigns possessing a minimum of military strength. The question attributed to Stalin during the last war:—"How many divisions does the Pope have?"—roughly interprets a traditional doctrine. A great power would feel it had been offended if it were not consulted when an important affair was discussed. Eventually, the great powers settled affairs involving lesser powers among themselves; sometimes they imposed a status (neutrality) or borders upon smaller states solely to avoid or to settle their own conflicts.

Nuclear weapons have not decisively modified this customary order of power. The present order is both more and less inegalitarian than international orders of the past. It is less so for two reasons. The first is the egalitarian ideal of modern civilization. The likening of "political units" to "collective persons" is suggested by the language we use, by the reigning ideology, by our anticolonialist passion. No distinction is made between the liberation of peoples and the liberation of individuals (or rather, the former is placed before the latter). The separation of ethnic groups, as we have seen, is a means of eliminating inequalities among individuals belonging to one or another of them. The old principle of European *ius gentium* (international law), implying a certain equality between states—an equality arising out of the recognized sovereignty of all states—is reinforced and enlarged by the egalitarian design of our period. The international law of the last century did not exclude the protectorate, foreign concessions (so-called unequal treaties), or the managing of certain public services in an independent state by bureaucrats from other countries representing the so-called community of civilized nations. Again, following World War I, the mandate principle implied a hierarchy among states, in that the mandatory states were by this very fact recognized as worthy of administering "dependent peoples," of working for their welfare and development. The liquidation in two decades of almost all colonial administrations consecrated the triumph of the egalitarian idea on the world level, but at the same time it increased the real inequalities between states that were juridically equal, at least in their sovereignty, and it enlarged the divergence between the legal theory espoused by the United Nations and the realities of international politics.

The elimination of protectorates, mandates, or colonies, the equal voting right of "Ruritania" and the United States in the United Nations General Assembly, consecrates the triumph of the egalitarian ideal in our century. But this has not been the sole agent of our historic revolution. The unarmed member of the Resistance, or the man armed with a submachine gun, Gandhi or Giap, forced the Europeans to recall the ideal they had proclaimed in Europe; and nuclear weapons at first promoted the revolt of the coloured peoples because the two states that possessed them had no colonies in the ordinary meaning of the term (although the Soviet Union maintains a multinational empire carved out by great sweeps of the sword, while Latin Americans denounce U.S. hegemony, if not Yankee imperialism).

This double equalization—in refusing a hierarchy between ethnic groups or states and in the dialectic of the submachine gun and advanced weapons—is likewise a function of the heterogeneity of the international system, whose members are held to be equal, while from all points of view (extent of territory, volume of population, per capita income, degree of development) they have never been so unequal in any of the systems of the past. We observe the denouement of this paradox every day: a combination of formal democracy and real oligarchy, to borrow our nouns from the Greeks and our adjectives from Marx. The two major powers, and especially the United States, possess all means of force—both conventional and nuclear weapons, and they can mobilize immense resources to back their foreign policy.

Anarchy continues to exist because there are two of them, and they cannot even agree to prevent the proliferation of nuclear weapons which is clearly in their common interest. The authority exercised by each of the major powers on its bloc is directly related to the fear aroused by the other. Peaceful coexistence therefore actually produces a loosening of the blocs. Elsewhere, in the Third World, the will of the major powers encounters the revolt of the masses and the submachine gun of the guerrilla.

The power of the two oligarchs is neither assured nor unlimited. Between now and the end of the century, two evolutions—the one probable, the other as certain as a historic evolution can be—will tend to curtail that power. Nuclear weapons have not been used militarily, but without them the Chinese Nationalists would not retain Quemoy and Matsu, and American bombers would not attack North Vietnam. The United States owes its freedom of action in Asia and even in Africa to its nuclear supremacy. It is probable that the military gap between first-rate and second-rate nuclear powers will decrease within the next decades and, by virtue of this, the planetary system will be less unified than it is today. Even though they may not be capable of striking American territory, the Chinese nuclear force will exercise a certain deterrence on American diplomacy. The superpowers will have to resign themselves to giving up their presence in the four corners of the globe.

One aspect of the deterrence which is not in doubt is the rise of China; this will almost certainly bring about the dissociation of the Soviet camp and the "nationalization" of the Marxist-Leninist party religions. It is permissible to speculate on the consequences of this prime factor, on the realignments that it will give rise to, on the relative weight of East and West, of Asia, America, and Europe in the world of the year 2000. But such is not within the scope of this chapter.

Our objective was more modest. The order of power—that is, the interstate order—has always been anarchical and oligarchical: anarchical because of the absence of a monopoly of legitimate violence, oligarchical (or hierarchic) in that, without civil society, rights depend largely on might. We asked ourselves how this traditional order had been adapted to technological civilization. Our conclusion is that this order has been transformed, but not overturned. Pessimists prophesy the collective suicide of mankind failing a kind of historic mutation such as would be denoted by the renunciation of military sovereignty by states. Optimists believe in peace through fear, in the end of the domination of peoples by peoples, since domination does not pay.

We have no grounds to decide in favour of one or the other. Mankind has always lived dangerously. The dangers are no longer the same, but they have not disappeared. One mankind, united under a single rational administration in order to exploit natural resources, would constitute one possible end of the human adventure. The adventure is still far from this final state, conforming not to *the* logic of history but to *a* partial logic that fascinates because it at once attracts and repels. Would man achieve fulfillment or perdition were he to arrive at the Promised Land of the world-state of technology?

10

On the Morality of Prudence

Idealism and Realism

We have tried to make the analysis of international relations independent of moral judgments and metaphysical concepts, taking as our point of departure the plurality of states, the shadow of a possible war hovering over the decisions of governments, the customary or legal rules more or less respected by the sovereigns but never interpreted by them as excluding a recourse to force in order to safeguard "vital interests" and "national honor." This analysis was neutral, as we see it, because it was a discernment of the *facts* (such has been, down through the centuries, the course of relations between states) and of the *subjective meanings* (statesmen, citizens, philosophers have always recognized a *difference in nature* between the internal order of states and the order between states).

Diplomatic-strategic conduct *has appeared* to us in the past to be a kind of mixture. It is social behavior; the actors—except in extreme cases—acknowledge each other's humanity, even their kinship, and do not believe they are entitled to abuse each other, whatever the pretext might be. But it is also anti-social behavior insofar as force decides the issue in case of conflict and constitutes the basis of what treaties might confirm as the norm. Now, insofar as diplomatic-strategic conduct is governed by the risk of or the preparation for war, it obeys, and cannot help but obey, the logic of rivalry; it ignores—and must ignore—the Christian virtues insofar as these are opposed to the needs of the competition.

Excerpts from chapters 19 and 20 of *Peace and War: A Theory of International Relations*, by Raymond Aron, translated by Richard Howard and Annette Baker Fox. © 1966, 1973 by Doubleday & Company, Inc. Reprinted by permission of Doubleday & Company, Inc., and Weidenfeld & Nicolson, Ltd. First published in French in 1961.

The double character of the relations between political units is the origin of praxeological and philosophical disputes. The actors—the political units or those who represent them—always try to justify themselves. But are they, should they feel obliged to stand by the juridical or ethical reasons they invoke, or should they act according to a calculation of forces or of opportunity? What role do nations and statesmen accord, or should they accord to principles, ideas, morality, necessity?

FROM IDEALIST ILLUSIONS TO PRUDENCE

In March 1936, on Chancellor Hitler's orders, German troops entered the Rhineland. The event constituted, without a doubt, a violation of the Versailles Treaty as well as the Treaty of Locarno. But the spokesmen of the Third Reich could plead that the disarmament of the left bank of the Rhine was unjust since France had fortified her own frontier. Equality of rights,[1] an ideology agreed upon by all, gave an appearance of equity to an action contrary to existing norms. Should the statesman or the moralist not party to the dispute have raised his voice in favor of legality or equity? Or else, observing that the reoccupation of the left bank of the Rhine would compromise the French system of alliances and put Czechoslovakia and Poland at the mercy of the Third Reich, should he have championed a military countermove in order to maintain a demilitarized zone, indispensable to the security of Europe?

Today's historian has no hesitation in answering these questions. We know that the German troops were ordered to withdraw if the French troops advanced. The attempt to punish by force the violation of a norm, regardless of the equality of rights, would have been justified because it might have prevented and, in any case, did delay the war of 1939; because it is morally legitimate to deny equality of rights to anyone who would make use of this same equality to deny it to others.

If, in 1933, France had heeded Marshal Pilsudski's advice and used force to overthrow Hitler, who had just come to power, she would have violated the *principle* of non-interference in the internal affairs of other states, she would have failed to recognize Germany's *right* of free choice with regard to regime and leader, she would have been denounced with indignation by American public opinion, by moralists and idealists hastening to the rescue, not of National Socialism, but of

---

1. It is, in fact, difficult to define equality of rights in a strict sense. In concrete terms, the rights of each, individual or collectivity, are different.

the will of the people or the rule of noninterference. The violence done to the German nation would have been stamped with the seal of infamy, and historians would never know from what miseries Hitler's disappearance would have saved humanity.

These ironic remarks about a past which did not come to pass are not intended surreptitiously to point a moral, but to bring to light some consequences of the true nature of relations between states. Since states have not renounced taking the law into their own hands and remaining sole judges of what their honor requires, the survival of political units depends, in the final analysis, on the balance of forces, and it is the *duty* of statesmen to be concerned, *first of all*, with the nation whose destiny is entrusted to them. The necessity of national egoism derives logically from what philosophers called the *state of nature* which rules among states.

Relations between states are not, for all that, comparable to those of beasts in the jungle. Political history is not purely natural. Diplomatic-strategic conduct tends to justify itself by ideas; it claims to obey *norms*, to submit to *principles*. We call *cynics* those who regard ideas, norms and principles as mere disguises of the desire for power, without real effectiveness. Those who repudiate the fact that all international order must be maintained by force are accused of *idealistic illusions*. The idealistic illusion assumes diverse forms, depending upon the character of the imperatives and the values invoked. *Ideological idealism* consists in considering a historical idea as the exclusive and sufficient criterion of the just and the unjust—for example, the right of peoples to self-determination, or the idea of nationalities. We use, with good reason, two different concepts, *right* and *idea*, because, in actual fact, both were and are used, and because the fluctuating vocabulary expresses the inevitable uncertainty of the thought.

The Germans did not bother to deny in 1871 that the majority of Alsatians wanted to remain French, but answered (when they did not confine themselves to brandishing the victorious sword) that violence had been done to the Alsatians by Louis XIV, two centuries before, and that belonging to German culture was more important than the accidental and transitory desires of one generation. In 1919 the Czechs did not claim that the Sudeten Germans wanted to be part of Czechoslovakia, but they asserted that, deprived of the territory inhabited by the Sudetens, they were doomed to subjection. Inevitably, the liberty of one or the other would have to be sacrificed, and the Czechs outnumbered the Sudetens.

The translation of a historical idea into territorial status does not proceed without uncertainty, either because the idea is open to several interpretations (what should be the fate of Alsatians of German culture and French preference?) or because the requirements of security prohibit its honest application (Bohemia, without the periphery inhabited by the Sudetens, is indefensible). The cynic will be tempted to conclude that in this case the idea serves only to mask appetites or interests, but he will not be right. Ideological idealism has little to do with reality: no state holds to *one* idea as an absolute to which all else must be sacrificed. That would be dangerous. Failure to appreciate strategic or economic necessity adds to the precariousness of a given status, even one allegedly consistent with the idea. But most states are reluctant to reject overtly an idea by which they justify, in the twentieth century, the annexation of peoples manifestly accustomed to and desirous of constituting independent nations.[2]

Juridical idealism consists in making decisions or carrying out strategy as a consequence of a more or less well-defined rule. George F. Kennan has often denounced this "legal idealism," and recent authors, even those who concede an important role to international law, are beginning to take into account the arguments formulated by the realists.

"The authors recognize the merits of criticisms that distinguished observers such as George Kennan have made regarding too great a reliance upon legal processes. American foreign policy has often been formulated without sufficient attention to the role of force and of national interests. We do not wish to encourage naïveté of the sort he describes as 'legal idealism,' a reliance upon abstract rules that are institutionally unsupported. We concede that nations often do act in partisan ways in support of immediate political objectives." But the writers are quick to add: "But we contend that much of international conduct is doctrinally consonant with normative standards, even though inconsistent with particular immediate interests, and that long-term self-interest can and does provide political support for internationally lawful conduct."[3]

Legal or semi-legal formulas by which American diplomats have expressed a given policy or concealed the absence of one are numerous and, in fact, well known: the Open-Door Policy in China, non-recognition of changes effected by force, outlawing of war as a political instrument, collective security. The first two formulas do not claim to

2. The victors nonetheless retain three possibilities: extermination, deportation, establishing the fifth column or a satellite state in power. The *historical idea* exerts a certain influence on the conduct of states; it does not guarantee survival.

3. Morton A. Kaplan and Nicholas de B. Katzenbach, *The Political Foundations of International Law*, New York, 1961, p. 10.

modify the essential features of politics among nations, while the last two tend to do so. But all four have the same character: they are abstract propositions, offered as normative, but stripped of all authority because they do not express needs genuinely felt by men, and because they are supported neither by force nor by institutions. Such formulas, then, do not constitute valid answers, effective solutions to immediate or eternal problems.

The Open-Door Policy was intended to protect China's independence and territorial integrity, an objective held to conform with the national interest and the ideal of the United States. However, the difficulty resulted not only from the imperialist ambitions of the European powers, but also from the disintegration of China's old regime and the absence of a central government in Peking capable of prevailing upon the provinces and being respected by foreign states. So long as a new dynasty had not received an indisputable mandate from heaven, European interference, with a view to gaining privileges or spheres of influence, easily overcame the obstacle of the Open-Door Policy.

Still more futile is the principle of the non-recognition of changes effected by force. Populations annexed against their will receive no help from the refusal of the government of the United States to accept a *fait accompli*. Men know that in the long run international law must bow to fact. A territorial status invariably ends up being legalized, provided it lasts. A great power that wants to forbid a rival from making conquests must arm and not proclaim in advance its moral disapproval and its abstention from force (such is the meaning of the non-recognition of changes affected by force).

The outlawing of war, in the Kellogg-Briand Pact, and the principle of collective security pose a basic problem which we shall consider in another chapter, namely: is it possible to devise and bring into being a juridical system which effectively assures the security of states and deprives them of the right to take the law into their own hands? But one thing is certain: between the two world wars such a system did not exist and had no chance of existing.

The authors cited above write: "The efforts to outlaw war eventuated in the supreme monument to human futility, the Kellogg-Briand Pact."[4] And elsewhere: "The presence or absence of institutional means of enforcement of legal principles determines whether a system of law exists or not. Municipal courts are able to call upon the assistance of sheriffs, or, if necessary, the total armed force of the state, to aid in the execution of sentence. The political arm of government is

4. Ibid., p. 43.

obligated to sustain legal process. And a municipal system of law that is not sustained by the cooperation of the body politic will not persist. The assertion that the Covenant and the Pact of Paris outlawed wars of aggression seems excessive when measured against the realities of the international society of the time. These were the statements of wishful thinking, not law."[5]

It would not be easy, as a result of the criterion established here, to determine the norms of international law which deserve to be considered as strictly juridical. But, on the subject of the Kellogg-Briand Pact, the conclusion seems to me indisputable: neither the moral state of the community of nations nor international institutions offered a basis for outlawing war. Anyone imagining he was guaranteeing peace by outlawing war was like a doctor imagining he was curing diseases by declaring them contrary to the aspirations of humanity.

Considering the background of international politics, the condemnation of wars of aggression as such would involve the traditional difficulties of application. If, in order to maintain the status quo and prevent the foreseeable attack of the Third Reich, France had taken the initiative in 1933, she would perhaps have been formally guilty of aggression (in 1936 this initiative would have been viewed as a juridical punishment of the violation of the Locarno Treaty), but this aggression would have had a limited and conservative objective. On the other hand, the day a rearmed Germany took the initiative, she sought to modify the status quo, but violating the treaties, she was not thereby morally guilty if the status quo were unjust. In other words, it is difficult to condemn, morally or historically, the initiative of a recourse to force for two reasons: this initiative may be the only means of preventing an attack that will ultimately be mortal; no tribunal, judging equitably, is in a position to say what peaceful changes are imperative and to compel respect for these decisions.

Likewise, if one postulates a system of militarily autonomous states, one must make many assumptions for the principle of collective security to be applicable. First of all, the states must agree on the definition of an aggressor. Hence they must be either disposed to subscribe to the status quo as such or else bring the same judgment in equity to bear on the acts of the states in conflict. A state having been unanimously recognized as an aggressor, legally and in equity (Italy, for example), the other states must feel sufficiently interested in safeguarding the juridical order to accept possible risks and sacrifices in view of an interest that is not strictly national and that is *their* interest

5. Ibid., p. 291.

at most in the long run (if we assume that all states not party to the conflict are interested in safeguarding the juridical order). Finally, one must assume that the coalition of states united against aggression is so superior in force to the state guilty of aggression that it has no other recourse but capitulation or a hopeless combat. If the aggressor state is, by itself, as strong as the coalition of states defending the law, collective security involves the generalization of a war, or localized, it runs the risk of leading to a general and total war. If several states refuse to accept the responsibilities involving sanctions against the aggressor, collective security paralyzes the defensive alliances without replacing them by a universal alliance.

The criticism of idealist illusion is not only pragmatic, it is also moral. Idealistic diplomacy slips too often into fanaticism; it divides states into good and evil, into peace-loving and bellicose. It envisions a permanent peace by the punishment of the latter and the triumph of the former. The idealist, believing he has broken with power politics, exaggerates its crimes. Sometimes states obey their principles and, with the excuse of punishing aggressors, go to the extreme of war and victory; sometimes, when their interests are at stake or circumstances oblige them to do so, they follow their opportunities. The United States did not hesitate to "interfere in Colombia's internal affairs" to provoke or favor the creation of a state of Panama, ready to concede it a perpetual sovereignty over the Canal Zone. To obtain (wrongly) a Russian intervention against Japan, Roosevelt yielded to Stalin's demands, even to those that could be satisfied only at the expense of the Chinese ally (whose government, it is true, was not hostile to these concessions).

States, engaged in incessant competition whose stake is their existence, do not all behave in the same manner at all times, but they are not divided, once and for all, into good and evil. It is rare that all the wrongs are committed by one side, that one camp is faultless. The first duty—political, but also moral—is to see international relations for what they are, so that each state, legitimately preoccupied with its own interests, will not be entirely blind to the interests of others. In this uncertain battle, in which the qualifications of the participants are not equivalent but in which it is rare that one of them has done absolutely no wrong, the best conduct—the best with regard to the values which the idealist himself wishes to achieve—is that dictated by *prudence*. To be prudent is to act in accordance with the particular situation and the concrete data, and not in accordance with some system or out of passive obedience to a norm or pseudo-norm; it is to prefer the limitation of violence to the punishment of the presumably guilty party or to a so-called absolute justice; it is to establish concrete accessible objectives conforming to the secular law of international relations and not to limitless and perhaps meaningless objectives, such as "a world safe for democracy" or "a world from which power politics will have disappeared."

Two quotations, borrowed from George F. Kennan, illustrate an analogous conception of the attitude at the same time most favorable to peace (or to the limitation of war) and to the relative morality of which states are capable:

"We must be gardeners and not mechanics in our approach to world affairs." And elsewhere: "This task will be best approached not through the establishment of rigid legal norms but rather by the traditional devices of political expediency. The sources of international tension are always specific, never general. They are always devoid of exact precedents or exact parallels. They are always in part unpredictable. If the resulting conflicts are to be effectively isolated and composed, they must be handled partly as matter of historical equity but partly, also, with an eye to the given relationships of power. Such conflicts, let us remember, usually touch people at the neuralgic points of their most violent political emotions. Few people are ever going to have an abstract devotion to the principles of international legality capable of competing with the impulses from which wars are apt to arise."[6]

The Idealism of Power Politics

The conclusion of the preceding section—prudence is the statesman's supreme virtue—seems to me obvious because it is based upon two incontestable facts: the particular character of each situation (which condemns the spirit of system or principle to irrelevance) and the frequency of a recourse to force by states in conflict,[7] a recourse which, despite attempts to "outlaw" war, still conforms to written and traditional international law. Hence we have not contrasted *prudence* and *idealism*, but prudence and *idealist illusion*, whether that illusion is juridical or ideological. . . .

6. *Realities of American Foreign Policy*, Princeton, 1954, p. 92, quoted by Kenneth W. Thompson, *Political Realism and the Crisis of World Politics*, Princeton, 1960, pp. 55 and 60–61. Kennan has expressed similar ideas in *American Diplomacy (1900–1950)*, Chicago, 1951.

7. The Kellogg-Briand Pact made not just any war, but "wars of aggression" a crime. And the non-aggressor states did not rely upon the pact to protect them.

What is true in all epochs is that the necessary reference to the calculation of forces and the endless diversity of circumstances requires statesmen to be *prudent*. But prudence does not always require either moderation or peace by compromise, or negotiations, or indifference to the internal regimes of enemy states or allies. Roman diplomacy was not moderate, the peace imposed by the Union on the Confederacy rejected all compromise. Negotiations with Hitler were most often fruitless or harmful. In a heterogeneous system, it is hardly possible for a statesman to model himself upon François I making an alliance with the Grand Turk, or upon Richelieu supporting the Protestant princes. True realism today consists in recognizing the action of ideologies upon diplomatic-strategic conduct. In our epoch, instead of repeating that all states, no matter what their institutions, have "the same kind of foreign policy," we should insist upon the truth that is more complementary than contradictory: no one understands the diplomatic strategy of a state if he does not understand its regime, if he has not studied the philosophy of those who govern it. To lay down as a rule that the heads of the Bolshevik party conceive the national interests of their state as did all other rulers of Russia is to doom oneself to misunderstanding the practices and ambitions of the Soviet Union.

The invitation made to the West today not to mix ideology and diplomacy assumes a paradoxical character in our epoch. The Soviet Union promises perpetual peace at the end of the world crisis, when socialism will have prevailed over capitalism permanently and universally. Can the West promise nothing? Can it not champion a type of institution within states, a type of relation among states? Must it resign itself to an inevitable war while the Communist world proclaims glorious tomorrows?

A true realism takes into account the whole of reality, dictates diplomatic-strategic conduct adapted not to the finished portrait of what international politics would be if statesmen were wise in their selfishness, but to the nature of the passions, the follies, the ideas and the violences of the century. . . .

States constitute a society of a unique type which imposes norms on its members and yet tolerates recourse to armed force. As long as international society preserves this mixed and, in a sense, contradictory character, the morality of international action will also be equivocal.

Relations between states are a test of wills, peaceful or bloody depending on the occasion. Peoples therefore cannot ignore the morality of struggle which enjoins individuals in collectivities to be courageous, disciplined and devoted, and urges them to respect promises and have a concern for honor. Why have the French passionately debated—and why do they continue to debate—the armistice of June 1940, both in and beyond its political and military consequences? Because the armistice raised a question: Did France, by leaving the war, break her word on honor? Was she violating the supreme rule that binds allied combatants? When the United States sided, in the United Nations, against the Franco-British Suez expedition, many Frenchmen and Englishmen felt that they had been "betrayed" by their ally. The United States, on the other hand, considered itself doubly innocent: it had not been forewarned; even if it had been, it would have subordinated the morality of struggle to the morality of law.

The morality of struggle is easily corrupted to a gang morality. Those who scorn the laws of society are not thereby "faithless and lawless." Obedience to the leader, gang solidarity, testify to a crude sense of discipline and honor which do not forbid the use of any means against other gangs and the orientation of collective behavior toward inadmissible goals. States are not always delicate in their choice of means; nor always faithful to the promises they make. The morality of struggle will have some meaning as long as war remains the final sanction of international relations, but it will never afford a prospect of lasting peace or universality.

The morality of law is the antithesis of the morality of struggle, because the law is valid for all, without consideration of persons, whereas the promises made by states or by gangsters are essentially linked to persons. But since international law is conservative, since states have never fully accepted its obligations, since, further, no tribunal, judging in equity, recommends the necessary changes, the states that invoke the morality of law often pass for hypocrites rather than heroes. A rare event in itself, respect for the law is too readily explained by national interest. If acted upon more frequently, this same respect would multiply wars and make them inexpiable.

The ambiguity of international society makes it impossible for a partial logic to be followed to its end, be it one of law or one of force. The only morality which transcends the morality of struggle and the morality of law is what I would call the morality of prudence, which attempts not only to consider each case in its concrete particularities, but also not to ignore any of the arguments of principle and opportunity, to forget neither the relation of forces nor the wills of peoples. Because it is complex, the judgment of prudence is never incontestable, and it satisfies completely neither the moralists nor the vulgar disciples of Machiavelli.

He who attempts to play the angel plays the beast. The statesman *ought* not forget that an international order is maintained only on condition that it is supported by forces capable of balancing those of dissatisfied or revolutionary states. If he neglects to calculate forces, he fails the obligations of his responsibility, hence the morality of his job and his vocation. He makes an error, since he compromises the security of the persons and values whose fate has been entrusted to him. Selfishness is no virtue, but it nonetheless prevails among states, whose survival is guaranteed by no one. But anyone who would play the beast does not play the angel. The Spenglerian realist, who asserts that man is a beast of prey and urges him to behave as such, ignores a whole side of human nature. Even in the relations between states, respect for ideas, aspiration to higher values and concern for obligations have been manifested. Rarely have collectivities acted as if they would stop at nothing with regard to one another.

The morality of prudence, the best on both the level of facts and that of values, does not resolve the antinomies of strategic-diplomatic conduct, but it does attempt to find in each case the most acceptable compromise. However, if the procession of states and empires continues endlessly, are the historical compromises between violence and moral aspiration little more than expedients? In the thermonuclear age, is a policy enough which reduces the frequency and the amount of violence? Proudhon proclaimed the right of force but also heralded an age of peace. Now that humanity possesses the means of destroying itself, have wars a meaning if they do not lead to peace?

11

On the Strategy of Peace

To Arm or Disarm?

The existence of thermonuclear weapons does not change the nature of the morality of diplomatic-strategic action: such is the conclusion of the foregoing chapters.

To be sure, it ridicules the traditional rhetoric concerning the regenerative influence of war or the courage of peoples. It makes clear the dissociation between the conditions of military force and the conditions of creative vitality or of the harmonious community. A state which, by virtue of its possession of thermonuclear arms and ballistic missiles, possesses the means to terrorize and even to exterminate the rest of the human race has not therefore given proof of the merits that would single it out as fit to rule the world. Perhaps it was too optimistic, but it was not absurd to have stated, as Proudhon did, that a people had no right to form an independent state unless they were capable of defending themselves. The same reasoning would suggest today that only a few giant states have a legitimate claim to independence.

If thermonculear weapons have perhaps changed the meaning of war, of martial virtues and of the independence of states, if the texts we borrowed from Treitschke manifestly belong to another age and not to the century of Hiroshima and Nagasaki, the practical-moral problems facing politicians are not fundamentally different; contrary to appearances, they have become more complex rather than simpler. All those who act, individuals and collectivities, have always had a

Excerpts from chapters 21 and 22 of *Peace and War: A Theory of International Relations*, by Raymond Aron, translated by Richard Howard and Annette Baker Fox. © 1966, 1973 by Doubleday & Company. Reprinted by permission of Doubleday & Company, Inc., and Weidenfeld & Nicolson, Ltd. First published in French in 1961.

tendency to consider the short rather than the long run, their own interests rather than those of the collectivity to which they belong, i.e., the advantages afforded by a certain action rather than the repercussions which this action will inevitably provoke. In the thermonuclear age this propensity on the part of the actors runs the risk of being fatal. The statesman who makes the decision, in France, to manufacture atomic bombs must, if he wants to be genuinely realistic, consider the consequences of the expansion of the atomic club and not only the advantage France might derive from being its fourth member. The statesman who, in the United States, wants Congress to approve a vast program of civil defense should consider the countermeasures which the Soviet Union would not fail to take. Finally—and this is both the simplest and the most important idea—*the aim of each of the super powers is to conquer the other without war and not to conquer "so oder so."*

The common interest of the two super powers, the common interest of mankind that there be no thermonuclear war,[1] is as great a consideration, and should be a greater one, than the limited stakes of each conflict. No statesman can define the national interest for which he is responsible without including in it the advantage of peace. Unfortunately, any statesman of the two super powers who was constantly aware of the disproportion between the stake and the cost of a potential war would condemn himself to beating a retreat each time there was or seemed to be a risk of explosion; thus he would condemn himself for losing, one after another, the stakes of all partial conflicts. But if each of these stakes is modest, are they still so all together?

The only way to resolve this antinomy—either to accept risks disproportionate to the particular stake or else to risk losing all the individual stakes—is for the two super powers[2] to create conditions such that they do not need to brandish the thermonuclear threat or, at least, that neither need brandish it except in circumstances so rare, for stakes so considerable, that the other cannot commit an error in judgment and has no temptation to risk its execution. How are such conditions to be created? I see two means: that of disarmament (in a broad sense which we shall specify), and that of a strategy–diplomacy reducing the role of deterrence and reinforcing that of defense. These two means intersect, and it is not easy to follow one or the other to its end.

---

1. It is not entirely true that this is the interest of the *whole* human race. Perhaps the Chinese would not be sorry to see a Russo-American war.

2. Or for whichever one is inclined to give in.

PEACE BY FEAR

The development of weapons of massive destruction has suggested a concept of possible if not eternal peace, which I have already referred to in passing and which a great many writers, in the course of the last few years, have entertained more or less seriously: the concept of peace by fear.

The idea is not new. It is over a century since the statement "war will kill itself" was advanced and found occasional acceptance, actually during periods of relative peace. Belied by a fresh outbreak of the monster of war, hope was soon rekindled by the development of a method of killing more men more quickly: the thermonuclear bomb, which amounted to a qualitative revolution so great was the quantitative increase in explosive power, gave this classic theme an actuality it had never had before. Friedrich Engels was mistaken when he thought that the development of military technique was nearly complete; the writers of the last century were mistaken when they counted on the machine gun and the cannon to prevent killing; the theorists of the period between the wars were mistaken when they prophesied the end of civilization in the event of a second world war: all these mistakes still do not prove that we are wrong to count on thermonuclear deterrence to prevent a third world war.

The thesis of "peace by fear" has three different versions, which are not always clearly distinguished but which are logically and historically separable. The extreme thesis would be that of *the possible generalization and duration* of peace by fear: the spread of atomic or thermonuclear arms would create by degrees the same kind of peace between all states as the peace that reigns today between the United States and the Soviet Union. A second version would be that of the peace between "nuclear" states which refuse to fight one another even with conventional weapons alone, for fear of escalation. Finally, a third, more modest version would merely hold that a thermonuclear war is impossible since the belligerents, even if they have access to these weapons, refuse to use them for fear of reprisal.

Of these three versions it is the first which is the most improbable, and it is also the only one that presents itself as a doctrine of peace. The other two amount to hypotheses concerning the possible course of events, given the present situation. They indicate the objectives of a conceivable strategy as much as they formulate hypotheses concerning the future. In any case, they operate within the context of the existing diplomatic strategy.

The extreme version of peace by fear can hardly be taken seriously, but it exercises a kind of fascination over a certain type of mind, it possesses a pseudo-logical probability, it lends itself to an allegedly rational formulation. Hence it is not entirely pointless to indicate why it cannot be accepted.

If it is enough for two states to have the means of "atomizing" one another for them to lay down their arms, why not give such means to all states? In this way eternal peace would presumably be established. The skeptics find themselves accused of the grim desire to "save war" by humanizing it (i.e., de-atomizing it). The error in this argument is twofold: peace between the possessors of thermonuclear forces *is not* assured. Assuming that it is at least probable, it is impossible to generalize it by promoting the spread of atomic arms.

Let us begin with the second proposition. The probability of peace between the possessors of thermonuclear arms is based on the hypothesis that reality resembles the model of "equality of crime and punishment," and not the two other possible models (the two gangsters, the disproportion of punishment to crime). But between two small states, at least during the coming phase, atomic arms are more likely to create the temptations and anxieties of "the two gangsters" than the security of justice. A state whose territory is small would be devastated before it exercised a posthumous vengeance (again, provided the means of retaliation are not destroyed by the attack which would have struck the peoples and their cities).

An increase in the number of states belonging to the atomic club would add two other factors of instability: the possibility of launching a war, whether intentional or not, between the super powers as a result of a small state's voluntary or involuntary action, and the greater probability of a war provoked by a statesman's so-called irrational decision.

The hypothesis of peace by fear between the super powers breaks down into a series of propositions. None of the advantages that might be brought about by victory could be compared to the calculated cost of a thermonuclear exchange. Each of the duopolists reasons in this way and knows that the other does so too. Neither lives with the obsession that the other is going to attack it. Neither one has its finger on the trigger. Each relies on both its capacity for reprisal and on what it calls the enemy's rationality. This kind of security would not withstand the indefinite expansion of the atomic club. The member of a bloc in possession of a small striking force would be in a position, under certain circumstances and by certain initiatives, to set off hostilities between the super powers against their will. In other words, the international structure of a duopoly involves fewer unknown factors than a structure characterized by an increasing number of military sovereignties. Two actors have a better chance of conducting a duel according to their intentions than four or five actors in conflict, with several possible groupings.

If an event which is not consistent with the desires of the super powers is rendered less probable by polyarchy, it renders the so-called irrational or irresponsible conduct of a diplomat-strategist more likely. We have not succeeded at any point in this book in giving an unambiguous definition of rational conduct, and on occasion we have even shown why the definitions that have been attempted failed in their purpose. We shall later muster the various arguments we have encountered in the course of our discussion. But, to avoid a pseudo-precision and to return to popular terminology, we shall merely say: the fear that future possessors of atomic or thermonuclear weapons will not conduct themselves in a "rational" manner is well founded.

It is not easy to determine whether the diplomatic use of the thermonuclear threat is ever "rational." Perhaps it would be irrational to execute this threat when the first blow struck by the enemy has destroyed the greater part of our thermonuclear forces. But at least let us assume that those in charge of the two major states and of the two thermonuclear forces are calm, reflective, that they do not act on impulse, that up to the last moment they will weigh the alternatives before giving orders the result of which might be millions of deaths. Let us also assume that on both sides such orders cannot be given on a lower level of the hierarchy, that the chain of command, like the network of communications, would stand the test of an international crisis. Such assumptions have less chance of being true for five states than for two, for states less precisely organized, less accustomed to the handling of modern technology than the duopolists.

The preceding remarks have a strictly limited meaning and objective. Between the two antinomic theses, each of which has its partisans—peace through the generalization of thermonuclear deterrence and the dangers created by enlargement of the atomic club—I do not hesitate to choose: the first is illusory, deceptively seductive, it has the characteristic appeal of sophistries. In short, *it is war which must be saved*, in other words, the possibility of tests of armed strength between states rather than eternal peace, which would have to be established by the constant threat of the thermonuclear holocaust.

We might go further still and consider whether a generalized peace by terror is actually a possible model for eternal peace (or even merely a lasting peace). Among the four models of international systems not yet realized but conceivable, Morton A. Kaplan has advanced what he calls the unit veto system, the system of the *liberum veto*. Just as a single dissenting voice paralyzed the Polish Diet, each actor—and not just each principal actor—would have not the right but the capacity to paralyze any other actor by actually threatening him with death. Every state would have the capacity to deter any other because it would have the means either to exercise mortal retaliation against the aggressor or to effect the extinction of the entire human race. The first hypothesis would require the small states to be in a position to render their thermonuclear force invulnerable, that is, in general, to locate it outside their territory, to bury it in the earth or disperse it in the depths of the ocean. The second hypothesis—that of a Doomsday device—will long, if not forever, exceed the resources of small or medium-size states. Even the super powers will probably not decide to construct a machine which, in the event of a "technical error," would seal the fate of mankind along with that of whichever state had constructed it.

The outclassing of the small states by the great does not therefore seem to be a phenomenon of short duration. We do not yet perceive on the historical horizon a reversal favorable to the small states. To be sure, it is conceivable that the latter may acquire weapons which, even in responding to aggression, would cause serious damage to the great power. But they would still be vulnerable to a strategy of intimidation, so great would be the disparity of dangers, and the smallness of their territory being a further cause of inferiority. It is true that other techniques—chemical, bacteriological—could be used for the mass extermination of human beings. It is not entirely impossible that these techniques might be less costly than thermonuclear and especially ballistic-missile technique, and that consequently they might offer the small states a chance to possess arms qualitatively similar to those of the great powers. But these do not seem to be immediate prospects.

Let us add that the international system of *liberum veto,* in all probability, would not be lasting. The great powers would rightfully regard it as intolerable. Well before it was put into effect, the great powers would have agreed to prevent the small states from jeopardizing their superiority. *No international system has ever been, or ever can be, equalitarian.* In the absence of a single authority, a reduction of the number of principal actors is indispensable to a minimum of order and predictability.

If the doctrinal version of peace by fear is, upon reflection, indefensible, the same is not true of the two moderate versions, the one whereby possessors of thermonuclear arms will not attack one another directly, even with conventional weapons, or at most will fight with conventional weapons. This is a hypothesis based on limited experience, and concerned with objectives which the duopolists can accept. The best method of estimating the degree of stability of peace by fear is to consider the circumstances under which the duopolists, by the desire of one or without the intention of either, might use against each other the weapons with which they threaten each other but which they do not intend to launch.

American writers have made up a list of the typical cases in which the "war nobody wants" would occur in spite of the fear it inspires. In one form or another, they arrive at approximately the following list:

1. The stability of peace by fear presupposes the approximate equality of crime and punishment. But this stability is not definitively acquired. It is constantly being threatened as a result of the "qualitative arms race." One of the super powers may acquire a superiority such that it considers itself in a position to eliminate its rival at a cost acceptable to itself or again may believe it can impose its will on its rival without the latter's daring to resist. In the first case it would take the initiative; in the second, it is the duopolist in an inferior position which would reply to an extreme provocation by an initiative motivated by fear but fatal to both. Let us say that the breaking of the balance of terror by a technical breakthrough would create a risk—difficult to evaluate but real—of the war for which men are preparing but which they do not want to wage.

2. Even if one of the super powers is not sure of a distinct superiority over its rival, it may happen that both imagine they are reduced to the situation of the two gangsters, each believing that the advantage of attacking first is enormous and constitutes the difference between (relative) victory and defeat, between survival and disappearance. The magnitude of the retaliation to be feared is still too great for either to launch its thermonuclear force in cold blood. But each will be tempted if it suspects its rival is about to do so. Hence all that is required is a misunderstanding concerning the other's intentions for either one of the duopolists to have a so-called rational motive for doing what fear presumably forbids. This second case, usually called *war by misunderstanding*, requires a certain instability in the balance, hence places a premium on initiative.

3. Finally, even assuming that the balance of terror persists, an "accident" may occur; the inaccurate reading of an instrument, the explosion of a bomb, may give the impression of an attack; a break in the system of communications or the hierarchy of command may enable

an officer of lower rank to give an order on his own responsibility that will provoke the explosion, etc. In other words, the "accident" can be either technical or social.

4. A fourth case is that of an escalation as a result of an armed conflict in which one or both of the super powers would be implicated. This escalation is obviously more to be feared in proportion to the advantage of striking first, and to the fear each of the duopolists entertains of its enemy's initiative, Escalation would therefore involve a certain element of misunderstanding or of *rage*.

5. A final eventuality is the one in which the explosion would be provoked by a third state, whether or not it possesses thermonuclear weapons. If it does possess them it may, voluntarily or not, involve the super powers in an inexpiable war which the latter do not desire but which would be consistent with the interest of the *tertius gaudens*. If it does not possess nuclear weapons, one of the duopolists may use or threaten to use its thermonuclear force against it and thereby provoke its rival's intervention.

No one can claim that this list is exhaustive, and the cases enumerated, though conceptually distinct, may be more or less mingled in reality. What is the probability of each of these eventualities? What is the probability of all these eventualities together? I am not sure that any observer, mathematician or political analyst is in a position to give a precise and sure answer. What we are dealing with is, in fact, neither a purely mathematical probability (if we increase the number of thermonuclear bombs, one day or another a bomb will explode by accident) nor a purely political probability (in the event of a duel between two states armed with thermonuclear forces, it is inevitable that one or the other or both will eventually decide to settle their differences by war). The probability is of a mixed character, it depends on technological factors (the results of the race for technological progress) and psychopolitical factors. It differs in kind from all known arms races.

For the time being let us waive this perhaps futile question: are these illusory fears, since the real fear inspired by thermonuclear war assures an effective protection against it? Let us merely confront the conclusions of the two analyses, one devoted to the doctrinal version of peace by fear, and the other to the two pragmatic versions. The first has led us to the following proposition: it is impossible to imagine a general and lasting peace by the spread of thermonuclear weapons to all states. The second has led us to the following proposition: even between two states that are the sole possessors of a thermonuclear force, fear does not guarantee peace. But obviously we have not disproved the self-evident proposition that the fear of thermonuclear war urges moderation upon diplomats. We shall add the proposition complementary to this: if atomic or thermonuclear weapons could be eliminated, given the international system as it is, a general war would be more rather than less likely. There is every reason to think that a general war, waged with ballistic missiles and thermonuclear bombs, would be more horrible than all those of the past, but there is no reason to think that the global system would be more peaceful than the partial systems of bygone millenniums if the great powers did not possess these terrifying weapons.

This fundamental antinomy obliges those who, like the author of this book, desire to reduce the role of force in international relations, to consider the function of disarmament in a strategy whose goal is peace or, at least, the diminution of the volume of historical violence.

PEACE BY DISARMAMENT

We have examined and, if possible, dissipated the illusion of *peace by fear*. Now, going to the other extreme, we should like to examine and dissipate the analogous illusion of *peace by disarmament*.

Traditionally, three expressions have been used: *disarmament, reduction of arms* and *arms control*. The first evokes the idea of a world in which states have renounced the means of fighting one another, that is, have put their battleships and airplane carriers on the scrap heap, have blown up their cannon and their fortifications, disbanded their regiments and kept only those police forces necessary, as they say, for the maintenance of order. Auguste Comte, always an extremist, did not hesitate to predict the transformation of standing armies into constabularies. This vision of the future, whether probable or possible, has always been Utopian in the pejorative sense of the word, in that it was a representation of a world different from the real one, incompatible with the nature of man and societies, and did not even indicate the path toward an accessible objective.

There is scarcely any need to prove at length that states, such as we know them in the 1960s, divided as to good and evil (or, to put it differently, as to the notion of the good society), convinced of their mutually hostile intentions, are neither capable nor desirous of renouncing the means of war, or in other words their capacity to defend their interests and to impose their wills by threats or arms. The hierarchy of the great and small powers would disappear in this imaginary universe; still, the inequality of the "police forces" necessary to "maintain order" would run the risk of re-establishing a hierarchy and provoking interminable debate over the matter of the "police forces" tolerated by the general and total disarmament treaty. A system without a hierarchy of power, without a supreme tribunal, without a monopoly of strength, is truly inconceivable. It is an ideal type, if you will, but one that is misconceived because it cannot be realized.

Fundamentally, the theory of peace by disarmament, for the millenniums preceding the development of weapons of massive destruction, was inapplicable for the following reasons: politicians have never regarded peace—or, if you prefer, the non-use of force—as more important for them than certain interests (territory, natural resources, booty). Only those who despaired in advance of surviving or emerging victorious from the test of war would therefore have subscribed to a peace by disarmament. Assuming that the princes would have agreed to submit their differences to a judgment other than that of arms, what could have been the nature of the tribunal of justice replacing the tribunal of war? Finally, the distinction between the force necessary to support the throne and the force necessary to conquer provinces was not sufficiently clear for even the idea of transforming all armies into police forces to have a meaning. The pacification of relations between states presupposes the pacification of relations between citizens (or parties, or provinces) within states. To some extent, all politics were violent, not only international politics.

Does intra-state or intra-bloc pacification make it possible to imagine, if not to achieve, a pacification of inter-state or inter-bloc relations? It seems to me that we must reluctantly but resolutely answer *no* to such a question. Within the nations longest established, like the French nation, no social group or political party has definitively renounced the use of force to defend either its assets or its ideals. The "police forces" necessary to "maintain order" against peasant uprisings or a Communist revolution should not be insignificant. But above all a large portion of humanity has not yet achieved national consciousness, either because individuals remain the prisoners of tribal customs, on this side of the state and the nation, or because the political units established today are unsure of themselves and of their future (either large and non-cohesive like India, or small and weak like Gabon or Mauritania). In both cases it is just as difficult to imagine the indefinite continuation of the status quo as the latter's non-violent transformation. Can nations grow without opposing one another, can they assert their existence without finding an enemy?

Let us grant for the moment that a tribunal of justice can theoretically, according to men's desires and economic-social circumstances, pronounce verdicts which may prevent or check bloodshed, which may enable nations to appear and to become aware of themselves without combating enemies within and without. Such a tribunal would presuppose an agreement among the great powers as to both a ratio of forces and the definition of just and unjust. Given the conflict between the duopolists, on the plane of force and on the plane of ideas, the third world is itself condemned to follow the path of violence with the sole hope that in their mutual interest, that of avoiding a total war, the two super powers will try to limit the hostilities which might break out in one place or another.

Finally, since the super powers are obliged, in order to maintain their positions, to retain a substantial quantity of conventional weapons, that disarmament which is held to be the prerequisite of peace would be concerned first and foremost with atomic and thermonuclear bombs on the one hand and with delivery systems on the other. But at this point a contradiction arises which is created by technology but which reveals a fundamental perplexity in the policy.

The elimination of atomic or thermonuclear weapons is all the more difficult as the verification of an eventual agreement is more uncertain and as the violation of the treaty would be likely to produce higher dividends. Let us remember the Washington Treaty on the limitations of naval armaments: no measure was provided to insure respect for the promises made. The five states—the United States, Great Britain, Japan, France, Italy—had less confidence in one another than they did in the ability of news to travel. It was considered impossible to build a battleship in secret. The commissions for control of German disarmament were not entirely effective. Nevertheless, until the time when the rearmament of the Third Reich was openly begun, Germany remained militarily weak and France, alone or with her network of alliances, would have been in a position to impose her will on Germany, if she had had a will.

Whether in the case of atomic bombs or of means of delivery, it is impossible to have a reasonable assurance that the agreement by which the two super powers promised to eliminate them would be respected. No one knows where, in the Soviet Union and the United States, the thermonuclear bombs are stockpiled. Even if officials were authorized to travel freely through the immense territory of the two super powers, they would have no chance of discovering all the places where such weapons were concealed, if we assume that one or the other power was firmly resolved to preserve a certain stock of ther-

monuclear bombs in violation of the treaty. The resources of conceal-
ment are, in the present state of affairs, greater than the resources of
inspection

Nor is it any more possible to eliminate the means of delivery. Underground launching platforms have become difficult to detect. In the
event of the elimination of ballistic missiles, any commercial airplane
would suffice, with or without modifications, to transport an atomic
or thermonuclear bomb. Finally, preparations for chemical and bacteriological warfare can be camouflaged even more easily. The principal
states possess stockpiles of gas bombs which attack the nerves and
cause either almost instantaneous death or a more or less temporary
paralysis. In the absence of atomic, thermonuclear or radiological
means, chemical weapons of mass destruction would still be available.

*Now, the advantages of fraud have not increased less rapidly than
the difficulties of control.* Let us suppose that one of the two super
powers, after having signed a treaty providing for the destruction of all
atomic and thermonuclear bombs, has managed to conceal several
hundred of these weapons: this power could terrorize the rest of the
world. The treaty limiting naval armaments was signed because it was
almost sure to be respected by all and because marginal violations had
only mediocre consequences. A treaty calling for wholesale atomic disarmament will never be signed because its control would be impossible
and because the possible consequences of fraud would be beyond measure. No one trusts a rival's honesty if the reward for breaking one's
word can be world dominion.

Reasoning of this kind has seemed so convincing to almost all who
have reflected on these problems that the thesis of peace by disarmament has scarcely any more partisans than the thesis of (general and
lasting) peace by fear. It is just as bizarre to imagine that industrial
societies will live in peace because they will no longer have the means
to fight as it is to imagine that they will live in peace because they will
all have the means to destroy each other in a few moments. The seemingly opposite intellectual error is actually the same in both cases. The
doctrinaire of peace by fear imagines an equality between states by the
capacity of the weakest to deal the strongest a mortal blow. The doctrinaire of peace by disarmament imagines the equality to consist in
the inability of the strongest to coerce the weakest. Neither equality is
attainable. Neither equality is or would be acceptable to the super
powers.

These two doctrines have yet another point in common: they are
based on a conception of an international system in which peace
would be insured automatically, as it were, without the intervention of

men and their free decisions. In order that the world of a thermonuclear *liberum veto* might not seem infernal, one presupposes a
rational *Homo diplomaticus,* in a certain number of examples. That
the world of states without weapons might seem secure, one presupposes citizens and states who are resolved never to resort to force on
the pretext that they have flung traditional or modern weapons on the
scrap heap or to the bottom of the sea. It is unjustifiable and absurd to
put politicians, individuals or groups, citizens or diplomats between
parentheses. There is no infallible "gimmick"—armament or disarmament—which will guarantee definitive peace to a violent and divided
humanity.

If general and total disarmament is no more the secret of eternal
peace than the generalization of the balance of terror, the policy of
armament, like the fear of a thermonuclear war, has a certain influence upon the risk of a conflict and the character the latter would
assume. Just as after having dissipated the illusion of peace by fear we
advanced the idea that the fear of war could be the beginning of
wisdom, similarly, after having dissipated the illusion of peace by disarmament, we do not exclude the possibility that the policy of armament may be one of the factors of peace and of war.

So long as there remains a plurality of military sovereignties, it is
impossible to assert that in and of itself the reduction of arms is favorable or unfavorable to the maintenance of peace. The limitation of one
type of arms (battleships) shifts rather than abolishes the rivalry. If one
of the great powers (the United States, for example) reduces its peacetime arms level below its potential, it encourages rival states to under-
rate the force it is capable of mobilizing or the resolution it will evince
in the course of the hostilities. Similarly, if one side does not rearm or
does not arm quickly enough, whereas the opposing side rushes into
an extensive arms program, this acceptance of inferiority is often of a
nature to precipitate rather than prevent the explosion. In the international system of which history provides examples, the balance of
power has never, in the long run, prevented wars, but the acceptance
of imbalance has sometimes hastened or provoked a particular conflict
which was not inevitable, at least at the time when it occurred.

Historically, the arms policies which seem to have been most favorable to the reduction of violence are policies of limitation, not the
result of a unilateral decision or a negotiated agreement, but the object
of an implicit agreement between the principal actors. The Washington naval treaty or the one Great Britain signed with Hitler in 1935
had, by the most generous interpretation, no effect—either favorable
or unfavorable—on the course of events. The two wars which it was

hoped could be avoided by preventing an arms race—the war between the United States and Japan, the war between Great Britain and the Third Reich—both took place, without even their dates having been affected, probably, by the treaties. On the other hand, during the nineteenth century the European states more or less deliberately avoided mobilizing, either in peacetime or in wartime, all the resources theoretically available.

That these implicit and half-conscious agreements of arms control have contributed most effectively to what we might call the "reduction of the volume of historical violence" is almost self-explanatory. When states can or will mobilize only a fraction of their theoretically available resources, it is either because internal regimes are restraining this mobilization, or because the people do not believe in an immediate danger, or because they do not attribute great significance to any foreseeable conflicts. In all cases, hostilities will be less frequent, and less costly in lives and in wealth.

On the other hand, the disparity of forces created by disarmament or even the slightest unilateral rearmament encourages the unsatisfied state or the side which has taken the initiative in rearmament. As for arms-control treaties, they are the symptom of the fears of peoples or governments. Disarmament conferences multiply when nations fear war and vaguely perceive the seriousness of conflicts on the international plane. Whether or not these conferences come to anything, they do not cure the evil, that is, the not artificial but real and justified hostility between states.

An arms policy, whether it involves increase or decrease, should not be judged in the abstract, but in terms of the situation.[3] It cannot be called good or bad in itself, but only in relation to circumstances, to the existing territorial status, to the ambitions of certain persons, to the comparative strength of revisionist and conservative states. What happens to this principle in the age of thermonuclear bombs and ballistic missiles? Actually, it remains valid but its application becomes more complex and involves certain new aspects.

The traditional arms policy sometimes sought to prevent war, but it always sought to win that war if it broke out in spite of everything. For the moment, the arms policy adopted by the two super powers seems virtually to overlook the concern for victory and to have no other object than the perpetuation of non-war (or at any rate non-ther-

---

3. It goes without saying that this statement presupposes that we judge an arms policy in terms of the probability of war or peace and of the volume of violence. Economically or morally, the reduction of arms may be considered good in itself.

monuclear war). To the extent that deterrence completely replaces defense, everything proceeds as if the actors were identifying peace with victory and were unconcerned with the future in the event that deterrence should fail. But no one would say that this strategy is reasonable; in fact, the arms policy should tend to reduce the volume of violence, even or especially if war breaks out.

Formerly, one would have said that the formula "to reduce the volume of violence" means to reduce the frequency and intensity of war. But already, throughout history, the intensity of wars has sometimes been all the greater when they were less frequent. Before 1914 European societies had lived in peace, at least on the Continent, for almost half a century. The security of individuals within the states was better insured than it had ever been before. Party rivalry occurred without or almost without recourse to physical force. Even strikes, the traditional means by which one social group seeks to force its will on another, rarely gave rise to violence and still more rarely to casualties. Living conditions, the stability of the administration, which had favored the pacification of social existence, favored the mobilization of human and material resources, once the call to arms was sounded. A government which acquires ways of imposing peace upon citizens thereby acquires the means of fighting abroad.

The classical antithesis between frequency and intensity is henceforth transformed by the availability of thermonuclear weapons. The strategy of deterrence, as expounded in the British white paper of 1957, presupposes the *possibility* that a thermonuclear war will never take place and the *probability* that this war, if it does break out, will be fought with all available weapons.

But almost without exception,[4] observers have realized that the threat of a war that would mean unlimited destruction could not be brandished on every occasion. The greater the horror of thermonuclear war, the less plausible the threat to resort to it, and the less improbable the eventuality of armed conflicts in which atomic or thermonuclear weapons would not be used.

Such, in effect, is the first dilemma confronting statesmen in our age: do they wish to save war or save humanity from a certain war (thermonuclear war)? Do they seek to erase the distinction between conventional and atomic weapons in the hope that, if the latter are used in any conflict, no one will resort to *any* weapon at all? Or,

---

4. The most notable exception is General Gallois who, for that matter, holds that all wars can be prevented by providing all states with atomic or thermonuclear arms. He proves this thesis by the argument of proportional deterrence.

convinced that states are not yet ready to settle their differences peacefully, do they anticipate the possibility of hostilities in which the belligerents would fight with conventional weapons for limited stakes? Up to now, the West has accepted the first alternative in Europe, the second in the rest of the world. Generally speaking, it is the second alternative which strikes me as the more reasonable. The first suffers from a fundamental contradiction: *one cannot maintain that the thermonuclear holocaust is too horrible for anyone to launch it and at the same time count on the effectiveness of this threat in most circumstances.* If the first assertion is true, there will rise a statesman who does not believe in a threat that the other party nonetheless made in earnest.

Let us restate the two propositions which we have tried to establish in this section: it is impossible to imagine, the international system being what it is, a controlled disarmament which would deprive the two super powers of their weapons of mass destruction. It is impossible to imagine the definitive abolition of armed conflict, even among members of the atomic club, by the strategy of deterrence, that is, the threat of using thermonuclear weapons. The translation into action of the traditional objective of "reducing the volume of violence" presupposes a difficult pursuit of a *political-military conduct according to which the two super powers would reduce to a minimum the risk of being involved in spite of themselves in a war they do not want to wage, without either of the two being favored in the prosecution of the cold war.* American writers have invented the new concept, *arms control,* to designate the military aspect of this proceeding that would correspond to the enemies' mutual interest by preserving them both from a war they fear without condemning either one to defeat.

The French expression *contrôle des armements* is ambiguous, suggesting the control of the agreements concluded between states, whereas the American writers have in mind the whole group of unilateral or coordinated measures, the ensemble of implicit or explicit agreements by which states are trying to reduce the volume of violence in the thermonuclear age, hence primarily but not exclusively to prevent thermonuclear war. But to prevent thermonuclear war is to reduce as much as possible the risks of a thermonuclear war by preemption, by misunderstanding, by technical or human accident, by escalation, by the diabolical ruse of a small power. The risks are a function of the total situation, of the relation between the forces and arms systems available to both sides. This is not all: the procedures implied by "arms control" also aim at reducing the volume of violence in the case of a limited war, whether tactical atomic weapons are employed or not. They aim, in short, at "limiting the volume of violence," even assuming ballistic missiles armed with thermonuclear warheads had been exchanged—that is, they seek to maintain communications between the enemies with a view to ending hostilities either by agreement between the two, or by the capitulation of one of them.

Thus conceived, arms control would be better designated by the terms *arms policy* or *policy of armament and disarmament*. The main idea is, in fact, that of the inevitable solidarity between what is done in peacetime and what will happen in wartime, between military preparations and diplomacy, between what I do and what my enemy does, between measures of national defense and the probability of war (or of a certain war). This main idea may be deduced from Clausewitz's two principles which we recalled in the first chapter of this work, namely the continuity of peaceful or warlike relations between states, the consequences of reciprocity of action[5] and the danger, as one reprisal leads to another, of escalation. But these two principles assume a more tragic meaning in our age than in the past, because the value of time and the destructive capacity of weapons have changed qualitatively. States have always waged war with weapons accumulated in time of peace. But from 1914 to 1918 they had time to continue their mobilization after the beginning of hostilities, and the intervention of neutral states tipped the scale. Even if the weapons are conventional or atomic tomorrow, time will be short. To avoid escalation, the hostilities must be brief: the troublemaker must create a *fait accompli* in order to assume a defensive position immediately and to force the conservative party or side to take the offensive or resign itself to losing the stake. With strategic bombers it required hours to reach Moscow from Washington (or Washington from Moscow). With ballistic missiles the duration of the trajectory is reckoned in minutes (thirty). As for the probable destruction, it was already great before 1939 but the progression is of kind, not of degree, since we have leaped from several tons to several million tons.

Arms control involves or may involve measures to reduce armaments, but it can also involve, on the rational level, measures to increase armaments: three hundred invulnerable ballistic missiles on both sides contribute more "stability" to the balance of terror than one hundred such missiles. Arms control is therefore the pursuit of a national defense adopted by one or several friendly or rival states, with a view to insuring each state and all together the maximum security of each with respect to a possible aggression. In short, this is a case of a

5. Or the dialectic of antagonism.

combined policy of armament and disarmament whose objective would be the control of the instruments of death by all mankind. If there existed only a single military sovereignty, mankind, at least in theory, would easily attain this control. Is this control attainable by mankind taken as a whole, as long as each sovereign power considers the measures proposed in relation to its *own* advantage in competition rather than in relation to the common interest of the system, that is, in the interest of avoiding thermonuclear violence? . . .

Is the arms race the cause of the political conflict or is the political conflict the cause of the arms race? This classic question, as we have said, admits of no categorical answer. The arms race is the result of the pursuit of security by force, it symbolizes the dialectic of hostility in peacetime, it is the non-warlike form of escalation. It is therefore capable, under certain circumstances, of intensifying the hostility from which it proceeds, of aggravating the insecurity felt by each of the rivals. Each rival arms because the other arms, and neither is capable of arresting this progression. This situation, obviously absurd for anyone who refuses to enter into the logic of the actors, may actually be created less by the suspicions each entertains toward the other than by the arms the latter acquires, less by the intentions each attributes to his rival than by the means of destruction he knows him to possess. Such, perhaps, is the present situation.

Advocates of "disarmament" or of "arms control" do not necessarily subscribe to the thesis that the sole or principal source of the danger is thermonuclear weapons. Indeed, some merely hold that these weapons do not eliminate the danger of war and that they would give war the character of an unprecedented catastrophe. Others maintain that the antagonism of position, power or ideology between the two super powers would not justify a major war and that the United States and the Soviet Union hate each other primarily because of the thought of the harm they might do each other. Yet others do not hold the weapons responsible either for the violence of the conflict or the hostile passions, but feel that the development of the weapons constitutes a supplementary and independent cause of a war which, as a result of this very development, would exceed in horror all the evils which men have inflicted upon one another throughout the ages.

The three arguments all contain at least an element of truth. Even if the weapons of mass destruction do not increase the risks of war, they obviously increase the cost of a potential war. They provide another dimension to the conflict, a greater bitterness to the passions, they may even give rise to real risks of explosion (misunderstanding, accident, etc.). The uncertainty has to do with *quantity:* does the fear inspired by war balance and outweigh the danger created by weapons and innovations? To this question I feel personally incapable of giving a categorical answer, but I am impressed by the fact that most American scientists incline toward pessimism. Even though thermonuclear war may be improbable at each moment, in each crisis, is it not probable in the long run if states continue both to multiply innovations and to brandish this threat?

Whatever the magnitude of the danger, I do not see how mankind, for the moment, can escape it. The inspection system earlier discussed for the nuclear test ban makes it possible to imagine the system required by an agreement on total disarmament and to explain why such an agreement will not be signed in the course of the next few years. Neither of the super powers will promise not to take the initiative in resorting to atomic or thermonuclear weapons: such a promise would require, on the part of the West, an effort at conventional rearmament which—wrongly, I suspect—they would refuse to make.

Not that the Big Two are acting as if the danger did not exist. On the contrary, they are acting partly as if they had listened to the partisans of "arms control"; they are trying to defend their interests by reducing the volume of violence, to prevent the enlargement of conflicts, to use only conventional weapons when recourse to force becomes inevitable, to reassure each other in time of crisis as to their peaceful intentions. But all these arguments, if agreement there be, are implicit, the measures taken are unilateral, and they do not eliminate what most experts regard as the most serious aspect of the present global rivalry: the qualitative arms race.

I do not underestimate the gravity, at once tragic and absurd, of this race. But I ask the question: short of a revolution in the heart of man and the nature of states, by what miracle could interplanetary space be preserved from military use? How could the United States and the Soviet Union each agree to relinquish their own plans and henceforth to have no more satellites except those they possessed in common? Why should the super powers agree not to proceed from bombs of a few megatons to bombs of several dozen megatons?[6] Why should they not perfect fusion bombs whose detonator would not consist of a fission bomb and which would kill men without destroying buildings?

To be sure, the two super powers would experience a sense of security if the balance of mutual deterrence were stabilized with a known number of missiles. The balance of deterrence would no longer

6. Unless the experts declare 100-megaton bombs to be "useless."

deserve the name of balance of terror. Why should we be surprised that this balance has not been the subject of a formal agreement, when the United States has not even been able to convince its allies to abandon these weapons?

In the course of the next few years perhaps technological progress will in fact stabilize mutual deterrence. We must not count on the diplomats to achieve this stabilization.

To Survive Is to Conquer

The goal of the West is not only to avoid thermonuclear war, but also to be victorious or not to be vanquished. If the sole goal were to avoid thermonuclear war, the rational decision, the one that gives the best chance of attaining the goal, would be capitulation. If the West is not capitulating, despite the thermonuclear bombs and ballistic missiles which were brandished by Mr. Khrushchev, it is because the stake of the struggle is worth the risks of resistance.

This last proposition, applied to a particular case, will perhaps seem paradoxical, and even absurd. Is the freedom of two million Berliners *worth* the risk of a thermonuclear war? No particular stake, in fact, will be comparable to the "lost wager" or to the "bluff." But once we consent to yield everything, each particular stake increases its desirability, more than itself, since it involves, in a sense, the fate of the whole. It is not just the fate of two million Berliners which is at stake, but virtually the choice of the West Germans (between unity under Soviet protection and freedom for the favored two-thirds), hence the destiny of Western Europe as a whole, hence, in the last analysis, of the West itself and all it represents.

But, the skeptic or cynic will object, does the "salvation of the West" ever deserve to be defended at the price of millions, of tens of millions of victims? This objection is spuriously rational. It is true that the West will not be saved if the thermonuclear war takes place. In the age of the strategy of defense, it was possible to save a nation or a civilization by war. In the age of the strategy of deterrence, it is not possible to save a nation or a civilization by war, *but neither is it possible to save them by capitulation.* The point therefore is to convince ourselves and others that the values which would perish along with the regime and the civilization of the West justify the danger which we are creating for tens of millions of people, a danger which capitulation would dissipate *temporarily.*

THE STAKE

It is not easy, in the age in which we live, to justify that which in other times would have seemed obvious. The difficulty springs not only from the enormity of the losses which would be entailed by a thermonuclear war and which has provoked numerous dignitaries of the Catholic Church to declarations that such traditional concepts as that of a righteous war are henceforth inapplicable. To "atomize" a population of "innocents"—men, women and children—because their leaders were guilty of aggression would be a wicked mockery. The (political) justice of the cause does not justify the use of such horrible means. Once again, the only answer to an objection of this kind consists, for the West, in not placing itself in a situation where it would have to take the initiative in resorting to such weapons. The problem we are raising is different: have we something to save in order to justify sacrifices and dangers?

Some will answer immediately that the mere fact of raising such a question is in itself a confession. If a "crusader for the cold war" resorts to expressing his doubts and cross-examining himself publicly, is this not one more proof among countless others that a declining civilization no longer believes in itself? The mere fact that we raise the question signifies, in my opinion, just the reverse. Only the fanatic and the barbarian cannot question themselves regarding the justification of war in an age when a single thermonuclear bomb can kill more people than all the Frenchmen killed by German shells, bombs and bullets in several years of fighting. He who, confronted by the dangers of thermonuclear war, has not asked himself at some time: does there exist a single cause that is comparable to the danger involved, does not deserve to be called a man.

That we cross-examine ourselves in public and that on the other side of the Iron Curtain people do not have the right to do so is the best introduction to the "defense and illustration of the West," our present theme. In Chapter XVIII, I analyzed *the enemy partners* by extending to its limit the effort of *neutrality*. I did not write as a committed Westerner; in fact, I adopted no viewpoint at all, neither that of the European who is critical of the United States, of which he knows himself to be an ally in spite of everything, nor that of the Indian who prefers the West to the Soviet world but fears the latter more than the former, nor any of the multiple and complex attitudes of the various types of non-aligned nations. In fact, with a pretension all the greater because it was well concealed, I posed as the "pure spectator" who understands and judges the whole composed of all points of view. But

I am not really this "pure spectator," and in the last analysis the latter does not grasp a part of what is essential, the meaning that men and states assign to their existence.

As long as we are comparing the structure and function of the political and economic regime on each side of the Iron Curtain, nothing is easier and, in a certain sense, more necessary than to note advantages and drawbacks of either authoritarian planning or market regulation imposed by state intervention; either a monopolistic and ideological party, or a plurality of parties competing according to constitutional law. Personally I hold that, even on the sociological level, with regard to the ideals both sides profess to cherish, the Western regime is, as a whole, preferable to a regime of the Soviet type, the advantages of the latter being characterized primarily by their relation to power (the capacity to maintain a higher rate of investment, to concentrate investment in certain vital sectors, etc.). But I am also prepared to recognize that this judgment as to which is preferable may be influenced by my prejudices or passions. I admit, in short, that the regime which is preferable in general or in the abstract is not always possible *hic et nunc*. It is not out of the question that the regime preferable in a given situation may be other than the one preferable if we were to compare two ideal types. When entrepreneurs and credit mechanisms are lacking, when only the state and its bureaucracy are capable of promoting industrialization, the regime of the monopolistic ideocratic party is potentially the least deplorable means of performing a historically necessary task.

But this way of looking at things which, even when applied to economic regimes, arouses some anxiety (after all, it is also the lives of men as well as of economic subjects which are determined by the regime), ignores the essential dimension of the phenomenon when it is applied to political regimes. A one-party regime and a multi-party regime may, of course, be analyzed and understood as the two typical solutions to a single problem as the two logically acceptable interpretations of democratic legitimacy, as two methods of performing the same functions. Since authority derives from the people, either they choose from among the candidates those who will govern and the plurality of possible choices will be the proof of liberty, or they ratify, by acclamation, the power of a party which knows, interprets and executes the true will of the masses (or of the class whose will is historically decisive). In both ideal cases the dialogue is maintained between government and governed; in both cases, the governed can feel that they are obeying their own representatives, while those who govern can be conscious of the legitimacy of their office; in both cases, political class is recruited from the party or parties.

Let us go further. Neither of the two regimes, in the abstract, guarantees the dialogue between government and governed, neither radically prevents the breakdown of communications, the despotism of minorities, the omnipotence of a charismatic leader, the reciprocal alienation of people and power. Below a certain threshold of popular participation, elections, even genuinely free ones, reinforce the oligarchy. Above a certain threshold of hostility between people and the monopolistic party, nothing of the democratic fiction remains.

This way of reducing the two current modes of democratic legitimacy to a common denominator for the sake of impartiality does not, however, overlook the reasons for which we commit ourselves to or against certain political institutions. Even more than economic institutions, political institutions are merely one aspect or one sector of existence itself. But, as individual or collective existences, these two kinds of regimes are radically heterogeneous. They are not distributed along a scale that ranges from less to more; they are opposed, as positive and negative.

Democratic legitimacy, which both blocs claim to represent, cannot and should not be realized in all collectivities by the same institutions, but institutions cannot honestly say that they exemplify this legitimacy unless they are characterized by one or another of the ideas of *constitutionality, representation* or *personal liberty.* The choice of rulers or the exercise of authority proceeds according to rules—not just anyone can assume power, and whoever has power cannot do whatever he likes; the people feel that they are represented by the rulers and the latter seek to be the representatives of the former; each citizen, within the limits prescribed by law, is entitled to think and act according to his desires—these, I think, are the three ideas (complementary in an ideal democracy but separable in any real democracy) which constitute democratic legitimacy. If any of the three is not even approximately realized, a regime that calls itself democratic is lying. That it is lying with or without realizing it matters little; the hoax still exists.

The one-party regime of the Soviet type remains unconstitutional in its country of origin. There is no mechanism that provides for the transmission of power in the event of the death of the chief. There is no visible relation between what happens and what is provided for by the Constitution which, enacted at the time of the great purge, guaranteed respect for all intellectual and personal liberties. Even today, the members of the Presidium are hardly the representatives of the Central

Committee, and the latter represents the members of the party only in a very vague sense. I do not mean that the members of the party are hostile to the Central Committee and do not feel that they are in touch with them: I mean simply that for the moment the leaders of the party choose those who are then said to represent the millions of members instead of the latter choosing their representatives. Finally, the Soviets are deprived of a great many concrete liberties—to travel freely outside their country, to listen to any foreign radio station, to write novels or paint pictures in their own way, liberties formerly enjoyed by a great many subjects of more or less enlightened despots and denied to members of the proletariat "liberated" by the victory of socialism.

To call the so-called regimes of popular democracy democratic is therefore to abuse the meaning of words or, to speak more cautiously for the time being, to admit that the same words do not have the same meaning in the East that they do in the West. But is this really true? In 1956 the Hungarians and the Poles strikingly demonstrated that they still gave what Mallarmé called "a pure meaning to the words of the tribe." As a matter of fact, neither in public nor in private, neither officially nor secretly do the Soviets regard as liberty what we regard as non-liberty.

Regimes of the Soviet type justify themselves first of all by the formula "for the people" if not "by the people." The absolute power of the party or, if one prefers, the leading role played by the avant-garde of the proletariat, is not presented as the expression of democratic orthodoxy, but as a historical necessity. Between the heterogeneous class society[7] and the homogeneous society of the future, dictatorship is exercised by the party in the name of the proletariat. Similarly, non-constitutionality of succession or of decisions and non-choice of representatives are by no means exalted as symbols of a superior legality or purpose. The best proof of this is the tribute paid by vice to virtue in the form of the Stalinist Constitution of 1936, the elections-by-acclamation or party Congresses. Will it be objected that these are concessions to propaganda or to bourgeois ideology? But such concessions, if that is the purpose of the Constitution or elections, would once agin prove that the Soviet leaders have no doubt about the meaning that their people, like other peoples, attach to democratic legitimacy. The Russians do not identify the omnipotence of the party with liberty any more than the Americans do: police terror was terror and

7. We are using the words *homogeneous* and *heterogeneous* here in the popular sense given them by the current idiom, not in the precise sense of a homogeneous or heterogeneous system.

not the fulfillment of humanism. Socialist realism, as Zhdanov imposed it, was tyrannical and not liberating.

The theory which, it seems to me, partisans and leaders believe, the true theory of this system of lies, is the historical theory. If plurality of parties and free elections are dismissed as bourgeois and denounced, it is not because the single party and phony elections are regarded as a higher form of democracy as such. But plurality of parties in the West, according to the historical vision of Marxism-Leninism, conceal the despotism of monopolistic capitalism, and only the Communist party is capable of overcoming this despotism and of opening the way for a classless society.

But the philosophy of history which serves as a foundation for these categorical condemnations and these confused justifications is false. Because their philosophy does not agree with the facts, the Soviets have been forced gradually to construct an extraordinary system of lies and to oblige conquered or converted peoples to live in a perpetual lie. Necessary progression from a capitalism defined by private ownership of the means of production to a socialism defined by planning and the power of the party identified with the proletariat, disappearance of all alienation with the disappearance of private ownership of the instruments of production and of capitalism, a classless and stateless society upon the accession of socialism—these are the major propositions which constitute the framework of the ideological construction. But these propositions are almost absurd. The party is not the proletariat, except in a mythology; the abolition of private ownership does not bring about the abolition of economic and social inequalities. However effective the organization of the economy, it will not eliminate the political order, the necessity for a state. Because they have done something different from what they believed they would do, because they pursued inaccessible goals, goals contrary to the nature of men and societies, the Communists lie as perhaps no other great historical movement before them has ever lied. The rejection of communism is for me above all the rejection of the enforced lie.

I can picture the smile of the skeptic, the scorn of the "leftist intellectual," who is convinced that the Soviet side, because it calls itself socialist, sustains and embodies the hopes of mankind. To make matters worse, I shall therefore carry my idea to its conclusion: those intellectuals who seek to be "humanitarians," who claim an association with the tradition of the Enlightenment and who either reserve their sympathy for the Soviet side or else refuse to distinguish between the two giants (or barbarians) seem to me to be suffering from a perversion of the moral sense. Between a society that is essentially totalitarian and a society that is essentially liberal, a man who, without being converted to the so-called new faith, chooses the former or sees no real difference between the two has become blind to fundamental values.

I would not be misunderstood: Western societies are imperfect and, in certain regards, perhaps more imperfect than Soviet societies. In particular, if one compares the United States and the Soviet Union, perhaps the former has more trouble putting into effect the principle of racial equality than the latter. Nothing prevents an observer from hating the commercialized radio and television from across the Atlantic more than the politicized radio and television from behind the Iron Curtain. But criticism of American civilization is an integral part of that civilization itself—which is not the case with Soviet civilization—and above all the negative aspect of the regime is not transformed into a positive one by dialectical jugglery. One may debate the share of power in the hands of monopolies (or large corporations). But it would never occur to any American theorist to claim that the more power such monopolies have, the more completely democracy is realized. *On the Soviet side, such an inversion of values is the foundation of the regime, since party is identified with class and the rule of the party with the realization of liberty.* From this point on, the deification of the party (or of the few or the one man incarnating it) corresponds to a necessity which is both psychological and logical. The party must be transfigured so that in obeying it the individual may feel he is obeying the highest reason. Why would the dictatorship of the party be indispensable to the liberation of the proletariat if history had not transferred to the party the mission which Marx and the first Marxists attributed to class? But, having become sacred, the party is entitled to extend its lawmaking indefinitely. Social man is total man, and the party is master and possessor of social man. A regime which claims to mold the totality of man is "totalitarian"; it is tyrannical by nature and not by accident because it is based on a false philosophy.

Once again I hear the skeptical reader countering with historical precedents. The French Revolution was also "totalitarian" at certain moments or in certain of its representatives. It, too, opposed the Church because it was of religious (in the broad sense of the word) inspiration. It, too, was denounced by the Church as incompatible with its traditional teachings. It withered away like all historical movements. The institutions which it finally resulted in—equal rights, individual freedoms, universal citizenship, representative government—far from contradicting the dogmas of Catholicism, have turned out to be consistent with Christian inspiration (at least with certain tendencies of that inspiration). Why should the same not be true of the Soviet Revolution? In the long run the latter will have contributed certain institutions—planned economy, accelerated industrialization, social rights of individuals—from which all the regimes of our time will borrow something. As for the Marxist-Leninist ideology, it will gradually fall into desuetude. The Soviets will salute the statue of Karl Marx with as much indifference as the Christian who has lost his faith continues to make the sign of the Cross when he enters a church.

This way of thinking—in the future perfect—has virtually become the rule among the intelligentsia of the West. It consists in putting oneself today in the place of those who will judge as *past* the events we are living through in the present. It adds to this a kind of popularized Marxism by devaluing the underlying *intention* of a historical movement and regarding as real only those institutions which emerge from it. In other words, we are asked not to regard Soviet totalitarianism as tragedy, because it is merely the "ideological point of honor" of economic planning and because it will have disappeared by the time our grandchildren are grown up.

That the totalitarian faith or purpose will eventually wither away it would be ungracious to deny, especially if one feels that totalitarianism is contrary to the eternal springs of human nature. But one would not be justified in deducing from this that the dogmatism of immanence, the claim to create a total man and a new man are merely superstructures or myths. Soviet society is indissolubly a group of institutions *and* the metaphysical intention of those who build it. That certain of these institutions may survive although emptied of the intention that inspires and distorts them is possible. But one cannot today consider this dissociation as already achieved. Our duty is to combat what we condemn and not to assume in advance the privileges of the pure spectator, as if our immediate future were already our distant past. I am the one who is deliberating and not my grandchildren. If they do not take the totalitarian threat as a tragedy, perhaps I may have helped to make their detachment possible by the very fact that I will have averted the danger. But to invoke a future detachment is really to seek an excuse for cowardice or abstention.

THE OBJECTIVE

But, my adversary—that is, myself—will again object, can I ignore the lessons of experience? How many historians manage today to share the fratricidal passions of the Spartans and Athenians or even, closer to our own day, of our fathers who fought the Germans from 1914 to

1918? How many historians sing the praises of the Roman Empire, in spite of the methods employed by those conquerors; were not the conquered peoples themselves, after several generations of peace, reconciled to their lot to the point of retaining, through barbarian centuries, a nostalgia for the vanished Empire? Wars to the death between related units within a single zone of civilization or wars of conquest: there is scarcely one example in which the judgment of the spectators, looking back, has coincided with the passions of the actors. Why should it be any different with our conflict and why should we not take this into account?

Indeed, we should take this into account and become conscious of exactly what we are fighting, of what we are fighting for. We have often, in our analysis of the current situation, noted phenomena of *asymmetry*. The West does not outlaw those who openly take the side of the enemy. The West, with a few exceptions, has not let itself be swept, by the logic of competition, into imitating its enemy. It has not imposed on the liberty of its citizens the same restrictions which Soviet regimes regard as normal and indispensable. The West speaks with many voices, the Soviet Union with only one; each country in the West, faced with an international crisis, displays its uncertainties and hesitations; the Soviet Union time and again employs several languages, combines threats and promises: but all its methods are coordinated by a single will.

This asymmetry appears on the highest level, that of the goals of war and of strategy. The leaders of the Soviet bloc, we have no reason to doubt, continue to think according to the Marxist frame of reference, as it has been revised by Lenin and by Mao Tse-tung. The conflict between the two blocs is for them only one aspect and one moment of the worldwide revolution, of the inevitable transition from capitalism to socialism. The United States is the only power capable of balancing the strength of the Soviet Union, but it is also the supreme expression of capitalism, and both the *national* enemy of Russia and the *ideological* enemy of the socialist world.

The rivalry between the two super powers is not, therefore, according to Marxist-Leninist philosophy, comparable to the rivalries between two candidates for the throne or for the empire; it exists within a context of revolutionary transformation of which it is, in one subperiod, the diplomatic expression. The point is not to bring this rivalry to an end by a lasting agreement based on the distribution of zones of influence or the principle of "live and let live." Peaceful coexistence is and can only be a particular mode temporarily assumed by a protracted conflict. The West tends to recognize, albeit unconsciously, the primacy of peace; also, faced with a conflict, it looks for a peaceful solution or settlement. The Marxist-Leninists, on the other hand, until the permanent and total spread of socialism, recognize the (beneficial) inevitability of conflict. The former are ready to be satisfied with a peace without victory. If the Soviets renounce the destruction of the West, the West will gladly let them live as they wish; it will abandon to them without too guilty a conscience those peoples whom the Red Army has "liberated" or "conquered." The Soviets, on the other hand, cannot even conceive of what a peace without victory might be. As long as a capitalist bloc remained, peace would not be certain (because capitalism is imperialist by nature) and the struggle would have to continue, not because men desire it but because the laws of history have so decreed. If such is the asymmetry of goals, has not the West lost in advance?

Such is the conviction of an American school, one of whose latest books, by Robert Strausz-Hupé, William R. Kintner and Stefan T. Possony, is entitled *A Forward Strategy for America*.[8] A few quotations suggest the strategic goal which the West, according to these writers, ought to choose for itself. "The first objective of any 'major' American strategy is, by all odds, the preservation and consolidation of our political system rather than keeping the peace. The realization of this objective may or may not require the establishment of systems compatible with ours throughout the entire world, but it does require the continuation or establishment of free systems compatible with ours in *certain* key parts of the world."[9]

The *survival* of the political regime of the United States being the first objective, a strategy of withdrawal to the American fortress is inconceivable because the United States, in a world entirely converted to the Soviet regime or to a totalitarian regime of one kind or another, could not preserve its free institutions.

But must the United States be content with this relative victory: assuring the survival of its government?

"The fundamental decision which faces us is this: must we accept the Communist concept of coexistence in one form or another, or must we bring about the final defeat of communism? If we choose the second line of conduct, we must decide whether we should rely on the defeat of communism as a result of fortuitous circumstances like internal erosion or revolution, or if we should multiply our efforts in order to attain this objective. We must decide whether a passive, wait-and-

8. New York, 1961.
9. P. 402.

see strategy does not in fact risk retarding the fall of communism while hastening our own. And, finally, we must decide why we really want to conquer communism. Is it because we hope to replace its 'economic order' with another? Or are we trying to overthrow a certain political system, to raze the intellectual concentration camp of communism, and to help the peoples of the Communist bloc to gain the right to govern themselves? Or do we base our policy on the belief that communism, in spite of its present hostility, might be an adversary less uncompromising than the system which would succeed it, assuming we lived long enough to see this successor? Once all these ideological resonances are eliminated, our policy should be based on the following premise: we cannot tolerate the survival of a political system which has both the increasing capacity and the inexorable desire to destroy us. We have no other choice than to adopt the strategy of Cato."[10]

And elsewhere, in a formulation just as clear:

"We feel that the permanent coexistence of systems as fundamentally opposed as closed and open societies is impossible, that the tightly contracted world of tomorrow will no more be able to tolerate being indefinitely partitioned by iron and bamboo curtains than the American Union in Lincoln's time could continue to live half slave and half free."[11]

In these two quotations all the problems raised by the pursuit of a strategy for the West are at least indicated. It is easy, and it is correct, to establish first of all that the survival of the United States—survival of the regime as well as of the body of the nation—is the first goal. Under what conditions can this goal be attained? Now the writers whom we are quoting, representatives of the offensive school, go on to say that the *indefinite* coexistence of closed and open societies is not possible. Unfortunately (or fortunately) the adjective—indefinite or permanent—makes such a statement utterly meaningless. Probably the American Union would not have been able, *in the long run*, to maintain the coexistence of slave states with free states: the War of Secession was not inevitable at the date when it took place; if it had been postponed, slavery might have been outlawed without war and the slaves would gradually have become free men. But above all, the reference to the situation of the Union in 1861 teaches us nothing about the future of the conflict between the two blocs. The Confederates and the Yankees both belonged to the Union, whose preservation or dissolution was at stake. The two blocs belong to the same interna-

10. Ibid., pp. 405–6.
11. Ibid., pp. 35–36.

tional system, not to the same political unit. Now, in the event of ideological conflict, the spokesmen of each regime tend to regard the citizens of the state of the opposing regime as slaves. The corrected formula, an international system cannot endure half slave and half free, would be equivalent to the statement: any bipolar and heterogeneous system inevitably leads to an inexpiable war which eliminates one of the candidates for mastery. We already know that this has been true countless times in the past, but we also know that the lesson we learn from history depends upon our choice of precedents. If we evoke the empires, lasting coexistence has been the rule (Parthians and Romans, Moslems and Christians). If we evoke zones of civilization which were eventually unified, there is generally to be found a Cato to repeat *delenda est Carthago,* and military leaders to follow these precepts. But which of the two precedents comes closest to the present situation? Obviously neither of the two comparisons teaches us as much as an analysis of the present.

The Soviet bloc and the Western bloc differ in countless respects from empires whose coexistence has been enduring. The peoples of Eastern Europe are temporarily resigned to the institutions in which they live, they are not devoted to them. The official preservation of state sovereignties, the survival of national and even nationalist sentiments prohibit the Kremlin leaders from placing the seal of legitimacy and of permanence on their conquests. The Soviet imperium remains precarious, lacerated by contradictions, held together by a force which neither consent nor law have yet consolidated or replaced. Nor is the American imperium proof against potential crises. How long will the West Germans prefer their liberty and prosperity to an attempt at reunification? After the fall of West Berlin and official acceptance of the partition of Germany and of Europe, would the citizens of the Federal Republic remain faithful to the European and Atlantic community? Will the French and the English, both nostalgic for a vanished greatness, ultimately accept a political status and military organization that stabilize the American imperium?

But the precariousness of the two empires is only one of the reasons for the instability of their coexistence. The two empires do not belong to the same political unit as did the South and the North, but nevertheless they are not as remote from one another as Moslems and Christians. Each of the two ideologies is directly aggressive toward the other. Men living under one of the regimes can imagine what their lives would be like if they belonged to the other. Finally and above all, technology intensifies the dialectic of mutual fear because it eliminates time and space, so to speak.

If one bases the impossibility of a lasting coexistence on the dialectic of fear, one must conclude logically, with Bertrand Russell, that a monopoly of the strategic weapons offers the only way out of the present crisis. That one of the two super powers has an open society and the other a closed society merely constitutes an aggravating circumstance. The fundamental fact is that ballistic missiles and thermonuclear bombs give any state which possesses them in sufficient quantity the means of destroying any other state in a few minutes or hours and that such a danger will eventually become intolerable to the two states, each of which holds this threat over the other. This argument is quite remote from the argument relating to Lincoln's phrase, and it is hopeless, for it would pose the final choice between the capitulation of the West and thermonuclear war.

Under these conditions the soundest argument for the thesis that the coexistence of the two blocs is impossible eventually comes down to the qualitative arms race, to the capacity possessed by each of the duopolists suddenly to inflict intolerable destruction upon the other. But this argument is not compatible with a "Catonian strategy." The destruction imagined—that of the Soviet Union or that of the Soviet imperium—can be conceived as physical or as political. Conceived as physical, it would imply the use of weapons of mass destruction. Such a Catonian strategy runs too great a risk of resulting in mutual suicide to be adopted in cold blood by men of good will. If the destruction is solely political, then it amounts more or less to the goal we have attributed to American strategy: the survival of American institutions will be assured only when the Kremlin no longer seeks to destroy them. *Each requires that for which the other must necessarily be its enemy.*

Even in this case, the symmetry is more apparent than real or, at any rate, the partial symmetry results from the dialectic of the struggle. The Russian nation has no reason to consider the American nation as an enemy, and conversely the American nation no reason to consider the Russian nation as an enemy—outside of the fact that they are the two super powers in the international system. Given the competition, each of the two more or less rightly imagines that it would be secure, or master of the world, if the other did not exist. What we have here, as we have shown, is at its origin a case of hostility without enmity, or better, of enmity proceeding from hostility.

But the absence of hate between the peoples does not mean an absence of enmity between the governing minorities. Regimes and ideas are opposed, and because of this, those embodying them on one side feel and actually are threatened by those embodying them on the other. The cold war is to a large extent an enterprise of subversion carried on by the so-called popular democracies against the so-called bourgeois democracies and by the latter against the former. Here again, there is no symmetry. But this time it is the appearance of asymmetry that is deceptive. Even when the so-called bourgeois democracies seem to be passive and to submit to the cold war waged by the Marxist-Leninists without answering them in kind, they are in fact agressive by their very existence, by the standard of living and the freedoms which they reserve for individuals.

Can this war of regimes be called a Catonian strategy? The answer must be a categorical negative. *The formula of a Catonian strategy makes no sense insofar as the West aims to destroy not the Soviet Union or the Soviet imperium but only the regime, and even the regime only insofar as the latter is forced, by ideological logic, to combat all regimes which resist the Marxist-Leninist gospel.* By evoking a Catonian strategy, one implies that in order to win the political or ideological battle against the Soviet Union or the Soviet imperium, the West has no choice but to completely destroy the latter and perhaps even the former. In reality, the West contemplates on the political level the elimination not even of Soviet institutions but only of those ideas and practices which oblige or encourage the Kremlin leaders to make war on the world of heretics, to consider themselves engaged in an enterprise whose end can only be the universal diffusion of what they call socialism. If the Soviets abandon this monopoly of hope, if they stop lying to others and to themselves, if they see their state for what it is—one type among others of modern government—peaceful competition will actually replace the cold war, controversy will replace subversion, and a dialogue of arguments will replace the dialectic of ideologies.

But the advocate of a Catonian strategy will object that dissociation between the rivalry for power and a purely political rivalry is impossible, since each is alternately means and end with respect to the other. To overthrow by subversion a regime favorable to the West is to weaken one side and strengthen the other. In this sense the ideological struggle serves the rivalry for power. But the power acquired by the Soviet bloc increases the spread of ideas and the authority of example. Countries will be converted to the Marxist-Leninist gospel because Moscow is the capital of the state strongest in military terms. All means—military, economic, diplomatic, ideological—are coordinated by Soviet strategists to an end which is inseparably the triumph of a regime and of the state that created it. If such is the end, if such are the means of one of the blocs, how could the other grant the subtle distinctions necessary to combat the universalist claims of the Soviet ideology without seeking to overcome the Soviet Union as such (even if, as men, we desire the fundamental freedoms to be restored to all men, anywhere in the world, who have been deprived of them)? I believe that these distinctions, though contrary to the passions of the struggle, are nevertheless necessary, that in the long run they offer a chance of peace-making without total war, without the total collapse of one of the contenders.

Of course, the West has a political-ideological enemy in the Soviet regime, which has decreed that constitutional-pluralist regimes are condemned to death by the law of history and which is making every effort to hasten the execution of the verdict. *But the West would cease regarding the Soviet regime as its enemy once the latter ceased denying its right to exist.* It will be objected that the Marxist-Leninist ideologists could not grant this right to exist without denying the very principles of their faith. Of course, this is only natural, and in this sense the West desires the death of the Soviet *ideology* just as the latter desires the death of the *West.* But the Soviet ideology, in our eyes, would be dead the day it recognized its own limitation. Whether such recognition is probable or improbable, at hand or remote, is a question of fact which we leave open for the moment. What concerns us here is the determination of the goal that Western strategy should bear in mind; it can be indicated in two words: survival and peace, physical survival by avoiding thermonuclear war, moral survival by the safeguarding of liberal civilization, peace by reciprocal acceptance by each bloc of the other's existence and of its right to existence. Survival in peace would also mean the victory of the West, for the latter would have convinced its enemy to give up the idea of destroying it, a renunciation which in turn is possible only by the conversion of the Marxist-Leninists to a more modest and more truthful self-interpretation. The day this conversion is achieved, we should be victorious without our enemies being therefore conquered: of all victories, the most fruitful, since it would have been obtained without bloodshed and would pave the way for reconciliation. . . .

THE STRATEGY OF PEACE

Bearing in mind not only the objectives of Western strategy as I outlined them in the second section, but also the facts of the situation as I just reviewed them in the third, what should be the principles of Western strategy in terms of these two analyses?

The West will never really enjoy security until the day the Soviet bloc no longer seeks the destruction of those regimes it calls capitalist, that is, the destruction of the West itself. Western Europe will never really enjoy security until the day the partition of Germany and of the Continent as a whole has been abolished. As long as the Russian armies are stationed two hundred kilometers from the Rhine, the doors of the temple of Janus will remain open. But these two statements must be supplemented by two others: since the United States was unwilling to take the slightest risk to liberate the nations of Eastern Europe at a time when it was strongest in military terms, it should not logically do so now. More generally, the West, short of being ready to wage a thermonuclear war, has no way of "destroying" the Soviet regime or imperium, and scarcely any way of influencing the internal development of this imperium, or relations between the Soviet Union and Communist China.

These four statements combined will seem characterized by a fundamental contradiction in the eyes of those who put a crude interpretation on the dialectic of antagonism and hope we will pay back with interest the hostility our enemies display toward us. The contradiction disappears the moment that we consider ourselves victorious on the day the Soviets have sincerely abandoned their enterprise. But since this conversion, assuming it someday occurs, is still remote, we must realize that the conflict will be prolonged and that short of a happy accident (the breakup of the Soviet bloc) or an unhappy accident (the breakup of the Atlantic bloc or war) the best we can hope for is a slackening of the Soviet advance in the third world and a gradual stabilization of relation of forces—political and not just military— between the two blocs. Whether we want to or not, we shall live under a military threat as long as there is no agreement on arms control, and under a political threat as long as the Marxist-Leninists remain true to their faith.

It is useless to evoke the strategy of rollback, as did James Burnham on the eve of the Republican return to power in the 1950s, or of *forward strategy,* as do the three writers we quoted above. The West, given its nature, has never had the political capacity for an offensive strategy, nor has it the material capacity for it today. It is not out of the question, however, that the weakened West may be more aggressive or more intransigent than the United States was just after the war, when it alone was intact and powerful. We know that democracies are inclined to make war when they are provoked, not when circumstances are favorable to them.

Granted that we have no way of "forcing" Soviet societies to become open or to "liberate" the countries of Eastern Europe, we must be prepared to live in a world that is "half free and half slave" for a long time to come, without excluding the possibility that the slave half of the world may change of itself. There is no question of subscribing to the simple-minded theory of some Marxists or pseudo-Marxists[12] whereby the Soviet regime will *necessarily* become democratic as the standard of living rises. But neither need we accept as a dogma that the Soviet regime cannot change or that Moscow's diplomacy-strategy is now and forever determined by the *intention* of Lenin or Stalin. Within the context of a philosophy which is for the moment invulnerable to experience, the Kremlin leaders act according to circumstances. The West can have an effect on the circumstances to which Moscow will deem it reasonable to adjust.

This strategy will be called a defensive strategy or a strategy of coexistence. And I do not deny that compared with a strategy whose goal is to destroy the Soviet Union or the Soviet imperium, to eliminate the Soviet threat once and for all, this strategy deserves to be called defensive, since it adopts the slogan of coexistence from the enemy, so to speak, with the difference that it gives it another interpretation. But the choice of a strategy must *also* be governed by an analysis of the relation of forces, and since the aim is to avoid thermonuclear war as well as to preserve liberal civilization, it seems to me preferable not to match the universalist intention of the Soviets with an intention equally universalist. It is by championing the rights of institutional pluralism against the monism of Marxism-Leninism that the West accurately defines its mission against totalitarianism, not by setting up a monism analogous and antagonistic to that we are combating.

Having accepted the fact of coexistence between the two blocs, the first requirement is the preservation of the balance between the global military forces. Or, to express myself more precisely, the major danger is still, for the present time, the military danger and not, as everyone insists, the danger of subversion or infiltration. That the majority of commentators think otherwise springs from the identification of urgency with importance, of visible crises with the unending and fundamental rivalry. It is very true that thermonuclear bombs and ballistic missiles do nothing to check Soviet expansion in southeast Asia and the Near East. It is very true that those—assuming they exist—who have counted on atomic strategy to contain the Soviet Union throughout the world were mistaken and that in this sense it is possible to speak of the failure of atomic strategy. But by definition a strategy of deterrence—politically defensive—can have only a negative

12. Isaac Deutscher, for example.

success. Since it aims no further than the status quo, it seems sterile as soon as one decides retrospectively that the status quo would have been maintained in any event.

The priority I accord to military considerations has the following significance: if the Soviet bloc were to become convinced that it possesses an incontestable superiority either as regards passive or active instruments of deterrence, or as regards military means in general, the danger would risk being fatal; the Kremlin leaders would feel that the time for the final struggle had come or, more probably, they would press their advantage to the point of forcing the West to choose between capitulation and war. Most of the time the struggle between the two blocs is not waged on military terrain, precisely because the balance of forces is maintained. Were the latter to be compromised, everything else would be jeopardized at the same time.

Now military equilibrium, in the probable absence of an agreement on arms control, presupposes a constant and large-scale effort of research and production which is far from being achieved once and for all by a minimum retaliatory capacity. This equilibrium, during the period beginning now, will make it increasingly difficult to tolerate a radical inferiority in any category of means—for example, in the area of conventional weapons. The probable development half a dozen years from now toward thermonuclear weapons which are increasingly terrible and increasingly invulnerable is accompanied by the probability, despite Soviet claims to the contrary, that conventional weapons may be used, even by the two super powers against one another and without escalation.

The primacy of military considerations is not just the result of the enormity of the risks involved in possible negligence: it has to do with another primacy, itself contrary to the opinion prevalent today—the primacy of Europe or of the theater of operations in which the two blocs confront one another with respect to the third world. Here again, the distinction is between *importance* and *urgency*. During those years which preceded Mr. Khrushchev's revival of the Berlin crisis, nothing seemed to be happening in Europe. Each of the two blocs was organizing: each found its territorial status unsatisfactory but preferable to the cost of a war, which seemed to be the only way to change it. Meanwhile, the war in Indo-China, or the nationalization of the Suez Canal, or the Algerian War, or the breakup of the Belgian Congo, or the revolt in Angola absorbed the attention of the leaders of the United States and of most of the European governments.

But the same is true of the "draw" in Europe as of the "balance of deterrence" on the global level: neither result is attained automatically or definitively. *Success or failure can be decisive only in the area of armaments or on the European Continent.* If the Federal Republic of Germany, in the hope of restoring its unity, were to turn to Moscow, Western Europe would be lost and so would the Atlantic Alliance. As long as Atlantic unity is preserved, all can still be saved; if Atlantic unity were shaken, all the West's other positions would be endangered.

I see still another reason to reduce the importance which Western strategists generally grant to the verbal or actual commitments of the Afro-Asian countries. In the short run, most of these countries, taken separately, would, were they to shift their allegiances, alter only slightly the balance of resources or of power between the blocs. In due time, if most of these countries adhered to one camp or the other, an imbalance would result on a universal scale, but the allegiances of these countries to one bloc or the other are circumstantial, revocable. They have no definitive character since it is obvious that an African or Latin American republic will not choose to be subject to the arbitrary power of Moscow once it ceases to fear European "colonialism" or "Yankee imperialism." If the two centers of force prevail in the Northern Hemisphere, neither will exercise a lasting domination over the Southern Hemisphere, because those countries which constitute stakes in the eyes of Moscow or Washington have above all a desire not to be subject to anyone, and express this desire today by the various modes of non-alignment or neutrality.

If we accept this hierarchy of importance, how can the West improve its diplomacy-strategy? Personally, I believe that the decisive answer, but also the most difficult, would be a tightening of the bonds among the Western countries, the taking of another step in the direction of an authentic Atlantic community. During the postwar phase, Atlantic unity, regarded as a zone of civilization, faced three tasks: the reconstruction of devastated regions (Western Europe), the giving up of colonial empires, and the organization of the community which required the presence of the United States in Europe from now on as indispensable. The first task was accomplished faster and better than anyone dared hope. The second was achieved without any real cooperation between the United States and the colonial states of Europe, the former making every effort to alienate neither its allies on the Continent nor the nationalists revolting against colonial power. It is easy to say in retrospect that with a little more clairvoyance here, a little more courage there, the process of decolonization could have been less costly, could have left less resentment in the hearts of the colonial peoples, less bitterness in the ex-imperial nations. But men—especially statesmen, rulers and citizens—do not always accept the events they foresee. The majority of French ministers foresaw decolonization, but this did not mean that they would have made the first move and, acting upon their accurate foresight, put into effect, in agreement with Washington, a ten- or fifteen-year program of accession to independence for the colonies or protectorates of North Africa. Perhaps the colonial peoples' violence was necessary to force the colonial powers to take seriously those ideas with which they prefer to play without acting upon them.

When all this has been said, it is still true that decolonization has been nearly completed without breaking either the alliance between the colonial powers and the anti-colonialist United States, or the internal unity of those European powers which have been forced to an awareness of something other than themselves and their mission.[13] Once the process of decolonization is over, the West will experience different, almost converse opportunities and problems. On the psychological level, in the war of propaganda, the West will be able to take the offensive and denounce Soviet colonialism. But nowhere will it be any longer in a position to exert an exclusive influence, nowhere will the ideas, the agents, the subversive influence of the Soviet bloc be absent, nowhere can it afford to ignore the new states, with their passions and their injustice, any more than its Marxist-Leninist enemy. The exchange of accusations between French and American public opinion on colonialism and anti-colonialism (what have you done to the Algerians? and what have you done to the Indians?) belong to the past (perhaps the roles are reversed in Latin America). But on the other hand, all those bases outside the countries of the Alliance are now preserved only precariously.

These disadvantages would be more than compensated if, released from the colonial mortgage, the countries of the Atlantic Alliance succeeded in conducting a unified diplomatic strategy, or at least a consistently coordinated one. Now the relative weakening of the United States, in relation to its enemy and its allies, threatens to exert an influence in the opposite direction. The economies of the Common Market countries henceforth do not depend upon the American economy more than it does on them. In military terms, France is trying, after Great Britain, to produce a national nuclear striking force. The Bonn Republic is less impressed than ever by Mr. McNamara's doc-

13. Portugal, if Mr. Salazar remains in power, is in serious danger of effecting its own ruin by fighting to the bitter end to maintain the fiction of the Lusitanian community.

trine. Where the latter sees a flexible strategy, his interlocutors in Bonn see the first signs of withdrawal.

The first condition for the Atlantic Pact to last and grow into an Atlantic community is for the leaders in Washington to realize that the time of the American (or Anglo-American) directorate is past (though this does not mean that the time of the *troika* directorate has arrived). In theory, perhaps, it might have been preferable to limit to the United States possession and disposition of the nuclear weapons within the Alliance. But it was contrary to the nature of states and their age-old aspirations to give up these decisive weapons once and for all. Today the problem is less to ascertain what formula would be best in itself than to avoid certain ill-fated consequences of the multiplication of costly national forces, which are of scant effectiveness and quickly outmoded by technological progress.

On the economic level President Kennedy set the tone with the word *partnership*. It is still too early to know how relations between the Common Market, Great Britain, the Commonwealth and the United States will actually be organized, but it is apparent that Europe's spectacular recovery, far from destroying the solidarity between the Western fringe of the Continent and the New World, is destroying the last vestiges of isolationism. The Six of the Common Market, which together are the leading international exporter and importer, constitute a great economic power, the indispensable partner to the prosperity as to the diplomacy of the United States.

On the military level the goal would be to insure the permanence and gravity of the American commitment while at the same time giving the Europeans a real participation in the strategy of deterrence. The long-term solution, once Great Britain and France have initiated national programs, seems to me the formation of a European force which, without officially depending upon the American deterrent, would act only in cooperation with it. In this way Europe would resume awareness of its responsibilities without the American commitment being thereby weakened. The tightening of bonds among Europeans would attentuate the inequality between *one* great power and *several* small ones. The Alliance would no longer be regarded as a kind of American protectorate, but as common undertaking.

As regards those zones outside the direct confrontation of the blocs, the analyses in the foregoing section have shown that there was neither an infallible formula, a universally valid priority (of economic aid or of military aid), nor a regime inherently suitable to the joint requirements of economic development and of Western interest. The greater

part of what is called the third world—Asia, Africa, Latin America—
is going through a phase of revolutionary upheaval whose causes are
in variable proportions political, economic, demographic and psychological.

Politically, the traditional powers are almost all weakened. Tradition and the past no longer constitute valid qualifications for the exercise of authority. Legitimacy has become democratic, but the realization of this formula of legitimacy by election generally encounters insurmountable obstacles. Those elected do not respect the decisions of
the electorate; these decisions are manipulated or fabricated. Between
the two formulas consistent with the idea, that of the constitutional
regime with several parties and that of the ideological and monopolistic party, intermediary experiments abound: conservative oligarchy
with or without an electoral facade, despots with or without parties,
modernists or reactionaries, military leader or junta of officers replacing a discredited or powerless parliament.

Economically, the peoples and, even more, the governing minorities
almost all desire not to remain on the margin of development, that is,
of industrialization, but whether the conditions necessary to development are or are not given in a country of Asia, Africa or Latin America
does not depend on American diplomacy. If necessary, the donor can
always build a few factories: such constructions solve none of the
problems of underdevelopment, neither the impatience of the elite and
the masses nor the disparity between the population and the volume of
resources.

Those countries which today are trying to make up for lost time
and to achieve the same revolution by which the favored third of mankind has shifted from the agricultural to the industrial stage enjoy one
advantage in relation to their elders: the technology to be inherited is
not that of one hundred and fifty years ago but that of today. The
knowledge available is not only natural but social. We know a little
more today than we did yesterday about social constants, the probable
consequences of fiscal measures, the requirements of a program of
investment, etc. The countries in the process of development are not
advancing into unfamiliar territory.

The advantage of coming *after* the West is purchased at a high
price. In certain cases the population has tripled or quadrupled (India)
before the process of industrialization has got under way. The effectiveness of investments in hygiene and medicine is such that the mor-
tality rate may be lowered without economic progress increasing
resources accordingly. Such is the case with the principal countries of

Asia (China, India), with the Near East (Egypt) and with Latin America.[14] Economic progress must catch up with demographic growth in order for living conditions to improve; the percentage of investment in relation to national income must reach 10 to 15 per cent in order for the advance to become cumulative, in order to make it increasingly easier to devote to current consumption a growing fraction of a national product which is expanding every year.

In addition to this fundamental difference between the situation of the Europeans in the eighteenth and nineteenth centuries and the situation of the Chinese, Indians and Latin Americans today, there are differences the consequences of which are not so easy to see. The traditional institutions of the political and social order were less weakened in Europe than they are in the countries of the third world in a comparable phase of development. The people were more passive, they were not aware of other possibilities, their demands were not justified by the example of advanced countries. The competition of the two super powers and the two ideologies, so long as the Communist party has not seized the state, sustains uncertainty, exploits the passions, diverts the energy of the elite toward civil strife. It is not just inevitable circumstances such as population pressure, the resistance of former privileged classes, the demands of the masses which favor adoption of the Soviet model of development; it is the Communist party itself wherever, by its opposition, it curbs any development from which its own ambitions would not benefit.

Half or two-thirds of mankind would be in revolution even if Moscow and Marxism-Leninism did not exist—a revolution which cannot but accompany the efforts of underdeveloped peoples to achieve the industrial type of society of which the West and the Soviets offer them two rival, but in certain respects similar, versions. The United States has never by itself had the power to control or channel this revolution. Whatever name we give it—revolution or rising expectations (revolution of hope, one might say) or revolution of the masses—we have here a universal phenomenon whose causes are a biological-economic imbalance and a social upheaval, and which will continue for decades if not centuries. To recognize the obvious facts and to impress on strategists the necessary *modesty* in the determination of objectives is the first step toward a reasonable policy.

It is now acknowledged, even in the United States, that certain political institutions (the multi-party system and representative govern-

14. Greater than the population of the United States right now (around two hundred million), the population of Latin America, at its present rate, will roughly triple between now and the end of the century.

ment) and economic institutions (the open market, freedom of entrepreneurs and consumers) are rarely suited to the requirements of initial phases of development. *The West should therefore prefer not those regimes which are closest to its own but those which have the best chance of promoting growth.* Also we must beware of the illusion that successful development will *insure* an attitude favorable, or at least neutral, to the West. No such guarantee exists. There are even circumstances in which economic progress will tend to strengthen the groups which incline toward the Soviet bloc, and thus to exert an influence contrary to our objectives. This could happen each time the West allows itself to be identified with the conservative or reactionary classes, leaving the quasi-monopoly of "progressive" slogans to the Communists or demi-Communists.

When things have reached this point, it would be futile to ask the American government to prefer an anti-Western regime because it accelerates development to a pro-Western regime which paralyzes it. But it is not impossible to convince American strategists first and foremost that no regime—whatever its institutions—need be called Communist as long as a party owing allegiance to Moscow is not in power. Next they must be convinced that even a regime in which the Communist party is in power, in Africa or in Latin America, is not the same as a regime imposed upon a country of Eastern Europe by the Red Army; in Asia, in Africa, in Latin America, revolutionary regimes, even if they declare their kinship with Moscow, will have an interest in not breaking with the West, if only to receive aid from both sides. In other words, instead of acting and above all talking as if our security were endangered each time "Ruritania" declares its allegiance to Moscow, it would be better to show detachment and a certain indifference, to expose in advance the Communist blackmail to which incompetent rulers are too frequently prone, wrongly convinced that the Americans would be damaged more than they themselves by a victory for Moscow. On the contrary, we should remember on every occasion that the relation of military forces in our age is not seriously affected by the vicissitudes of the cold war.

These precepts—to isolate the enemy by recognizing as such only the Communist party, to accept any socialist party or regime, to prefer rulers effective in their own countries to those repeating declarations of allegiance, to aid development because such is our human obligation and in the long run our political interest, but to be neither disappointed nor surprised if India or Brazil become more nationalist and more neutralist in proportion to their acquisition of an industry—will seem to some to be pervaded with the spirit of Munich. But this is a radically inaccurate interpretation. Since, even ninety miles off the coast of Florida, the United States refused to send Marines to put down a regime hostile to it in Cuba, we might better draw conclusions from this refusal to resort to armed force as well as from the dissociation between the vicissitudes of the cold war and the balance of deterrence.

These precepts in no way keep us from waging the cold war on the three battlefronts of economics, subversion and debate. On the first, two changes are desirable, one which is being made, the other scarcely recognized as yet. Since aid is futile if the government is weak and the anachronistic structure of ownership is maintained, it is better to concentrate resources, which will always be limited, where those conditions indispensable to a good return on investment are realized or can be realized as a result of outside pressure. Gifts or long-term loans are and must be an element of an over-all policy by which the West contributes, within its means, to the industrialization of the Southern Hemisphere. But even now, and increasingly during the years to come, it is the whole of the West's commercial policy which adds to or subtracts from the available resources of the third world. It has not been possible to do much about stabilizing the markets of raw materials. Another problem arises, and will arise tomorrow in even more acute form: that of the entry into developed countries of those simple manufactured products (textiles) which countries in the process of development are relying on in order to acquire foreign currency. At the present time, trade is tending to become increasingly free between Western countries, the Common Market having given an additional impetus to a movement which had already started. But since the United States is having increasing difficulty assuring itself the foreign currency necessary to finance gifts or loans, it is probable that aid will increasingly take the form of long-term credit with the obligation to buy in the creditor country. Moreover, in order to avoid the possibility of inter-European or inter-Atlantic free trade having unfavorable consequences on the third world, some measures inspired by a directed economy will probably be inevitable—price guarantees for the purchase of raw materials, the opening of Atlantic markets to the merchandise of countries with cheap labor, loans entailing purchases on a fixed market.

Economic aid needs time to be effective. Where subversion is about to win the day, countersubversion (or counterguerrilla activity) alone is an effective countermeasure. On this point it is prudent to call attention to a few commonplace ideas which are too often forgotten. Subversion has been successful in colonial territories because technological and tactical opposition came up against a decisive fact: the revolutionaries spoke the same language and belonged to the same race as the populations who were the stake in the conflict between subversion and repression. Even in Algeria, where the Moslem population was never unanimously won over the FLN, the presence of a European minority established by right of conquest and obviously privileged, paralyzed the psychological and political efforts of the French army to pit slogan against slogan, the liberation of individuals against the liberation of Algeria, or a free Algeria in association with France against an independent Algeria. Where circumstances do not assure the forces of subversion such an advantage over those of repression, why should the former have won out in advance?

It is true that a small minority is enough to make repeated attacks and to foster a climate of insecurity. It is true that the Viet-minh commandos from the north raid the villages by night, terrify the villagers and apparently succeed in rallying the population, whereas the latter, had they not been subjected to threats of violence, would incline to the other side. In short, the techniques of subversive warfare not only reveal a pre-existing popular will, they are also capable in many circumstances of creating it. But precisely because this will does not exist, countersubversion—repression or counterguerrilla activity—*provided it uses suitable means,* does not have, *a priori,* less opportunity to succeed than the aggression it opposes. Do these *suitable means* entail, and to what degree, adopting the enemy's methods of leadership, of parallel organization, of inflexible discipline within the insurrectional core, of terror with respect to wavering crowds? It would be hypocritical to deny that almost through necessity adversaries are obliged by their dialectic to imitate one another when they fight. And the Soviet side has a twofold advantage: the spontaneous organization of the Communist party is immediately adaptable to the necessities of underground fighting (Lenin's principles of organization corresponded to these necessities); once in power, the Communists deny their enemies those liberties they have often enjoyed.

Repression is always necessary when subversion has reached the guerrilla state. It is rarely effective against propaganda, infiltration, attempts to seduce intellectuals, to exploit popular unrest, to convince the vacillating of the moral or historical superiority of the Soviet bloc. The fundamental principle which, like all strategic principles, is simple albeit difficult to apply, is that for every weapon there is an appropriate response, that on every kind of terrain the defense must erect an obstacle against the attack, and that one cannot afford to overlook any theater of operation. We are beginning to understand that the thermonuclear threat is no protection for territory liable to conquest by subversion. But we have not yet learned that too pronounced an inferiority in one kind of armament is dangerous and that one does not combat guerrilla forces by economic aid, any more than one combats propaganda by police methods. To be sure, there are cases in which one must also use the police against the enemy's propagandists: after all, the Marxist-Leninists are not above this. But the police force in a totalitarian regime is at the service of an enterprise of indoctrination. The police alone, without the aid of organization and persuasion, are ultimately ineffectual.

To say that we should follow the enemy on all kinds of terrain does not mean that we ought to model ourselves after him. On the contrary, whether we are talking about strategy or tactics, persuasion or subversion, asymmetry is inevitable. We are not trying to destroy the power that wants to destroy us, but to convert that power to tolerance and peace. We do not seek to persuade men that our institutions alone offer hope, but on the contrary to persuade our enemies and the third world too, that mankind, aside from respect for certain principles, has a natural bent toward diversity. Countries with democratic regimes cannot use the same tactics as countries with totalitarian regimes, and when they deny their principles they pay dearly in the end for a temporary advantage. They are neither able nor willing to sow revolution; they are neither able nor willing to forbid nations to seek their salvation, each according to their nature. But as long as the two worlds remain as they are, the freedom the West enjoys will have a subversive meaning on the other side of the Iron Curtain—a revolutionary meaning which Western strategists will never renounce but whose gradual disappearance they themselves desire. The day the Soviets have the same right to read, write, criticize and travel as Western nationals, the competition will have become truly peaceful.

This outline of a strategy will seem disappointing to all, to the school of offensive strategy and the school of peace alike. I am not unaware of the arguments of either school. The real question is to determine to what degree the prince's adviser has the right to conceive of the world as different from what it really is.

Personally, I think that it would have been possible, for several years after 1945, to liberate Eastern Europe without serious risk of war. Even in 1956, at the time of the Polish and Hungarian revolts, the West had an opportunity which it did not know how to take. But the possibility we are asserting without proof was altogether material; it presupposes that the United States and Western Europe were different then than they are now, with different institutions, different leaders, a different state of mind. But what was materially but not politically possible yesterday has for the time being ceased to be materially possible. Given the balance of power, the Kremlin leaders would probably prefer war to the loss of an important part of their imperium. Territorially, the West is in no position to aspire beyond self-defense.

If the West, under the protection of an approximate balance of deterrence capacities and of over-all military strength, keeps abreast in every theater of operations, it can hope not to suffer any serious defeat, but it cannot hope for any spectacular victory, barring either the conversion of the Soviets or a break between the Russians and the Chinese—possibilities it would be just as absurd to count on in the near future as it would to dismiss forever.

To the school of peace, this strategy, which involves a qualitative arms race, a continuation of the cold war with countersubversion and counterpropaganda, will seem warmongering and fraught with immeasurable dangers. How long can the two blocs oppose one another in this way on every continent and by every means, while threatening one another with the worst punishments and without executing their threats?

The first school censures this strategy for running the risk of gradual defeat which it involves, the second the risk of thermonuclear war which it sustains. Both these reproaches are justified. The West runs the risk of being gradually smothered by the advance of the totalitarian regimes, buried by the wave of subversion. It could also be devastated by the monstrous weapons which its enemy, like itself, possesses. But the risk of suffocation could not be eliminated or reduced without increasing the risk of the thermonuclear catastrophe. And the risk of the military catastrophe could not be eliminated or reduced without accepting a greater risk of being forced to capitulate.

So the moderate strategy seems to me to offer the best chance of simultaneously averting these two kinds of danger—the danger of suffocation, the danger of violent death. If these two dangers are averted, the West's survival will be assured, a survival which in our time is the best, if not the only expression of victory.

Part Six

Max Weber and Modern Social Science

The final part of this volume consists of an introduction that Aron wrote in 1959 for the French edition of two famous lectures by Max Weber, "Wissenschaft als Beruf" (Science as a Profession) and "Politik als Beruf" (Politics as a Profession).

Aron's thought was formed under the influence of Weber's work. For Aron, Weber was a model of rigor and clarity in thinking, though Aron was never one of his disciples. Here, Aron attempts to formulate what he has in common with and what separates him from Weber. He accepts Weber's phenomenological description of the condition of man, that is, the antinomies of human thought and action, but he does not transpose them into a philosophy of inexpiable conflicts.

The piece includes an argument with Leo Strauss over Strauss's interpretation of Weber's work.

12

Max Weber and Modern Social Science

Max Weber was a scholar, and occasionally a political journalist; he was not a politician or statesman. But he was, throughout his life, passionately concerned with matters of state, and he never ceased to feel a kind of nostalgia for politics, giving the impression that the ultimate aim of his thought was participation in action.

He belonged to the generation that came of age during the height of the German empire, that witnessed the fall of Bismarck and the assumption of responsibility by the young emperor Wilhelm II. The last fifteen years of the nineteenth century, which saw him through his formative years (from the age of twenty to thirty-five), were simultaneously marked by the development of social legislation, by the emperor's first personal interventions in diplomacy, and, even more deeply, by reflection on the Bismarckian heritage. What would Germany's mission be, once unity was achieved? What would be her role in the world? What regime was most likely to reestablish national unity? Weber's generation could not desist from asking itself these questions; they were questions to which history was to provide tragic responses.

More personal reasons, as well, explain his attitude. He consistently stressed that politics had no place in academic lecture halls, and he repeatedly stated that the virtues of the politician and those of the scholar were incompatible. But his care to separate the two was not greater than his awareness of the bonds between them. One cannot be *at the same time* a man of action and a scholar without damaging the dignity of both professions, or without falling short of the

Translated by Charles Krance from Raymond Aron's Introduction to *Le savant et le politique,* by Max Weber (Paris: Plon, 1959). Reproduced by permission of Editions Julliard.

requirements of each. But one can take political positions outside of the university, and the possession of objective knowledge, if not altogether indispensable, is surely beneficial to rational action. In short, the relations between science and politics, in Weber's thought, are not characterized exclusively, as is so often claimed, by the necessary disjunction between them. The science he envisages is one that is capable of serving the man of action; by the same token, the latter's attitude differs, in terms of its ends but not in its constructs, from that of the scientist.

The man of action is one who, at a singular and unique moment, makes his choice in accordance with his values, and introduces a new element into the chain of causal connections. The consequences of the decision acted on are not clearly foreseeable, insofar as the moment of action is unique. There can be no scientific prediction except for sequences of events likely to repeat themselves or (in other words) of relationships perceived not just in concrete particularity but on a certain level of generality. Reasonable decision, nonetheless, requires that one apply all of the abstract knowledge at one's disposal to the unique situation as it exists at the moment, not in order to eliminate but to delineate and isolate the element of unpredictable uniqueness. A science that analyzes the relations between cause and effect, such as Weber intended, in theory, is therefore the very science that answers the needs of the man of action.

The theory of historical causality, founded on retrospective calculations of probability—What would happen if . . . ?—is nothing more than the approximate reconstruction of the deliberations that were made, or might have been made, by the actors in the event.

To act rationally is to make a decision, after reflection, that offers the best chance of attaining the desired goal. A theory of action is a theory of *risk* at the same time that it is a theory of *causality*. The historian who asks himself questions about historical causality restores, after the fact and in his imagination, the vanished possibilities that were, or may have been, considered by the actors in the course of the deliberations that preceded their decision.

Causal analysis does not apply to the deliberate actions of individuals. The question, What would happen if . . . ? may also be asked with regard to events that no one desired (intervening physical phenomena, storms, the depletion of gold mines, defeat or victory in a battle, etc.) as well as with regard to personal decisions. The effort to avoid the retrospective deterministic illusion regarding events or actions is no less characteristic of the political historian—the historian who, interested in individuals and their struggles, and bent on evoking the past, wants to respect the proper dimension of action: namely, uncertainty with regard to the future, an uncertainty that could be respected by the historian only if he insisted (against the undeniable existence of events once they occurred) that those events were not prescribed beforehand and that the course of historical events could have been quite different, depending on particular individuals or circumstances.

The connection postulated by Weber between science and politics appears just as close if one examines the other aspect—not that of causality but of values: the relationship to values, in the case of science, and the affirmation of values, in the case of action. The choice of facts, the elaboration of concepts, and the delineation of the object, Weber wrote, are marked by the direction of our curiosity. From the infinitude of immediately perceptible data, natural science selects those phenomena that are likely to be repeated, and constructs a system of laws. The science of "culture," on the other hand, selects what is related to values—whether those held by contemporaries or those of the historian—from among the infinitude of human events, and develops either a history (if the scholar fixes his attention on the unique sequence of events or societies), or the various social sciences, which study repetitive sequences or relatively stable patterns.

Historical science, or the science of "culture," as Weber understood it, is the understanding of the manner in which men have lived, of the meaning they have given to their existence, and of the hierarchy they have established between values; political action, meanwhile, is the effort made, in circumstances not of our own choosing, to promote those values that are constitutive of our community and our very being.

Understanding other persons does not necessarily imply a concomitant understanding of self. Understanding the action taken by others in the past does not necessarily lead to the will to act in the present. There is, nonetheless, philosophically—and, to use a currently fashionable term, existentially—a connection between self-knowledge and knowledge of others, just as there is between the act of evoking the conflicts between men long dead and the decision, in the present, to take a certain position.

Practically speaking, there is no lack of historians who try to understand the lives led by others without examining their own. There is no lack of politicians today who fail to align their profession with the ultimate meaning that they themselves, or the collectivity, give to their existence. The exploration of the past cannot rightfully be separated from the act of becoming conscious of oneself; rightfully, action can be human only on the condition that it be situated in the course of events and with reference to its ultimate ends. The reciprocity between encounter with the other and discovery of self is inherent in the very activity of the historian. The reciprocal relationship between knowledge and action is immanent in man's existence in history, but this is not the case for the historian. Weber forbade professors to take a partisan position in public contentions when they were acting in their academic capacity; yet he could not help considering action, if no more than by speech or writing, as being the fulfillment of his work.

To what extent were Weber's own ideas adequately expressed in Heinrich Rickert's neo-Kantian vocabulary and categories? The phenomenology of Husserl, with which he was familiar although he made very little use of it, would surely have provided him with the philosophical and logical tool that he was seeking. It would have helped him, in his analysis of understanding, to avoid oscillating between Jaspers's "psychologism" (at a time when the latter was writing his *Allgemeine Psychopathologie*) and the indirect paths of neo-Kantianism which lead to meaning only by way of values. One may just as well ask to what degree Weber's practice conforms with his theoretical scheme. Does the analysis of causal relations play as large a role in his practice as it does in this theory? Is not the essential feature of his studies on the sociology of religion the exploration of different systems of belief and of thought, the purpose of which is to show the interlacing of ideas and institutions (i.e., the connection between religious values and social attitude) rather than to delineate what is causally efficacious in each of the various elements? Is not the essential feature of his *Wirtschaft und Gesellschaft* a bringing to light of the intelligible structure characteristic of the various types of power and economy? It is not sufficient that a comprehensive relation be understandable in order to be true in a given situation, but verification does not have much in common with the coincidence of comprehensive relation and causal relation.

Weber certainly simplified both the multiplicity of intelligible relations perceived by historians or sociologists, and the complexity of relations between understanding and explanation, or the immanent relationship between data and relationships elaborated by retrospective calculations of probability. There are different types of meaningful conduct, or motivated action, ranging from conduct that conforms to the laws of abstract economy, to conduct following from the interpretation of a certain doctrine of salvation, and conduct called for by the logic of resentment. Verification takes on different aspects according to one or another of these meaningful relationships, which

Weber tended to conflate in his methodological analysis of understanding. Connections and extensions, in this regard, would not make any serious difference to the principal theme of our study. In certain cases, on the contrary, in dealing with economic theory or when explaining an event by comparing it with the interpretative scheme, one should, it seems to me, emphasize accessible objectivity and universality. But fundamental revision should not be obligatory.

Let us take the case of understanding. It has been said that love and hatred are the true sources of understanding. It is futile to recommend objectivity if the latter term is taken to mean indifference toward values where men, past and present, and their works, blessed or cursed, are concerned. One cannot plumb the depths of the souls of these departed beings without experiencing similar feelings toward them as are aroused by the living. Weber would probably have had little difficulty recognizing the truth contained in these remarks, but he might have said that they applied to the psychology of research rather than to the logic of science. He would have upheld both the moral imperative of striving toward understanding *sine ira et studio* and the duty to see life and works as objects to be known, not as values to be appreciated.

As for his economic or sociological propositions, whose truthfulness is probably less closely tied to the present than Weber suggests, whether they deal with particular societies or, at a higher level of abstraction, all societies, those propositions do not in essential respects affect the analysis of choice and action. These truths are partial and incomplete; the values to which individuals relate are multiple; it is rare that the predictable consequences of a course of action conform to all our values and are agreeable to all individuals. It is not the subjectivity and relativity of scientific knowledge that make choice necessary but, rather, the *partial* character of scientific truths and the plurality of values.

To object to Weber's phenomenology of political choice on the grounds that he used outdated concepts like fact and value, means and ends, misses the essential point, in my view. It will be readily admitted that the fact with which value is contrasted was not constructed without the historian's referring to values. Values are not affirmed or invented apart from the ceaseless exchanges between individuals and their social environment; these exchanges are characteristic of human historicity. Likewise, the proximate end becomes the means of a subsequent action, just as the current means has been the end of an earlier action. What is more, it is doubtful that the attitude adopted by the individual can be reduced to such a distinction. In opting for a certain view of history, one is already very close to joining a party and subscribing to a technique of organization and action. Global perspective is as much a question of choosing means as of choosing an end.

Max Weber was not unaware of this. The Marxist thinks he possesses the true interpretation of a change in history that is both necessary and desirable, and that this interpretation involves joining a party and accepting a method of action. Experience has shown that this philosophy did not eliminate doubt, with regard either to parties or to methods. The most unrelenting antagonists are those who claim allegiance to the same master. Even barring this experience, Weber would have denied that a philosophy of history could at the same time announce a certain future and imperatively dictate an attitude. Seeing into the future presupposes determinism, a determinism oriented toward an end yet to come and thus as partial as, and even more probabilistic than, retrospective determinism. The characteristics of future society to which, in the best of cases, we can be privy in advance leave room for contradictory value judgments because those same characteristics do not satisfy all human aspirations. We are never morally compelled to like what science proclaims. Free to speed up or slow down the evolution that we have been told is inevitable, we face the choice of a global perspective yet are in the position of a man of action facing a particular situation: we observe facts, we wish for determined ends, and we choose at our own risk and peril, without recourse to a totality (which is inaccessible to us), a necessity (which is a mere alibi of our resignation or of our faith), or a reconciliation between men and gods (which is no more than an idea on the horizon of history).

What is in question is neither the means-end correlation, which is admittedly too simple, nor the facts-values distinction, whose philosophical significance is debatable. In order to refute Max Weber's thought, one would have to demonstrate either that science reveals to us the truth of history as a whole, or that it has foreknowledge of a predetermined future, or that it promises the resolution of conflicts between collectivities and values.

Weber was bent on demonstrating the fact that, although in the end it would strip the world of its charms, and although incompleteness was its very essence, science had meaning and was worth devoting oneself to.

He fought on two fronts: against those who threatened to corrupt the purity of rational thought by bringing in political convictions or sentimental outpourings, and those who falsified the meaning of science by attributing to it the capability of unlocking the secret of nature or of man. The "défense et illustration" of science, in Weber's writings, have an overtone of pathos; one can almost hear a muffled echo of nostalgia and sense the impatience of a man of action: nostalgia for the times when knowledge was not merely a link in an endless chain but plenitude and completion; the impatience of a man of action who demands of science the knowledge of means and consequences but who knows in advance that it will not free him from the obligation to choose, because the gods are many and the values contradictory.

Die Entzauberung der Welt durch die Wissenschaft, the disenchantment of the world through science, continues. Less than ever before does authentic science, whether physics or sociology, give us a complete picture of the universe, whether cosmic or human, in which we might discern our destiny or our duty. But two phenomena have intervened, causing a heavy weight of mute anxiety to hang over the universities, at least in Europe. The means of destruction, which have been placed at the disposal of civilian or military leaders by the progress of science, have increased to such a degree that the scientists responsible for the discoveries and their application question themselves about their responsibilities. We know that in our century there have been, and still are, effective and unsentimental tyrannies that do not stop at imposing on scientists an oath of loyalty to the state (such an oath, although it may be odious to individuals, is not necessarily a mortal blow to science)—tyrannies for which the act of seeking out and speaking the truth *objectively* is intolerable. These tyrannies are intent on imposing on the universities doctrines that are presented as all-encompassing but that are nothing more than derisive caricatures of the great religious syntheses of the past.

I will say little about the first phenomenon. Every increase in the capacity of production has, over the past few centuries, been accompanied by an increase in the capacity of destruction. Newness lies strictly in the order of magnitude. It is the increase in quality that creates the difference in quality. Individually, the scientist cannot take precautionary measures against the exploitation of his work by the war industry. Collectively, if he shirks service to the state, he is encouraging other states, especially those which do most to reduce individual liberty. Scientists' associations, when they start to discuss war or peace, are political and no longer scientific. Their appeals would be more convincing if they did not so often manifest as great a naïveté in diplomatic matters as their justly recognized authority in matters of nuclear physics.

For those of us who are concerned with human science, the second phenomenon—the serious threat that certain political regimes present to the universities—is of greater importance. In the past we have witnessed "Aryan mathematics"; today we see a state cutting short the scientific debate concerning the heredity of acquired characteristics, or the Mendelian theory. The two examples I offer here differ in nature. I don't think there were many German mathematicians who took the distinction between "Aryan mathematics" and "Hebraized mathematics" very seriously, nor many physicists who considered Einstein disqualified because of his race or religion. But it was a very serious matter that in a country like Germany so many scientists had to tolerate in silence this disgraceful sham as if they did take it seriously, and thereby cast a serious slur on this international community of minds that constitutes the natural and requisite society of scholars.

Nothing is farther from the truth than the idea that the scientist can work alone, left to his whims or to his genius. Mathematicians, physicists, biologists, though separated by borders and scattered across the planet, are held together by invisible and powerful ties: they thus form a research community, constituted by intellectual rules which, though unformulated, are binding. The problems to be resolved are provided them by the state of progression of the sciences (this explains the frequency of simultaneous discoveries). An implicit and quasi-spontaneous conception of what constitutes a truth induces scientists to push aside certain types of solutions, to accept reciprocal criticisms, and to refine their knowledge through exchanges.

Some research, whether mathematical or physical, has become so subtle that its world scientific community consists of only a few members. Their speculative investigations are rightfully universal nonetheless: they are addressed to all minds capable of grasping them and of resisting extraneous arguments or extrinsic influences. My friend Cavaillès, who was a mathematician and philosopher, wrote a work on mathematical logic while he was being pursued by the police. As a Frenchman and a soldier he fought against the occupying forces. As a logician he remained a disciple of Cantor, Hilbert, and Husserl. In front of the examining magistrate he bore testimony to his admiration of what was best in German culture. The idea never occurred to him that collective conflicts—especially those which he took upon himself to the point of giving up his life—could penetrate the sanctuary of thought that remained faithful to his vocation, namely, the search for truth.

When a state or a party sets out to dictate what the research objectives or procedures of science are to be, when it sees fit to exclude such and such individual or race, when it goes so far as to arbitrate controversies that relate to experimentation or that stem from reasoned argumentation, it is not enough to protest (quoting the commonplace formula) the oppression of individuals by the collectivity. For what is really involved is the illegitimate intervention of a political collectivity in the activity of a spiritual collectivity; in other words, totalitarianism at its most radical. The invention of totalitarianism is most fearsome when it subordinates the multiplicity of human endeavors to the exclusive will of a party, sometimes of a single man. Georg Simmel, in his *Sociology*, brilliantly described the plurality of social circles to which each of us belongs, and he saw this plurality as requisite to the progressive liberation of individuals. This reminder allows us to judge the efforts of totalitarianism for what they are: truly reactionary attempts to bring societies back to their primitive stages, in which the disciplinary rules of the social order covered all individuals as well as each individual in his entirety.

It may well be noted that science is *in part* determined by social, historical, and possibly even racial factors. It is not inconceivable that such and such a race may be more talented than another when it comes to certain types of work, or more inclined than another to conceptualize the world in a certain manner, although it is almost impossible to pinpoint the influence of race. Most generalizations in this area have been proved false. Others are unprovable. But to whatever degree science—as well as the questions it raises and the philosophical notions on which it is based—may be said to be determined by external circumstances, those who call upon such de facto determinism to justify authoritarian dictates, decreed by public authorities, as to the direction that science should take commit a fatal error.

Scientists are also individuals who live in a particular society and in a particular time. The orientation and genre of research are marked by the characters of individuals as well as of scientists, for the two are never strictly separable from one another. In spite of everything, there remains a fundamental difference between the influence that the social environment, of its own accord and in combination with the unconstrained participation of scientists, exerts upon science, and the influence that political leaders would exert if they arrogated the right to determine what the objectives, methods, and even the results of science are to be. In the first case, the scientific community continues to obey, essentially, its specific laws. In the other case, it would abdicate its autonomy and with the same stroke imperil its mission and its further progress.

Great Britain itself, right after the war, was witness to discussions on the independence of science. A few scientists, impressed by the Soviet example, recommended that plans for research be established, with a rational apportionment of material and human resources among the various laboratories, each receiving its particular mission. The British scientists rejected this pragmatic concept; they denied the state the right to mark out for them the objects of their research. Abandonment or subordination of theoretical research would be not only fatal to the progress of technology (one never knows beforehand which theory will lead to which application), but would constitute the first stage of the scientific community's abdication, thereby alienating its autonomy. The disappearance of Mendelian biologists, or the necessity of physicists to shroud their results in the jargon of dialectical materialism, illustrate what could be the final stage.

The social sciences are threatened by totalitarianisms in a different manner from the natural sciences. Tyrants need the latter in order to accumulate the means of power: there is a limit, set by a concern for effectiveness, to their interventions. Physicists in such cases are obliged to acknowledge dialectical materialism; their equations, however, are not dictated to them. When all is said and done, there is a great deal of interest in the development of nuclear physics. There is nothing to prevent the Marxist theories of surplus value and wages from being held, and imposed, as definitive truths: no irreparable damage will be done to concrete planification. Orthodoxy, not being directly harmful to administrative efficiency, becomes an instrument of artificial unanimity, which despotisms view as a guarantee of stability.

The resistance of social sciences to the intrusion of politics has always been more difficult than in the case of natural sciences. In the past, there has been an incontestable solidarity between certain types of analysis and certain political preferences, or certain political concepts. Nothing is easier, or more tempting, in political economy than to confuse ideal schemes with reality. The latter is generally credited with the merits that belong (if at all) to the former. If we accept the classic theory that a balanced state of the market implies the maximization of the forces of production in society and the use of the best resources, it does not necessarily follow that those actual economies that we call liberal (when they are in fact only partially liberal) are the best, or that it is advisable to allow the imperfect mechanisms of the marketplace to be set in motion on the pretext that if these mechanisms were to somehow achieve perfection they would bring about the best solution. Karl Manheim gave the name *Wissenssoziologie* to the discipline that strives to elucidate the diverse modalities of relations between historical circumstances and intellectual constructs.

We would not dream of denying that the social sciences never start with a clean slate, or that the posing of problems is suggested by events, or that method is not independent of philosophy or historical background, or that results are often influenced by national and class interests. It would be no less fatal to draw the conclusion that the social sciences are nothing more than class or racial ideologies, and that the orthodoxy imposed by a totalitarian state does not differ in nature from the free research conducted in pluralistic societies. There does exist, no matter what one says, a *community of social sciences,* which, though it may be less autonomous than the community of natural sciences, is nevertheless real.

What are the rules that constitute this community of social sciences?

1. First of all, *the absence of restrictions in research and the establishing of the facts themselves,* the right to present fundamental facts and to distinguish them from interpretations. It can no doubt be maintained, in the spirit of philosophical precision, that every historical fact is a construct and therefore implies selection and interpretation. When applied, these distinctions preserve their full implications. It is either true or false that Trotsky played a considerable role in organizing the Red Army; it is either true or false that Zinoviev or Bukharin plotted the assassination of Stalin; it is either true or false that Wall Street manipulates American politicians and is organizing an anti-Soviet crusade. All totalitarian states outlaw certain facts on the grounds that they do not fit in the official scheme of things. Every totalitarian state exaggerates, to the point of absurdity, the interdependence of fact and interpretation.

2. Next, *the absence of all restriction on the right of discussion and criticism, applying not only to partial results, but also to groundwork and methodology.* Social knowledge rises to the level of science insofar as it is accompanied by an exact awareness of its significance, and also of the limits of its validity. In political economy, for example, theory makes progress by constructing new models, but also by recognizing the precise conditions in which a given model, even if long established, applies. Keynes's general theory owes its originality to many factors: the situation that presented the problem (so-called permanent unemployment); the effort to reexamine the classic theory by way of a new, schematic plan, as a particular and valid case in point concerning the hypothesis of full employment; the characterization of a few concrete facts (invariability of nominal wages) as necessary; a psychology of the entrepreneur as being different from the rational psychology of the economic subject in traditional theory; and so forth. The contribution and significance of the *general theory* can only be understood if these diverse elements are considered simultaneously, in terms of fact and of method. The theory of knowledge, as concerns social science, is inseparable from knowledge itself. Any doctrine, be it liberal or Marxist,

that elevates equivocal propositions and imprecise schemata to the level of dogma slides from science to mythology. Critical consciousness in sociology or political economy is constitutive of scientific consciousness itself.

3. Finally, *the absence of restriction on the right to disenchant the real.*[1] There is a significant gap between the idea of a certain regime and the actual functioning of that regime, or between the democracy that we all have dreamed about when under tyranny and the system of parties that has been established in Western Europe. But this disappointment is in part inevitable. All democracies are oligarchic, all institutions are imperfectly representative; any government that must obtain the assent of groups or of a plurality of people acts slowly and must take human foolishness and selfishness into account. The first lesson a sociologist must transmit to his students, even if it threatens their eagerness to believe and to serve, is that there has never been a perfect regime.

It is rare for a scientist to use these three freedoms simultaneously and without any limitations; he would have to be almost inhuman to do so. The function of the community of social sciences is precisely to create, by dialogue and mutual criticism, the equivalent of these three freedoms. The *other* shows me the range of interpretation implicit in the fundamental facts that I must ascertain, or the troublesome consequences of institutions that I was tempted to recognize as exclusively meritorious. It is within and through the whole community that the social sciences strive not to dismiss any fact, not to spare any value from legitimate criticism, and to accumulate, at one and the same time, certainties and doubts by relentlessly specifying the external conditions and the provisional hypotheses to which the truth of general propositions is attached.

By the same token, it is plain what this free community of social sciences sees as its goal, and why so many rulers fear it. Only a critical science can prevent history or sociology from sliding from constructive knowledge to mythology; many regimes, however, make no effort to prevent such sliding.

The events of history have all that it takes to be transfigured into

---

1. H. H. Gerth and C. Wright Mills remind us that "Weber liked to quote Friedrich Schiller's phrase, the 'disenchantment of the world.'" *From Max Weber: Essays in Sociology,* ed. and trans. Hans H. Gerth and C. Wright Mills (Oxford University Press, 1946), p. 51. Accordingly, I have translated Aron's phrase, *désenchanter le réel,* literally here (see also p. 341 above). Elsewhere, however, I have given the phrase a less verbatim translation (see below, p. 348).—Trans.

mythology. They are close to us, they are human: we are inevitably tempted to attribute them to the clear and resolute will of a few individuals (or groups), who are made out to be angelic or monstrous by virtue of the immeasurable good or evil that they supposedly spread. Most twentieth-century individuals are incapable of explaining phenomena that not long ago would have been considered miraculous, such as heavier-than-air aviation, or long-distance transmission of sound and image, but they know that these phenomena can be explained rationally. Electricity is magic only to children. Capitalism, Communism, and Wall Street are demons for millions of adults. History abets mythology by its very structure, by the contrast between partial intelligibility and the mystery of the whole, or between the obvious role of human will and the no less evident failures that events inflict upon the will; and by the spectator's vacillation between indignation—as if we were responsible, one and all, for what happens—and passive horror—as if we were in the presence of an inhuman fate.

If we are not careful, the concepts of science can sometimes become characters of mythology. One need only confuse schemata with the real, forget the multiple meanings of widespread phenomena that are designated by terms such as capitalism or socialism, and the substitution is soon complete. We are then no longer in the presence of men and institutions, of meanings immanent in the behavior of the former and in the structure of the latter; instead, we sense in them a mysterious force which, although it has preserved the full strength of its original meaning, has lost contact with fact. History, henceforth designated with a capital, becomes the site of mighty struggles between Ideas. The historical sciences do not dispel the mystery of supraindividual aggregates, but they do depoeticize them. Scientists' dialogue on the evolution of collectivities teaches neither skepticism nor lack of respect, but it does prevent the divinization of temporal things, it does bring back to earth those men or those regimes that are raised above the common lot.

Despotic governments are bound to resent the social sciences as soon as the latter go beyond the study of administrative techniques and carry their mission to its conclusion.

Even if, for reasons of prudence or necessity, the sociologist or the historian abstains from studying the characteristics of Caesarisms (both ancient and modern), even if he limits his study to regimes different from the one under which he lives, the student cannot fail to understand that the same method ought to apply to his masters and would thereby remove their halo of perfection and infallibility. For fear of being accused of harboring antidemocratic views, let us not cease analyzing parliamentary institutions such as they presently function in Europe.

Science will not tell us that we must be favorably inclined toward democracy, or that democracy is, as such, superior to other feasible forms of government in our century. Science does show the unlimited risks that single-party regimes bring to bear upon certain values which the academic, although devoted to the secular tradition of universities, holds sacred. It shows what relative guarantees are provided by multi-party systems, with regard both to a certain respect for personal rights and to the constitutional character of the exercising of power. It also shows what risks are immanent in this type of regime: the instability of the executive branch in the case where there is no clear majority; social disintegration when the party or class struggles surpass a certain level of violence; paralysis of the rulers when all the particular interest groups plead their cases too loudly.

Fears are often expressed to the effect that political science is dangerous for democracies because it shows them as they are, in their inevitable and bourgeois imperfection. I see no danger here at all. Let us not forget: democracy is the only regime that admits—what am I saying?—that proclaims that the history of states is and must be written not in verse but in prose.[2]

Whether dealing with science or with politics, Max Weber had the same goal in mind: to highlight the ethics peculiar to a given activity in such a way that the former could be seen as conforming to the finality of the latter. The scientist must repress the feelings that bind him to the object under study, and refrain from the value judgments that spontaneously surge within him and shape his attitude concerning society—both the society of the past, which he explores, and the society of the present, which, whatever he may say, he wants to safeguard, destroy, or change. One must accept the indefinite character of constructive research, and, for the benefit of an inquiry whose end is unknown, dispel the magic aura that surrounds the world of nature and of men—such was the pathos that Weber put forth to his hearers and called upon them to accept as their own, for the sake of the scientific career they had chosen.

The pathos of action was linked, as he saw it, to the antithesis of two moral codes: the ethics of responsibility and the ethics of convic-

2. The relative playfulness with which Aron concludes this section of his article can be explained, in part, by his allusions here to Molière's *Le Bourgeois Gentilhomme* (not to mention certain parallel allusions to part 1 of Marx's *The Eighteenth Brumaire of Louis Bonaparte*).—Trans.

tion. Either I act according to my convictions—pacifist or revolutionary, it makes no difference which—without concerning myself with the consequences of my acts, or I hold myself accountable for what I do even if I didn't intend to do it, and in that case good intentions and a pure heart no longer suffice to justify an actor.

At the same time, Weber never tired of emphasizing the gap between the projects of man and the consequences of his acts. What one generation has freely opted for becomes inexorable fate for the next generation. The Puritans chose to be craftsmen; the men of today have to follow suit. We can hardly deny the perpetual gap between men's aspirations and their actual experiences when we think of Lenin's hopes and observe the realities of Stalinism, or when we recall the faith that inspired so many young Germans in 1932 or 1933 and contemplate the horrors of Nazism. History is the tragedy of a humanity that creates its own history but does not know what history it is creating. Political action is nothing other than a tireless effort to act in an enlightened manner and to avoid being betrayed by certain consequences of that action.

The ethics of a man of action are certainly those of responsibility. But such an affirmation should not be taken lightly. It does not include submission to the rules of a formal ethic such as Kant had devised, or submission to the sublime imperatives of the Sermon on the Mount. The state is the institution which, in a given collectivity, has a monopoly on legitimate violence. To enter into politics is to participate in conflicts whose stakes are power—the power to influence the state and thereby the collectivity. By the same token, one is bound to submit to laws of action, even if they go against our individual preferences or the Ten Commandments; a pact is made with infernal powers, and the individual condemns himself to the logic of efficiency.

Who bore the brunt of Weber's criticism when in the aftermath of the First World War he wrote *Politik als Beruf*? I believe he was taking aim at two categories of people in particular: those we would call, in French, *pacifistes d'inspiration chrétienne* (pacifists of a Christian stripe), and principaled revolutionaries. The first group, for whom Weber had a certain amount of respect, he blamed for not taking into account the consequences of their arguments or writings. To lay the burden of all responsibilities upon one's country does not help reestablish peace among nations. By weakening the moral position of the defeated adversary, one in fact lays the groundwork for a treaty so harsh and unjust as to prevent pacification and reconciliation. The second group he blamed for converting a legitimate goal—the transformation of the economic and social regime—into an absolute value, in such a way that the revolution, in the eyes of the faithful, could never be paid for dearly enough.

The dialogue with the so-called Christian pacifists is, in my opinion, irrelevant nowadays. There are hardly any of these pacificists left in a world in which war has become quasi-permanent. Those who pass themselves off as such are usually disguising a position that is more political than spiritual. A more thoughtful pacifism today would be one based on the reasonable conviction that, for those who are its victims and whose territory serves as field of battle, modern warfare is an unqualified catastrophe. This conviction could become a factor of peace only on condition that it were shared by all statesmen and all peoples. Communists, however, are bound by their doctrine to believe that the historical phase, which they call world revolution, will be filled with gigantic struggles that will necessarily lead to universal socialism. For such an end, even atomic warfare would not be too high a price.

As for the revolutionaries, whom Weber condemned, they were idealists above all: some shared views similar to those held by the so-called Christian pacifists, others leaned more toward the anarchists or utopians. Today's revolutionaries are technicians of subversion and tyranny who nevertheless continue to think in terms of millennia: they endow one event—the revolution—with a unique value, which places it outside of the immanent progression of human history. In this perspective, nothing will be possible until the day of History's transfiguration, and from that day on, everything will be possible; no means should be spared to attain that supreme objective, which, moreover, is historically inevitable.

It is easy to imagine Weber's response to such a philosophy. It may be, he would have said, that Western societies are necessarily (or, in more precise terms, probably) evolving toward a regime of collective property or planification.[3] But it cannot be postulated in advance that one and the same party must necessarily accomplish this transformation in all the countries involved. As for the advantages and disadvantages of such a regime, they are certainly debatable; but science does not allow us to affirm, or even to believe, that the advantages are sufficient to decisively modify the secular traits of human societies.

Such argumentation is unlikely to affect the faithful, but it does make them stand out in their true light: they appeal to science as their

---

3. Thirty years ago Weber was not convinced of this. He held the necessary tendencies of evolution to be rationalization and bureaucratization, not a given type of ownership or regulation.

authority, while they are the protectors of a faith that drapes itself in the tawdriness of an outworn science on the one hand or a popularized philosophy on the other. Max Weber, whose studies should have led him to broad overviews of history, had adopted a more modest point of view. Rather than raise questions about the society of the future, he pondered the tasks of the here-and-now. Thirty years ago, the major task was the reconstruction of the state and its politics.

Some of his analyses bear upon a historical situation and have thus lost part of their currency. He was obsessed by hostility toward the emperor, whom he charged with major responsibility for the German catastrophe. He considered the recruitment of political leaders from among civil servants to be one of the essential causes for the failings of the Wilhelmian empire. "Parliamentarization," i.e., the transfer of effective responsibilities to parliament, would allow those who were energetic, pugnacious, or prompted by the desire for power and struggle to have better chances in rising to positions of authority.

Weber traced the development of one social category and one type of man through the centuries: he called this type of individual the professional politician, meaning a person who draws his substance from politics, who lives *by* and at the same time *for* politics. Depending on the centuries and countries involved, it was the clergy, the intellectuals, the English aristocracy, or the jurists who held the top positions, with the relations (again, varying from one nation to the next) between monarch, traditional nobility, and bourgeoisie determining the alliances or conflicts among these various groups. Without going deeply into these analyses, which are deservedly renowned, I will dwell on one point that Weber himself stressed: the decisive contrast between two types of parties—those that are made up of notables, and those that are more properly mass (or popular) parties, with jurists and lawyers, state or party officials, and otherwise prominent citizens constituting the principal types of professional politicians in our era.

What is the situation today? The opposition between parties of notables and mass parties, a distinction that has almost disappeared in certain countries (the Conservative party in Great Britain has become a mass party almost to the same degree as the Labour party), continues to exist, as I see it, in both Germany and in France. The Radical-Socialists and independents do not constitute mass parties in the same sense as does the Section française de l'Internationale ouvrière, or even, up to a certain point, the Mouvement républicain populaire. The Christian Democratic Union seems still to preserve a few characteristics of the parties of notables, in spite of efforts to transform it into a mass organization. The need for such an organization varies according to the degree of the society's urbanization and the balloting methods in practice. During the current phase, in continental Europe, the structural difference between right-wing and left-wing parties is diminishing but is unlikely to disappear entirely.

Difference in party structure is accompanied by a difference in the recruitment of political leaders. In all political regimes, and in democracies more than in any other, it is on the recruitment of leaders that success or failure invariably depends. In Germany, the principal leaders still belong to the pre-Hitlerian generation, who spent most of their lives during the Wilhelmian empire or the Weimar Republic. In France, the leaders are for the most part survivors of the Third Republic who, after 1945, were promoted to the top ranks, having long held secondary positions; they were joined during the same period by a few prominent figures of the Resistance or Gaullists. Those men with established careers as party or trade union officials, an important category in Germany, have almost no leading role to play in France.

For the academic who wants to enter politics, the difficulty lies in party discipline and doctrine. There is not a single sociologist or economist who is likely, at any time in history, in any country in the world, to accept, word for word, the platform of any political party. At best, he can agree with it to varying degrees, but only if he makes free use of what in religious matters used to be called symbolic interpretations. In a state of struggle, the opposition has never been known to refrain from unfair or deceitful arguments that blame the government for failing to achieve what no other government could ever achieve, or for making concessions that no other government, for that matter, could have avoided making. For the social science professor who wants to be politically active, this state of affairs creates a permanent source of tension.

The tension can vary in intensity according to the degree of dishonesty characterizing political discussions—a degree of dishonesty which, in turn, varies from country to country and according to the degree of discipline demanded of party members—and depending on the historical moment. Each of us finds his own answer to this personal problem of the relationship between science and politics. Those who participate in parliamentary procedures cannot afford the luxury of unhampered liberty. The vocation of science is an unconditional appeal to truth. The avocation of the politician does not always tolerate the utterance of truth.

The problem of individual subordination to the party may be less serious today than it was twenty years ago, thanks to the skepticism that has eroded partisan beliefs. Fortunately, neither the leaders nor the rank and file of Social Democracy even affect loyalty to Marxism or to the dogmatism of collective property. Parties are what they appear to be and what they must be: organizations that aim at the exercise of power, that defend certain interests, and that promise to govern according to vague, general concepts. Unfortunately, however, parties sometimes compensate for their increased flexibility in doctrine by increased violence in controversies of the moment.

Max Weber was concerned about the quality of democratic recruitment. Those who lack personal wealth cannot launch into a political career without accepting both the hazards of the profession and financial insecurity. In Germany today, apparently, most politicians keep up, and are forced to keep up, their previous or secondary professions, often as civil servants. Only party officials can be full-time professional politicians. The parliamentary game is so formalized and so purged of unpredictability and the spirit of contest that it no longer constitutes a basis for selection. It is in the party rather than in the legislative assembly that you have to assert yourself in order to get ahead. Political life in France, having preserved its rather unstable and whimsical characteristics, remains less predictable. From time to time a particular personality will stand out and be noticed, not *within* but *on the fringe* of political parties. The current style of politics in Germany cannot be said to encourage the emergence of top-rank personalities—those demagogues that Max Weber dreamed of, who devote themselves to their work while earning their living at it, and who strangely combine clear-headed passion with a sense of responsibility and proportion.

But Weber may have been asking too much of politicians in modern democracies. He fancied the best of them as being draped in a kind of charismatic authority. It is true that democracies are perpetually threatened by the decadence brought on by the anonymity of power, the mediocrity of rulers, and the passivity of spiritless masses. In tragic circumstances, when the life of the nation is at stake or the constitution needs to be restored, the masses yearn for a leader to follow and laws to obey. It is then that the demagogue steps forward: in the Roman Republic he was known as dictator, and political writers of the past have referred to him as the Legislator. Current and durable regimes give rise, in critical moments, to persons who are capable of saving them. In periods of tranquillity, the leaders of democracies are honorable administrators and occasionally good organizers, though they are more often pacifiers. That they should also have the breadth of vision, the clear-sightedness, and the clear-headed passion of great statesmen is a stroke of fortune that one can hardly count on.

*   *   *

A few years ago, Leo Strauss dedicated a chapter of his book *Natural Right and History* to an investigation of Max Weber's views. The ultimate intention of his critical analysis is to reduce (so to speak) Weber to nihilism. In other words, Strauss intends to show that man, because he lacks scientific or, at least, rational judgment, surrenders to the arbitrariness of decisions that are all equally justifiable or unjustifiable. For his part, however, Strauss does not clearly indicate what regime, in itself, is best, or how reason succeeds in specifying the characteristics of such a regime and establishing its universal validity. Strauss's philosophy could be reduced to a suprahistorical dogmatism, just as he reduces Weber's relativism to nihilism. We will disregard, for the time being, the ultimate consequences of these two theses and consider the objections addressed by the philosopher, who is in search of natural right, to the sociologist, who is concerned with establishing an objective science and who is convinced of the irreducible diversity of human epochs.

1. Strauss's first objection might be expressed in these terms: *to prohibit value judgments is meaningless, of itself, because neither historian nor sociologist could respect the prohibition without compromising the quality of his science.* Or, in Strauss's own terms: "[Weber's] work would be not merely dull but absolutely meaningless if he did not speak almost constantly of practically all intellectual and moral virtues and vices in the appropriate language, i.e., in the language of praise and blame." Or again: "Weber, like every other man who ever discussed social matters in a relevant manner, could not avoid speaking of avarice, greed, unscrupulousness, vanity, devotion, sense of proportion, and similar things, i.e., making value judgments" (*Natural Right and History* [Chicago: University of Chicago Press, 1953], pp. 51, 52).

Strauss may, admittedly, be right on the first point; but since Weber, according to his critic, violated the rule he laid down in his own theory, we must find out why a scientist so concerned with precision and clarity could have failed to recognize the inconsistency in his practice.

A historian or sociologist incapable of distinguishing between a true prophet and a charlatan would, by the same token, be incapable of genuine understanding. An art historian unable to distinguish be-

tween the paintings of Leonardo da Vinci and those of his imitators could not grasp the specific meaning of the historical object—in other words, the quality of the work. A sociologist who put Hitler and Washington, or Boulanger and Charles de Gaulle, a politician whose sole interest was power and a statesman impassioned with the sense of his nation's greatness, all in the same basket would throw everything into confusion on the pretext of not taking sides.

These three examples suggest the same general proposition: a historian cannot help but include value judgments in the description or interpretation of events or individual achievements, to the extent that value judgments themselves are inherent in the world of action or thought and are therefore constituent elements of reality itself. In order to avoid value judgments of these kinds, the historian would have to limit himself to historical propositions in the strict sense of the word, to analyzing, for example, the origin of paintings while ignoring their mediocrity or excellence, or to identifying successive styles without establishing a hierarchy (whether among the various styles, or within any one style) between the accomplishments of the original creators and those of their imitators.

Weber adhered to this type of analytic rigor without being fully aware of it; at least, he restricted himself to maintaining the formula of "reference to values" against that of "value judgment." To be sure, this distinction is strangely summary in nature.

To declare that a temple in India is beautiful or ugly by referring to the canon of Greek beauty would be the type of value judgment proscribed by Weber in the name of the objectivity of the social sciences. But to range the diverse accomplishments of the architecture and sculpture of India on a hierarchical scale is, in the last analysis, inevitable; how can one avoid comparisons between the temples of the past and those that are built today—ostensibly in imitation of the ancient style but in fact mere caricatures of an art long since dead? Similarly, in matters of religion or politics a man of faith or a man of action is supposedly judged by references to the meaning that each of these men accorded to his own preachings or undertakings. Weber did not define what he really understood by "value." There is nothing to prevent us from replacing the concept of *value* by terms that concretely define the objectives of an action or a creation and, concomitantly, the rules to which actor or creator must be bound.

Weber, judging from his own point of view, might have consented to this revision, which has less to do with his thought than with the way he expressed it. The only objections he would have raised would apply to a later phase of the argument. He would certainly have ac-

cepted the principle that one can and must distinguish between Leonardo da Vinci and his imitators—but can a historian really establish a hierarchy between Persian miniatures and Italian painting, or between Hindu statues of the Elephanta and the statuary art of Phidias? Within a sphere that possesses its own criteria for valuation, the historian cannot avoid appraisal without falsifying his comprehension of the real. When the criteria are fundamentally different, or when the spheres in question are disparate, the historian could make his appraisals only if he took sides, thereby ceasing to be a scientist.

Our examination of this first objection—which is a valid one but nonetheless susceptible of being mistaken for Weber's own thought on the matter—brings us to a second objection, which also offers us a second theme for reflection: what is the meaning of this diversity of spheres?

2. *The acceptance of a radical diversity among different epochs would, in the final analysis, destroy the full significance of historical sociology itself.* Indeed, the sociologist cannot comprehend a society without the aid of a conceptual scheme. Now if he uses his own conceptual scheme, his understanding of the foreign society in question will be different from the self-understanding of that same society, and, by the same token, he will have falsified its significance (unless, of course, he understands that society better than it has understood itself). Understanding of the other by reference to our own conceptual system is relative to the latter, and, to the extent that this system can change, our understanding can change right along with it; far from being universal, it is tied to history and to one's own time as well. When the sociologist tries to establish a comparative science of institutions, he will either make use of a quantity of categories, whose validity surpasses the limits of a specific time, or else his work will be ephemeral and, in the last analysis, insignificant.

The objection that we have thus formulated, in terms slightly different from those used by Strauss, calls for an incontestable conclusion, which Weber himself accepted. Historic or social science is universally valid, but its universality is hypothetical: it is dependent on initial hypotheses, as well as on choice of and reference to values—none of which present themselves to all individuals in the same way, and all of which change from epoch to epoch. It might be argued that the mathematical and, for that matter, the physical sciences too are valid only for those who are concerned with this type of truth. But there is a decisive difference between the natural sciences and the "cultural" sciences, as Max Weber interprets them; once mathematical or physical

truth is sought, the evolution of these sciences is based on accumulation. Even in cases of theoretical revision, yesterday's propositions can be accommodated, with due regard to their degree of accuracy, in today's structures. On the other hand, if the questions raised by historians and sociologists change from epoch to epoch, an individual living in the twenty-first century, even if he is seeking an objective truth, does not have to take an interest in the questions raised by his precursor in the twentieth century.

Weber accepted this consequence of his own principles without any hesitation, for two reasons—the one explicit and the other unexpressed. The questions are raised by the scientist, he said, but the answers are universally valid once the questions have been raised. On the other hand, and although he did not say so, he could not help but believe that the questions he himself raised with regard to the past would continue to be relevant, even for the individual in times to come. It is this unexpressed reason that establishes the validity of historical sciences so much more firmly than the objectivity of the answers.

What Weber understood by *question,* or *reference* to values, does not merely determine the object or limits of research; it also leads to conceptual formulation. How could scientific propositions (the answer) be anything but inseparable from the questions? Weber himself oscillated between diverse formulas: the answer being both understanding and causality, propositions are confirmed, by the latter, in their hypothetically universal validity. But this formula presupposes that history or the social sciences were formed (woven, as it were) by causal relations, which is not the case. It is not causality that establishes the validity of Max Weber's interpretation of Calvinism but, rather, the understanding of Calvinists—regardless of their actions in the earliest phase of capitalism—to which Weber devotes the major part of his study.

What can the *truth* of this interpretation consist of if the interpretation presupposes a whole system of concepts and if the system, in turn, is the expression of both the interpreter and his time? The interpretation must of course be compatible with the available facts or documents, but, according to Weber himself, several interpretations are compatible with a given set of data. Unless analysis is further pursued, epistemology gets mired down in this incoherent plurality. In order to go beyond it, we must have recourse to more subtle analyses.

Weber lay stress on the notion of subjective meaning, the meaning experienced by historical actors. This, and not true meaning, is what historians and sociologists relate to. But experienced meaning is complex: the charlatan can take himself to be a true prophet, and the demagogue can see himself as a charismatic leader. The expression that actors give to their experiences, their self-consciousness (or what they claim as such), does not necessarily constitute historical truth. If all meanings are interchangeable, if they all have equal weight, there is no way the historical and social sciences can avoid chaos. In fact, plurality of meaning is undeniable, but it is plurality of a particular kind.

If the demagogue is a charlatan, a historian who sees him as a charismatic leader is mistaken. If the prophet is authentic, a historian who sees him as a mere hoaxer is equally mistaken. This differentiation is another example of value judgments inherent in those spheres that Weber did not account for in his explicit epistemology. When different interpretations are given of a historical oddity (such as those mentioned above), a hierarchy spontaneously arises; the meaning in relation to the milieu, the significance attributed to the unusual individual by his disciples, and that same individual's self-definition are not juxtaposed. The meaning of a religious creed or of a philosophical system is first and foremost the one it has been given by the prophet (or theologian) and the philosopher. It is by reference to this intrinsic meaning that the other meanings are derived. And the historian must first rediscover this primary meaning before looking for others.

But—one may interject—if the historian applies his concepts to the interpretation of this intrinsic meaning, he will in effect be altering it. Assuredly. But the only conclusion to be drawn is that in the absence of an inherent order in the religious or philosophical sphere, the resulting interpretations would be as incoherent as the sequence of individual events within that sphere. This proposition, moreover, is self-evident if one thinks about it. There is no history of humanity if humanity does not exist. There is no history of philosophy if philosophy per se does not exist.

Let us clearly understand the thrust of these affirmations. It is not necessary for humanity to subscribe to a single, unique idea of itself to have unity: all that is required is that the various ideas that it has had of itself fall into a certain pattern, so that they do not appear to be unconnected or unreasonable. Likewise, philosophy acquires the unity of a history from the moment that the question, or questions, connect, even if the answers oppose one another.

Weber's historical sociology, in a similar vein, presupposes that the institutions of diverse societies are not incompatible, and that it is possible to set up a universally valid system of concepts. Strauss, for his part, blames Weber for failing to recognize the possibility and necessity of a universally valid system of categories, and—once having admitted this system's historical relativity—for falsifying his sociology of universal history by the very provincialism of his scheme. The "distinction of three ideal types of legitimacy (traditional, rational, and charismatic)," he writes, "reflects the situation as it existed in Continental Europe after the French Revolution when the struggle between the residues of the pre-Revolutionary regimes was understood as a contest between tradition and reason." The third type of power [or, as it appears in Strauss's text, "legitimacy"], charismatic power, is added to create "the impression that the scheme [is] now comprehensive."[4]

Our purpose here is not to discuss the merits (or deficiencies) of the differentiation between these three types of power. But—and on this point Strauss is right to criticize Weber's explicit epistemology—the distinction is significant if (and to the degree that) the innumerable types of power can be subsumed under three types; in other words, if (and to the degree that) historical diversity is not radically incoherent. But nonincoherence does not, of itself, imply—and here, at this stage of the argument at least, Weber has the upper hand—that there is a trans-historical order, and only one, in which all historical singularities must be consolidated. It is true that the rivalry between the ancien régime and the Revolution has been wrongly confused with the antinomy of tradition and reason. It is possible that the tradition-reason antithesis characterizes a certain historical period, and only one. But the Weberian scheme, nonetheless, has (in my opinion) a far-reaching effect that Strauss refuses to acknowledge.

The three terms—tradition, reason, charisma—correspond to three principles of obedience. The individual obeys leaders who are established by virtue of custom, designated by reason, or elevated above all others by virtue of their inspiration: the elders, the organizers, and the prophets symbolize these three sources of legitimacy (Strauss should have been able to accept these types, since they constitute models very much like the ones familiar to the nonphilosopher citizen who thinks according to everyday notions). Furthermore, the authority that is placed in the hands of officeholders, or the powers that be, and that either tradition or advanced age continues to exercise, is, in our own age, in the process of rationalization. But this rational authority is never enough: at the highest level, the leader does not appeal to reason alone. In the last analysis he is transfigured by a tradition, even if in

4. Since the second half of this paragraph constitutes, essentially, a direct quotation from Leo Strauss, *Natural Right and History*, p. 57—although Aron does not clearly identify it as such (cf. above, p. 354)—I have provided Strauss's own words here, and have included quotation marks that are not present in Aron's original text.—Trans.

the form of rational mechanisms or by the enthusiasm of the crowd. The Weberian scheme helps to grasp the core of the political problem of our civilization.

It is true that, stated in these terms, the political problem does not allow for an optimal solution. We can therefore conceive of another possible thesis, while admitting the partial legitimacy of the Weberian scheme. Allowing for the fact that historical diversity is not incoherent, the opposition remains between these two theses: Max Weber's, which precludes the search for the ideal regime and the universally valid order of diversity, and thereby implies the legitimacy of a comparative science and the historical renewal of this science; and Leo Strauss's, which connects comparative science to the trans-historical order which, in turn, consolidates historical diversity.

3. Just as the radical diversity of epochs, or of institutions through time, would devalorize historical sociology, so *the radical irrationality of decisions would devalorize the concern for a rigorous differentiation between science and politics, and between references to values and value judgments.* After all, why not pass politics off as science if, in the last analysis, honesty is just a choice among many, neither more nor less valid than the contrary choice between cynicism, hypocrisy, or confusion? The danger is all the more real as Weber seems at times to be passing off each individual's duty to obey his god or his demon as the ideal and supreme consequence of his own choice. Become what you are; this would be the last word, in terms of what would probably have to be called a "personal ethic" rather than a moral science or wisdom.

Considered in relation to the philosophical tradition, Weber appears to be almost Nietzschean. He refuses to place the formal rules of morality above historical relativity. Thus, Kantian imperatives are no less characteristic of one attitude among many than is the attachment to Christian dogmas or the cult of vitalistic values. "Do not do unto others what you do not want done unto you": this commandment demands suppression of the will to power and submission to the principles of equality and reciprocity among individuals. The individual who has chosen to do his own will in the manner of Callicles will refuse to yield to prohibitions that are promulgated by the weak in order to protect themselves from the strong, or by slaves in order to put their masters in chains.

It is beyond all question that formal rules are not independent of a material ethic, and that the latter is incompatible with the cult of vitalistic values or the will to power. But if the imperative of reciprocity and the rejection of that imperative are placed on the same level, then there is no room for doubt: we fall into nihilism, pure and simple. Everything is equivalent. "Thou shalt not kill," in the last analysis, is no plainer than "Do what you have ventured to do to the limit, even if it's over your mother's body." If the only thing remaining is the obligation of being faithful to oneself, then the Nietzschean who stops at nothing is better than the violent individual who is stopped by scruples.

The nihilistic implications of some of Weber's texts are incontestable. I might add that this was one of the tendencies of his thought. "God is dead, everything is permitted." Or at least "God is dead, everyone chooses his god, who may turn out to be a devil." But this is not the only tendency that runs through his thought. The Nietzschean nihilism with which his thought sometimes converged was less the object of a definite choice than the semi-involuntary consequence of a principle which, in his eyes, was fundamental: the impossibility of scientifically demonstrating a value judgment or a moral imperative.

One can grant him that the truth of prohibitions—such as "Do not do unto others what you would not want done unto you," or "Thou shalt not kill"—is not of the same order as the truth of the law of gravity or the equations of relativity. Having affirmed the heterogeneity between the universal truth arrived at by the modern, natural sciences and all else, Weber did his utmost to circumscribe, within the "cultural" sciences, a domain in which a truth similar to that of physics could be affirmed, casting everything else into the outer darkness.

His error was twofold: the differentiation between (arbitrary) questions and (objective) answers is not as easy to infer as his analyses would lead one to think. If everything that is not a scientific truth is arbitrary, scientific truth itself would theoretically be the object of a preference as ungrounded as the opposite preference for myths and vitalistic values.

Weber could have worked his way out of the circle in which he enclosed himself. Indeed, if he chose what in his own terms he called scientific truth, it was because this truth was universal and, as such, constituted the proper grounds and domicile of a community of minds, across political boundaries and through the centuries. The cult of vitalistic values and the affirmation of the will to power result in the denial of universality: rivalry among rather than community of individuals would then constitute the essence of humanity. Even if one admits that, logically, the truth of "$2 \times 2 = 4$" is not the same type as that of "Thou shalt not kill," the fact remains that the ultimate meaning of arithmetical equivalence is pertinent to all men, a universality found in a different form in the prohibition against killing.

What is more, the formal rules of the rationalist ethic—rooted in Christianity but reaching their full expression in the philosophy of Kant—are not a simple matter of taste like that of color preference. They are, instead, the logical development of the notion of humanity, of the universal society of man, an idea inseparable from the profound significance of scientific truth. These rules are formal because the institutions which, from century to century, embody them cannot resist change as a function of material and social technology.

4. Little does it matter, Weber might have replied, whether or not the philosopher establishes multiple categories of propositions or nonscientific commandments: "I have not been nor did I intend to be a philosopher. I ventured out on the philosophical terrain only to mark off the limits of science and the antinomies and paradoxes of action." *The intention of universality that animates formal ethics is not imparted to men of action when they are faced with decisions.* In other words, and to use terminology different from Weber's, Weberian phenomenology of action remains valid even if one separates formal ethics [or, ethical formalism] from historical relativity.

Let us resume, one by one, the essential characteristics of this phenomenology. Are there two essentially distinct ethics, the one having to do with responsibility and the other with personal conviction? It is tempting to respond, as Leo Strauss does [cf. Strauss, *Natural Right and History,* pp. 69–70], that to act exclusively according to one's convictions is not moral. No one has the right to disregard the consequences of his acts. What is more, the concern for consequences completes, rather than contradicts, the motives of an action. We act *according to* our convictions and *in order to* obtain certain results.

These objections are too summary to be convincing. Weber did not mean to imply that the moralist who is concerned with responsibility has no convictions, or that the moralist who is preoccupied with the problem of individual convictions has no sense of responsibility. He *is* suggesting that, in extreme situations, the two attitudes can be contradictory, and that in the last analysis the one gives preference to the uncompromising affirmation of his convictions over success, while the other sacrifices his convictions for the necessities of success; both, however, are ethical within their respective conceptions of morality. From the point of view of the ethicist of responsibility, Romain

Rolland[5] is guilty of having weakened the confidence of the French in the justice of their cause; he is not considered guilty from the point of view of the ethicist of personal convictions,[6] who holds the respect for truth, or brotherhood, to be loftier aims than the triumph of an individual country—even if the latter were the bearer of a relatively pure cause.

This response, in turn, seems to us to be both convincing and comprehensive. If it is true that the "ethicist of convictions" is interested in the consequences of his acts, it is no less true that the "ethicist of responsibility" is often tempted to violate formal rules or sacrifice concrete values in order to attain specific ends. Nothing contributes more to the effectiveness of a struggle than the good conscience of the combatant. This good conscience is more often forged by mythology or falsehood than by staunch fidelity to truth. Max Weber would have subscribed to the pat statements that Julien Benda made at the time of the Dreyfus affair: as an intellectual, I defend the truth, that is, I proclaim Dreyfus's innocence; but let it not be said that in so doing I am serving either my country or the army. Quite the contrary: by compro-

5. The French biographer and novelist Romain Rolland (1868–1944) was widely criticized during the First World War for expounding his convictions as a pacifist and disinterested internationalist.—Trans.

6. Aron structures his discussion of Weberian phenomenology (and Strauss's reactions to it)—as it relates to the "two ethics" in the preceding paragraph—on the antithetical relationship between *le moraliste de la responsabilité* and *le moraliste de la conviction*. Up to this point in this section I have given these expressions a more explicit equivalent, for the purpose of contextual clarity. At this juncture, however, and for the purpose of economy, I have translated these expressions as "ethicist of responsibility" and "ethicist of (personal) convictions." My choice of terms in translating these expressions is based on the following considerations: (1) the English translation of the text by Max Weber that serves as the background for this discussion distinguishes between the "ethic of responsibility" on the one hand, and "the absolute ethic" or "ethic of ultimate ends" on the other. Weber illustrates his discussion of the latter of these two ethics (namely, the one dealing with "absolute" or "ultimate ends") with the examples of "a convinced syndicalist, believing in an ethic of ultimate ends," and "the believer in an ethic of ultimate ends [who] feels 'responsible' only for seeing to it that the flame of pure intentions is not squelched" ("Politics as a Vocation," in *From Max Weber*, pp. 120–21); (2) Leo Strauss, drawing on the same text of Weber, refers to the "ethics of responsibility" and the "ethics of intention" (Strauss, pp. 69–70); (3) Aron, for his part, gives the Weberian distinction a more concrete interpretation, by giving more weight to "the believer in [the] ethic," namely, the *moraliste*. By translating these expressions as I did, I have tried to reflect the nuances of agreement as well as disagreement that run through the three texts—Weber's, Strauss's, and Aron's—while at the same time avoiding a literal (and, in my opinion, more awkward) translation, i.e., "moralist of responsibility" and "moralist of conviction."—Trans.

mising the prestige of the general staff, I am jeopardizing the necessary authority of the military leaders. But I am responsible for the truth, and not for the military powers of the French nation.

I do not think Leo Strauss would deny these facts. The question is to determine the role that political philosophy should assign to the inevitable antinomies of action. There is a whole school of thought, with Machiavelli as its most illustrious representative, that maintains that the essence of politics is revealed, precisely, in extreme situations. A politician must be both convinced and responsible. But when it is a question of lying or losing, of killing or being defeated, which is the righteous choice? Truth, answers the "ethicist of convictions"; success, replies the "ethicist of responsibility." Both choices are moral, provided that the success willed by the latter is that of the republic and not his own.

The antinomy is essential, I believe, even though in the majority of cases prudence would dictate a reasonable compromise. The extreme situation, in which compromise becomes difficult if not impossible, is not exceptional; the element of risk emerges as soon as there is conflict. Weber, not without reason, regarded politics as essentially conflict between nations, parties, and individuals. No one has ever suggested that the formal rules of Kantian ethics can also be used efficaciously by antagonists in political battle. The historical examples of the ethics of conviction that Weber offers us, though debatable in themselves, were not chosen at random: the pacifist refuses to go to war, the revolutionary trade-unionist—such as Weber represents him—pushes the will to war to its ultimate end. Both totally reject prudence—for which the ethicist of responsibility rightfully rebukes them—but they can both just as easily reply that they don't want to get involved, the one in war, and the other in a regime that he abhors. The unconditional, absolute *no*, uttered at the risk of losing all, is the ultimate expression of what Weber called the ethics of conviction. There is no responsible individual who, for that matter, one day or another, doesn't find himself backed into a corner, forced to say no, whatever the cost, *weil er nicht anders kann,* because he cannot do otherwise. In short, with the human world being what it is, the prudence that normally accompanies an affirmation of will and a concern for consequences runs the risk, at any moment, of being knocked off its feet when confronted by the contradiction between universal ethics and the demands of the struggle. War is inseparable from politics, and the man of good intentions who enters politics can neither entirely submit to, nor free himself of, the obligations of the combatant. He rationalizes his own contradictions within the antinomy of the two ethics; this antinomy, on the level of the phenomenology of political action, seems to be a faithful conceptualization of the tortured conscience typical of the "intellectual in politics."

"To save one's soul or to save the state": Christians, throughout history, have not considered these phrases incompatible. Nor do I mean to imply that they are. But politics is war, while the universal ethic (whether Christ's or Kant's), which had remained intact in Weber's unconscious as *the* ethic, is peace. Perhaps wisdom teaches philosophers not to engage in war. If they do, perhaps they will be prudent. Will they be truthful? Will they be pure?

5. Many philosophers will be tempted to view the antinomy of the two ethics as being artificial—two tendencies, complementary although sometimes divergent, that are presented in the form of two contradictory phrases. On the contrary, Weber saw in this antinomy the authentic mark of the human condition. He met with this contradiction on three levels: (a) political controversy, (b) the foundations of a just order, and (c) the ultimate ends of action or human existence.

a. Weber never tired of showing that no concrete measure adopted— such as a tariff, an increase or decrease in a tax, or a subsidy—could pervert the dignity of a scientific truth. It is impossible to favor one group without unfavorably affecting another, impossible to demonstrate that progress in general production is not too dearly paid for by the ruin of small businessmen or the decline of an underprivileged region, impossible to prove that the consequences of a given fiscal policy that are deplorable in themselves are compensated for by the anticipated benefits. This line of argument is both indisputable and without much significance. It does little more than address itself to the henceforth classic problematics of collective versus individual interests.

Let us place ourselves in the world of modern economics. No measure taken can be said, with certainty, to conform to the common good unless it increases the satisfaction of some without decreasing the satisfaction of others (satisfaction, or compensation, being measured in terms of their objective expression, i.e., available incomes). Even in this hypothesis, which draws on Pareto's definition of the maximum of interest designed to *favor* a collectivity, there remains, strictly speaking, an uncertainty: a measure that would increase some people's incomes without reducing anyone else's could also increase the degree of dissatisfaction created by unfairness in cases where the betterment of the whole would make the inequality of distribution more pronounced. Let us suppose that a given measure is favorable to some but not to others: this in itself does not mean that the choice, which certainly is not rigorously scientific, is arbitrary; nor that, lacking a universally valid demonstration, all that is left is an endless struggle with no possibility of an equitable settlement. The controversy within industrial society is a permanent one, but it is not a fight to the death, for it does not preclude reasonable debate and negotiated solution.

The goal is stated openly: an increase in the national product and a decrease in the inequalities of distribution. These two objectives—growth, and reduction of inequalities—do not always imply identical decisions. By putting too much stress on equality, one runs the risk of compromising growth. Obsession with growth, on the other hand, leads one to disregard the sufferings of men and to sacrifice the living for the generations to come. There is no so-called technical measure (interest rate, customs duty, tax) that does not have political and social implications—in other words, that does not affect the distribution of wealth and power at the same time as the development of the whole. The hypotheses on which the doctrine of welfare is established (for example, that an equitable distribution of a certain amount of income increases satisfaction, with the income that is transferred from the rich to the poor increasing the latter's satisfaction to a greater degree than it decreases the former's) are all debatable; in any case, they are not scientific. But it would be wrong to present science and arbitrary decisions as alternative options. Between the rational proposition—valid for all, because it can be demonstrated according to methods that apply to all—and the choice made by each individual alone, without binding anyone else, there is room for a reasonable decision, i.e., a decision founded on reason, although it may run contrary to the interests of a few.

Discussion and reasonable choice are at the very heart of industrial civilization, and, indeed, of certain, particular regimes. Whoever remains hostile to industrialization, or unconditionally rejects private ownership of the means of production, does not enter into this reasonable discussion: he is relegated to history, and history is made up of a ceaseless struggle among men, parties, and gods.

b. Also without end, in Weber's view, are conflicts centered on the definition of a just order. What are the exigencies of the notion of equality? This is what the debate over a just order must eventually come around to. Now, said Weber, there are two equally valid replies: either more is owed to the one who accomplishes more, or else more is asked of him. Should the elite be favored and helped to flourish? Or, on the contrary, should legislation act in the opposite direction to nature and continually reestablish the equality that nature, just as persistently, strives to destroy? Leo Strauss (not without reason) considers that Weber formulated the antinomy with insufficient precision, and was even less precise as concerns the thesis of "equality at all costs," with the result that this latter thesis seems as plausible as the opposing thesis of natural inequalities, which every society must accept.

It would be impossible to deal adequately with the problem of the "just order" and stay within the limits of this essay. A few remarks will therefore suffice to bring out what appears indisputable in the Weberian notion of the antinomies of equality, as well as what is valid in Strauss's rejection of this tragic transformation of antinomies.

Let us consider political doctrinaires as well as party heads. The fact is that one group is concerned with allowing free rein to individual talents, while the other is concerned with preventing the disparities of social rank from standing out. It is worth rereading Alain: this philosopher of radicalism[7] recognized, along with Auguste Comte, that the rich and the powerful exist in every society; but he was more concerned with preventing the abuses of wealth and power than with granting the most productive individuals their deserved rewards. Other writers lean in the opposite direction and ask themselves how the selection of an elite and the authority of the best that society has to offer can be assured. Whether it is a question of income or power, it is fairly clear to me that two tendencies are emerging in socioeconomic ideologies. The first favors the idea of assuring all individuals as similar living conditions as possible, and of preventing rulers (even the best of them) from exercising unlimited power. The second favors the idea of increasing the bonus for the most productive individuals, and consolidating the reign of rulers who are worthy of their functions.

These divergent preferences inevitably come into play when a specific problem has to be resolved. Whether with respect to fiscal policy, the educational system, or the ownership of the means of production, the doctrinaire of equality will lean one way, while the doctrinaire of natural and social hierarchy will lean in another. In this sense, Weber was not wrong in indicating the heterogeneity of political decision and scientific demonstration. But was he right in assimilating divergent preferences to a fundamental and irreconcilable contradiction?

This assimilation derived from the following postulates: (1) individuals are naturally unequal, but as this natural inequality is both the predominant and original injustice, the political theoretician or practitioner is entitled to believe that it should be erased and that everything

7. Alain, whose real name was Emile Chartier (1868–1951), was the theoretician of the Third Republic and philosopher of the Radical-Socialist Party. Significantly influenced by the philosophical systems of Kant and Auguste Comte, he published his *Eléments d'une doctrine radicale* (Principles of a Radical Doctrine) in 1925.—Trans.

must be done toward that end; (2) society needs those individuals that are most gifted intellectually or spiritually, but someone inspired by a passion for equality is entitled to overlook pragmatic considerations so as to obey the single imperative of justice as he interprets it; (3) when various and, to some extent, divergent considerations present themselves simultaneously, someone who ignores one of them is no less worthy than someone who strives to keep them all together: in other words, the extremist is on a par with the moderate, and the man with the fixed idea (the "mono-ideist") is on the same level as the sage.

We need only formulate these postulates to see that they are, at the very least, debatable, and that they all have the same origin, which is noticeably more psychological than logical. Outside of science there could be only free choice, and since this choice is essentially unscientific, one could hardly condemn the man who acts on his convictions to the fullest, even if they were to lead him to the point of fanaticism. One need only accept the plurality of considerations (or, if you like, of values), without postulating an irreconcilable antinomy between them, in order to see the way out. Concern for the equal dignity of all individuals and, in our societies, for the reduction of economic inequalities; acceptance of natural inequalities and the need to encourage the development of individual talents; awareness of the social hierarchy accompanied by the will to make it equitable through the proper selection of rulers, and acceptable to those that are ruled, by restrictions on the prerogatives of the powerful: whoever chooses to ignore one or another of these fundamental ideas may not be guilty of scientific error or moral deficiency, but he *is* unreasonable. Perhaps Weber would simply reply: certainly, but why is it better to be reasonable than impassioned? Perhaps the criteria of a just order are manifold rather than contradictory; perhaps the antitheses exist in the sphere of concrete, historical solutions and not in the domain of principles which, at the highest level of abstraction, are complementary rather than contradictory. The fact remains that the requirements of each person, of each civilization, of each epoch, cannot be compared. Every living being has his God, and the gods are in a state of struggle.

c. Let us come to the third, the most deep-seated, and—if it is authentic—the most decisive contradiction, namely, that of values. Weber alluded to the contradiction of values as if it were self-evident; he did not demonstrate it, and the examples he does give are not all convincing. Something can be beautiful precisely because it is not good; thus, said Weber, we have *Les Fleurs du Mal (The Flowers of Evil)*. Certainly, Baudelaire's work is moral neither in form, nor in purpose, nor perhaps even in its creator's intentions—assuming, for that matter, that the poet's intentions can be judged according to ethical criteria. The beauty of *Les Fleurs du Mal*, however, is not due to the immorality of the themes or the (assumed) immorality of the creator. It is not a question of irreconcilable conflict between the specific meaning of the work of art and the finality of self-proclaimed moral conduct, or between beauty and obligation, but simply of a plurality, comparable to that of the castes of India.

No demonstration, Weber continues, can settle the question of the respective value of German culture and French culture. Certainly; but is the question meaningful? At a pinch, a hierarchy can be established among the works in a given sphere, but not among bodies of historical fact, each one of which contributes to the richness of total history and brings something that the other does not possess.

These observations are so obvious that it is difficult to imagine that Weber failed to recognize them.

Let us therefore resume with the most characteristic statement: "It is commonplace to observe that something may be true although it is not beautiful and not holy and not good. Indeed it may be true in precisely those aspects" [*From Max Weber*, p. 148]. Why did Weber conclude from this commonplace wisdom that Greek polytheism rightfully evoked a struggle of the gods, rather than the fact that each of the spiritual domains had its own laws?[8]

Man cannot conduct himself simultaneously according to the requirements of saintliness and of temporal ethics. Turning the other cheek is undignified conduct when it is not a sign of saintliness. Moreover, if it is true that Apollo and Mars, or Venus and Minerva, are not condemned to do battle, then no individual or collective body can simultaneously offer sacrifices to all the gods. The philosopher can certainly conceptualize the diversity of human accomplishments as being an enrichment; man, alone among others, cannot choose to achieve one task without giving up others. A society cannot simultaneously excel in all categories of action, saintliness, art, and meditation. In this sense, all existence is choice, and choice requires more noes than yesses: it condemns everyone to reckon on more enemies than supporters or loyal friends.

It is obvious that the individual never realizes but a small portion of his, or humanity's, potential. It is also obvious that a given period is a

8. Cf. Weber: "But all these are only the most elementary cases of the struggle that the gods of the various orders and values are engaged in. . . . We live as did the ancients when their world was not yet disenchanted of its gods and demons, only we live in a different sense. . . . One can only understand what the godhead is for the one order or for the other, or better, what godhead is in the one or in the other order" (ibid.).—Trans.

captive of its own ideas concerning beauty. But Phidias did not choose Greek statuary art in preference to the Hindu Elephanta, any more than the individual who chooses the scientist's profession does so in preference to the ethics of soldiering. The particularity of each historical accomplishment does not bring about a conflict between these particularities when considered side by side. At the very most that particularity would create a spiritual chaos if relativity pure and simple were the last word in reflecting on history.

War between the gods, or at least between their faithful followers, breaks out if the worship due one god directly contradicts that due another. In the state, the citizen or man of action must take a stand for a party or cause, against other parties and causes, as all parties appeal to the highest values. In the age when Christians were fighting the Roman pantheon, the actors of history believed in gods and were therefore committed to a struggle to the death. The same was true (to a lesser degree) when the French revolutionaries smashed thrones and altars. The same holds true today, when Communists dissolve parliaments and nationalize the means of production. Whatever the philosopher's judgment may be, historical existence is made up of uncertain struggles in which no cause is pure, no decision without risk, no action without unforeseeable consequences. The philosopher may perhaps discern the brotherhood of the gods above the tumult; the historian, for his part, ascertains the fratricidal fury of the churches.

The war of the churches is not the same thing as the war of the gods, but Weber's reflection suggests a transition from one to the other: Turning the other cheek is undignified conduct when it is not a sign of saintliness. The same act can be good or bad, depending on the meaning one gives to one's life.

To illustrate the notion of contradiction, Weber speaks of attitudes toward the enemy; his choice of example, though it may seem accidental, has a clear motive. Kant's ethic and the ethic of the Sermon on the Mount both apply to men of peace and goodwill. On this earth, however, men are at war within the state, and states are at war on the global stage. Every state defends a cause that in itself is valid (how can a hierarchy be established among nations, or between German and French cultures?). The warring parties, whose means or immediate ends are the least justifiable, can bring about long-term benefits that will greatly satisfy our children's children. Once again, Weber sees only one way out for anyone who does not submit to the imperatives of combat: indifference with regard to the consequences. This indifference, then, is what lies beneath the ethics of conviction and behind the saintliness of individual nonresistance (as a sign of faithfulness to certain teachings of Christ).

The saint and the hero cannot act similarly at the same juncture. Is the religious command to "turn the other cheek" the same thing as recommending nonresistance to evil? All societies in one way or another have recognized the plurality that Weber chose to view as bellicose and pathetic. The warrior does not always understand the Brahmin, but the Brahmin never ignores the warrior: he hesitates between the utopia of a state where the warrior would obey his orders, and wisdom, which dictates that he be satisfied with a state where philosophers will have the leisure to think but not the ambition to reign, resigned to a "tale full of sound and fury, signifying nothing." Whatever his choice is, he will not witness a "war of the gods." If the philosopher sticks to his utopia, he preserves the hope of reconciliation. If he is wise, therefore resigned to the nonwisdom of others, why would he see an irreconcilable conflict between himself and the senseless, between those who meditate and those who fight? The hero neither ignores nor scorns the saint: he scorns the individual who turns the other cheek out of cowardice, not the one who does it out of a superior courage.

Why was Max Weber so assured that the conflicts of Olympus are irreconcilable? Both because these conflicts were his own, and because they constitute the prerogative of sociological study. The rationalist recognizes the conflict between faith and unbelief; he admits that neither is scientifically demonstrable. Subscribing to the truth of unbelief, he concludes that there will be either progressive dissemination of enlightenment or continuing illusion—but not that there will be a war of the gods. In the eyes of the believer, on the other hand, it is faith that determines the meaning of skepticism. The expression *war of the gods* is the result of translating an indisputable fact (individuals have conjured up incompatible representations of the world) into a philosophy that no one lives by nor subscribes to, because it is contradictory (all representations are equivalent, none being either true or false).

Weber could indeed have thought that this philosophy was translated into real acts. As a nonbeliever, he hung on to a nostalgia of faith, and he was convinced that religion brought about a loss of irreplaceable spiritual values. As a Kantian, he was an enthusiast of political action, and he saw an irreconcilable antinomy between the rules of formal ethics and the requirements of action, that is to say of struggle. As a sociologist, he observed that civilizations, nations, and parties think and act according to value systems and interpretations that diverge from one another if they are not in direct opposition to one another. The discord caused by unbelief, the antinomy of ethics and politics, and the diversity of cultures, in Weber's writings, all become so many proofs of the "war of the gods." Phenomenological analyses that in themselves were truthful found themselves expressed in a humanly unthinkable philosophy.

Max Weber's methodology, as Leo Strauss among many others has said, is inseparable from his philosophy. From this indisputable remark, however, Strauss probably draws conclusions contrary to those that I myself would draw. He suggests that Weber's methodology was probably warped by his philosophy. I agree, on certain points: his Neo-Kantian language (the distinction between facts and values, the reference to values and value judgments) compromised the elaboration of a theory of understanding; it also prevented him from drawing on observations that are linked to understanding itself, in the case of works whose meaning is inseparable from their quality. The essential point, however, is not so much that the methodology suffered because of his philosophy, as the fact that the methodology wrongly inspired his philosophy. The limits of science, the antinomies of thought and action, are authentic contributions to a phenomenological description of the human condition. The philosophy of discord (if one can use such a phrase) translates these fundamental ideas into another language and gives them a different meaning. This translation, or transposition, implies a refusal to differentiate between vitalistic values and reasonable accomplishment; its hypotheses include the total irrationality of choices between political parties or among the various images of the world in conflict, and the moral and spiritual equivalence of various attitudes—those of the sage and of the madman, of the fanatic and of the moderate.

Because of his undying nostalgia for the faith that he had lost, Weber, in the last analysis, judged the science to which he dedicated his life to be unjustifiable. Decision seemed all the more human to him as it was freer. But he did not ask himself if a decision could be made for no particular reason, or, if it could not, whether a reason did not inevitably refer to universal principles. The historical diversity of values, beliefs, and cultures is a primary fact that neither historian nor sociologist can fail to ascertain. But they would not be able to present that fact as ultimate without making the science of this diversity impossible. Does the order of this diversity allow one to establish the one and only end of the adventure as the natural and ultimate destination of man or societies? I do not claim, in the preceding pages, to have answered this question.

The choices to which historical man is condemned—because science is limited, the future is unforeseeable, and short-term values are contradictory—are not demonstrable. But the necessity of historical choices does not imply that thought should yield to, or be dependent on, decisions that are essentially irrational—or that existence can be fully realized in the kind of liberty that would refuse to yield, even to Truth.

Index